POLICING VULNERABILITY

POLICING VULNERABILITY

Editors

Isabelle Bartkowiak-Théron

Nicole Asquith

THE FEDERATION PRESS
2012

Published in Sydney by
    The Federation Press
    PO Box 45, Annandale, NSW, 2038.
    71 John St, Leichhardt, NSW, 2040.
    Ph (02) 9552 2200. Fax (02) 9552 1681.
    E-mail: info@federationpress.com.au
    Website: http://www.federationpress.com.au

National Library of Australia
Cataloguing-in-Publication entry

    Bartkowiak-Théron, Isabelle.
    Policing vulnerability / Isabelle Bartkowiak-Théron; Nicole Asquith.

    Includes index.
    ISBN 978 186287 897 6 (pbk)

    Police – Australia.
    Police administration – Australia.
    Police training – Moral and ethical aspects – Australia
    Police-community relations – Australia.
    Law enforcement – Moral and ethical aspects – Australia.

363.20994

Typeset by The Federation Press, Leichhardt, NSW.
    Printed by Ligare Pty Ltd, Riverwood, NSW.

Foreword

Professor Peter Grabosky

Some three decades ago, I was asked by officials in the NSW Government to suggest some issues that might provide policy opportunities for the then Attorney-General. Having recently worked in South Australia, where the needs of victims of crime had risen quickly on the policy agenda, I suggested that crime victims might be a worthwhile group for the Minister to champion. Their traditional neglect by agencies of the criminal justice system had been substantial, and one could see how the issue was being strategically exploited in the United States as a means of offender-bashing. The potential for mimicry in Australia was self evident. Unfortunately, my suggestion that the Minister might like to become identified with crime victims met with a distinct lack of enthusiasm.

I went back to the drawing board, and soon returned with another suggestion: the legal needs of the elderly. As we know, "demography is destiny". Australia's population had begun to age, and the population of older Australians could only grow. Older voters also tend to be more conservative, and appealing to them could be a good idea for the young, progressive, upwardly mobile politician whose ear I was seeking. Alas, the suggestion that the Minister might seek to advance the legal needs of older Australians went over like the proverbial lead balloon. At this point, I decided to take a step back and see what kinds of issues the Minister chose publicly to embrace. Within a couple of days, an article appeared in the paper describing his launching of a halfway house for transsexual ex-prisoners.

Thirty years later, I still think crime victims, and elderly Australians, represent worthy causes. But I will give full points to the Minister, who saw much further than I did. Moreover, he passed up the easy (and politically advantageous) options, and took aim at a very marginalised and vulnerable group. His choice of issues may not have been good politics, but it was almost certainly compassionate policy.

A book on policing vulnerable members of society is nothing if not timely. Our increasingly neo-liberal society may or may not be producing more vulnerable people than in the past. Whatever the case, we are certainly more conscious of the vulnerability that surrounds us. Vulnerability can arise from a variety of causes; some natural, some the result of human intervention (or neglect). Correlatively, vulnerability can be mitigated by a number of solutions, implemented by a number of institutions, public and private. The police are but one of these.

Policing does not occur in an organisational vacuum, but rather in a policy *system* (or *set* of systems) comprised of various governmental and non-state institutions. These institutions impact on each other. Shortcomings of the mental health system may result in an increase in the number of people who pose a greater risk to themselves and others. Consequently, safety of the mentally ill and those around them is one of the greatest challenges facing police today. When schools are inattentive to truancy in general and to truants in particular, police are likely to become busier. To the extent that correctional authorities provide insufficient support and surveillance of probationers and parolees, individuals from these vulnerable groups are more likely to attract police attention. Family dysfunction can produce damaged or victimised children, who are more likely to be clients, in some form or another, of the police. Suffice it to say that when an element of the social policy system breaks, the police are the ones who have to pick up the pieces. In other words, much police work arises from the malfunctioning of other social institutions. You can be sure that the police know this, too.

Vulnerability is not always uni-dimensional. The worst-off of our fellow citizens may bear the weight of multiple vulnerabilities. The homeless may have mental health issues. The ex-prisoner may have substance abuse problems. Both may be at greater risk of criminal victimisation. Vulnerability begets vulnerability. One of the most significant criminological research findings of the 1990s involved multiple victimisation (Farrell, 1992; Farrell and Pease, 1993). Simply stated, premises that had experienced a break and enter were significantly more likely to suffer a subsequent victimisation within a month. One solution to this was to provide the vulnerable householder with the knowledge enabling him or her to "harden the target" against subsequent attempts at intrusion. This was a relatively easy solution, as it was something that police could achieve, alone or in collabora-tion with victim assistance or neighbourhood watch groups. More difficult are the compound vulnerabilities that transcend institutional boundaries. Four decades ago, the eminent Australian psychiatrist Eric Cunningham-Dax called attention to "multi-problem families", whose members were simultaneously clients of mental health, social welfare, and criminal justice systems (Davies and Dax, 1974; Cunningham-Dax, 1977). The decades that have ensued since Cunningham-Dax's observations have seen a degree of inter-agency coordination, but much remains to be achieved. The degree to which police are able to recognise vulnerability, and to engage with or mobilise the most appropriate institution for its prevention and control, will help both the vulnerable *and* the police themselves.

Few professionals, certainly police and academics, enjoy being told how to do their job. Both professions have been slow to change. In years past, one could rightfully suggest that police were lacking in sensitivity to the more vulnerable members of society. Among the most prominent of these were victims of sexual assault and domestic violence. Until quite recently, police in most English-speaking democracies have been overwhelmingly male, and did not regard violence against women as a high priority. Gradual sensitisation occurred in response to vocal protest from, or on behalf of, vulnerable citizens.

One of the more frustrating aspects of vulnerability is that not all of its mani-festations elicit compassion. For those whose vulnerability arises from conscious lifestyle choices, the issue remains, how coercive should the state become? How paternalistic? Should one be allowed to "live fast and die young"? Are there certain individuals who should be free to live their life as they wish, free of state attention?

To what lengths should police go to save people from themselves? When does intervention become counterproductive? Police negotiators spend a great deal of time seeking to dissuade individuals who threaten to take their own lives. Few would regard this as an inappropriate allocation of police resources. One can make a compelling case for enforcing seat belt and child restraint laws, but perhaps not for laws that prohibit less harmful forms of drug use.

Does it help to distinguish between those who refuse to help themselves, and those who are unable or less able to help themselves? One could perhaps argue that protection of the latter is certainly appropriate. Protection of the former, however, should depend to some extent on whether the individuals and activities in question abridge the liberties of their fellow citizens.

The growth of technology may also facilitate attention to vulnerable citizens. The good news is that this may be freedom enhancing. Children, the developmentally challenged and the elderly may now be equipped with tracking and communications devices that can facilitate rescue if they venture into harm's way. But technology is a double-edged sword. There are those who lead high-risk lifestyles but who may not wish to be under constant surveillance.

In the best of all worlds, there would be no vulnerability. In the next-best world, there would be sufficient resources to minimise the risk of becoming vulnerable, and to mitigate the vulnerability that does exist. In our real world of today, there are never enough resources to go around, and attention to the vulnerable must be rationed. This raises the question on what basis should attention to the vulnerable be allocated? Should one look to the individuals and groups whose needs are most acute, or should one look at the largest class of those afflicted? One might also think in terms of moral agency, where adults who may have contributed to their circumstances may be accorded less attention than those born with (or into) circumstances of extreme adversity. Is it even possible to identify the individuals and groups who are more deserving of care?

One might also ask whether there are limits to the use of the term "vulnerable". By labelling someone as such, is there a risk that they may internalise that identity, and come to perceive themselves as different from, or inferior, to the mainstream? In other words, can labelling theory be applied to the afflicted as well as to offenders? It would appear that police and other agencies should address vulnerability in a non-stigmatising way, to permit as many fellow citizens as possible to regard themselves as ordinary members of society.

The role of police in a democratic society is one of considerable complexity. The challenge they face is to weigh the various claims on their services, and to allocate their resources appropriately. Unfortunately, the most vocal members of the community are not always in need of police attention, and those most in need are often inarticulate.

Some members of society lack the skills and capacity to articulate their vulnerability with sufficient clarity that they are recognised by police or by other agencies of government. Historically, when police were customarily reactive, tending to focus on incidents rather than patterns, they would not always perceive a problem. More recently, police have become more outward looking and proactive. As such, they may be in a position to identify such hidden vulnerabilities and to respond to them appropriately.

It is important for all members of society to be conscious of vulnerabilities and how best to deal with them. Many of us are preoccupied with our own day-to-day problems, and remain ignorant of those less fortunate, especially when they may be small in number or geographically isolated. Three decades ago, transsexual ex-prisoners were not on my radar screen. Community education is therefore, an important strategy in the overall reduction of vulnerability. So too is the education and training of police in issues relating to vulnerabilities in our society and how best to manage them.

As mentioned above, policing vulnerable people is not something that should be left to police alone. To the extent that police can persuade (upstream) institutions to modify their practices or expand their services so that the vulnerable members of society are better looked after, the police and the vulnerable both benefit. This requires certain social and political skills that may not be taught at the police academy. The potential for police to play a role of policy broker or entrepreneur should not be overlooked. Every member of the police service, from the commissioner to the probationary constable, should be alert to the indicia of vulnerability, and to the array of institutions that may contribute to its alleviation. They should, to the best of their abilities, engage with other institutions of both government and civil society in furtherance of optimal solutions. One might even suggest that police might even play a leadership role in this regard.

Like it or not, we live in an era of globalisation. People, finance, ideas, commodities and diseases are all on the move, and a reversal of these trends appears most unlikely. Diversity includes vulnerability, and societies almost everywhere are becoming more diverse. One way in which progressive police services have adapted to the diversity of the public they serve is to become more diverse themselves. Greater diversity in police ranks, in terms of race, gender, ethnicity and sexuality, are likely to lead to more attentiveness to the vulnerable, and to more sensitive ways of serving them.

It has been said that the quality of a society will be evident in the way it treats its most vulnerable citizens. This book stands to make an important contribution to improving the quality of those societies which heed its guidance.

References

Cunningham-Dax, E, 1977, "Multiproblem Families and Their Psychiatric Significance" 11 *Australian and New Zealand Journal of Psychiatry* 227.

Davies, L and Dax, EC, 1974, "The Criminal and Social Aspects of Families with a Multiplicity of Problems" 7 *Australia and New Zealand Journal of Criminology* 4.

Farrell, G, 1992, "Multiple Victimisation: Its Extent and Significance" 2 *International Review of Victimology* 85.

Farrell, G and Pease, K, 1993, *Once Bitten, Twice Bitten: Repeat Victimisation and its Implications for Crime Prevention*, Home Office, London.

Contents

PART FIVE

Pathways to Sentencing and Punishment

Acknowledgments

The editors would like to acknowledge the unreserved support of Professor Jenny Fleming (University of Southampton, UK), Professor Rob White and Associate Professor Roberta Julian (University of Tasmania, Australia), who immediately saw the value of this collection and its contribution to the literature. Our heartfelt thanks also go to Associate Professor Jen Wood (Temple University, USA), for her advice and early comments on our book proposal. We acknowledge the resilience and patience of all authors who contributed to this book, and this important field of policing. We also thank Chris Holt, Ann Cunningham, Rebecca Fung and Josephine Romeo at The Federation Press, who recognised the importance of the collection and supported the editors throughout the publishing process.

We both feel very privileged to be in a position to work directly with police organisations and partner agencies on an everyday basis, in our respective teaching, research and community engagement specialties. We would therefore like to thank all the police officers we have worked with throughout the years, in Australia, the UK, Canada and the USA, as well as the victims, offenders and community members who have contributed their thoughts to this collection and to our work in general.

Isabelle would also like to particularly thank Professor Sophie Body-Gendrot (Université de La Sorbonne-Paris IV, France), without whom nothing of this would have ever been possible in the first place. Her thanks also go to Professor Peter Grabosky, for unwavering mentoring and advice since she arrived in Australia. She dedicates this book to Jean-Yves, for his infinite, medal-deserving patience and understanding, and also, to "les Gens du Nord". Particulièrement Monique, René, Valérie, Sabine et Elisabeth, pour une éthique et des valeurs familiales sans faille, des discussions passionnantes, des fous rire beaucoup trop réguliers pour être bons pour la santé et pour ne lui avoir jamais demandé de prouver quoi que ce soit. Et puis, à Praline et Althaea ... parce que pourquoi pas.

Nicole dedicates this book to Liz – for her honesty and love, and her practical insights from the "other side" – and Jan, for her lifelong support. She would also like to thank Professor Scott Poynting (Manchester Metropolitan University, UK) for his sharp wit, great cooking, critical eye and wise words over the last ten years.

Isabelle Bartkowiak-Théron and Nicole L Asquith

Contributors

Nicole L Asquith (Editor) – Deakin University

Nicole is a Senior Lecturer in the School of Humanities and Social Sciences at Deakin University, and Associate Senior Research Fellow with the Tasmania Institute of Law Enforcement Studies, University of Tasmania. Nicole has worked as a practitioner and academic in the areas of policing hate crime, and policing in culturally and linguistically diverse societies, for over 15 years. Her current research with the London Metropolitan Police Service uses forensic linguistics to understand the context of hate speech in hate crime. Her work has been published in a range of edited collections and journals, and she is the co-author (with Rob White and Janine Haines) of *Crime and Criminology*.

Lorana Bartels – University of Canberra

Lorana is a Senior Lecturer in the School of Law at the University of Canberra, where she teaches criminology and criminal law. She has previously held research and policy positions at the Family Court of Australia, NSW Office of the Director of Public Prosecutions, NSW Attorney-General's Office, NSW Public Defenders Office, ACT Law Reform Advisory Council and the Australian Institute of Criminology. Her first book, *Qualitative Criminology: Stories from the Field* (co-edited with Kelly Richards) was published in 2011. She has published widely on a range of criminology issues, including domestic violence, Indigenous women in the criminal justice system and sentencing law.

Isabelle Bartkowiak-Théron (Editor) – University of Tasmania

Isabelle is Discipline Coordinator of Police Studies at the University of Tasmania and a Senior Researcher at the Tasmanian Institute of Police Studies. Isabelle teaches and researches policing, and specialises in the topic of vulnerable populations and policing. She teaches this very topic at the Tasmania Police Academy, a role she was already undertaking with the New South Wales Police Force, when she was working at Charles Sturt University. She is a member of the Australian University Community Engagement Alliance Scholarship Committee, a member of the Ethical Review and Research Governance Advisory Committee of the Australian Institute of Police Management. She is an Associate Investigator at the Centre of Excellence in Policing and Security, and a member of the Australian Crime Prevention Council. She is an Adjunct Senior Lecturer at Charles Sturt University, in the School of Police Studies.

Katrina Clifford – University of Tasmania

Katrina is a Lecturer in Journalism, Media and Communications at the University of Tasmania. She has over 10 years' experience as a journalist, magazine editor and communications consultant. Prior to joining UTAS, Katrina was a tutor and guest lecturer at the University of Wollongong, and a research assistant on the independent evaluation of the NSW Police Force Mental Health Intervention Team. Her current research examines the ways in which fatal police-involved shootings of mentally ill individuals in crisis are represented and interpreted by and between news media and people traumatised by these critical incidents.

Anna Corbo Crehan – Charles Sturt University

Anna is a Lecturer in Policing Studies at Charles Sturt University's Australian Graduate School of Policing, and a Research Fellow in the Centre for Applied Philosophy and Public Ethics. She works in the areas of police ethics (with particular focus on professional distance issues, use of discretion and vulnerable people). Currently, she is undertaking research on obedience to authority and police students, teaching interdisciplinary professional ethics, and deaths in police custody. Anna is a member of two Human Research Ethics Committees, and has a particular interest in the issues of justice facing Indigenous peoples.

Penelope Egan-Vine, AM – Murray Valley Sanctuary Refugee Group

Penny is a Trauma and Grief Counsellor in Albury, NSW. She is also the Chairperson of the Murray Valley Sanctuary Refugee Group, whose vision is to assist refugees in order that they can achieve independence and integration. The MVSRG has recently progressed a project with UTAS on the bridging of the relationship gap between police and refugees. Penny is a Member of the Order of Australia.

Katie Fraser – Street Law

Katie Fraser is a solicitor currently working in Canberra as the manager of Street Law, a free legal service for people who are homeless or at risk of homelessness. She also works as the project manager of the National Legal Aid Community Legal Education Strategy for New Arrivals. In her previous role at the Footscray Community Legal Centre, she completed two reports that documented the legal problems experienced by refugees (*Out of Africa and into Court*, 2009), and ways in which common legal problems might be prevented (*Prevention is Better than Cure*, 2011). In 2010, Ms Fraser was appointed to the Department of Immigration's Orientation Consultative Committee.

Peter Grabosky – Australian National University

Peter Grabosky is a Professor in the Regulatory Institutions Network, at the Australian National University. His interests lie in areas of policing, regulation, computer-related crime, and the role of non-state actors in public policy. He is a Fellow of the Academy of the Social Sciences in Australia and has received the Sellin-Glueck Award of the American Society of Criminology, and the Hermann Mannheim Prize of the Centre International de Criminologie Comparée de l'université de Montreal, for his contributions to comparative and international criminology.

Hannah Graham – University of Tasmania

Hannah Graham is a PhD candidate and Associate Lecturer in Sociology & Criminology in the School of Sociology & Social Work at the University of Tasmania. Together with Rob White, she is the co-author of the book *Working with Offenders: A Guide to Concepts and Practices* (Willan/Routledge, 2010). Her PhD research involves examining the perspectives and experiences of Tasmanian practitioners in offender management and the alcohol and other drugs sector working with people with complex needs.

Terese Henning – University of Tasmania

Terese Henning has expertise in the law of evidence, criminal process, human rights and law reform. Her research has resulted in major reforms to the law of evidence and sexual offences in Tasmania. Currently her research and law reform interest are human rights law, specifically the enactment of human rights instruments at a State and Federal level. She is a Senior Lecturer in the Faculty of Law at the University of Tasmania. She is co-author with Jeremy Gans, Jill Hunter and Kate Warner of *Criminal Process and Human Rights* (Federation Press, 2011).

Victoria Herrington – Australian Institute of Police Management

Victoria is the Director (Research and Learning) at the Australian Institute of Police Management, and an Associate Investigator with the Centre of Excellence in Policing and Security, Australian National University. She was a Senior Lecturer at Charles Sturt University and Research Fellow at King's College London before joining the AIPM. Victoria has conducted research for the UK's Association of Chief Police Officers, New South Wales Police and the London Metropolitan Police Service.

James Huntley – Australian National University

James is Senior Psychologist at the Southern Area Brain Injury Service, based in Goulburn, NSW. In addition to conducting clinical and neuropsychological assessments and advising on cognitive and behavioural outcomes, Dr Huntley has also serves as an Expert Witness for the Magistrates, District and Supreme Courts of NSW. He is a Clinical Lecturer at the School of Psychology at the Australian National University, and lectures at the NSW Police Academy to senior police officers as part of the Safe Custody course. His chapter emanates largely from discussions with almost 1000 police officers who have taken this course.

Catherine Layton – University of Wollongong

Catherine is an academic developer at the University of Wollongong and coordinates the University of Wollongong University Learning and Teaching Course. As a former Associate Professor from Charles Sturt University, Catherine has worked in police education since 1989. She contributed extensively to the design of the NSW Police Force Constable Development Program, including writing and delivering distance education for the Charles Sturt University Associate Diploma in Policing Practice. She was awarded a HERDSA Fellowship in 2006.

Kelly Richards – Australian Institute of Criminology

Kelly is a Principal Research Analyst with the Australian Institute of Criminology, and a Visiting Fellow in the Centre for Restorative Justice at the Australian National University. Her areas of expertise include restorative justice, juvenile justice, sexual violence, human trafficking and qualitative methodologies. Kelly has previously worked as a lecturer at Sydney University and the University of Western Sydney. In 2010, she was awarded the ACT Government Audrey Fagan Churchill Fellowship to research methods of reintegrating child sex offenders in the United States of America, Canada and the United Kingdom. Her first book (co-edited with Lorana Bartels), *Qualitative Criminology: Stories from the Field* was published in 2011 (Hawkins Press).

Karl Roberts – Macquarie University

Karl is a Forensic Psychologist, with expertise in the field of policing; particularly, investigative skills focusing upon psychological and behavioural assessment, investigative interviewing and risk assessment and management. He has interests in the investigation of violent crimes such as terrorism, honour violence and stalking and the psychological motivation of offenders. Karl is Associate Editor of the journal *Behavioral Sciences of Terrorism and Political Aggression*, was recently (June 2011) Guest Editor of the *British Journal of Forensic Practice* for a special edition on Investigative Interviewing and has just secured a book contract with Taylor Francis for a volume on policing honour based violence with colleagues from the London Metropolitan Police. Karl works closely with the police and other agencies providing behavioural advice in the form of risk assessments, interview strategies and offender profiles to major investigations and has provided advice to over four hundred major investigations throughout Australia, the United Kingdom, Europe and the USA.

Angela Robinson – Tasmania Police

Angela is a Senior Constable with Tasmania Police, and former Police Prosecutor with the Magistrates Court of Tasmania (Drug Diversion and Youth Justice courts). Angela is currently studying her Honours degree in Criminology at the University of Tasmania, completing her thesis on youth bail curfew breaches and associated formal criminal justice responses. Angela was also a Research Intern at the Australian Institute of Criminology in 2012. During this internship, she contributed to an examination of Indigenous Youth Justice programs and an evaluation of the Australian Classification Education System, as well as researching disability access to the criminal justice system.

Sonya Stanford – University of Tasmania

Dr Sonya Stanford is a nationally awarded Social Work lecturer in the School of Sociology and Social Work at the University of Tasmania. She coordinates the first year program of the Social Work program, and teaches into undergraduate and postgraduate program. Sonya has practised as a social worker in the fields of sexual assault, aged and disability support and income support. Sonya's research program has focused upon how risk operates in the organisation and provision of welfare services. Her research responds to the expressed concern that risk thinking and practices can potentially distort and undermine liberatory, progressive policy and professional goals. Given these concerns, Sonya's research explores the social justice issues that interface with the logic and practices of risk in policy and service delivery contexts.

Rosemarie Winter – University of Tasmania

Romy is an experienced applied social researcher who operates a consultancy practice specialising in social research and program evaluation. Romy works with the government and non-government sectors in generating the evidence base for programs that target vulnerable families. Romy's PhD with the Tasmanian Institute of Law Enforcement Studies focused on the implementation of a criminal justice response to family violence. Other research interests are community capacity building, Aboriginal health and wellbeing and women's labour market issues.

Part One

The Emergence and Contexts of Vulnerable People Policing

Chapter 1

Vulnerability and Diversity in Policing

Nicole L Asquith and Isabelle Bartkowiak-Théron

In an international backdrop of economic and political instability, policing is becoming more professionalised, and the human rights of victims and offenders are increasingly scrutinised. Police organisations and their personnel (sworn and unsworn) are required to do more, often with fewer public resources. At the same time, developments in police management (including the pluralisation of policing and the resurgence of the idea that police should provide a due service to the community) have led to whole-of-government responses to crime. These responses commonly require the "co-production" (Friedmann, 1990) of security with other government and non-government partners and, more locally, communities. The capacity of communities (and individuals qualified to represent the "community") to participate in this co-production is not evenly shared, with the result that some communities are better able to help shape responses to crime. Having the social resources to participate in the development of preventative and reactive responses to crime and criminal behaviour is marked by a range of social, demographic, biological and economic factors. We suggest that some communities are left out of this social development of the criminal justice system – that is, not invited to participate and/or not capable of participating. Most of those left out of shaping the system are, paradoxically, the targets of greater and greater surveillance by the police, by way of specific legislation, guidelines and operational protocols. These social groups are commonly referred to as being "at risk" groups, or "vulnerable people". But what do these terms mean? Who is "vulnerable"? How is vulnerability assessed, and why? How does this influence policing practices? Can we measure vulnerability? Do some vulnerabilities supersede others? This collection begins to answer some of these important questions in relation to the policing of vulnerable communities, or "vulnerable people", as we choose to use in this book. Contributors have considered what police officers need to know about vulnerable people, in order for them to do their job well. They have also considered the impact of legal categories of vulnerability on police operational procedures. Each chapter offers a critical evaluation of contemporary practices at each point of the

3

policing process, and provides practical solutions for strengthening frontline and management capacity in vulnerable people policing.

When vulnerable people policing is considered from the perspectives of criminal justice processes, it becomes clear that there are experiential patterns in how police approach vulnerable people, and respectively, how vulnerable people react to their contact with police. This collection comes at a time when we question whether these patterns of shared experiences provide a basis for consolidated policies and practices. We also question:

1. The absence of consolidated literature on vulnerable people at a time when additional training relating to vulnerable populations is requested by policing organisations
2. The erratic multiplication of academic and policy terminology relating to such populations (with consistency across Australian states or internationally difficult to achieve)
3. The balkanisation of the literature on some categories of vulnerable people, but not other categories of vulnerability
4. The pressing demands for police to know anything and everything about these categories of the population
5. The demands on police to pay careful attention to vulnerable people, in a constantly evolving context of performance management, accountability and risk assessment

To make this collection as relevant as possible to police organisations, recruits and more senior officers, and key stakeholders, we have reached out to colleagues experienced in the policing of vulnerable populations. Contributing authors are actively involved in vulnerable people policing, either as academics specialising in policing and/or socio-legal issues, as police educators or serving police officers. All have hands-on experience in each step of the processes described in this collection. Some authors work with police on particular vulnerability issues (Penny Egan-Vine, Katie Fraser, and Nicole Asquith), while others are involved in the education of police officers or in the provision of professional development courses to police (Isabelle Bartkowiak-Théron, Victoria Herrington, James Huntley, Catherine Layton and Anna Corbo Crehan), or in the evaluation or analysis of police work with vulnerable populations (Terese Henning, Karl Roberts, Hannah Graham, Lorana Bartels, Kelly Richards, Sonya Stanford, Katrina Clifford and Rosemarie Winter). Some have also been involved in research and education matters for police organisations, as well as in the design and improvement of police operations (Isabelle Bartkowiak-Théron, Nicole Asquith and Victoria Herrington). One contributor is a police officer (Angela Robinson). Their chapters provide analytical, theoretical and empirical insight on vulnerable people policing and reflect on critical issues in a domain that is increasingly subject to media and political scrutiny, and speedy conversion from policy to practice. The contributions provide an evaluation of contemporary strategies in policing (and, in some cases, the wider criminal justice system) and offer critical insights into the conversion of research into policing practices.

Vulnerable People Policing

Vulnerable people policing is in its infancy, and as such, little is known about how executive principles convert to frontline practices, nor what the benefits and shortfalls are of particular approaches. Importantly, the language of policing vulnerabilities is not universal, with some countries using other vernacular to describe the same individuals. An extensive review of literature over the past 10 years relating to the topic of vulnerable people in policing unveils such terms and expressions as: at risk, disadvantaged, risky, problem-people, vulnerable populations, vulnerable adults, vulnerable witnesses, vulnerable children, at risk children, to name but a few. "Vulnerable people" is offered as an innovative umbrella term. It moves away conceptually from older ideas of disorderly people as "police property" (Reiner, 2000) and complements practices intended to manage diversity, particularly models such as productive diversity (Cope and Kalantzis, 1997).

As a general rule, vulnerable people are featured in legislation and/or policy throughout Australia in *consolidated or piecemeal* legislation. The legal classification of people, albeit normative in nature, is intended to give direction to policing practices, and to act as a checklist for correct procedures. These policies and legislation consider those who need the most support from government and non-government agencies, but also those social groups known for having historically tense relationships with police, or those deemed a potential "procedural risk" for police. In Australia, vulnerable populations are understood to include: young people, the elderly, people with a culturally and linguistically diverse background, the mentally ill, the disabled, victims of crime, Indigenous Australians, people with addictive behaviours, and sexually and gender diverse communities (see Bartkowiak-Théron and Corbo Crehan, 2010; Henning, 2011). In some jurisdictions, the homeless are also recognised as a vulnerable population. These groups can be recognised as vulnerable populations in generalist language, but some terminology can further compartmentalise specific categories of vulnerability. For example, the expression "culturally and linguistically diverse" (CALD) is often used in policy documentation as an umbrella term for people who are from a "non-English speaking background" (NESB – mostly used in legislation) and/or "humanitarian refugee".

In this labelling exercise, it is now acknowledged however, that social categorisation has to take into account the complex nature of individuality, and that an individual identity may be fractured across several categories at once. Recognising the multiple facets of individual identity complements Weber's concept of "status groups", which are not defined according to "economic markets (such as the rich and the poor, for example), but according to non-economic, social indicators" (Germov and Poole, 2011: 212), such as their way of life, physical and psychological capacities, and cultural affiliations. From a socio-legal point of view, vulnerable people are those deemed at a disadvantage within the criminal justice system when compared with others. Their vulnerability means that by virtue of a particular characteristic (language, disability, illness, age, sexual or gender identity), they are more susceptible to abuse, discrimination, misunderstanding or miscommunication. They therefore need additional support to navigate the intricacies of the system. Vulnerable people policing is therefore a paradigmatic way to look at forms of policing that are specifically attuned to policy, rules, regulations and protocols that focus on vulnerability.

This said, at the level of policing practice, the focus remains on specific categories of "vulnerable people", often without consideration of the common experiences shared between vulnerable groups as victims and offenders. While greater attention to the issues encountered by specific groups has "grounded" the work of policing, and provided clear practice direction, it has done little to maximise the skills and competency of police officers when working with multiple and intersecting vulnerabilities. Vulnerable people policing requires officers and organisations to challenge silo *ad hoc* responses for specific groups; in its place, this approach requires organisations to identify the possible vulnerabilities that can be experienced at each stage of the policing process, and develop practices that mitigate that vulnerability. This approach acknowledges the pervasive nature of vulnerability in the criminal justice system, and normalises it within policing practices.

As documented in this collection, people who come in contact with policing organisations – from non-criminal interactions to detention and investigation – most commonly experience at least one form of vulnerability. Structuring policing practices around the presence of this vulnerability not only makes operational sense, it also brings policing practices in line with human rights legislation. We suggest that when vulnerability is normalised in policing practices, frontline officers will acquire new competencies that will enable them to move police encounters from "risky" and dangerous to "at risk" and vulnerable (Stanford, in this collection, Ch 2). In time, it may also lead to greater professional awareness and reflective practice about the vulnerabilities experienced by police officers themselves.

Contemporary Policing: The Context of Vulnerable People Policing

From the 1960s onwards, a number of social movements denounced the criminal justice system for failing to equitably account for all experiences of crime and disorder (Bartkowiak and Jaccoud, 2008: 209). Empowering communities, to enable them to become co-producers of law and order (Friedmann, 1990), was seen as a solution to an increased dissatisfaction with the administration of justice, particularly, increasing levels of fear-of-crime. As documented by Bayley (1989) and Crawford (1997), police began to reach out to the communities they policed, including the enclaves of privilege where Neighbourhood Watch provided a direct communication conduit between the police and those interested in maintaining law and order (Bennett, 1989; Fleming, 2005). However, in less privileged communities, these traditional structures for co-production failed to reduce distrust, and in some cases, outright hostility, between the police and their communities (Hirschfield and Bowers, 1997; Fleming, 2005; Innes and Roberts, 2008). To re-build trust, policing organisations were required to develop alternative mechanisms; strategies that uniquely meshed with the social, economic and cultural attributes of particular communities. These tentative steps towards building stronger police-community relationships emerged just as the political contexts of law and order coalesced around a new punitiveness (see, for example, Pratt et al, 2005).

Central to the innovations in the structuring and operationalising of policing in the 21st century has been the blind faith that community-based strategies were the panacea to under-reporting, re-offending, and lack of trust in police (Friedmann, 1990; Brogden, 1999). While these approaches have fundamentally changed the landscape of contemporary policing, and have assisted in reducing fear-of-crime and the building of trust and rapport, some communities are better able to take up the opportunities that come with collaborative partnership with the police. Indeed, some of these are, for example, wealthier, healthier, more stable, and have easier access to services. This privileged social positioning offers these communities a better chance to seize opportunities for co-production of community security, health and wellbeing. On the other hand, under-resourced and marginalised communities have limited opportunities to co-produce law and order. Even in the best circumstances – where communities are empowered to participate, and policing organisations are able to resource, support and integrate community-based approaches into their wider agenda – this approach is not a quick fix (Bartkowiak-Théron, 2011). Building trust and rapport are time consuming activities, which require consistency and sustainability in order for them to achieve measurable success. However, the success or failure of community policing does not lie solely with police organisations; the capacities of communities are also important factors in co-production.

Policies, especially public policies, do not emerge in a social vacuum; nor are they objectively crafted by policymakers in a political vacuum. How police do their work is an area of public policy that is of interest not only to politicians and policy makers, but also, importantly, the media and the public. Commentary on talk back radio and online is saturated by public discussions of law and order; at times, with lay arguments and fiction competing equally with professional arguments (of politicians, policy makers, stakeholders, even scientists) – especially when "wicked issues" (Fleming and Wood, 2006) are under discussion. What is crime, and what we, as a society, should do about criminal behaviour are as much moral and ethical questions, as they are about legal reasoning. Answers to these two questions are also socially and historically contingent; they change across time, and between peoples. It is no wonder, then, that solutions to these two problems are hotly contested.

Given that the social characteristics of communities can inform the success or failure of any innovation in policing, it is important to understand the various ways in which the social contexts of offenders and victims influence crime and criminal behaviour, and in turn, criminal justice responses. The social norms and values that influence the structuring of social life have been transformed in the last 50 years. The social changes present in the 1960s and 70s that led to the emergence of community policing and a greater awareness of vulnerable people and populations appeared, at the time, to be revolutionary. It appeared that the universal human rights developed in the 1940s and 50s were being given life through the increasing demands of both the public and political institutions. In turn, this opened up discussions and policy/practice developments to a wider array of voices; some with more success than others.

By the 1990s, an increased awareness of diversity led to institutional reforms that did more than pay lip service to community engagement. Throughout these periods of revolution and reform, social relationships and structures – such as work, family, identity and community – were changing. Globalisation was breaking down normative understandings of geographic, social, cultural, economic and national borders, whilst policing organisations were asked to manage crime within the contours of the old social boundaries of geography and culture. As social life was becoming more global, so was crime. It became disconnected from the physical world of "bobbies on the beat", "community" roundtables and nation states. It required, then, for policing organisations to be capable of shifting and adapting to the new meanings of community, just as they were beginning to understand and respond to the new meanings of crime.

Models for Change[1]

Justice personnel, especially those in daily contact with the public (that is, primarily, the police) have been required to be more "attuned" to the needs of the communit*ies* they serve. The plural is important here. It is recognised that the social fabric is not composed of one single community, but of many groups (May, 1987). In policing and criminology, acknowledging that police serve different publics has been discussed by many, especially as it relates to class, age, gender, and, most extensively, ethnicity. However, such communities now transcend these conventional social boundaries. While such categories are important to acknowledge in societies that claim to be multicultural, they are but just a few of the facets that make up society as a whole.

If police have to be familiar with the needs of community members, it is also important that they understand both communit*ies* and their needs. Police therefore have to be versed in what constitutes a vulnerability, and how they can work with vulnerable people (see Bartkowiak-Théron and Layton, in this collection, Ch 4). The concept of cultural competency was initially raised in the context of policing as early as the late-1990s, and later operationalised by different jurisdictions through silo training and management, or as an integrated philosophy of productive diversity (Cope and Kalantzis, 1997). Cultural competency, in its most basic form, consists of the acquisition of the knowledge and skills required to effectively and appropriately operate within a culturally diverse environment (Cope and Kalantzis, 1997). In this framework of cultural competency, vulnerabilities are addressed individually in training or management (such as a workshop on "Indigenous issues"), and police officers are expected to become better informed about the specific issues experienced by a single group. However, in its most advanced form, "productive diversity" not only seeks to make individuals better aware of the differences experienced by some vulnerable groups, but also expects that the responses to this diversity and vulnerability are part of a fundamental change in the cultural framework of the organisation as a whole (Cope and Kalantzis, 1997). This approach also requires individuals and organisations to be aware of, and make room for integrating cultural differences into the standard operating procedures of the organisations. In this sense, cultural diversity (and cultural competency) is an asset to policing, not a problem to be fixed by increasing levels of accountability and oversight.

Managing Diversity

The use of expressions such as managing diversity, productive diversity, valuing diversity and cultural diversity has exploded in recent years. Each of these expressions is subject to a variety of interpretations and, in some cases, the distinctions between these interpretations are quite meaningful. Confusion also arises with regard to terms such as anti-discrimination or equal employment opportunity, and the role of such programs in managing diversity. "Diversity" can be defined in broad or narrow terms. Narrow definitions are consistent with procedural justice, and reflect the language used in equal opportunity and anti-discrimination law; they define diversity in terms of race, gender, ethnicity, age, religion, disability, and in some jurisdictions, sexual and gender identity. Broader definitions are consistent with distributive justice and may also include values, personality characteristics, education, language(s), nation of origin, physical appearance, marital status, lifestyle, beliefs, and characteristics such as geographic origin and economic status.

The diagram below provides a framework for understanding the various components central to an operational definition of diversity (adapted from Gardenswartz and Rowe, 1994). As is clear, at the core of the framework is the individual. All individuals bring to their interactions a set of norms and values, which influence their personality and interactive styles. These individual attributes can contribute to a level of vulnerability. Graham (in this collection: 268) points out that these also contribute to desistance from crime, including the importance of individual identity, life narrative, and readiness and capacity for change.

Figure 1: Dimensions of Diversity

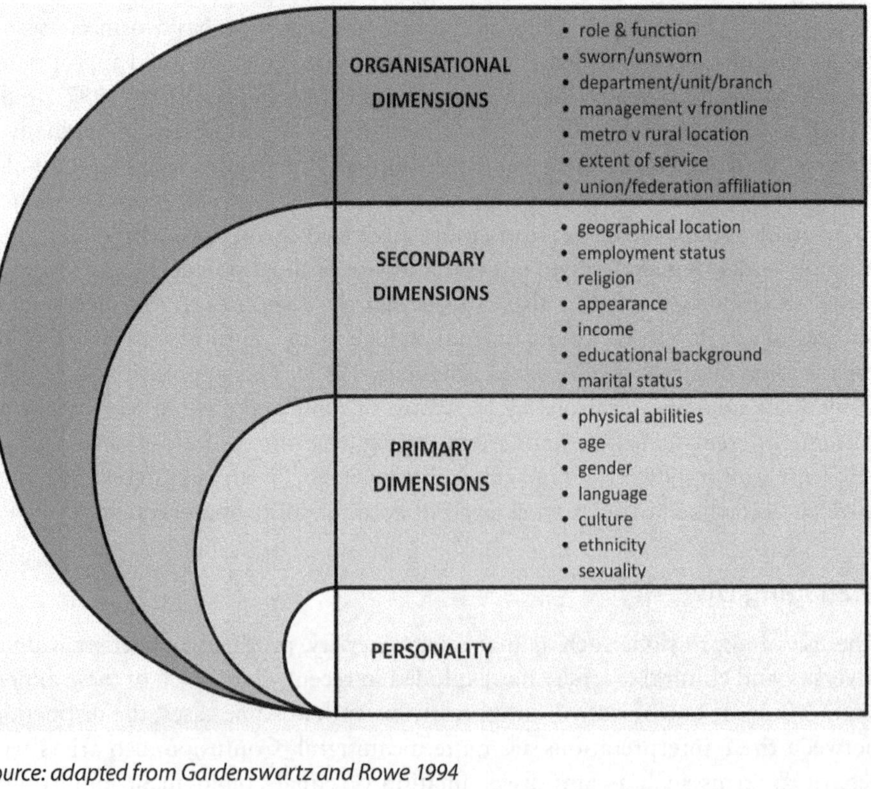

ORGANISATIONAL DIMENSIONS	• role & function • sworn/unsworn • department/unit/branch • management v frontline • metro v rural location • extent of service • union/federation affiliation
SECONDARY DIMENSIONS	• geographical location • employment status • religion • appearance • income • educational background • marital status
PRIMARY DIMENSIONS	• physical abilities • age • gender • language • culture • ethnicity • sexuality
PERSONALITY	

Source: adapted from Gardenswartz and Rowe 1994

The next level is that of the primary dimensions of age, culture, ethnicity, sexual and gender identities and physical and psychological abilities. This level has been the focus of traditional techniques of managing diversity and vulnerability. These are core characteristics of all people, which rarely change; at the same time, these characteristics are those upon which people commonly judge others. These are the way the world sees us irrespective of whether or not we consider these dimensions most important, or whether we wish to respond to them. Importantly to our approach, focussing on this level alone can lead to increased vulnerability for those who have multiple, and at times, contradictory primary identities. Silo approaches to managing diversity that operate at this level are incapable of adjusting to the ways in which, for example, a young person could have a physical disability and identify as transgendered. The variations and combinations of diversity and vulnerability are almost without end.

When considerations of diversity take into account the individual and primary dimensions, along with the broader social (secondary) and institutional (organisation) dimensions, the variations in vulnerability can be managed as part of an integrative approach of policing, rather than a problem to be solved in an *ad hoc* manner. The secondary dimensions (including education, religion, socio-economic status, and geographic location) are those that are acquired, can be flexible over time and become a part of the social capital used by individuals and communities to negotiate their way through the social world, including the criminal justice system. They are also fundamental in understanding the road to desistance, especially in relation to opportunity and mobility, capacity, responsibility and "generativity" (Graham, in this collection: 268). Finally, the organisational dimensions structure how diversity is "given life" and converted into policies and practices. Just as different ethnic cultures construct their norms and values within a specific social context; so too, do criminal justice agents, including police officers. How "management" understands diversity (its value to the organisation and the problems adhered to it) differs greatly to the operational realities of frontline officers. The conflict between the two policing cultures can lead to a hybrid that neither talks the talk, nor walks the walk.

Productive Diversity and Cultural Competency: Pathways to Manage Vulnerability

In line with the broader understandings of culture documented above (and what Herring and Henderson (2012) called "critical diversity"), Cope and Kalantzis (1997) argue that organisations who integrate diversity across operational practices (and mission statements and policies) are better placed to maximise the advantages that come from the diverse individual and social experiences of its workers, clients and stakeholders. Contrary to the traditional view that organisations must present themselves as homogenous entities where individual differences are subsumed within a wider culture, Cope and Kalantzis (1997) suggest that the global imperatives of modern business demand flexibility and heterogeneity. Flexibility, however, is not limited to the roles undertaken by individual workers or the systems of production. Flexibility, in their operationalisation of the term, also incorporates the organisation's ability to flexibly adapt to working with increasingly diverse client groups. Productive diversity approaches differ from traditional equal opportunity approaches in the following ways.

Table 1: Comparison of Traditional and Productive Diversity Approaches to Managing Diversity

	TRADITIONAL APPROACHES	PRODUCTIVE DIVERSITY APPROACHES
MUTUAL ADAPTATION PROCESSES	Individuals will make the necessary adjustments on their own in order to adapt to the needs of the organisation and its stakeholders	Stakeholders will adapt to suit the requirements of each other, thereby creating organisational cultures with high levels of flexibility and adaptability
UTILISATION OF POTENTIAL	Focuses on participation of previously "disadvantaged" or "vulnerable" people within a particular aspect of the organisational structure (both as police officers and stakeholders)	Focuses on the full utilisation of the potential of all participants at all levels of the organisation
EVOLUTIONARY APPROACH	Focuses on quick fix solutions to identified gaps	Prioritises evidence-based approaches that ensure the broader organisational needs are identified and then addressed through strategic planning
ORGANISATIONAL MATTERS	Driving forces behind many equal opportunity approaches are legal requirements, moral prescription or social responsibility	Organisationally motivated in order to optimally utilise diversity to improve productivity and effectiveness

Traditional strategies for managing diversity (such as equal opportunity) continue to be important at the level of individual experiences. Productive diversity does not simply replace the objectives of these older approaches; rather, the two are complementary, with productive diversity succeeding only when the equity considerations of equal opportunity are reinforced. The two approaches, however, diverge in their capacity to bring about productive cultural change in organisations. Whereas equal opportunity is focussed on the specific, recognised individual characteristics of vulnerable people (as outlined in diversity procedures and legislation), productive diversity harnesses the full range of cultural attributes of individuals and organisations (as documented in Figure 1 *see page 10*) to create dynamic social environments where complementarity rather than sameness is fostered. In this sense, diversity, and the paradoxes that emerge when we manage diversity, is not to be seen as a problem or matter to be fixed (Cope and Kalantzis, 1997: 3). Conversely, managing diversity through the lens of complementarity – not sameness – creates the conditions for innovation and organisational success (Cope and Kalantzis, 1997: 132).

In this collection, we adopt a cultural competency framework broader than has been documented elsewhere, or employed in most policing organisations. The concept of "culture" has been applied to identities other than ethnicity, nationality or race. In this collection, we have adopted Herring and Henderson's (2011) model of "critical diversity", which is also linked to age, sexual and gender identities, class, health and well-being, citizenship status, and physical and psychological capacities. This expansion of the cultural competency framework follows the work that police and other professionals in the criminal justice system have done in the past 50 years in response to the demands of various social movements. Importantly, unlike the deeper framework of productive diversity, the contributions in this collection are not focussed on the ways in which diversity can be better understood as a "positive" feature within the criminal justice system. In fact, we argue that until the vulnerabilities associated with diversity are neutralised, it will be difficult to maximise the advantages that come from plural, inclusive organisations. The contributors to this collection highlight how normalising difference and vulnerability, in the long term, provides policing organisations with a significant dividend in terms of intelligence-led, and human rights-informed, policing practices.

Relevance to Policing

The acknowledgment of cultural diversity has resulted in increasingly complex policing practices, which have in turn contributed to a steep increase in police powers in their interaction with vulnerable people, along with stronger demands in protective provisions and duties attributed to liaison, arrest, custody and investigative officers. The premise of this protectionist and interventionist agenda is threefold: to protect the rights of vulnerable individuals; proactively cater for their vulnerability within the criminal justice system; and, to secure police operations and protocols within strict guidelines (Bartkowiak-Théron and Corbo Crehan, 2010). This response to vulnerability in the criminal justice system, however, has not emerged solely as a product of state paternalism; rather, the growing interest in vulnerable populations is also the result of changes in public sector and policing management. In particular, performance management and professional development strategies and technologies have led to increasing levels of duty of care for, and oversight of, all "users" of the criminal justice system, whether a vulnerability exists or not (Fielding and Innes, 2006). At the same time, officer discretion is reduced, and "clients" are documented and subject to standard operating procedures, no matter the social and crime context of each policing encounter. The duty of care for their "clients" and/or "users" necessarily requires policing organisations to become:

- better informed about the diversity of their communities
- engaged with their communities in the development of policies and practices
- critically aware of shared human rights, and the ways these ethical stances and legal structures can lead to better practice outcomes for vulnerable people and populations, and all "users" more generally.

The competencies most commonly associated with community policing, such as those listed above, do not come naturally to many police recruits. Yet they are vitally important in an era where operational benchmarks and co-production of law and order define what police "do". When police recruits are taught to think about their roles and functions through the lens of the most vulnerable victims and offenders, the skills and competencies they acquire are transferable across their policing work. They also resonate throughout the criminal justice process; just as vulnerable people policing is more likely to be community-oriented, it also has a practice affinity with restorative and therapeutic justice in the legal and penal systems.

Finally, vulnerability is relevant to policing because frontline officers are often first responders. As "front-of-house" staff, police officers have enormous power over vulnerable people's "career" in, and experiential knowledge of, the criminal justice system. The labels used, the discretion applied and the cultural values brought to each encounter by police officers can determine how vulnerable people experience the system as a whole. They are not just gatekeepers to the system; they also inform the experiences of vulnerable people passing from police, to lawyers and judges, to prison and rehabilitation officers. Their first actions can inform whether criminal justice is *just* at all.

Structuring the Debate

This collection provides the context for a new form of policing – vulnerable people policing – and guides the reader through the policing process as it is experienced by police officers, victims, offenders, witnesses and stakeholders of policing services. The legal classification of vulnerable populations is extensive and differs from one jurisdiction to another, and lends itself to an exercise in labelling theory that we would like to circumvent as much as possible. Rather than becoming the feature of each chapter, specific vulnerabilities are presented as case studies for a single step in this policing process: from police recruit education on vulnerable people; to initial point of contact; through to custody and investigative interviewing; and, the final transfer of vulnerable people into the other criminal justice agencies. The specific populations discussed in this collection do not represent all those communities and individuals who are, or may be, vulnerable in policing encounters. Rather, the case studies reflect the interests of individual contributors.

The book is divided into five parts. In Part One, Professor Peter Grabosky and the editors document the emergence of vulnerable people categories in the Australian and international contexts and offer a new way to conceptualise diversity and vulnerability within the criminal justice system. This introductory material is contextualised by Stanford's discussion of the concepts and terminology that underpin policy and practice, and Bartkowiak-Théron and Corbo Crehan's examination of the major ethical concerns at stake in how legislative and policing organisations have approached policies and operational interactions with vulnerable people. As a first step into the policing process, Bartkowiak-Théron and Layton examine how police are (and should be) trained in matters of vulnerability.

Part Two introduces the first point of contact between police and vulnerable people, commonly in non-confrontational and non-arrest situations. It displays the work of police in keeping the peace and networking with the community they serve. Winter and Asquith critically examine the relevance of community-based policing in broadacre public housing estates, whilst Clifford considers how police interactions with vulnerable people are portrayed in the media, and Bartkowiak-Théron analyses the synchronisation role of police liaison officers as a first policing approach to vulnerability.

Part Three establishes the role of police when first responding to deviance and anti-social behaviour. With the exception of Asquith's consideration of complaint-making procedures for vulnerable victims (applying the case study of sexually and gender diverse communities), in this part of the book, the contributors begin to turn their attention from victims and victimised communities to vulnerable suspects and offenders. Herrington and Clifford document the experiences of people with mental illness, focussing on people in mental health crisis, whilst Egan-Vine and Fraser analyse the relationship between police and newly-emerging communities, especially in light of non-violent crimes such as driving offences.

Part Four introduces the chain of custody, and the consequences of detaining vulnerable people. Chapters in this section follow the work of police in the very first steps of the investigation, interviewing and prosecution of vulnerable offenders. Bartels provides a much needed update as to the progress of Australian police organisations in relation to the recommendations of Royal Commission into Aboriginal Deaths in Custody, Roberts and Herrington unpick the complexities of investigating and interviewing psychologically vulnerable offenders, whilst Huntley provides, for the very first time in policing literature, insight into the complexities of having a person with acquired brain injury in custody. Henning provides, as a backdrop to these three discussions, the legal provisions that underpin the need to support vulnerable offenders throughout the investigation process.

Part Five explores the work of police when vulnerable people are released from their custody, and transferred into diversion or court processes. Robinson looks at the options police have in diverting vulnerable people (especially youth) from the criminal justice system, Bartels and Richards provide a thought-provoking analysis of how vulnerabilities can translate in the courtroom and how they could be addressed, whilst Graham, reflecting on vulnerability as a concept, makes a deep connection between vulnerability factors, resilience and desistance from crime. The editors conclude the collection with a discussion of the overall solutions offered in adopting vulnerable people policing as a new paradigmatic way to view police business. They also consider the ways policing organisations can enhance their operational capacities and their relationships with vulnerable communities at the same time.

Conclusion

The discussions presented in this collection are offered to police recruits as an overview of key themes and concepts; for more advanced readers, these chapters provide a first step to the research, analyses and practices of each of the topics. For teaching staff, this collection provides a framework for talking about diversity and vulnerability that neither tokenises specific groups, nor bypasses the specific cultural experiences of those who pass through the policing and criminal justice processes. For criminal justice practitioners, the authors have provided grounded examples and case studies, which translate the academic literature into operational models, including details about national and international best practices.

This collection brings together practitioners and researchers who have sought to find a way to maximise the opportunities that come from recognising and integrating diversity. The risks in not addressing diversity holistically are too great; social exclusion will deepen, vulnerabilities will become entrenched and relationships between the police and their communities will become more estranged. Alternatively, making hard decisions now will lead to more effective policing practices, greater co-production of law and order (with communities, and other members of the "police extended family", Johnston, 2005), more rewarding career development for individual officers (including deeper competency and skill sets), and a system of policing deeply embedded in human rights principles.

Vulnerable people policing, as a distinct approach to managing diversity in policing organisations, is a new concept, and one that is just beginning to emerge at both practice and research levels. As such, this collection is a first attempt to survey the field, and to bring together specialists in the areas of vulnerability and policing. We expect that the chapters in this book will generate further debate about how to operationalise these approaches, and how to measure the success and impact of this framework. Re-imaging how diversity and vulnerability can be integrated into the policies and practices of policing takes time. Necessarily, these changes will also be socially and culturally specific as they are based in the relationships between police and their communities. The capacity to participate is variable for local communities generally, and more vulnerable communities specifically. Some of these more vulnerable communities will need additional assistance to build their "co-production" skills. As such, there will remain concerns about whether there is sufficient political leverage and government resourcing (including, legislation, policy, and funding) to sustain this change, at this time. Yet, there are also significant financial and organisational gains that can be extracted for policing organisations by adopting vulnerable people policing as a process model.

Endnote

1   This section has been adapted from work undertaken by Asquith in collaboration with Maria Dimopoulos (MyriaD Consultants) and Chitrita Mukerjee (NSW Police Force), for the Australasian Police Multicultural Advisory Bureau (APMAB). The models for managing diversity documented in this section were central to an unpublished 2005 report on the recruitment and retention of culturally and linguistically diverse police officers. Dimopolous and Mukerjee were expert advisors to APMAB during this project, and, in this research, they combined their extensive practical experience of managing diversity to construct this national approach for modelling change in policing organisations.

References

Bartkowiak-Théron, I, 2011, "Community Engagement and Public Trust in the Police: A Pragmatic View on Police and Community Relationships and Liaison Schemes", 3 *Australasian Policing: A Journal of Professional Practice and Research* 2.

Bartkowiak-Théron, I, and Corbo Crehan, A, 2010, "A new movement in community policing? From Community Policing to Vulnerable People Policing", *Community Policing: Current and Future Directions for Australia – Research and Public Policy* (Ed J Putt), Australian Institute of Criminology, Canberra.

Bartkowiak-Théron, I and Jaccoud, M, 2008, "New Directions in Justice in Canada: From Top-down to Community 'Representatives'", *Justice and Community and Civil Society: A Contested Terrain* (Ed J Shapland), Willan Publishing, Cullompton, UK.

Bayley, DH, 1989, "Community Policing in Australia: An Appraisal", *Australian Policing: Contemporary Issues* (Eds D Chappell and P Wilson),Butterworths, Sydney, 63.

Bennett, T, 1989, "Factors Related to Participation in Neighbourhood Watch Schemes" 29 *British Journal of Criminology* 207.

Brogden, M, 1999, "Community Policing as Cherry Pie", *Policing across the World: Issues for the Twenty-first Century* (Ed RI Mawby), UCL Press, London, 167.

Cope, B and Kalantzis, M, 1997, *Productive Diversity - A New, Australian Approach to Work and Management*, Pluto Press, Sydney.

Crawford, A, 1997, *The Local Governance of Crime: Appeals to Partnerships*, Clarendon Press, London.

Fielding, N and Innes, M, 2006, "Reassurance Policing, Community Policing and Measuring Police Performance" 16 *Policing and Society* 127.

Fleming, J, 2005, "'Working Together': Neighbourhood Watch, Reassurance Policing and the Potential of Partnerships", *Trends and Issues in Crime and Criminal Justice*, 303, Australian Institute of Criminology, Canberra.

Fleming, J and Wood, J, Eds, 2006 *Fighting Crime Together: The Challenges of Policing and Security Networks*, University of New South Press, Sydney.

Friedmann, RR, 1990, "Community Policing: Promises and Challenges" 6 *Journal of Contemporary Criminal Justice* 79.

Gardenswartz, L and Rowe, A, 1994, *Diverse Teams at Work*, Irwin Professional Publications, Chicago.

Germov, J and Poole, M, 2011, *Public Sociology: An Introduction to Australian Society*, 2nd ed, Allen and Unwin, Sydney.

Henning, T, 2011, *Consolidation of Arrest Laws in Tasmania*, Tasmania Law Reform Institute, Hobart.

Herring, C and Henderson, l, 2011 "From Affirmative Action to Diversity: Toward a Critical Diversity Perspective" 38 *Critical Sociology* 629.

Hirschfield, A and Bowers, KJ, 1997, "The Effect of Social Cohesion on Levels of Recorded Crime in Disadvantaged Areas" 34 *Urban Studies* 1275.

Innes, M and Roberts, C, 2008, "Reassurance Policing, Community Intelligence and the Co-Production of Neighbourhood Order", *The Handbook of Knowledge-Based Policing: Current Conceptions and Future Directions* (Ed T Williamson), John Wiley & Sons, Ltd, Chichester, UK.

Johnston, L, 2005, "From 'Community' to 'Neighbourhood' Policing: Police Community Support Officers and the 'Police Extended Family' in London" 15 *Journal of Community and Applied Social Psychology* 14.

May, L, 1987, *The Morality of Groups*, University of Notre Dame, Notre Dame, Indiana, USA.

Pratt, J, Brown, D, Hallsworth, S and Morrison, W, Eds, 2005, *The New Punitiveness: Trends, Theories, Perspectives*, Willan, Cullompton, UK.

Reiner, R, 2000, *The Politics of the Police*, fourth ed, Oxford University Press, Oxford, UK.

Chapter 2

Critically Reflecting on Being "at Risk" and "a Risk" in Vulnerable People Policing

Sonya Stanford

Risk and vulnerability are related concepts. When speaking about vulnerability, we often suggest that people are "at risk" in some way; either from individual traits and experiences (such as dependency, disability or psychological distress) or from external factors located in people's environments (such as, lack of access to affordable housing, living in areas with high crime rates or from experiencing discrimination). For example, in policing, risk assessments are done to identify the likelihood of crimes occurring in particular locations or to specific people. Assessments are done to determine which individuals and communities are at risk of criminal acts. Similarly, profiles are conducted of who is likely to commit a crime. Hence assessments are done to determine which individuals and groups of people are likely to commit crimes. I argue in this chapter that ideas about risk, vulnerability and dangerousness are often spoken about in taken-for-granted terms; that is, we assume that what and who is "at risk" (that is, vulnerable) and what and who is "a risk" (that is, dangerous) is a matter of common sense. This means that our assumptions about what seems "natural" about risk – and hence ideas about vulnerability and dangerousness – can remain unexamined and this can be problematic in the policing context because of the potential to unwittingly reinforce ideas about individuals and communities that disrupt the social goals of policing.

In this chapter, I argue the importance of cultivating reflective police practitioners and organisational cultures that critically examine, as a part of their day-to-day operations, the taken-for-granted assumptions that are located in constructions of who is defined as "at risk" (that is, vulnerable) or "a risk" (that is, dangerous). To begin, I consider how ideas about risk can be understood as socially constructed. That is, rather than thinking about risk as natural, I discuss how ideas about what or who is called "risky" and "vulnerable" reflects a process that is imbued with moral and political meaning. I note that when understood in these terms, it is possible to see that risk is a personally, *and* also politically, moralised concept. This enables an examination of how ideas about who is "at risk" and "a risk" serve to advance the interests of some whilst concomitantly interfering, undermining or disadvantaging the interests of others. From this constructivist standpoint it is possible to apply a critical lens to explore how ideas about risk operate within social institutions and professions.

Constructing Risk

There is little doubt that assessing and responding to risk has been, and continues to be a central preoccupation of policing across many domains, and more broadly within the criminal justice system in western societies. It is not surprising then, that Campbell (2004: 696) refers to police as the "risk profession". However, even the most cursory glance at criminal justice policy, and criminology and policing literature reveals that ideas about risk are complex and disputed. The same can be said of literature that discusses the assessment and response to risk by other key risk professions (such as social work and health workers) within the human services sector who are commonly involved in policing networks and partnerships. A common theme of the combined literature of these risk professions is a recent move towards questioning the political motivations and moral imperatives that are embedded within the structures and the measures utilised to define and operationalise responses to risk. This literature impresses the view that there is nothing natural about risk; it is understood as a deeply contextual, "manufactured" concept that reinforces political interests and normative standards (Adam and Van Loon, 2000). Consequently what or who is defined as "at risk" or "a risk" needs to be understood as a reflection of a complex interplay of competing knowledge claims, interests, politics, ideologies, technologies, emotions and moralities. In turn, it is important to realise that there is nothing "commonsensical" (Armstrong, 2004, cited by Dwyer, 2011: 5) about risk, although this is often purported to be the case within our work and other contexts.

Acknowledging that little can be taken-for-granted about the nature and operations of risk may in itself appear risky; it highlights the extent to which uncertainty prevails within service systems and work contexts that expressly value knowledge (along with those who produce such knowledge), and generate predictability of outcomes (Maguire, 2000; Lennings, 2005; O'Malley, 2006). Policing is a prime example of such a context, a point that is emphasised by Ericson and Haggerty (1997) and evidenced by the burgeoning use of information communication technologies in policing, and the focus upon intelligence-led crime control (Maguire, 2000; O'Malley, 2006). I argue there is much to be gained from the realisation that risk is a constructed concept; it means that risk professionals can have an impact upon how ideas about risk, and in turn vulnerability, are recognised and implemented in practice. This requires individuals and organisations to use a critical lens to identify and explore how risk thinking can undermine the aspirations of modern policing organisations to be socially responsible and culturally relevant and responsive (Bartkowiak-Théron and Corbo Crehan, 2010), and, in turn, consciously work towards more socially just practice responses. This ambitious moral agenda inscribes the importance of fostering the ethical and moral agency of police and their community partners as human service workers who do "risk work" (Horlick-Jones, 2005) in the service of creating safe and secure communities, and this final point is the concluding focus of the chapter.

Applying a Critical Lens to Risk

Critical theories about risk, such as Ulrich Beck's "risk society" thesis (2003, 2004), the governmentality perspective that derives from Michel Foucault's work and discussed by writers such as Dean (1999), Culpitt (1999) and Rose (2000), and Mary Douglas's (2003) cultural and anthropological studies of the forensic attributes and functions of risk, have illuminated the "problematics of risk" (Kelly, 2000, 2001). This analysis highlights how ideas about risk and the language of risk act as predominantly repressive political, social and cultural forces in contemporary society. It is argued that risk thinking dominates (to ill-effect) how we determine, progress and evaluate the 'public interest' and how we think about and evaluate others and ourselves within public and private spheres of life (Culpitt, 1999). Accordingly, a core theme of this analysis is that risk operates as a morally conservative construct in the neoliberal context of the risk society (Beck, 2003, 2004; Culpitt, 1999). The organisation, definition and implementation of policing is positioned in this broad political and social context. Therefore, I summarise key arguments of this critical literature as a means of supporting the development of a critical awareness of how ideas about risk operate in policing practice.

Replacing Needs-led with Risk-focused Policy and Practice Approaches

According to the risk society thesis, pre-empting and protecting oneself against risks preoccupies citizens and governments in their attempts to secure order, balance and stability whilst also striving to progress modernisation in order to generate capital (Beck, 2003, 2004; Giddens, 2003). Hence, safety and security operate as the predominant normative goals of modern society (Furedi, 2008); they are accorded high social value. It is argued, however, that the focus on security has undermined social responses to distress and need (Culpitt, 1999; Kemshall, 2002). Consequentially, a risk-focused (rather than needs-led) approach has come to dominate the logic and organisation of social and community services (Webb, 2006). The consequences of this risk-focused approach are discussed as being:

- increasingly devolved responsibility to communities and individuals for social care and order (Rose, 1996a, 1996b, 2000; Green, 2004) where often less resourced groups are unfairly burdened and less able to respond to this responsibility compared to more socially advantaged groups and individuals (Gilling, 2001; Kemshall, 2011)
- restricted entitlement and reduced provision of, and accessibility to, health and welfare supports that correspondingly reinforces and perpetuates individual and structural disadvantage thereby increasing peoples' vulnerability (Culpitt, 1999; Kemshall, 2002)
- an increased emphasis on efficiency and effectiveness targets in the coordination and delivery of human services that can lead to under-resourcing of programs and the displacement of humanitarian service goals (McDonald, 2006)
- greater demands for professional accountability that engenders a more defensive mentality towards "taking risks" in practice (Titterton, 2006), and
- attempts to standardise practice interventions thereby devaluing and de-professionalising practice (Campbell, 2004).

It is therefore argued that "new risks" are created by the expansion of the "risk business" of policing, particularly in relation to "implications for human rights, the shape and tenor of social control, and the future of criminal justice" (Maguire, 2000: 333). Critical risk theorists argue that this serves the function of exerting control over practitioners, individuals and communities. As Rose explains, the role of practitioners is now to:

> calculate and reduce the risk of their professional conduct, instruct the subjects of their authority in the riskiness of their practices and procedures in which they are engaged and manage their clients in the light of the imperative to reduce the risk they may pose to others (Rose, 1996a: 349).

Hence managing risk has become an individualised responsibility.

Responsibilising Citizens and Communities for Risk

According to governmentality literature, risk operates as a constituent of what comprises "good" citizens. Good citizens are constructed in neoliberal discourse as individuals who activate their economic citizenship (Culpitt, 1999; McDonald, 2006; Rose and Miller, 2010) by making rational choices to maximise their capacity to avoid or respond effectively to risks, thereby protecting and advancing the economic interests of the market society. Citizens are held responsible for risk at a personal and community level in the domains of preventative health care, income protection and crime prevention, for example. As prudential subjects, people are required to constantly engage in the calculation and management of their risks. Moral judgments are made about individuals and groups based on the extent to which people are deemed to have accepted their responsibility to be autonomous and self-reliant citizens (Culpitt, 1999; Rose and Miller, 2010) and these risk-based moral judgements are defining of peoples' and groups' identities. There is a distinct insidiousness to this logic of responsibilisation; no matter the level or nature of disadvantage which people experience they are regarded as needing to be active agents in the exercise of their "remoralisation" and capacity for autonomy (Rose, 2000). Accordingly, risk discourses operate as powerful forces in the construction of individual and group identities that are essentialised (that is, people *are* risk) and totalised (that is, people are *just* risk) (Stanford, 2008).

Risk Identities are Problem Identities

Polarised identities cumulate around notions of risk – dangerousness and vulnerability; independence and dependence, responsibility and irresponsibility, trustworthiness and untrustworthiness, and culpability and innocence (Stanford, 2010: 1066). Constructions of risk, then, reflect ideas about what is considered to be good and bad. When risk is located in or attached to people, moral values are ascribed to them. Hence risk-based identities are moral identities (Stanford, 2008); people are deemed to be good or bad on the basis of their risk identities.

Consideration has recently been given to how people's identities are constructed as risk identities in direct practice contexts (see, for example, Stanford, 2008, 2010; also Pollack, 2010; Dwyer, 2011). Hence, risk is understood as embodied. It is important to note that people are not simply constructed as "at risk" (for example, of harm by others) or "a risk" of harming others, however. Research demonstrates that when ascribing risk identities to people, service providers recognise service users as being both "at risk" and "a risk" (Stanford, 2008, 2010). Consequently peoples' constructed moral identities reflect both their innocence (by construct-ing them as vulnerable) and culpability (by virtue of constructing them as being dangerous). Within the context of people being held responsible for avoiding and managing their risk, vulnerability is not necessarily an innocent subject position. As mentioned above, to be vulnerable within neoliberal discourse means that individuals are seen not to have made prudent decisions to avert their misfor-tune. Consequently, they have compromised their safety and, in turn, they have compromised the economic and social wellbeing of others given their dependence on resources and services (Culpitt, 1999). Thus risk identities are essentially flawed identities and on this basis they enable the moral recognition of risky problematic "others". Risk therefore operates as a moral concept that establishes systems and measures of social inclusion and exclusion (Rose, 2000). This point is impressed by Dwyer (2011) in her research about lesbian, gay, bisexual and transgendered

(LGBT) young people's interactions with police. Dwyer notes that when young people are seen to embody youthful vulnerability to harm, police take action to protect them. However, participants of her study suggested "that the behaviour easily moves from protection to targeting" as LGBT young people are "pulled up for no reason a few too many times" (Dwyer, 2011: 4).

Human service workers are directly implicated in the construction of risk identities through assessments (formal and informal) and interventions (Horlick-Jones, 2005; Broadhurst, Hall, Wastell, White and Pithouse, 2010; Kemshall, 2010; Stanford, 2010). When a focus on risk predominates, service provision becomes founded upon the assessment of people as risk factors. As a calculated object of high risk, people are subject to a range of practices that act to reform, control and contain the potential of harm to or by them. As a calculated object of low risk, services can be denied in spite of apparent need (Stanford, 2010). The consequence of being identified through a risk lens is that service users are invited to see themselves and are recognised by others in terms of a deficit model of self for which they are charged with the responsibility for resolving. And if they fail in this undertaking, those of us charged with controlling risk in our risk management roles are considered justified in employing paternalistic or punitive interventionist strategies (see, for example, Winter and Asquith's study of this in relation to public housing residents, in this collection, Ch 5). Accordingly, a risk focus in police practice can undermine seeing people in more humanitarian terms such as appreciating the contextuality of people's lived experience, such as their cultural contexts.

It is important to note that practitioners are also subject to moralised constructions of them being "at risk" and "a risk" in their work contexts. Practitioners' "at risk" identities reflect a sense of their vulnerability from several sources, which in policing can include people who pose a threat to their physical and/or emotional/ psychological wellbeing, critical colleagues and managers, and a suspicious, hostile public. Practitioners are also constructed as being "a risk" (and therefore a danger) to people if they respond inappropriately to the risk of vulnerable others. The intense public scrutiny of police actions such as high speed car pursuits, officer-involved shootings (see Clifford, in this collection, Ch 7) and detention that results in the death of young people, people diagnosed with mental illness, and people from non-white backgrounds are examples of how "dangerous" identities are constructed and examined in the public domain. At issue within critical literature is not a dispute about professions, such as police, being confronted by serious risks to their wellbeing during the course of their work, nor is it disputed that police can pose threats to others in the conduct of their work. The critical risk literature high-lights the importance of not assuming the truthfulness of the totalising accounts of people as being "at risk" or "a risk". Instead, this literature emphasises critically examining how a predominant view of others and ourselves through a risk lens creates and constrains our vision of how we can understand others and ourselves. Critical researchers and writers note that what is left unexamined in the context of moralised risk identities is how positions of social advantage and privilege are reinforced on the basis of the moral logic of risk (Culpitt, 1999; Gilling, 2001). As Stanko comments, risk can mask "the socially unequal distribution of violence, exclusion and fear produced by a society 'that has not rid itself of the persistent remnants of hierarchies founded in the historical legacies of colonialism, patriarchy, heterosexism and class'" (2000: 28, cited by O'Malley, 2006: 52).

Risk and White Privilege

In recent work, Stanford and Taylor (forthcoming) have undertaken a critical analysis of how formal rationalities of risk that are embedded in neoliberal social and community services reflect the privilege of "whiteness". To clarify, privilege refers to "systematically conferred advantages individuals enjoy by virtue of their membership of dominant groups with access to resources and institutional power that are beyond the common advantages of marginalised citizens" (Bailey, 1998, cited by Pease, 2010: 8). Privilege is largely invisible, normative, naturalised and considered an entitlement (Pease, 2010: 9-16). The racial context of whiteness is a form of privilege. Moreton-Robinson (2004: vii) notes, "Whiteness is the invisible norm against which other races are judged in the construction of identity, representation, subjectivity, nationalism and the law". Critical cultural literature argues that the good neoliberal citizen is a raced white citizen (Goldberg, 2009; Roberts and Mahatani, 2010; Davis, 2007). The invisible privilege of white neoliberalism is evident, at the most basic level, by the white majority ownership of the market and the disproportionate over-representation of "non-whites" (and "not-white enough" and "not-equally-white" people) (Haylett, 2001) across key measures of social vulnerability.

Stanford and Taylor argue that formal risk rationalities operate to reinforce the privilege of white neoliberalism. We note that the embodied privilege accorded to whiteness remains under-examined in the conduct of risk assessment and management practices. The focus of risk in these practices is upon risky (non-white) others (as "at risk" and "a risk") as opposed to systems, policies and interventions that create and perpetuate economic and social disadvantage (Gillings, 2001). Indeed, within neoliberal discourse, such a claim would appear defunct given that we are told we are now living in a "post-race" era (Davis, 2007; Howard-Wagner, 2007; Walter, 2010). The "risk gaze" is firmly upon non-white others as opposed to individuals and groups privileged by whiteness who design, organise, deliver and implement risk strategies.

Summary: the Moral Dilemmas of Risk for Policing

Risk, as an embodied concept, poses significant moral dilemmas for those of us doing risk work and who aspire to contribute to social inclusion and to promote individual and community wellbeing. This is a particular challenge for policing as a risk profession, which has an expressed aspiration to work more sensitively with vulnerable groups. The resolution of this dilemma becomes a very personal issue for us as human service workers in our frontline service contexts as we determine how others, and we, are "at risk" and vulnerable, and "a risk" and dangerous or problematic in some way. The challenge police face is how to act with moral and ethical integrity within the socio-political and cultural mentality of risk discourse that is so dominant in neoliberal society.

The Reflective Practitioner in 'Risk Work'

Green (2004) notes that organisations face an enormous challenge in their management of the ethical and moral dilemmas of risk within the context of neoliberalism. He states that these dilemmas produce "policy and practice issues of considerable complexity. Unfortunately most risk frameworks provide little assistance in their resolution, or do not even recognise their existence" (Green 2004: 4). In the absence of clear organisational frameworks of response, the resolution of the moral and ethical dilemmas of risk becomes a matter for individual practitioners to manage in their day-to-day working contexts (Stanford, 2010).

Responding to these dilemmas has become a central focus of recent research and commentary in criminal justice, and health and welfare disciplines. A key question posed by this research is whether it is possible for practitioners to act contrary to the morally conservative impetus embedded in modern notions of risk. This is an important question to ask as it opens up the possibility of locating sites of resistance to the overall risk ideology. It could also be strategically used to advance alternative ways of thinking about problems and their solutions. As O'Malley (2006: 54-55) notes, the critical issue is not about risk per se but the implications of what we do for how offenders and victims are thought about and treated, and the implications for questions of distributive and procedural justice (Bartkowiak-Théron and Asquith, in this collection: 285).

Kemshall (2011) demonstrates that numerous empirical studies indicate that a risk ethos does not operate as a totalising system of rule in personal and professional life. Campbell (2004) provides evidence of this in policing. Campbell studied how police subvert the "communication formats" they are subject to as "risk-knowledge-brokers" in the risk society. Campbell reviewed police arrest sheets, analysing the information and language that was recorded and their effect. The writing of these accounts was formally governed by strident protocols that attempted to limit the amount and type of police narrativity of policing practice

– itself a risk management practice. Police defied the proscription about what and how they should record their arrests and in the process narrated a story of operational policing as highly professional, successful and accomplished. Campbell (2004) states that "storying" their arrest accounts in these ways was an important practice in the context of police feeling under pressure to move away from traditional policing practice to more routinised, standardised, and some might argue, de-professionalised practice.

Consideration of whether it is possible to "speak back" to the moral conservatism of risk in professional practice has also been a core focus of my research. I have considered this question in relation to social workers' practice (Stanford, 2008, 2010, 2011). Reflecting the arguments that are presented in this chapter, this research found that risk operated as an identity-defining construct in social workers' practice. In many cases, both clients and practitioners were ascribed both "at risk" and "a risk" identities; that is, clients were seen as "vulnerable" and "dangerous" and practitioners also saw themselves as "vulnerable" and "dangerous" or problematic in some way. Responding to risk in practice then became a very personal issue for these practitioners. The moral dilemma they faced was whose and what risk identities they would respond to in their interventions. Predominantly, these dilemmas pivoted upon whether to attend to the client's vulnerable identity and or dangerous/problematic identity and/or the practitioner's vulnerable identity and or dangerous/problematic identity. In other words, practitioners faced a dilemma about whether to take a stand for or against their client, and for or against themselves. Those practitioners who were able to resolve this dilemma in a manner that was consistent with a social justice focus, did so on the basis of reflecting upon:

- personal and professional moral, ethical and value frameworks;
- their positions of power and privilege relative to clients;
- their belief in the possibility for change for clients; and
- theory and practice frameworks.

Conversely, social workers adopted a more controlling and dismissive approach in their practice when:

- they did not reflect upon their positions of power and privilege relative to clients;
- they did not think change was possible for clients; and
- they did not refer to theory and practice frameworks.

When the findings of this and other research are applied to policing vulnerability and encouraging culturally appropriate policing responses, it is evident that thoughtful, reflective practice is crucial. Being a reflective practitioner means using evaluative criteria that consider the ethics of interventions and the use of personal and institutional power. The importance of these evaluative criteria was clearly demonstrated in my research when social workers determined how to construct a moral response to their client's and their own sense of risk. In the absence of such an evaluative stance, practitioners' interventions tended to be autocratic and they were dismissive of their client's needs and interests. Risk loomed large for those practitioners who took a stand against their seemingly dangerous, problematic clients. Interestingly, while their fears for their own wellbeing were strong, they did not face any substantial threat to their physical, economic or social wellbeing. These risks were clearly apparent for their vulnerable clients, however. The initial assumptions about risk that were embedded in these practitioners' constructions of risk were never challenged – they were accepted as a given, as truth. Risk had become a static concept within their practice context and arguably played a role in them responding in unhelpful ways.

Critical reflection offers a way of reflecting on practice in which these taken-for-granted assumptions about risk can be reviewed, contested and reconstructed if required. Critically reflective questions can trouble hidden assumptions about power and privilege located within constructions of others and ourselves through a risk lens. I argue there is a need to reflect upon who does and does not benefit from risk thinking and how this compares to stated police service goals. There is also a need to question what other identities could be ascribed to others and ourselves that might be more enabling of people. Many more questions could be developed along these lines and Fook (2002) gives some direction how to form these questions. They lend themselves to personal reflection as well as being integrated into supervision and leadership contexts of policing.

Conclusion

Risk, it is argued, is used to legitimise the conservatism of the socio-economic policies and practices of neoliberal governments couched within the rhetoric of security, independence and economic freedom. The political and ethical ramifications of risk within this form of governance have perhaps unsurprisingly come to be spoken of in negative terms within the developing critical risk literature. Nonetheless, it is important to recognise that the dominance of the morally conservative rhetoric of risk is not total in the contexts of policing and other risk professions. There is an abundance of research that indicates that practitioners rely on situated informal rationalities in their direct practice (Horlick-Jones, 2005; Broadhurst et al, 2010), and that these reflect alternative landscapes of reason, emotion and morality that may reflect more socially just principles (Kemshall, 2010; Stanford, 2010). This knowledge impresses upon us the importance of including critical reflections upon risk as an available strategy for examining the implied socio-political and cultural contexts that form the ethics of direct practice encounters. I have proposed that critical reflection can create an ethical and moral professional space that is not captivated by the mentality of neoliberal risk ideology. In this space, vulnerability need not be framed as a culpable construct, but instead understood as a consequence of preceding "misrecognitions" (Lister, 2007) in institutional and interpersonal contexts. Such a practice may well support a more culturally productive and ethical response in the policing of vulnerability and responding productively to cultural diversity.

References

Adam, B and Van Loon, J, 2000, "Introduction: Repositioning Risk: the Challenge for Social Theory", *The Risk Society and Beyond: Critical Issues for Social Theory*, (Eds B Adam, U Beck and J Van Loon), Sage, London, 1.

Bartkowiak-Théron, I and Corbo Crehan, A, 2010, "A New Movement in Community Policing? From Community Policing to Vulnerable People Policing", *Community Policing in Australia: Research and Public Policy Series*, 111, (Ed J Putt), Australian Institute of Criminology, Canberra, ACT.

Beck, U, 2004, *Risk Society: Towards a New Modernity*, Sage, London.

Beck, U, 2003, *World Risk Society*, Polity Press, Cambridge, UK.

Broadhurst, K, Hall, C, Wastell, D, White, S and Pithouse, A, 2010, "Risk, Instrumentalism and the Humane Project in Social Work: Identifying the Informal Logics of Risk Management in Children's Statutory Services" 40 *British Journal of Social Work* 1046.

Campbell, E, 2004, "Police Narrativity in the Risk Society" 44 *British Journal of Criminology* 695.

Culpitt, I, 1999, *Social Policy and Risk*, Sage, London.

Davis, D-A, 2007, "Narrating the Mute: Racializing and Racism in a Neoliberal Movement" 9 *Souls* 346.

Dean, M, 1999, "Risk, calculable and incalculable", *Risk and Socio-cultural Theory: New Directions and Perspectives* (Ed D Lupton), Cambridge University Press, Cambridge, 131.

Douglas, M, 2003, *Risk and Blame: Essays in Cultural Theory*, (reprint), Routledge, London.

Dwyer, A, 2011, "'Damaged Goods': Riskiness and Lesbian, Gay, Bisexual and Transgender Young People's Interactions with Police", *Proceedings for the 2010 Australian and New Zealand Critical Criminology Conference*, 1-2 July 2010, Sydney.

Ericson, RV and Haggerty, KD, 1997, *Policing the Risk Society*, Clarendon Press, Oxford, UK.

Fook, J, 2002, *Social Work: Critical Theory and Practice*, Sage, London.

Furedi, F, 2008, "Fear and Security: a Vulnerability-led Policy Response" 42 *Social Policy and Administration* 645.

Giddens, A, 2003, *Runaway World: How Globalization is Reshaping our Lives*, Routledge, New York.

Gilling, D, 2001, "Community Safety and Social Policy" 9 *European Journal of Criminal Policy and Research* 381.

Goldberg, DT, 2009, *The Threat of Race: Reflections on Racial Neoliberalism*, Blackwell Publishing, USA.

Green, D, 2004, *The Risk Society and the Protection of Rights: Implications for an Ethical Practice*, Office of the Public Advocate. Viewed on 11 November 2004, <David-Green-Presentation-paper-2004-e6fa34bd-495d-45fa-a5bd-52688b892be6.pdf>.

Haylett, C, 2001, "Illegitimate Subjects?: Abject Whites, Neoliberal Modernization, and Middle-class Multiculturalism" 19 *Environment and Planning D: Society and Space* 351.

Horlick-Jones, T, 2005, "On 'Risk Work': Professional Discourse, Accountability, and Everyday Action" 7 *Health, Risk & Society* 293.

Kelly, P, 2001, "Youth at Risk: Process of Individualisation and Responsibilisation in the Risk Society" 22 *Discourse: Studies in the Cultural Politics of Education* 23.

Kelly, P, 2000, "The Dangerousness of Youth-at-risk: the Possibilities of Surveillance and Intervention in Uncertain Times" 23 *Journal of Adolescence* 463.

Kemshall, H, 2011, "Crime and Risk: Contested Territory for Risk Theorising" 39 *International Journal of Law, Crime and Justice* 218.

Kemshall, H, 2010, "Risk Rationalities in Contemporary Social Work Policy and Practice" 40 *British Journal of Social Work* 1247.

Kemshall, H, 2002, *Risk, Social Policy and Welfare: Introducing Social Policy*, Open University Press, Buckingham, UK.

Lennings, C, 2005, "Risk Assessment in Care and Protection: the Case for Actuarial Approaches" 4 *Australian e-Journal for the Advancement of Mental Health*. Viewed on 11 November 2006, <auseinet.com/journal/vol4iss1/lennings.pdf>.

Lister, R, 2007, "(Mis)recognition, Social Inequality and Social Justice: a Critical Social Policy Perspective", *(Mis)recognition, Social Inequality and Social Justice: Nancy Fraser and Pierre Bourdieu*, (Ed T Lovell), Routledge, Oxon, 157.

Maguire, M, 2000, "Policing by Risks and Targets: some Dimensions and Implications of Intelligence-led Crime Control, Policing and Society" 9 *Policing and Society: an International Journal of Research and Policy* 315.

McDonald, C, 2006, *Challenging Social Work: the Institutional Context of Practice*, Palgrave Macmillan, Houndsmills, UK.

Moreton-Robinson, A 2005, "Whiteness, Epistemology and Indigenous Representation", *Whitening Race: Essays in Social and Cultural Criticism* (Ed A Moreton-Robinson), Aboriginal Studies Press, Canberra, ACT.

O'Malley, P, 2006, "Criminology and Risk", *Beyond the Risk Society: Critical Reflection on Risk and Human Security* (Eds G Mythen and S Walklate), Open University Press, Maidenhead, UK, 43.

Pease, B, 2010, *Undoing Privilege: Unearned Advantage in a Divided World*, Zed Books, London.

Pollack, S, 2010, "Labelling Clients 'Risky': Social Work and the Neo-liberal Welfare State" 40 *British Journal of Social Work* 1263.

Roberts, DJ and Mahatani, M, 2010, "Neoliberalizing Race, Racing Neoliberalism: Placing 'Race' in Neoliberal Discourses" 42 *Antipode* 248.

Rose, N, 2000, "Government and Control" 40 *British Journal of Criminology* 321.

Rose, N, 1996a, "Governing 'Advanced' Liberal Democracies", *Foucault and Political Reason: Liberalism, Neoliberalism and Rationalities of Government* (Eds A Barry, T Osborne and N Rose), UCL Press, London, 37.

Rose, N, 1996b, "The Death of the Social?: Re-figuring the Territory of Government" 25 *Economy and Society* 327.

Rose, N and Miller, P, 2010, "Political Power beyond the State: Problematic of Government" 61 *British Journal of Sociology* 271.

Stanford, SN, 2011, "Constructing Moral Responses to Risk: a Framework for Hopeful Social Work Practice" 41 *British Journal of Social Work* 1514.

Stanford, SN, 2010, "'Speaking Back' to Fear: Responding to the Moral Dilemmas of Risk in Social Work Practice", *British Journal of Social Work* 1065.

Stanford, SN, 2008, "Taking a Stand or Playing it Safe?: Resisting the Moral Conservatism of Risk in Social Work Practice" 11 *European Journal of Social Work* 209.

Titterton, M, 2006, *Risk and Risk Taking in Health and Social Welfare*, Jessica Kingsley Publishers, London.

Walter, M, 2010, "Market Forces and Indigenous Resistance Paradigms" 9 *Social Movement Studies* 121.

Webb, SA, 2006, *Social Work in a Risk Society*, Palgrave Macmillan, Houndsmills, UK.

Chapter 3

"For when equality is given to unequals, the result is inequality":* The Socio-legal Ethics of Vulnerable People

Isabelle Bartkowiak-Théron and Anna Corbo Crehan

In many jurisdictions, categories of "vulnerable people" have been created with the intention of addressing the impaired ability[1] of some individuals to defend themselves and pursue their own best interests when involved with the judicial process. The most extensive provisions related to these categories impact on police work; that is, at people's first point of contact with the criminal justice system. In some cases, the relevant provisions identify a number of *mandatory* defence and support mechanisms that must be activated. Indeed, if such mechanisms are not activated, then evidence may not be admissible in court. This chapter takes as a fundamental premise that current criminal justice practice in relation to vulnerable people is essentially aimed at ensuring equality before the law for these people, consistent with a key aspect of the rule of law. The authors identify a number of ethical issues that arise in this context and assess their specific impacts on the goal of ensuring equality before the law. In particular, attention is paid to ethical matters triggered by the *blanket* provision of defence and support mechanisms for people who legally belong to a vulnerability category, but who arguably are not as disadvantaged as others in that same category – and, who may well be considered not vulnerable at all. With this information in hand, consideration will then be given to the impact this has for policing. We question how these ethical issues can addressed and, if not, whether they so undermine the goal of ensuring equality before the law that the whole idea of classifications of vulnerability should be revisited.

Rule of Law and Equality before the Law

The rule of law, which can be understood to be the fundamental impetus for laws and policies specific to vulnerable people, was given its classic formulation by AV Dicey (1914). He stated that the rule of law has three meanings:

The absolute supremacy or predominance of regular law as opposed to the influence of arbitrary power, and [it] excludes the existence of arbitrariness, of prerogative, or even of wide discretionary authority on the part of the government...

It means, again, equality before the law, or the equal subjection of all classes to the ordinary law of the land administered by the ordinary Law Courts; the "rule of law" in this sense excludes the idea of any exemption of officials or others from the duty of obedience to the law which governs other citizens or from the jurisdiction of the ordinary tribunals (Dicey, 1914).

Here, Dicey refers to equality before the law, which we consider to be the specific rationale for current criminal justice practices in relation to vulnerable people. Under the rule of law, a person cannot be punished for anything other than a breach of law – which implies, *inter alia*, that a person cannot be punished for having a disability which limits their understanding of everyday social interactions, their ability to contribute to their own defence, or their understanding of police practices or court proceedings. Typically, conceptions of the rule of law are now more nuanced and contain more concepts than Dicey's original three. For example, the Law Council of NSW (2011) listed eight "principles of the rule of law", and Gleeson in 2001 identified eleven "practical conclusions said to be required by the principle of the rule of law" as indicated by High Court judgments (2001). Nonetheless, the notion of equality before the law is common to all such conceptions viewed for the preparation of this chapter.

This notion was recently stated by the Law Council of Australia (2011) in the following terms: "The law should be applied to all people equally and should not discriminate between people on arbitrary or irrational grounds". The Judicial Commission of NSW in their *Equality Before the Law Bench Book* identified some such "arbitrary or irrational grounds" in its list of characteristics that can, but should not be allowed to, lead to unfairness in the treatment of people: "gender, ethnicity, disability, sexuality, age, religious affiliation, socio-economic background, size or nature of family, literacy level or any other such characteristic" (2011: 1103). To further expand their point, the authors then refer to McHugh J's statement that "discrimination can arise just as readily from an act which treats as equals those who are different as it can from an act which treats differently persons whose circumstances are not materially different" (*Waters v Public Transport Corporation*). This idea is captured in one of Gleeson's eleven "practical conclusions", namely, "that the criminal law should operate uniformly in circumstances which are not materially different" (2001); and, by extension, differently in cases that are "materially different".[2]

The various vulnerabilities that are identified by the criminal justice system and other agencies are one way of distinguishing certain circumstances as "materially different" to others. A situation where one person can understand a court's proceedings or a police officer's interview questions is substantively distinct from a situation where he/she does not understand the language in which those proceedings or questions are delivered. Similarly, a child's ability to negotiate the power imbalance involved in dealings with police is substantively different to an adult's abilities to negotiate that imbalance. It is also clear why laws and policies concerning vulnerable people are needed, to ensure that criminal laws "operate uniformly" and not in an ad hoc way. In short, only a brief acquaintance with the concepts of the rule of law and equality before the law is needed to demonstrate that specific processes and practices were introduced into the criminal justice system to address the various vulnerabilities that mean some people have an impaired ability to defend themselves within the judicial process and pursue their own best interests. With these systems of support, vulnerable people can supposedly better approach and navigate the criminal justice process, and are able to better communicate, understand proceedings and are in a better position to avoid abuse. According to Spigelman J, former Chief Justice of the Supreme Court of NSW, "the law is a system to be used by citizens for their own protection and their own advancement in their relations with the state and with other citizens" (2003). People who are vulnerable in various ways may not be fully able to use the law in this way (without some sort of specific assistance) and so risk falling outside the protections that are meant to be available to all.

Vulnerable People: An Overview

Various sorts of vulnerability have been identified as affecting whether someone does receive equal treatment before the law, and conversely as providing reasons for treating people differently in their dealings with the criminal justice system. For example, children are identified as vulnerable due, *inter alia*, to their underdeveloped reasoning and predictive skills; those whose first language differs from the language used in their respective justice system are identified as vulnerable due to the risk of them misunderstanding spoken and written information; and the mentally ill are identified for similar reasons.

In New South Wales, vulnerable people have been legally defined thus in cl 24 of the *Law Enforcement (Powers and Responsibilities) Regulation 2005* (LEPRR):

24 Vulnerable persons
(1) A reference in this Division to a vulnerable person is a reference to a person who falls within one or more of the following categories:
    (a) children,
    (b) persons who have impaired intellectual functioning,
    (c) persons who have impaired physical functioning,
    (d) persons who are Aboriginal persons or Torres Strait Islanders,
    (e) persons who are of non-English speaking background,

but does not include a person whom the custody manager reasonably believes is not a person falling within any of those categories.

In its *Consolidation of Arrest Laws in Tasmania*, the Tasmania Law Reform Institute (TLRI) recommends that "the proposed *Arrest Act* should include protective provisions for vulnerable persons" and that

> A vulnerable person should be defined as a person who falls into one or more of the following categories:
> - Young persons;
> - Persons who have impaired intellectual functioning;
> - Persons who have impaired physical functioning;
> - Aborigines and Torres Strait Islanders;
> - Persons who are of non-English speaking background (TLRI, 2011, p vi).

And the Queensland Police Service provides a 14 item list of which people count as vulnerable:

> **Identifying a Vulnerable Person**
> While it is not possible to supply an exhaustive list of persons who may be vulnerable in the criminal justice system, the following could be considered a guide:
> - (i) immaturity, either in terms of age or development;
> - (ii) any infirmity, including early dementia or disease;
> - (iii) mental illness;
> - (iv) intellectual disability;
> - (v) illiteracy or limited education which may impair a person's capacity to understand police questions;
> - (vi) inability or limited ability to speak or understand the English language;
> - (vii) chronic alcoholism;
> - (viii) physical disabilities including deafness or loss of sight;
> - (ix) drug dependence;
> - (x) cultural, ethnic or religious factors including those relating to gender attitudes;
> - (xi) intoxication, if at the time of contact with police the person is under the influence of alcohol or a drug to such an extent as to make them unable to look after or manage their own needs;
> - (xii) Aboriginal people and Torres Strait Islanders;
> - (xiii) children; and
> - (xiv) persons with impaired capacity (10 April 2012).

Apart from indicating the range of people that can be, and are, classified as vulnerable, the preceding lists also indicate the generality with which determinations of vulnerability are made. Not all mental illnesses, for instance, are such as to make a person vulnerable in their dealings with police (for example, mild depression), nor are all Indigenous Australians going to be vulnerable in their dealings with police (for example, a case where an Indigenous lawyer is arrested). Moreover, sometimes vulnerability, or levels of vulnerability, will depend on the reason for the interaction with police – whether someone is a victim, a witness or a suspect. Arguably, there is so much at stake when a person is treated by police as a suspect that unaddressed vulnerabilities are likely to have a significant effect. Conversely, vulnerable victims are likely to receive sensitive and considerate treatment from police – given that they are victims – and so their vulnerabilities are likely to be taken into account, even if only coincidentally.

These sorts of generalities are, of course, unavoidable features of policy-making and legislative development. It is not possible for policies or laws to be written that can cover all relevant situations, and there is a *prima facie* case to be made for "erring on the side of caution" and developing policies and laws that are too broad, rather than too narrow, especially in high risk situations, a description which typically fits dealings between police and vulnerable people.

Implications of Vulnerable Status for Police and Other Justice Personnel

As noted above, the legal classification of vulnerable people by the criminal justice system is for the purpose of providing those people with a series of services intended to address the inequalities they would otherwise encounter in their dealings with the criminal justice system. In most instances, police have no discretion in relation to "activating" the relevant processes or accessing the relevant services. For example, the *Police Powers and Responsibilities Regulation 2000* (Qld) provides at s 36(1) of Sch 10 that "A police officer who is about to question a relevant person the police officer reasonably suspects is an adult Aborigine or Torres Strait Islander *must*, unless he or she already knows the relevant person, first ask questions necessary to establish the person's level of education and understanding" (emphasis added). And similarly, in s 36(6), "If the police officer reasonably suspects the person is at a disadvantage in comparison with members of the Australian community generally, and the person has not arranged for a support person to be present during the questioning, the police officer *must* arrange for a support person to be present" (emphasis added).

There are provisions in the respective legislation enabling police to choose not to implement a specific provision, but during the authors' overview of relevant legislation (which they do not claim to have been exhaustive), it appears that such exceptions applied only to Indigenous Australians. The Commonwealth *Crimes Act 1914* includes the following: "An investigating official is not required to comply with subsection (1), (2) or (2B) in respect of a person if the official believes on reasonable grounds that, having regard to the person's level of education and understanding, the person is not at a disadvantage in respect of the questioning referred to in that subsection in comparison with members of the Australian community generally" (where sub-ss (1), (2) and (2B) identify the support people that must be contacted when an Aboriginal or Torres Strait Islander person is to be questioned as a suspect). A similar provision is included in the respective Queensland legislation.

But such provisions are exceptions to the rule; in most cases legislation and policy concerning vulnerable people make the provision of support mechanisms and "safeguards" (Morawa, 2003: 144) – such as translation services, psychological support, *certain* police actions, and specific follow up – mandatory, and to be in place for *all* members of these populations. The compulsory nature of these provisions means that, amongst other things, evidence obtained in situations where vulnerable people are not offered the relevant protections and services may be ruled inadmissible at court (Gudjonsson, Hayes and Rowlands, 2000; Bartkowiak-Théron and Lee, 2006). Put another way, there is a risk of significant injustice (cases in which the guilty go free or the non-guilty are punished) if the protective mechanisms in place for vulnerable people are not activated by police officers or other front-line representatives of the criminal justice system.

Ethical Issue One: Issues of Definition

The aforementioned lists of vulnerable people trigger immediate questions as to their non-exhaustive nature. It also reveals the absence of a single piece of legislation that not only brings these groups together under an official statute, but also makes a specific determination of what exactly constitutes the vulnerability of the individuals who fall within each group.[3] "Vulnerable", under LEPRR, is defined as nothing but the list mentioned above (LEPRR, Division 3, cl 24), and neither the Act (*Law Enforcement (Powers and Responsibilities) Act 2002 – LEPRA*) nor the Regulation provides a semantic or sociological explanation of the expression for the benefit of either readers or law enforcement professionals. The Queensland Police Service Vulnerable Persons Policy includes some text that might be thought to approximate an explanation. For example, "[those] who are vulnerable could encounter difficulties in accessing or receiving equitable or fair treatment during their contact with the QPS as a victim, witness or suspect", and "a defendant must be given procedural fairness or natural justice - the ability to participate in the defence of the charges brought against them, the ability to understand what is happening and being given the opportunity to be heard and present a defence" (QPS, 10 April 2012). But other statements in the same section apply generally to victims, witnesses or suspects, irrespective of a specific vulnerability; for example, "Victims and witnesses may feel intimidated by the court process or may not understand or know what is required of them" (Ibid). Clearly, what is being referred to here is the vulnerability consequent upon being a witness or victim, rather than the sorts of vulnerability characteristics on which this chapter (and, indeed, the rest of the Queensland policy) focuses.

While preparing a syllabus some years ago, one of the authors found an interesting gap in the literature about the very definition of vulnerable people.[4] Since most of the literature related to risk and vulnerability does not delimit semantics, and thus is not in a position to inform legislation and police policy, the first ethical issue we have identified is the need to fill this gap and set some specific parameters as to how vulnerability and vulnerable people should be understood (Bartkowiak-Théron and Lee, 2006). It is even more important given that the expression is used indiscriminately as a synonym for other people (see Asquith and Bartkowiak-Théron, Ch 1), which confuses the debates. It is sometimes used in very general ways, which do not capture the specific sense implied in legislation and policies for vulnerable people. Some clarification is needed here.

Vulnerability is inextricably related to the idea of risk. The Oxford English Dictionary (2008) states the main definition of *risk* as one of an external danger, a peril that one might face. Risks are often external factors coming from society or one's physical or psychological environment. Being *at risk* is being in a state or condition marked by a high level of risk or susceptibility, being exposed to harm, particular threats or to danger in general (see also Chapter 2 in this collection). *Vulnerability*, quite distinctly, defines somebody as being either *defenceless* (an interpretation we believe may be too strong in the current context) in the face of potential risks or having a compromised capacity to defend themselves in relation to potential risks. The etymology traces the word back to a late Latin meaning of wound or injury (*vulner-, vulnus*) and highlights one's susceptibility to being physically or emotionally wounded, open to attack or damage, and/or assailable. Although 'vulnerable' and 'at risk' are now used as synonyms, including in the context of legal definitions, we are of the view that the differences in their initial definitions highlight an important distinction which causes systemic problems (from both theoretical and practical perspectives) when the distinction is not maintained. Specifically, we believe that vulnerability – in the current context – should be understood as an impaired ability to defend oneself in the face of specific sorts of risks; an understanding which captures the idea of susceptibility as per the term's original etymology.

Ethical Issue Two: Gaps and Omissions

The aforementioned semantics of the expressions highlight, in a rather interesting manner, the limits of the legalistic classification of people into the categories mentioned above. Notwithstanding the fact that the various policies and pieces of legislation referred to above sometimes apply to people at specific stages of the criminal justice system (for example, in custody), there are glaring omissions from the lists of who counts as vulnerable. Among the omitted groups, one could consider women, people released from prison (or, perhaps, only those recently released), members of some professions, religious minorities, and people from a disadvantaged economic situation[5] (although we agree that some of these are debatable, from, for example, a feminist position). It can be argued that members of these additional categories would also have impaired defences in the face of at least some aspects of the judicial process, and could therefore fruitfully avail themselves of some support when going through the justice system. Nonetheless, while they can indeed be considered vulnerable from a logical and analytical point of view, none of these categories have been identified in legislation reviewed for this chapter. This is the first gap we have identified.

Moreover, it is arguable that if the vulnerability status of at least some groups (Indigenous Australians are a case in point) rests partly on the grounds of the discriminatory harm done to their communities in the past, then that same status should be granted to other populations who were also discriminated against in the (near or distant) past, such as Jews, Muslims, South-East Asian refugees, or even gay men and lesbians. A discourse seems to be held for particular categories of people in a rather arbitrary manner, while not considering other groups who are alike in respect of relevant vulnerability factors (see our earlier reference, in the title of the chapter, to Aristotle's statement of the principle that it is unjust not to treat like cases alike). As before, this raises a very fundamental ethical discrepancy, which stands in need of either remedy or justification.

Despite classifications of vulnerability being intended as a way to provide certain forms of support to people, it is nonetheless true that being categorised as vulnerable is not necessarily a good thing, nor necessarily something that a person would want for themselves. There are some more or less reasonable arguments that might be put forward for declining the label of legal vulnerability (by both those already recognised as such and those who could be so recognised). Richardson (2008) argues that in the context of mental illness, the determination of vulnerability "on the grounds of mental impairment" bears a negative and discriminatory label that can act to the detriment of defendants. In another domain of consideration, one could also argue that in the context of a society facing threats of terrorism post-9/11, being "granted" vulnerable status may do no more than bring you within a sphere of control and surveillance which could seriously affect your enjoyment of various human and civil rights. Put another way, the conferring of vulnerable status may be another form of stereotyping, providing a means of discriminating against a group. If we consider the recent Queensland case of Dr Mohammed Haneef[6], it is easy to see how fear and uncertainty can lead to dangerous liberties being taken with one's rights – a possibility which would, arguably, be magnified for members of any group deemed vulnerable and thus subject to mandatory legal actions. This presents us with a deep and fundamental ethical problem that is partly rooted, according to Hörnqvist (2004: 37), in the emergence of security, rather than law, as a foundational element in the negotiation and articulation of judicial matters[7].

Another gap exists in relation to principles of non-interference and self-determination (Williams, 2002: 303), perhaps better known as the moral obligation to respect another's autonomy, all things being equal (see, for example, Dworkin, 1988: 20). Being given a vulnerability status can seriously undermine one's autonomy, one's interest in being able to formulate one's own preferences, plans and values, and in being able to act on decisions about the pursuit of those preferences, plans and values. For instance, it is now generally agreed that being a woman does not automatically make a person vulnerable, and feminist movements throughout the world have demonstrated the aptitude of women in the face of hardship and their capacity for independence and self-defence in the face of risk. And we can now see how the status of vulnerability limited the sorts of choices women were able to make and the sorts of interests they could pursue.

Similar conclusions can be drawn about contemporary legally defined categories of vulnerable people. For example, although elder abuse is a significant problem for modern societies (Williams, 2002: 294), people do not automatically become vulnerable in our sense (that is, having an impaired ability to defend themselves against certain sorts of threats) as soon as, and just because, they reach a certain age. However, all elderly people are recognised as vulnerable under several pieces of legislation or policy documentation on guardianship, for example. This means that they can be "subjected to" actions which interfere with their ability to make and act on their own decisions. Another example would be that of individuals from non-English speaking backgrounds who are granted vulnerability status under LEPRR in NSW. Clearly, having a first language other than English does not necessarily impede one's English skills, which might be excellent and not hinder one's understanding of legal issues, and to presume otherwise would amount to a disregard for a person's ability to act for themselves and make their own decisions. In some cases (see the references above to the Commonwealth and Queensland legislation that allows vulnerability status to be withheld from Indigenous people) the law indeed considers an individual's background. However, this is an exception. And while it would appear possible that in some cases a police officer would have the discretion to determine actual needs and risks, and therefore modulate actual vulnerability levels, this itself is ethically problematic, given the subjectivity of such judgments and the ways they might be impacted on by irrelevant considerations (for example, avoiding the time it would take to find a support person or interpreter).

Finally, the law leaves a gap in that it does not specifically mention issues of multiple vulnerabilities in the articulation of protective mechanisms for vulnerable people. It is common to find persons displaying multiple vulnerability factors. Let's have, as an example, a homeless, elderly, non-English-speaking, Indigenous person with a history of mental illness, or a young victim of crime addicted to prohibited substances displaying signs of bipolar disorder. The provision of the relevant multiple services in such cases demands careful attention to not only detail (have all vulnerabilities been addressed?), but also the priority with which they should be addressed (where do authorities start? Which vulnerability factor has the highest level of urgency and who decides this?). The scope for breaches of a person's rights seems significant in these cases – might the young victim of crime receive less than optimal attention from police if she identifies as a user of prohibited substances while being interviewed by police? Should police seek medical advice for her apparent bipolar disorder before taking a statement from her? Is it justifiable for police to intervene in relation to her health if she voluntarily seeks their assistance for another matter? For police in charge of such cases, risk considerations are labyrinthine. We do not think it is possible to specify, *a priori*, how vulnerabilities and corresponding rights should be prioritised. We simply argue that legal and policy guidelines on addressing vulnerabilities should provide specific information in relation to people with multiple vulnerabilities; and that a justifiable prioritisation of vulnerabilities needs to pay adequate attention to corresponding issues of rights.

Ethical Issue Three: Overlaps and Redundancies

The provision of protection and support mechanisms for those at the other extreme of the scale – those who fall into a legal classification of vulnerable, but in fact are not disadvantaged – is also ethically worrying. The classifications fail to create a 'level playing field'. While vulnerable categories have been set up to amend the situations of the most disadvantaged, the *blanket provision of services* to people who fit these categories is problematic for those who belong to these categories *per se*, but are *de facto* much less vulnerable than others. Granted, such an impact is often true of many policies and pieces of legislation that simply cannot include various distinctions between individuals. And there may be good utilitarian reasons for maintaining blanket approaches, even when they "scoop up" people unneces-sarily. If police do not have to make distinctions between people who are putatively members of a vulnerable group, there is less chance of them "doing something wrong" and missing a step in protocols that might put future legal action at risk. Nonetheless, the question remains whether the impact on non-vulnerable members of vulnerable groups is so disproportionate as to require attention? Does it go so far as to have the opposite effect on some who are assigned (unnecessarily) membership of vulnerable groups?

Clearly, the conferring of legal vulnerability status is not linked to an indi-vidual's actual capacities, which could be verified *in situ* and on a case by case basis. What is considered instead is the individual's belonging to a group of people that has been pre-determined as probably "lacking capacity" (Williams, 2002: 303) with no regard for their actual individual capacities. This contradicts people's right to autonomy, and their membership of "an externally coherent group" becomes the sole reason for their being subject to specific treatment. Externally coherent groups, a term included in the work of Larry May (1987), are groups whose coherence is based on the "strong identification of individual persons as group members by external observers" (May, 1987: 115). Such groups are generally unorganised social groups, the members of which share characteristics which make them identifiable to others as group members. Indigenous Australians, African-Americans, women, and homeless people constitute the sorts of groups to which May is referring. When a person's treatment is based solely on their group membership, they are being "reduced to a mere token of the [relevant] type ... There is no other morally significant type of which any given ... [group member] is thought to be a token" (May, 1987: 116). Such considerations lean towards a paternalistic discourse of structural inequalities, where the disadvantaged are determined according to their standing at the margins or even outside the social majority.

Blatantly missing from the categorisation exercise, then, are the other aspects of the person which may render an apparent vulnerability factor moot. As recognised by the Commonwealth and Queensland governments, being of Indigenous descent may often be an indicator of vulnerability; an Indigenous person's language skills, professional standing or education may ensure that they are not at all vulnerable. We believe that such 'additional factors' ought to be considered in the allocation of 'mandatory' support mechanisms under vulnerable persons legislation. For one thing, it is morally culpable to be wasteful of scarce resources by allocating them to situations where they are not needed. Perhaps more importantly though, classifications of vulnerability – as we have argued – can impact in significantly negative ways on a person's autonomy. So, if it is possible to ensure that such negative impacts do not occur – and the Commonwealth and Queensland have clearly demonstrated that it is possible – then such impacts ought to be ensured against.

This is not necessarily to argue that sweeping discretionary powers should be at the forefront of authorities' decision making in ascribing vulnerability status: some vulnerabilities may not be readily observable (for example, some learning disabilities), while others might go unobserved for any number of reasons (for example, the person may go to some lengths to disguise a disability, or a police officer may have certain biases that mean they do not "see" some vulnerabilities). Policies and legislation can include guidelines that provide police with indications as to characteristics and skills that would justify withholding vulnerable status. Discourses of equity and of the rule of law should be reiterated here. Allocating specific services to one person and none or fewer to another, without new guidelines to ensure fairness, undermines the principle of equality before the law and risks an imbalance wherein some individuals are granted privileges and some are "denied" the same support for no apparent good reason. The cycle of inequality is therefore reproduced, despite initial efforts to mend the gap, and Aristotle's assertion, quoted in the title of this chapter, still seems to apply. And yet, the principle of "epikeia"[8] justice (Shanske, 2008) and the notions of procedural and distributive justice should be driving the articulation and application of the law, alongside the principles and ideals of the rule of law. The current understanding of classifying vulnerable people has triggered a hermetic system of precautionary measures, which focuses exclusively on one extreme of the scale (the disadvantaged) without considering the other extreme (ones who do not need additional protection or already have the skills to protect themselves).

Some Conclusions about the Ethical Difficulties of Striving for Equality before the Law

As we stated initially, we believe current criminal justice practice in relation to vulnerable people is essentially aimed at ensuring equality before the law for these people, consistent with a key aspect of the rule of law. However, the preceding discussion has revealed a number of ways in which this objective is not fully met. These include the apparently arbitrary designation of who counts as a vulnerable person, a situation exacerbated by the lack of any rigorous definition of what "vulnerable" means – both in general and in this context – and the lack of specific guidelines for people with multiple vulnerabilities. It has also been demonstrated that the over-reach of vulnerable people policies and legislation is avoidable and, due to the injustices it can cause, ought to be avoided. More generally, then, what this chapter has demonstrated is that the negative consequences of current criminal justice system practices in relation to vulnerable people can be addressed in ways that preserve their intent of providing vulnerable people with a series of services intended to address the inequalities they would otherwise encounter in their dealings with the criminal justice system. Addressing those negative consequences need not become an exercise where a proverbial baby (the provision of relevant services to those who genuinely need them) is thrown out with the respective (and equally proverbial!) bathwater.

Endnotes

* The quote in the title is one version of a phrase usually attributed to Aristotle in his *Nicomachean Ethics*; see note 8 also.

1 Clearly, this ability will be so impaired in some people as to render them totally defenceless. However, we will retain use of the more complex term as it captures the range of possibilities.

2 This maxim is usually traced to Aristotle's *Nicomachean Ethics*.

3   Tasmania has recently called for a consolidation of Arrest Laws, with a clear definition of disadvantaged groups; see Henning (2011).

4   This is confirmed by Morawa (2002: 150).

5   Some of these, but not all, are included in international legislation (see, for example, the European Convention on Human Rights). They are also the focus of policy documents in Australia and internationally, but are not clearly mentioned in legislation.

6   An interesting discussion of some of the ethical aspects of this case can be found in Keim (2010).

7   Hörnqvist (2004: 36-37) implies that the importance of the rule of law and the law in general has been "down graded" in the particular post-9/11 context and that terrorist threats and moral panics have led the criminal justice system to consider security rather than law as more of a priority.

8   What is appropriate, seeming or proper.

References

Human Rights Act 1998 (UK).

Aristotle, 1983, *Nicomachean Ethics* (Trans JAK, Thomson), Penguin, UK.

Bartkowiak-Théron, I and Lee, M, 2006, "Modelling Risks and Vulnerabilities: Legal Implications and Protection of the Law", Paper presented at the 23rd Australasian Law and Society Conference, University of Wollongong, 13-15 December 2006.

Council of Europe, 1970, *Convention for the Protection of Human Rights and Fundamental Freedoms*, European Court of Human Rights.

Dicey, AV, 1914, *Introduction to the Study of the Law of the Constitution.* Viewed on 10 April 2012, <www.constitution.org/cmt/avd/law_con.htm>.

Dworkin, G, 1988, *The Theory and Practice of Autonomy*, Cambridge University Press, New York.

Germov, J and Poole, M, 2011, *Public Sociology: An Introduction to Australian Society*, 2nd ed, Allen and Unwin, Sydney.

Gleeson, M, 2001, *Courts and the Rule of Law.* Viewed on 10 April 2012, <www.hcourt.gov.au/assets/publications/speeches/former-justices/gleesoncj/cj_ruleo-flaw.htm>.

Gudjonsson, GH, Hayes, GD, and Rowlands, P, 2000, "Fitness to be Interviewed and Psychological Vulnerability: the views of Doctors, Lawyers and Police Officers", 11 *The Journal of Forensic Psychiatry* 18.

Henning, T, 2011, *Consolidation of Arrest Laws in Tasmania*, Tasmania Law Reform Institute, Hobart.

Hörnqvist, M, 2004, "The birth of public order policy", 46 *Race and Class* 22.

Judicial Commission of NSW, 2011, *Equality Before the Law*. Viewed on 10 April 2012, <www.judcom.nsw.gov.au/publications/benchbks/equality>.

Kahn, PW, 1997, *The Reign of Law: Marbury v. Madison and the Construction of America*, Yale University Press, New Haven, USA.

Keim, S, 2010, "Ethics of the Advocate: a Theoretical and Practical Examination", 11 *Australian Journal of Professional and Applied Ethics* 81.

Law Council of Australia, *Rule of Law*. Viewed on 10 April 2012, <www.lawcouncil.asn.au/programs/international/rule-of-law.cfm>.

List, C, 2006, "Republican freedom and the rule of law", 5 *Politics, Philosophy and Economics* 19.

May, L, 1987, *The Morality of Groups*, University of Notre Dame, Notre Dame, Indiana, USA.

Morawa, AHE, 2003, "Vulnerability as a Concept of International Human Rights Law", 6 *Journal of International Relations and Development* 18.

Moroni, S, 2007, "Planning, Liberty and the Rule of Law" 6 *Planning Theory, Special Issue: Land-use, Planning and the Law* 17.

Oxford English Dictionary, 2008, Risk, OUP, UK.

Queensland Police Service, *QPS Vulnerable Persons Policy*. Viewed 10 April 2012, <www.police.qld.gov.au/rti/published/policies/>.

Richardson, E, 2008, "Mental Health Courts and Diversion Programs for Mentally Ill Offenders: The Australian context", Paper presented at the *8th Annual International Association for Forensic Mental Health Services Conference*, Brisbane, 25-26 October 2008.

Shanske, D, 2008, "Revitalizing Aristotle's Doctrine of Equity", 4 *Law, Culture and the Humanities* 29.

Simons, KW, 2001, "On Equality, Bias Crimes, and Just Deserts", 91 *The Journal of Criminal Law and Criminology* 30.

Spigelman, J, 2003, "The Rule of Law and Enforcement", 26(1) *University of New South Wales Law Journal*.

Tasmania Law Reform Institute, 2011, *Consolidation of Arrest Laws in Tasmania*. Viewed 10 April 2012, <www.law.utas.edu.au/reform/documents/Consolidation_of_Arrest_Laws_in_Tasmania.pdf>.

Williams, J, 2002, "Public Law Protection of Vulnerable Adults: The Debate Continues, So Does the Abuse", 2 *Journal of Social Work* 23.

Chapter 4

Educating for Vulnerability

Isabelle Bartkowiak-Théron and Catherine Layton

Educating police about vulnerability is a complex process, with harm minimisation essential for non-police and police alike, and against a background of longstanding stereotypes. Reiner (1998) suggests that police see vulnerabilities in others by way of social distinctions, including "police property" (scum, radicals, gays); "rubbish" (domestics); and "disarmers" (worthy victims), and see themselves as "macho"; that is, without vulnerability. It is probable that past police education has contributed to these stereotypes. But when vulnerable populations are now said to represent about 75 per cent of police encounters in the field, how do police officers prepare for their task? McLaughlin and Whatman (2008) argue that deconstructing cultural assumptions starts with a critical enquiry into the ways in which attitudes and behaviours are framed by our own cultures. If students are to appreciate the ways in which the "other" is framed, they must recognise the complexities of social interaction and the difficulties of achieving mutual understanding. Could a model developed for intercultural competence be of value in redeveloping police education to better cater for the needs of the vulnerable, and for officers to recognise their own vulnerability? In the policing context, there is a delicate balance to be achieved between experimenting during encounters with vulnerable people, implementing protocols, de-escalating crises and delivering, as immediately as possible, the best services to community members.

In this chapter, we examine two possible paths forward, based on our own combined experiences of changing police education in two Australian states, Tasmania and New South Wales. We base our view of learning on the holistic approaches to learning from experiences delineated by Boud and Miller (1997) and Boud, Cohen and Walker (1996). We suggest that people's interpretations of, and actions upon, their experiences at work and in training inevitably involve improvising their way through experiences and interactions with the tools and models they have to hand and in the light of perceived possibilities. This model recognises the inevitable interaction between individuals' personal histories and their specific work and training contexts. However, we recognise that this is not the model that has been prominent in police education, even though apprenticeship, where students learn through practice, has dominated. We will show how teaching perspectives can overlap or be combined to satisfy the requirements of police operational and academic education, whilst also initiating circles of engagement and trust with community members.

Educational Options

Teaching police recruits involves primarily the deconstruction of "taken-for-granted" attitudes amongst individuals before they enter police organisations. These attitudes are embedded in routine practices. Unfortunately, the critical thinking skills underpinning how police interact with vulnerability are rarely well taught, if at all, and rarely acquired (Sipress and Voelker, 2006; Angelo, 1995). Besides cultural barriers, hindrance to the critical thinking that underpins the deconstruction of social situatedness includes:

- Self-delusion, narrow-mindedness, and prejudice
- Fear, defensiveness, projection, hiding behind rules
- Habits and routines
- Bureaucratic monitoring and testing
- Ignorance
- Resistance to doing the intellectual work necessary (Paul, 2007; Hirschhorn, 1988).

To what extent can education offer a pathway out of this impasse? There are many competing educational theories upon which we could draw, and many categorisations of these theories (for example, Ramsden, 2003; Saddington, 1998; Stewart, 2004; and Warner Weil and McGill, 1989). Here, we draw on Pratt, Collins and Selinger (2005), as their work encompasses both well-used and less frequently used perspectives, with the latter more likely to engender a process of perspective deconstruction at an individual level. They characterised current Western theoretical frameworks on teaching as having five dimensions: transmission, apprenticeship, developmental, nurturing and social reform perspectives. Of these, the first two are most common in policing. Table 1 describes them in detail, with references to police education.

We used these five perspectives on learning and teaching to analyse our own classroom and curriculum development practices (using the Teaching Practices Inventory; Pratt and Collins, 2001). Both of us have strong profiles in everything other than the transmission model. Given the limitations of the transmission model in deconstructing assumptions, and the potential of the other approaches to engender change, this is a fruitful starting point for our discussion.

Table 1: Brief Summary of Teaching Perspectives

Transmission Perspective	Teachers have mastery of the subject matter, and represent it accurately, efficiently and memorably. There are clear objectives, planned lectures, timely feedback, corrections, directions, and high assessment standards. Delivered by specialised academics or experienced police officers, this style is the dominant delivery mode in police academies. However, this rational "sage on the stage" model has allowed for organisational defences to become entrenched, and is unlikely to generate the sorts of experiences that can help students deconstruct their assumptions about vulnerability.
Apprenticeship Perspective	Students adopt social norms and ways of working in a graduated way, from direction, through guidance, to independent practice. The model relies highly on the quality of the "workshop", the "apprentices" and the "master". Professional virtues and guidance are essential – well-meaning amateurs can perpetuate or create problems in students' understanding of vulnerability (Layton, 2004), or stereotypes about police character and roles (Berg, 1990). Again, only if practices change might this approach be effective.
Developmental perspective	Students are supported in developing increasingly sophisticated ways of understanding content through challenging questions, cases and problems. This approach, highly scientific, rational and cognitive in its origins, has framed the notion of constructivist and of problem-based learning approaches in education, and the parallel development of problem-oriented policing. It goes from starting with learners' understandings as a basis for structuring learning in classroom contexts, to a practice-centred, experiential approach. But in policing, simulated patrol depends on fellow students "acting" the client-role, and debriefing may not be about the "client" and "officer" experience, but, rather, about what was and was not done correctly.
Nurturing Perspective	Teachers develop a climate of trust and support to foster everyone's capacity to achieve an approach atypical of institutional contexts. This is a possible component of police education, and of police management that would address vulnerability within the service, but, of our experiences in police education, two phrases come to mind, "Get used to it!" and "Build a bridge and get over it!", which are not conducive to such an approach.
Social Reform Perspective	Teachers and students deconstruct discourses and practices that perpetuate disadvantage. The focus is not so much on how knowledge is created; rather by whom and for what purpose. It thus empowers students to take social action to improve their lives. In this model, education for practice is fundamentally a political act; the knowledge of those who have been excluded from society must be profoundly respected, valued, and worked with as legitimate (Freire, 1998). This critical engagement has three key aspects: • collaborative learning, • the examination of power, how things come to be the way they are, and how to improve the situation for the most excluded, and • interacting with communities in ways that emphasise self-determination, co-ownership of processes and outcomes, open participation and distributed leadership (Smyth, Angus, Down, and McInerney, 2008: 2-7). The applicability of this type of perspective to police education is discussed below.

Context of Police Education on Vulnerability

The premise for this discussion is an awareness of the complexities of police working in a heavily politicised, multicultural and diverse environment, and of its consequences on police education. The conservative view of policing is that it is the benign crystallisation of the power of the people (Reiner, 1998), represented in many ways – uniforms, weapons, the right to ask questions, to caution, to arrest. It is not in the state's interest for police to seed revolution and dissent by working on behalf of the dominated and devalued – they can provide a service, but challenging the status quo is likely to be a very different matter. Despite an acknowledgment that societies are increasingly pluralised (Chan, 1997), Schattschneider (1960) suggests that, "The flaw in the pluralist heaven is that the heavenly chorus sings with a strong upper-class accent".

Their very role therefore puts police at the centre of interactions within a framework of unequal power. Within this framework, stereotypes and the behaviours that can perpetuate them may stem from a distancing of authorities from the communities they serve based on mutual misunderstandings, lack of awareness, fear, dislike, differences in values and so on. Whether we look at the concept of "vulnerable populations" from a Marxist or Weberian perspective, this places police officers at the centre of a rather tense dynamic, where they are in charge of keeping the peace, enforcing the law, and also deal with a variety of tasks mandated by rule of law and duty of care principles. This implies significant juggling, as police are stuck between their accountability to higher authorities, to their organisation, and externally to the community itself. Nonetheless, we must be cautious about taking a one-size-fits-all approach, or assuming that police organisations, like the police within them, are divorced from wider social contexts. Three issues are discussed here: differing national/state contexts, political and economic constraints, and the extent to which centralised power feeds into everyday interactions.

First of all, curriculum issues relate not just to power, but also to the ways in which it is used and communicated across widely differing nation states, individuals, populations, geographies, and situations. For example, in countries where the segmentation of society according to "vulnerabilities" would be ill-advised, categories of population may not even be legally recognised, and therefore ineligible for special attention (Bartkowiak-Théron and Corbo Crehan, in this collection, Ch 3; see also Bartkowiak-Théron and Corbo Crehan, 2010). In France, for example, matters of ethnicity, race or religion are acknowledged but not grounds for specific attention, as the particularisation of the French society into segmented communities goes against the republican ideal. Australia is at the other end of this spectrum, with strong policies based on multiculturalism.

Secondly, state-related concerns will dominate, in terms of finances, electoral platforms and contemporary normative tendencies. Budget management and priorities (Dupont, 2002) will strongly impact on the timing and delivery of education: in paring down costs, education may be stripped to the bone, suffer cuts to student intakes or costly aspects of the curriculum, or be wholly or partly tendered out to other providers. The 2010 state budget cuts in Tasmania, for example, have cancelled all police recruitment for the foreseeable future. Along the same vein, election promises that increase throughput of recruits increase class sizes and tend towards processes that ignore social inclusion within the classroom. This "industrialisation" of police education might mean that the assessment focuses on content through rapid, multiple choice exams – ill-suited to the social domain because the assessment invariably moves away from critical reflection and analysis.

Finally, there is also a danger in focusing people's attention on large-scale descriptions and stereotypes of police as agents of the state, not recognising that, in most Western democracies, the reach of the state is limited. As Gidden suggests, the "juggernaut of modernity ... is not an engine made up of integrated machinery, but one in which there is a tensionful, contradictory, push-and-pull of different influences" (1991: 139); each police officer will have to communicate and make decisions that either confirm or negate vulnerability. Indeed, the notion of vulnerability is decontextualised in policy and in legislation: very different people are grouped together as a "population" to be dealt with more or less effectively, and making the day-to-day interactions in which effective practice finds its place invisible (Foucault, 1981). For example, differences between sub-categories of non-English speaking background individuals are brushed over, hiding vast deviations between them in terms of cultural proficiency with social norms, language skills and familiarity with a "European-based" criminal justice system. However, the logistics of police curriculum often mean that shortcuts are needed to see to the prompt operationalisation of officers, especially recruits. We offer solutions to this later in our chapter, by providing examples of how this can be avoided, and how complex teaching practice grounded in multiple teaching perspectives and beliefs can contribute to competence building.

Police and Vulnerability

Police organisations are more often a "force" rather than a "service", typified by a highly masculinised occupation, where vulnerabilities amongst the "members" are shunned, including:

- physically (entry requirements, expectations of readiness for action, and injury-related early retirement);
- mentally and intellectually (entry requirements and early retirement); and
- emotionally (absence of routine practices for debriefing other than at major disaster level – official solace for the traumatised has traditionally been found in conversations with police chaplains and recent Employee Assistance Programs).

This has meant an important gap in employee support services, reflecting and perpetuating "macho" stereotypes. Indeed, Reynolds, Scott and Austin (2000) draw attention to studies which demonstrate that empathetic responses to clients will be absent if the work environment is not supportive. Hirschhorn (1992) concluded that organisations often had institutionalised defence mechanisms which workers adopted to avoid direct and painful encounters with the emotional significance of what they were to do. This is not a problem solely for police – other occupational groups have had to think through these issues too (see for example, Stanford, in this collection, Ch 2).

The illusion of strength and control in everyday policing can mean that not only is no attention paid to vulnerability amongst clients, fellow officers and subordinates, there is insufficient recognition of everyday complexities. However, this lack of attention to the emotional well-being of those who are doing the policing is not true of all police organisations. For example, those investigating child abuse at a national level have a psychologist available to them in the workplace. Also, this is not true of all police – just as communities do not fit the stereotypes commonly found amongst police, nor do police fit community stereotypes of them. Even when the backgrounds are seemingly uniform, there are differences of personal values, responses to challenges and changes, people and vulnerability.

Furthermore, recent progress in policing education encourages, at early recruitment and education stages, an acknowledgment of future officers' awareness of their own "weaknesses". This implies that teachers, via a series of questions or exercises, encourage students to look at their own prejudices (we all have some, however benign) and how biased they might be (we all are) on some issues. In police education, this transpires into a broader organisational outlook on practices, with awareness raising lectures on topics such as institutional racism, affirmative action practices, and anti-discriminatory guidelines.

Relationships with the Education Sector

Historically isolated and insular in terms of the education sector, the origins of police education lie, like much of Western education, in the creation of "disciplined bodies" (Foucault, 1977), and, in many cases, this is where police education has largely stayed. In English-speaking countries, the starting point for policing as we know it lies in developments early in the nineteenth century, particularly the creation of the Metropolitan Police in 1829 by Robert Peel. Walker (1999: 21) described three elements from this period that form part of the framework of modern policing: a mission of crime prevention; a strategy of maintaining a visible presence through preventive patrol; and a quasi-military structure, "including uniforms, rank designations, and the authoritarian system of command and discipline" to ensure that the police actually undertook the beats on which preventative patrol depended. Police*men* had to be six feet tall (or as near as possible), have no history of wrong-doing, and were required to wear their uniforms both on and off duty. King (1956) described the ways in which geography, the social composition of the colony, available money and human resources, the spread of the pastoral industry and of Sydney – combined with ideas and techniques imported from the "mother country" – shaped policing in New South Wales. The hierarchical observation, normalising judgments, controlled activities and moral correction through disciplining bodies typical of this period have their place in aspects of police curricula today, particularly weapons training, fitness and drill.

Over time, loose connections emerged between TAFE-style apprenticeship systems and police training, in that periods of training and workplace experience were interspersed, but the brevity of the training meant that the parallel is that of a "crude craft model" (Bradley, 1997). Attempts to define policing as a profession, with ethics the predominant issue, have been relatively recent. There have been different models, each having to swim against a tide of pragmatism and aversion to theory. As an example of this trend, here we look at the New South Wales experience.

In New South Wales, before World War II, police training involved a daily one or two hours of law, shorthand and physical training, followed by time at the police station. After the war, there were two weeks of initial training, followed by nine months at the station, six weeks of training in law, procedures, reports, arithmetic, pistol-shooting and drill (Lusher, 1981). Less than five per cent of the curriculum was socially oriented.

The appointment of John Avery as Commissioner in 1985 triggered what became a lengthy series of educational reforms, starting with a new Police Recruit Education Program in 1988, with problem-based learning introduced in 1991. The curriculum was again redesigned in 1997, in response to the Wood Royal Commission's recommendation that recruit education be placed in the hands of universities in order, in part, to overcome insularity. The NSW Police Service developed a collaborative model for which universities tendered; Charles Sturt University (CSU), which already had a presence at the (then) NSW Police Academy, was the successful bidder. A new, comprehensive curriculum was designed. The program explicitly addressed the recommendations of the Wood report in relation to vulnerable populations, acknowledging that:

> Some minority or disadvantaged groups are particularly vulnerable by reason of their limited resources, cultural backgrounds, or unfamiliarity with the English language, to extortion and corrupt conduct on the part of the police (Wood, 1997: 139).

The NSW Police story is offered merely as an example of changes in police education with which we are familiar. Across many nations, the general movement for contemporary police education was and remains complex, with police officers expected to have knowledge in sociology, criminology, public policy, and of course, law. The move towards the professionalisation of policing has led to a growing number of partnerships with universities, and to the requirement for police officers to be accredited professionals. These partnerships offer a jointly designed curriculum at recruit level, which transitions into opportunities for ongoing professional development for police officers.

Training Police to Deal with Vulnerability

In this section, we describe two different types of educational practice; one which works at a whole of curriculum level – recognising the constraints of, and innovations in, police practice (Bartkowiak-Théron) – and the other that works at an individual level (Layton). Our discussion is based on our thirty years of experience, between us, in a period of change in police education in two Australian states. We have also both been players in these initiatives as members of the academic community, whilst simultaneously engaging in operational practice (ride along, observation, research).

Police Curriculum and Vulnerable Populations

Police curriculum is fraught with (very justifiable) limitations. In an increasingly diverse environment, police are required to familiarise themselves with a complex array of information. In the area of vulnerable people, many government and non-government agencies lobbied throughout the 1990s and 2000s for police officers to be more knowledgeable in some specifics relating, for example, to disability, sexuality, brain injury, and mental health conditions. These demands were for tweaks to the curriculum to recognise particular needs. However, the sheer number and weight of requests eventuated in added scrutiny as to what police officers *should* know, versus what police officers *have to* know according to their core-business.

A fairly sophisticated exercise ensued, where police education authorities (often Directors of Studies, curriculum designers, senior police officers, partner agencies and academics) analysed and balanced the required knowledge according to the realities of the field. As a result, curricula were redesigned to take into account the subtle, yet well-documented move toward more inclusive and collaborative forms of policing. Since the 1960s, a better understanding of crime and social, psychological, and physical vulnerabilities has implied that police take into account a range of factors that can impact on the commission of a crime. These call for more holistic and encompassing modes of governance, requiring an improved integration of otherwise fragmented services:

> Taken in isolation, these factors are the responsibility of a number of government and non-government agencies that specialise in markets, psychology, education, family services, and so-on, and are not particularly "police trade" …Clearly, police cannot solve such wicked issues on their own and do not hold either the answers, or the resources to address such problems (Bartkowiak-Théron, 2011a: 183)

Reframed in the area of vulnerability, this meant two things. First of all, that while police are the first port of call for a number of matters – considering their ability to respond to incidents on a 24/7 basis – they cannot specialise in all of these. The example of police not being "street corner psychiatrists" is well known amongst practitioners (see Herrington and Clifford, in this collection: 123). However, it is important that police are aware of referencing protocols to specialist agencies, and of existing support resources in the communities they serve. Secondly, it means that police curriculum should follow this line of thought, and that frontline police should be taught how to determine signs of vulnerability, and how to address emergencies and follow incident-response protocols, before referring people to appropriate services. It is important that they be aware of the complexity linked to vulnerability, and that both specialist community agencies and police at senior levels are better suited to addressing more complex cases.

The initial question framing curriculum redesign, then, was "what do police officers need to know in order to do what they do?" This question was deemed too reductionist, as police officers have to be aware of a variety of causal (proximate or distal) factors before acting. Therefore, the question took a more academic twist, and became: "what do police officers need to be aware of, and need to know absolutely, in order to provide their community with the best service possible, and according to the best practice possible, within whole of government principles?". In the area of vulnerability, this was answered as follows: police officers need to observe and identify signs of vulnerability, assess these signs, answer emergencies, and refer to specialist agencies, after addressing immediate policing needs (protection of persons of interests, of themselves, of the public and enforcement of the law).

From a teaching and learning perspective, this meant that police officers were to be skilled in a number of areas (socio-legal studies, criminology, sociology and public policy, and tactical and operational protocols, to mention a few), but also that they had to be able to employ higher order thinking (see Bloom, Engelhart, Furst, Hill and Krathwohl's taxonomy, 1956). Besides retaining information such as portions of legislation – which is the lowest level of thought – and understanding their social and professional environment, they have to:

- *apply* protocols;
- *critically* analyse events;
- *formulate* strategies when facing unfamiliar or unforeseen events;
- *implement* these strategies; and
- *evaluate* their actions (which constitutes *reflection*).

All of these latter thought processes constitute higher order thinking.

Community Placement and Vulnerability

Field placements are used in education across areas of professional practice such as social work, education, psychology, law, and management. Their rationales are to introduce students to the domain of practice and its variations; to generate direct engagement, and hands-on, experiential learning; to allow students to learn how to become a professional; to increase sensitivity to individual and cultural needs; to apply theory learnt in the classroom to practice; to test the theories; to encourage reflection; and to foster self-knowledge (Amerson, 2001; Layton, 2004). Students are placed in a quasi-apprenticeship relationship with communities of practice (in this case, the police organisation, via a police station or a regional command). Apprenticeships allow exposure to common sets of problems, practices and language associated with dealing with these problems; a shared sense of purpose, and grasp of how others contribute to problem-solving (Wenger, 1998: 56).

From the end of the 1990s, police recruits have seen part of their curriculum take the form of placement in a "community", either that in which they will be posted after graduation, or one determined randomly. This occurs either during their time as probationary officers (during which they keep on studying part time), after graduating from the Academy, or as a few weeks stint in the community, full-time, during which they work on a field assignment, before returning to class.

Learning in field placements is unlikely to be simply just action, or detached observation, or a quasi-scientific process. There will be unanticipated outcomes as a result of experiencing a new world, in work environments which have political dimensions. Field placement allows for a more direct exposure to vulnerabilities than classroom teachers are able to showcase. Both of us have often met students back from placement, who indicated that the first incident they had to go to involved a type of vulnerability. Such exposure reveals the complexity of living and working in an environment where risks are omnipresent, and where co-morbidity is more often the case than not (that is, vulnerabilities coexist, like a young person living with a mental illness). Direct exposure to communities also reveals a variety of community groups and service agencies. Police officers need to be aware of such resources, as they may be needed in a time of crisis, or can be a catalyst for further community engagement and problem solving.

Table 2: A Model for Combining Teaching Perspectives with Higher Order Thinking – Curriculum Components for Police Recruits

	TRANSMISSION	APPRENTICESHIP	DEVELOPMENTAL	NURTURING	SOCIAL REFORM
Retention of Information					
Understanding of Environment	Students provided with information on law and socio-legal items, to "rote" learn and for further assessment; teachers provide contextualisation of these, showing students how policies have evolved through time, or how police have "learnt by mistake", analysing examples of events or inquiries into police services.	"Hands on experience" and "in situ" learning, either in scenario or role playing, observation (a few days), during community placement (several weeks, in uniform) in a police station; students take part in police operations, familiarise themselves with the policing and community environment.	Students think through their own views of society (work on possible bias or prejudice).	Encouragement to ask senior officers for pointers on field tasks, community characteristics and local resources.	Introduction to good practice models, multi-agency partnership.
Protocol Implementation	For example, the deinstitutionalisation of the mentally ill, the Burnley or Cronulla Riots, the Wood Inquiry, the Henderson inquiry on multiculturalism.		Inclusion of multiple partnering agencies in policy implementation.	Students are encouraged to reach out to prominent members of the community (such as elders, parents, teachers), especially among "target" vulnerable groups, to build problem solving from the ground up. This pushes them to value local knowledge: everyone has an opportunity to be consulted, participate and engage with the police.	
Strategy Formulation	Introduction to concepts such as whole of government approaches, local or nodal governance.				
Implementation of Strategies	Teachers showcase event-management or provide examples of successful problem-solving strategies by police and/or partnering agencies.	Students take part or observe the unfolding of protocols and how they work.	By choosing a repeat crime incident involving vulnerable people, or the study of a hotspot involving vulnerable people, students are invited to use problem-oriented policing to address a problem in the community they serve. Students are encouraged to develop a full plan of action, building on their local knowledge of the community, their own experience and on their "fresh" perspectives on policing (that they have learnt and experienced so far). Students are encouraged to think proactively through potential obstacles to their strategy, and to think of possible ways to circumvent them.		
Evaluation	Students are introduced to policing research (especially collaborative research) and how it can help enhance police services.	Notebooks are reviewed by senior officers.	Students are also asked by police course coordinators or directors to reflect on their experience in the field, and use self-assessment exercise, to gauge police students' capacity to learn from their mistakes, or to think of better ways to serve their community.		
Reflexivity		Notebooks as a catalyst for reflexivity.	In Tasmania, should students receive a grade high than a Distinction to their work, they receive a merit certificate, and a further joint assessment of their work by senior police or academics might see their assignment considered for implementation.		
Critical Analysis					
Creativity					

Therefore, the aims of community placement for police recruits are:

1. for the student to gain understanding of social inequality and power in society within the context of policing, and
2. for the student to practice basic skills in social investigation. Various dimensions of social inequality and their impact on policing including class, status, gender, education, employment, family, locale, ethnicity and aboriginality are surveyed. Social investigative skills include observation, interviewing, reflection and critical analysis (CSU, 1998).

These goals explicitly address the application of knowledge and skills, and the exercise of critical and reflective judgment; a higher order thinking skill essential to the Social Reform agenda. In the case of NSW Police Force recruits, during community placement, students were required to develop a highly prescribed learning contract with their senior officers, keep a daily log (a standard police work practice), and to familiarise themselves with a number of policing tasks. However, learning materials did not make it explicit that the aim was to help students deconstruct their own social situatedness, and increase their capacity to empathise with people when they are vulnerable. It was the *process* that was to achieve this goal.

Deconstructing one's situatedness is a process that develops in the following stages:

1. mindless adherence to one's own rules and traditions;
2. recognising the differences, wanting to know more, and seeking simple rules of thumb;
3. seeing how others' norms and rules are comprehensible and even reasonable, and acting on this;
4. assimilating; and
5. proactively supporting the other culture (Thomas and Inkson, 2003: 68).

What Thomas and Inkson do not mention is the emotional dimension of, and the inherent vulnerabilities in, the changes involved. In the examples below, feelings and vulnerabilities can partly be identified by the language used by our students, and are present as component of the changes described by them. But students also used their experiences to reflect on their own lives, in ways that are likely to affect the ways in which they conduct themselves as police.

In New South Wales, over eleven trimesters, 2233 students undertook placements in 678 organisations (Layton, 2004). All of them wrote diaries as part of the assessment process. Assessing these diaries led to an in-depth, qualitative study of how and whether their identities changed as a consequence of their placements. Did they start with stereotypical understandings? How did they conclude – did their understanding of what it means to be "other" change at all? Table 3 provides sample comments from students who contributed to the study (Layton, 2004).

Table 3: Students' Perceptions in Community Placements

Adhere to own rules & traditions	I would not leave my dog in that place.
Recognising differences	I noticed that kids who tend to be a pain in the butt only do it to seek attention. I observed that when someone is yelling at you, the way you react is going to intensify or pacify the situation.
Acting on understanding	I learnt so much, most of which the kids actually taught me. My attitude changed from pure shock and anger to that of understanding and sadness. I have realised that some things aren't as they seem. You have to look deeper and ask WHY?
Assimilating	Here we are sitting down in a circle with underprivileged juveniles, learning from and interacting with them in such non-threatening or confrontational circumstances.
Proactively supporting	Undoubtedly the most interesting was the domestic violence issues. I will become a member of the domestic violence Committee in order to raise awareness and gather knowledge... Service for the community is what it's all about, and I've gained a real sense of empowerment – I know I can create tailor-made responses to the situations I face.
Feeling & trauma	This made me very depressed and also appreciate what I have [reading the file of a victim of physical and sexual abuse]. At first I thought this was torture. Now at the end I don't feel I could have entered policing without experiencing the other side.

There are clearly different impacts, from none at all to major changes in self-positioning, and in understanding how this experience should translate into practice. A lack of change was generally attributable to strong allegiance to stereotypical understandings of what it meant to be a police officer. The extent of any change was largely, but not always, related to the characteristics of the agencies in which students were placed. Thus, with careful selection of agencies, the potential impact of placements on students' supportive treatment of vulnerable individuals is significant. Models of professional practice matter to the ways in which intending police conceptualise and respond to their own and others' vulnerabilities.

We therefore encourage the further practice of police student placement, especially in relation to exposing recruits to social vulnerabilities. While this exposure in currently *incidental* to placement, we suggest that placement locations (taking risks into account) target areas where students are *specifically* more likely to experience their own vulnerability as well as others'. This could not only contribute to building their own social competence, but the student experiences featured in the above table indicate that they can go a long way in improving community engagement practices, at a time where police officers, because of budget and field constraints, seem to have less time to engage in such activities (Bartkowiak-Théron, 2011b).

Conclusion

In this chapter, we have considered how education might lead to improvements in not only policing vulnerable populations, but also in addressing the often well-hidden sense of vulnerability that recruits experience as they encounter emotionally challenging situations. It was suggested by McLaughlin and Whatman (2008) that a process of critical enquiry into one's own social situatedness is required, and we wondered whether this individualised approach would work with large organisations, such as the police. Our examples show the diversity of approaches integral to curriculum development when it is closely tied to practice, and the potential of community placements for radical change.

It is unclear, at this stage, whether and how large scale curriculum changes, and concomitant changes in police practice will impact on the quality of service provided to vulnerable populations, or on students' sense of vulnerability. However, given that professionals and professional practices are shown to have a positive impact on both of these dimensions, the likelihood is that an increasingly professionalised service, with internal specialists, will have a positive impact.

Our experience, then, suggests that changes are required in several areas for education about one's own and others' vulnerabilities to be effective. Firstly, greater clarity is needed within police organisations about how and when to connect with partner agencies and client services, when and where specialist police should be called, and when and how individual officers might require or be provided with support. Secondly, in the sphere of education, a whole-of-curriculum perspective is needed, to ensure that all aspects of the curriculum drive towards the same point – recognition of the needs of vulnerable people in all of their complexity, without fragmenting into quick-fixes that new crises often demand. Thirdly, placements in the community appear to have a particularly powerful impact on recruits' understanding of their own social situatedness, the nature of vulnerability, and what these might mean for their practice.

References

Amerson, RM, 2001, "Cultural Nursing Care: The Planning, Implementation, and Development of a Learning Experience" 17 *Journal for Nurses in Staff Development* 20.

Angelo, TA, 1995, "Beginning the Dialogue: Thoughts on Promoting Critical Thinking – Classroom Assessment for Critical Thinking" 22 *Teaching of Psychology* 6.

Bartkowiak-Théron, I and Corbo Crehan, A, 2010, "A new movement in community policing? From community policing to vulnerable people policing",

Community Policing: Current and Future Directions for Australia – Research and Public Policy (Ed, J Putt), Australian Institute of Criminology, Canberra.

Bartkowiak-Théron, I, 2011a, "Partnership Policing for Police Organisations", *Policing in Practice* (Eds V Herrington and P Birch), MacMillan, London.

Bartkowiak-Théron, I, 2011b, "Community Engagement and Public Trust in the Police: a Pragmatic View on Police and Community Relationships and Liaison Schemes" 3 *Australasian Policing: A Journal of Professional Practice and Research* 4.

Berg, B, 1990, "Who should teach police? A typology and assessment of police academy instructors" 95 *American Journal of Police* 79.

Bloom, BS, Engelhart, MD, Furst, EJ, Hill, WH and Krathwohl, DR, 1956, *Taxonomy of Educational Objectives: The Classification of Educational Goals; Handbook I: Cognitive Domain*, Longmans Green, New York.

Bradley, D, 1997, *Outside Plato's Cave: Some Questions Concerning the Possibility of the Development of a Full Professional Model for Reflective Police Practice*, Goulburn, New South Wales Police College.

Boud, D and Miller, N, 1997, *Working with Experience: Animating Learning*, Routledge, London.

Boud, D, Cohen, R and Walker, D, 1996, *Using Experience for Learning*, The Society for Research into Higher Education & Open University Press, Buckingham, UK.

Chan, J, 1997, *Changing Police Culture: Policing in a Multicultural Society*, Cambridge University Press, Cambridge, MA.

Charles Sturt University, 1998, *Undergraduate Handbook,* Charles Sturt University, Wagga Wagga.

Dupont, B, 2002, The New Governance of Australian Police Services. Unpublished paper, Goulburn, New South Wales. Viewed 18 February 2011, <www.crim. umontreal.ca/cours/cri1600/revue/dupont3.pdf>.

Foucault, M, 1977, *Discipline and Punish: the Birth of the Prison*, Random House, New York.

Foucault, M, 1981, "Questions of Method: An Interview" 8 *I & C: Power and Desire – Diagrams of the Social,* 3.

Giddens, A, 1991, *The Consequences of Modernity*, Polity Press, Cambridge, UK.

Goldstein, H, 1990, *Problem-Oriented Policing*, McGraw-Hill, New York.

Hammer, MR, 2002, "The Intercultural Conflict Style Inventory: A Conceptual Framework and Measure of Intercultural Conflict Approaches" 29 *International Journal of Intercultural Relations* 6.

Hirschhorn, L, 1988, *The Workplace Within: Psychodynamics of Organisational Life,* MIT Press, Cambridge, MA.

King, H, 1956, "Some Aspects of Police Administration in New South Wales, 1825-1851" 42 *Journal of the Royal Australian Historical Society* 205.

Layton, C, 2004, *Learning Selves: A Study of Police Students' Learning in Community Placements, Using Diaries.* Unpublished PhD thesis, UTS, Sydney.

Lusher, E, 1981, *Report of the Commission to enquire into New South Wales Police Administration*, NSW Government, Sydney.

Matheson, C and Matheson, D, 2008 "Community Development: Freire and Grameen in the Barrowfield Project, Glasgow, Scotland" 18 *Development in Practice* 30.

Matsumoto, D, 2004, "Reflections on Culture and Competence", *Culture and Competence: Contexts of Life Success* (Eds RJ Sterberg and EL Grigorenko), American Psychological Association, Washington DC.

McLaughlin, JM and Whatman, SL 2008, "Embedding Indigenous Perspectives in University Teaching and Learning: Lessons Learnt and Possibilities of Reforming/Decolonising Curriculum", *Fourth International Conference on Indigenous Education: Asia/ Pacific*, 19-22 July, Vancouver, Canada.

Paul, R, 2007, "Critical Thinking in Every Domain of Knowledge and Belief", *The 27th Annual International Conference on Critical Thinking*, 23-26 July, Berkeley, CA.

Potts, B, 1994, "Strategies for Teaching Critical Thinking" 4 *Practical Assessment, Research & Evaluation* . Viewed February 26, 2012, <PAREonline.net/getvn.asp?v=4&n=3>.

Pratt, DD and Collins, JB 2001 "Teaching Perspectives Inventory (TPI)". Viewed February 26, 2012 from <teachingperspectives.com/html/tpi_frames.htm>

Pratt, DD, Collins, JB and Selinger, SJ, 2005, "Development and Use of the Teaching Perspectives Inventory (TPI)". Viewed 7 December 2011, <www.crim.umontreal.ca/cours/cri1600/revue/dupont3.pdf>.

Ramsden, P, 2003, *Learning to Teach in Higher Education*, 2nd ed, Routledge, London.

Reiner, R, 1998, *The Politics of the Police*, 3rd ed, Oxford University Press, Oxford, UK.

Reynolds, WJ, Scott, B and Austin, W, 2000, "Nursing, Empathy and Perception of the Moral" 32 *Journal of Advanced Nursing* 235.

Saddington, T, 1998, "Exploring the Roots and Branches of Experiential Learning" 3 *Lifelong Learning in Europe* 133.

Schattschneider, EE, 1960, *The Semi-Sovereign People*, Holt, Rinehart and Winston, New York.

Sipress, JM and Voelker, DJ 2006, "From Learning History to Doing History", *Exploring Signature Pedagogies: Approaches to Teaching Disciplinary Habits of Mind*, (Eds RAR Gurung, NL Chick and A Haynie),Stylus, Sterling, Virginia, USA.

Smyth, J, Angus, L, Down, B and McInerney, P, 2008 *Critically Engaged Learning: Connecting to Young Lives*, Peter Lang, New York.

Stewart, M, 2004, "Learning Through Research: An Introduction to the Main Theories of Learning", *James Madison University Learning and Teaching Press* Harrisonburg, VI: James Madison University. Viewed July 6 2010, <www.ljmu. ac.uk/lid/lid_docs/Learning_theories_intro.pdf>.

Thomas, DC and Inkson, K, 2003 *Cultural Intelligence: People Skills for Global Business*, Berrett-Koehler Publishers Inc, San Francisco.

Walker, S, 1999 *The Police in America*, 3rd ed, McGraw-Hill College, Boston, MA.

Warner Weil, S and McGill, I, Eds, 1989, *Making Sense of Experiential Learning: Diversity in Theory and Practice*, Society for Research into Higher Education and Open University Press, Milton Keynes, UK.

Wenger, E, 1998, *Communities of Practice: Learning, Meaning, and Identity*, Cambridge University Press, Cambridge, MA.

Wood, JRT, 1997, *Royal Commission into the New South Wales Police Service: Final Report*, Vols 1-3, The Government of the State of New South Wales, Sydney.

Part Two

Police and Vulnerable Populations: First Contacts

Chapter 5

Quality of Life Policing in Broadacre Housing Estates

Rosemarie E Winter and Nicole L Asquith

The terms "community policing", "quality of life policing" and "reassurance polic-ing" are commonly used to denote population-based crime prevention strategies, models and programs. Essentially, these are strategies that stress greater interaction with the community regarding crime control and prevention, with the aim to improve residents' sense of security, reduce anti-social behaviour and offences that affect quality of life, improve confidence in the police, and increase the capacity of communities to 'co-produce' law and order (Innes and Roberts, 2008). While community policing (CP) is thought to be a catch-all phrase, there are significant differences between the goals of various community-based strategies. This chapter seeks to highlight that, in some communities, particularly *disadvantaged* communi-ties, community policing is reduced to "quality of life policing" (QOLP), in part because the wider goals of CP are unattainable without significant prior investment in solutions to non-criminal problems (such as education, health and welfare). In these vulnerable communities, such as broadacre public housing estates, the community-based policing practices most commonly adopted coincide with the limited goals and objectives of QOLP, which require little or no community consultation or engagement.

This chapter first identifies the differences in operationalising community-based approaches, before turning to a critical study of two programs adopted in Tasmania (Officer Next Door, and Safe at Home). These contrasting programs were chosen to illustrate the diverse models adopted under the banner of community-based polic-ing, and the limitations in the introduction of these approaches in public housing estates. The former, Officer Next Door (OND), is a crime prevention program managed within the community policing division of Tasmania Police, yet involved no consultation with the community about its implementation or operation. The latter, Safe at Home, was introduced in 2004 in response to community pressure and consultation, and despite being a crime control strategy based on a pro-arrest, zero-tolerance approach to family violence, was, in fact, created to prevent what was perceived as an unacceptably high homicide rate for intimate partner violence. These case studies of "soft" and "hard" community-based policing highlight, in their own ways, the social and individual barriers to successful policing strategies in broadacre public housing estates, and the impact that limited social and economic capital can have on community participation in the "co-production" of law and order.

Community-based Policing

During the late-1960s and 1970s, policing organisations across the world experienced a crisis in their mission as crime-fighters, which was fuelled by economic constraints on "big government", increased civil unrest, public mistrust of policing services, amplified attention on police corruption and rising crime rates. The traditional crime detection and prosecution focus had resulted in a disconnection between the police and their communities. Motorised patrols and radios – where contact between police and the people is reduced to emergency situations and focussed on interactions with distressed victims/witnesses – had the unintended consequence of increasing the social distance between the police and "the policed" (Reisig and Parks, 2004). While the mobile patrols enabled police to respond to emergency calls much faster and reduced the time wasted between incidents, they were also less effective because they did not engage with communities to the same extent as foot patrols. To remedy some of these emerging problems, and in a return to the principles advocated by Peel in the nineteenth century, policing organisations sought to re-fashion their officers as members of the communities in which they patrolled.

There are three basic principles involved in community-based strategies. First, "reassurance policing" requires that police are visible, accessible and familiar to communities. Second, "quality of life policing" focuses on crimes and anti-social behaviour that most affect the community's sense of security and fear-of-crime. Finally, "community policing" facilitates community participation in order for informal, subtle and complex social controls to be developed (Duffee et al, 1999; Innes, 2004, 2005; Innes and Roberts, 2008). In this sense, "community policing" differs from the other two approaches in terms of the quality of the interactions between the community and their policing services. While "reassurance policing" and "quality of life policing" may ask communities about their experiences of crime, and use their responses to shape strategies, "community policing" requires that communities become partners in crime control. True community policing means listening to communities, putting the right sort of resources in place to deal with the local problems of neighbourhoods, and integrating communities into the identification and problem-solving stages of policing responses.

Just as community policing (CP) was emerging as a viable policing option, other related theories appeared, which linked escalating crime with social disorder. These were called incivilities or social disorganisation theories; colloquially, "broken windows" or "quality of life" theories (Vitale, 2005; Wilson and Kelling, 2006). According to these perspectives, neighbourhoods with limited informal social controls (and/or neighbours who interact reluctantly) are vulnerable to criminal invasion. A central principle of the incivilities thesis is that disorderliness creates fear. Disorder, in this sense, can be both behavioural (such as anti-social behaviour) and environmental (such as litter, abandoned properties, and burnt out cars). It was believed that graffiti and untidy environments create a feeling that the area is uncontrolled with the effect that members of the community are intimidated and less likely to report crime (Wilson and Kelling, 1982). Broken windows or quality of life policing (QOLP) concentrates on eliminating these kinds of visible disorder and everyday annoyances using approaches such as zero tolerance, hot-spot targeting, stop and search, civil enforcement, and by creating laws to criminalise anti-social behaviour (Vitale, 2005).

In contrast, the main strength of the CP ethos lies in its capacity to increase the flow of information to the police in order to either prevent or prosecute criminal activity. However, this is not easy to achieve in practice. The core objective of CP solutions is to create the conditions within communities that will allow for private (family and close friends), parochial (neighbours) and public (police) social control mechanisms to emerge, flourish and, as a consequence, to assist communities to prevent the conditions which allow violence and crime to take hold (Duffee et al, 1999). It is thought that policing in this way will build strong connections between communities and their police, which facilitates information exchange and leads to an increased capacity to detect crimes and prosecute offenders, and influences the levels of fear-of-crime.

However, broad CP programs in public housing estates often encounter problems beyond the purview of policing. Society's most vulnerable groups live in these neighbourhoods. These neighbourhoods are characterised by high concentrations of poverty and residents with low levels of resources in terms of housing, transportation, employment, and urban development (Blokland, 2008; Duffee et al, 1999; Reisig and Parks, 2004). Schneider's (1999) research in Vancouver highlighted that community policing fails in socially disadvantaged neighbourhoods because police fail to recognise how communication with these communities continually reproduces a negative power relationship. Schneider's (1999) research showed that communication is most commonly one way; citizens felt that they were expected to be the eyes and ears of police but got little feedback and did not feel that they had a say in the way in which policing occurred in their neighbourhood. This gave the impression that nothing was done and led to apathy and lack of cooperation with the police (Schneider, 1999).

Achieving a successful community policing outcome in broadacre public housing estates is more complex than it first appears. The ability of police to secure community buy-in is hampered by confusion about the communities' role in the implementation of programs. This is alongside the very real fear of retaliation from the "trouble-makers" in the community (Long et al, 2002). Further, Blokland (2008) argues that, in some cases, participation in community-based programs can be counter-productive for individuals, especially when their actions can result in the arrest and detention of loved ones (such as children and intimate partners). In the case of the latter, beyond the emotional trauma, cooperation with the police could also lead to significant economic hardship, particular for women with children. Geographically defined communities are also filled with divisions and tensions because of the inherent heterogeneity of their populations (Hughes and Rowe, 2007). This makes it difficult to form communities that remain stable enough for the purposes of governance and also impacts on neighbourhoods' ability to maintain order through informal social controls. The two case studies that follow illustrate the difficulties that emerge when the rhetoric of community-based approaches is faced with the multiple vulnerabilities found in public housing estates.

Officer Next Door[1]

The Australian adoption of community-based models of policing in the early to mid-80s coincided with an increased concern about fear of crime. In particular, the barriers created by fear of crime and therefore, the limitations on the co-production of law and order, became central to community policing strategies. In response to these developments, in 1988, Tasmania Police in conjunction with Housing Tasmania created the Officer Next Door (OND) program. On its tenth anniversary, the partners contracted the Tasmanian Institute of Law Enforcement Studies to evaluate the business and community policing case for this program (Asquith et al, 2009). In evaluating the efficacy of the OND program, the research highlighted the conditions under which community-based approaches may achieve their stated goals, and the barriers to achieving those goals. But more importantly for this chapter, this research also investigated whether this approach was the most appropriate model for reducing fear-of-crime, and if there was a direct relationship between experiences of crime and fear-of-crime in broadacre public housing estates.

From the review of international literature (including policing and housing policy and practice), the OND program is unique; perhaps, in large part, due to the unique social contexts of public housing in Tasmania. At the core of the Officer Next Door program was a desire to find additional, alternative means to respond to a perceived heightened level of criminal and anti-social behaviour in broadacre public housing estates, including many cases of arson against public housing properties. In essence, the program involves Housing Tasmania providing Tasmania Police officers with accommodation in public housing at a substantially reduced weekly rent. As part of their contract, Officers Next Door were expected to participate in local programs such as Neighbourhood Watch (though most preferred to work directly with young people in the community), report criminal and anti-social behaviour in their community, and to act as role models of good social citizenship.

As with many community-based programs, perceptions about the aims, requirements and successes of the Officer Next Door (OND) program varied considerably between research sites (nine sites including, North-West sea-changers, and inner-city estates in Launceston and Hobart) and stakeholders (Housing Tasmania Tenancy Officers, Housing Tasmania Area Managers, Tasmania Police Inspectors, Officers Next Door (ONDs) and Housing Tasmania residents). Despite the differences in perceptions of OND, participants in the review (Asquith et al, 2009) identified six key program objectives:

1. Visible police presence in "at-risk" communities and neighbourhoods, including informal uniformed presence such as driving/walking/jogging around the neighbourhood and role-modelling
2. Management of social conditions outside the purview of Tasmania Police or Housing Tasmania, such as anti-social behaviour
3. Informal contact point for residents encountering criminal/anti-social behaviour
4. Informal communication network between Housing Tasmania, Tasmania Police and Housing Tasmania residents
5. Monitoring of the problematic parts of the estates
6. Local police involvement in community policing initiatives (such as Neighbourhood Watch)

Importantly, residents' opinions were not officially recorded at any time during the ten-year operation of the program; nor had there been any attempt to educate Housing Tasmania residents about the goals of the program. These issues are significant in light of previous research into community policing which illustrate that the success of these types of interventions are dependent upon the "co-production" of safety by those who are the targets of the intervention (Innes and Roberts, 2008). The absence of community input into the design, implementation and operation of the program fundamentally precludes OND from being considered a true community policing strategy. While the rhetoric was about informal communication networks, in contrast to other strategies which are based upon two-way communication between communities and policing services, OND – particularly from the perspective of communities – was simply a mechanism through which to manage the perceived "quality of life" issues in these estates.

The social contexts of communities are fundamental to the adoption, effectiveness, and ongoing success of community-based strategies. Too often, those communities who least need community policing interventions are those that become role models of the approach – Neighbourhood Watch being a classic example of this asymmetrical deployment of CP (Bennett, 1989; Fleming, 2005). As highlighted above, high levels of social capital and social efficacy have been found to correlate positively to successful community policing programs. While social capital is capable of being generated in any community, it is most likely to be found in communities with housing and economic security, low unemployment, high levels of education, and cultural homogeneity. With this in mind, a community policing model is not an ideal approach to adopt in the types of communities subject to the OND program.

This is particularly the case for one of the evaluation sites in the Hobart suburbs. From the outset of Officer Next Door program review, stakeholders identified Tudordale[2] as a key site for analysis. This was not only because of the perception that this community faced extreme issues of crime and anti-social behaviour, but just as importantly, it had been the host of many Officers Next Door – some of whom are considered the most successful participants in the program. As with many public housing communities, the social context of Tudordale is one of marginalisation and dislocation. Vulnerable communities such as Tudordale have been correlated in previous research to low up-take of community building and participation in crime prevention programs (Reisig and Parks, 2004). However, under the right circumstances, this relatively time-rich population could also be ideally suited to the development of positive social capital, and critical community interventions that may radically transform the lives of residents.

Tudordale is a cul-de-sac of cul-de-sacs, with only two main streets into the community – both of which begin from the same major road. It is not a suburb to be travelled through or, in fact, entered without a reason. Further, there are limited social and business services that would draw people into the community. For a large part of the day, it is only serviced by public transport on an hourly basis, with no services after 10.30pm. Tudordale, in this sense, is a forgotten community, hidden from passing traffic. When the community does come under the public gaze (via media reports), it is invariably because of a range of criminal and anti-social behaviour, particularly the deliberate and accidental burning of Housing Tasmania properties by arsonists and unsupervised children, respectively. A large proportion of offences reported to Tasmania Police are connected to Housing Tasmania properties in and around the northern (and most common) entrance to the community. Not only does this inform the "feel" of the community as soon as residents and visitors enter the broadacre estate from this approach, it also affects the security of services and businesses at that end of the community.

Crime rates varied considerably across the nine OND research sites, and, within Tudordale, varied at the level of streets. As can be seen in Figure 1, the crime rate for Tudordale was up to three times higher than the Australian average reported by the ABS in *Crime and Safety, Australia* (2005), and twice as high as the OND average. Within Tudordale, the crime rate was much higher in particular streets; specifically, up to 36 per cent of reported incidents occurred in one street alone, which represented a doubling of the crime rate as a proportion of the properties in that street (Asquith et al, 2009). In fact, the street itself (rather than households)

**Figure 1: Comparative Analysis of Victimisation Rates
(Tudordale, Officer Next Door, *Crime and Safety, Australia*)***

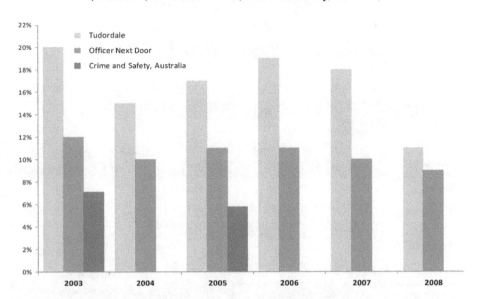

Source: Australian Bureau of Statistics (2005) and Tasmania Police (2009)

was the site of most criminal activity, predominantly related to hooning, public violence and drug offences. Traditional fear-of-crime measures have their problems, not least of which is the inability to measure intensity and longevity of fear, or the impact of media representations on fear-of-crime. However, when taken purely as a comparable measure (rather than robust indicator of fear), Figure 2 (*over page*) shows that residents who participated in the OND research reported that they were up to ten times more fearful than the Australian average reported in *Crime and Safety, Australia* (2005)

While Tudordale residents reported much higher levels of fear-of-crime than their Australia-wide peers, their vulnerability is comparable to their public housing peers in the other eight evaluation sites. This is despite higher levels of actual crime victimisation reported to the police. There was however an exception to this consistency across the OND sites; Tudordale residents reported significantly lower levels of social support (being able to ask for help from neighbours). Further, while the other aggregate figures are consistent across the nine research sites, when

* The data collected for the Officer Next Door research used the same set of fear-of-crime questions as *Crime and Safety, Australia* (2005). However, unlike *Crime and Safety, Australia*, which is random sample of the Australian population, all public housing residents were offered the opportunity to respond to the victimisation survey as part of the Officer Next Door research. Response rates were comparable. Tudordale and Officer Next Door data for 2008 was collected only until October of that year.

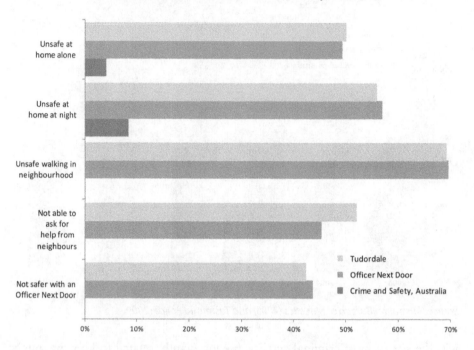

Figure 2: Comparative Analysis of Fear-of-Crime Measures
(Tudordale, Officer Next Door, *Crime and Safety, Australia*)

Source: Australian Bureau of Statistics (2005) and Tasmania Police (2009)

the data is disaggregated to the street level in Tudordale, the situation changes dramatically. Respondents from one street reported significantly higher rates of fear, particularly in relation to being unsafe at home at night (77 per cent compared with 56 per cent), and walking around the neighbourhood (82 per cent compared with 69 per cent). One respondent living in this street stated:

> We can't leave our house alone at any time and never get to go out as a family since I've lived here 'cause the neighbours have threatened to burn us out (Female, under 35 years, Tudordale).

While residents indicated that they felt safer with having Police Officers living in their community, their qualitative statements painted a completely different picture. Of the nine research sites, it was only Tudordale respondents who explicitly commented on the OND program. This may reveal recognition of the OND brand in Tudordale (something not found in any of the other research sites), however, from respondents' comments, this recognition stems predominantly from a perceived failure of the program, including:

> I feel that having police living in the community is about as useless as tits on bulls (Female, 36-60 years, Tudordale)
>
> I have lived in my community for over thirty years and I cannot see the sense in having a $5 a week police officer living in the area ... For what they do, they might as well sit on the roof and clap hands at the hoons in the streets (Male, 36-60 years, Tudordale).

Without the support of residents, a program such as OND can become irrelevant to the community, and its community-capacity building. However, for some residents who live in the immediate vicinity of the OND properties, the presence of ONDs has ameliorated some of the crime and safety issues faced by residents. This best illustrates the strength of the program – supporting and/or protecting "at-risk" residents – but also its greatest flaw – the temporal and geographical influence is transient.

The evaluation of the Officer Next Door program raised several significant issues. The most important to this chapter include:

- High rates of crime and fear-of-crime in public housing generally
- High rates of crime lead to the normalisation of violence, which "inoculates" against fear of crime
- A lack of knowledge and understanding of community policing principles
- Failures in two-way communication between public housing residents, stakeholders and the police, and
- A failure to integrate the program into broader Housing Tasmania and Tasmania Police strategies

Each of these issues point to a failure of OND to live up to principles of community-based policing. At its core, the Officer Next Door program is a shadow of community policing. It is more "quality of life" policing than a deliberate policy or practice of community engagement to co-produce law and order. This is perhaps due to the vulnerabilities that public housing residents experience on a daily basis, especially in relation to the social capital required to "co-produce" law and order. Violence and disorder becomes normalised to the extent that residents cannot imagine a life without crime, or without fear-of-crime. The loss of social controls – or the capacity to build social networks to respond to crime – means that these communities are left with "hard" quality of life approaches about which they are not consulted.

Safe at Home

Safe at Home is a coordinated community response for addressing intimate partner violence in Tasmania, and was introduced as part of the *Family Violence Act 2004* (Tas). This was the first legislation in Australia to define economic and emotional abuse and intimidation as criminal offences and grounds for obtaining restraint orders. The *Act* signified a radical change of direction in placing family violence within a criminal justice framework, with significant consequences for offenders and greater protection and recognition of the vulnerabilities of adult and child victims. Safe at Home involves a pro-arrest, pro-prosecution and pro-interventionist approach to incidents of family violence. Under the act, police received additional powers of entry, as well as the power to create Police Family Violence Orders (PFVO), where the risk of reoccurrence was low or medium. Penalties for breaches of orders were increased. Any breach which exposed a child to violence was considered an aggravating circumstance and attracted a more severe sentence. Police were also empowered to conduct risk assessments, safety audits and were mandated to notify Child Protection Services if a child is present during a family violence incident. The coordinated agency response included a 24 hour police crisis line and the creation of specialist police Victim Safety Response Teams (VSRT). Under the Act, victims also have access to an expanded range of services including court support and victim liaison services, including a child witness program.

In an investigation of the implementation of legislation designed to elicit social change, semi-structured interviews were undertaken with 43 personnel involved in operationalising the Safe at Home policy framework; these included operational police, police managers, police prosecutors, magistrates, legal professionals and victim advocates. In addition, this project involved extensive observation of operational police in the field including during family violence training and over 100 hours riding along with Victim Safety Response Teams (Winter, 2011).

The major finding of this research pertaining to policing family violence in broadacre estates was the power of the discourse in the prevailing culture that a substantial proportion of victims were less than genuine, or not vulnerable to the specific harms generated out of family violence. The discourse of the genuine victim is experienced as mistrust of the veracity of victims' complaints and operationalised by actors in terms of rhetoric and behaviours which demonstrate bias against certain groups of victims. Police subscribe to an *underclass* storyline (Hajer, 1995) in their perception that 80 per cent of their callouts are to the same group of people; those people from low socio-economic classes, exhibiting high levels of alcohol and drug use, and an intergenerational usage of violence to solve conflict.

Broadacre estates are often both geographically and socially isolated, and Mama (1989) suggests that some sectors of these communities were more likely to call the police than others. Those who frequently contact police do so because they lack family and community supports, and because police are the only emergency service available 24 hours. The research that found that this highly vulnerable section of the community was most likely to be regarded as less than genuine by the police.

Popular conception would have us believe that intimate partner violence affects the lower socioeconomic communities more so than others; that is, they are the most frequent sites of interpersonal violence in the home. This underclass discourse describes people who are not just vulnerable due to low income. The men in the family are unable to keep jobs for more than a few weeks. Drunkenness and drug use is common, homes are untidy and in need of repair. Children are badly behaved, ill-schooled and are the young males are "barbarians" who are responsible for most of the anti-social behaviour in a jurisdiction. This underclass is further characterised by criminal behaviour, teenage parenthood and homelessness. This stereotype is continually reinforced in the media, and police, particularly younger officers, were clearly influenced by this narrative. In this study of a coordinated community response to intimate partner violence, lower socioeconomic groups, including those living in broadacre estates, were seen by police as the predominant site of family violence incidents:

> When you see it in a proper household it's a bit different, like your parents or something, you can think geeze this could happen to your parent's group. But when you see it with the crooks and all that, it isn't, because you just think that's how they are (Operational Police Officer 2 in Winter, 2011).

In almost all the interviews with frontline officers, there was some level of doubt cast on the truth of complaints made by a substantial group of victims. Officers were doubtful about the legitimacy of many complaints, and questioned whether the level of response was warranted in the incidents that they attended. In essence, responding officers questioned whether the victims of family violence in public housing estates were, in fact, vulnerable. Officers estimated that only between ten and fifty per cent of cases were legitimate. These officers held these views for a number of reasons. In the first instance, police expressed frustration that victims would often return to their violent partners, which led to the conclusion that the violence must have been exaggerated or that the victim was in some way complicit in the violence. Victims were accused of lying on their risk assessment forms in order to get their partner out of the house for the weekend. They were perceived as dishonest because they either withdrew their complaints early in the following week, refused to go to court, breached their FVOs or incited such breaches. Police spoke of victims being "savvy" with the system to the extent of "preparing" statements that would result in the arrest of their partner (Winter, 2011). They accused this group of victims of using the system to manage the rough patches in their relationships. Police voiced suspicions of victims that chose not to follow the prescribed legal process, such as in the provision of the victim statement to the alleged offender during an application for a court issued family violence order (Winter, 2011). In this storyline, they were joined by some magistrates and lawyers who defended this practice as the process of natural justice. The victim's vulnerability to retaliation, which motivates a withdrawal of the application, is interpreted by police and the legal profession as evidence of fabrication of the allegation or exaggeration of its severity.

This complements an interrelated narrative of "if it were so bad then she would leave". Officers and the public face a predicament in interpreting the behaviour of victims who chose to stay in violent relationships. On the one hand, this is consistent with the behaviour of someone who has been victimised. On the other hand, officers make assessments based on common sense, which dictates that rational people do not willingly expose themselves to situations in which they are likely to be assaulted. Police continue to subscribe to this narrative in spite of the evidence and case law introduced in their training, which clearly demonstrates that there is an increased vulnerability to serious injury or homicide triggered by separation from a violent partner (Winter, 2011). Campbell et al (2003) found that the risk of intimate partner femicide increased ninefold by the combination of a highly controlling abuser and the couple's separation after living together. The attitude of "if I can't have her then no one can" recurs in homicide and homicide/suicide cases. In these cases, there is commonly a history of sub-lethal violence or threats to kill, which is often used as a coercive tactic to terrorise women and keep them under their partner's control. Women are particularly vulnerable in the first two months of separation and immediately prior to divorce proceedings. After the relationship is officially declared to be over, the risk of violence usually decreases (Winter, 2011).

Training of Victim Safety Response Teams consists primarily of modules about police powers and processes but places little emphasis on victimology, and the specific vulnerabilities faced by women and children with little or no economic, social or cultural capital. VSRT training included some information to enable police to recognise a victim's agency and to honour all the choices they make (including staying); however, police in this study had considerable difficulty imagining that these victims faced increased vulnerability. The interviews with police often revealed their sense of helplessness and frustration about victims going back into a relationship with a partner that had been violent (Winter, 2011). Even when officers displayed and reported significant empathy, they did not have a language that understood the constraints associated with being a victim. The language they use to discuss victims (and offenders) is often less than sympathetic. For example, police referred to chronic offenders as "snoozers", "bucket-heads", "losers", "gorillas" and "bantam roosters" (Winter, 2011).

A number of officers, one magistrate and the general public often deployed a storyline of provocation to understand these cases of family violence in public housing estates. In this storyline, they describe scenarios in which the victim may have nagged the perpetrator to "breaking point" or even instigated the violence which has then "got out of hand". This attitude suggests that there was a collusion with perpetrators around the permissibility of violence, and if sufficient provocation exists, this narrative of "mutual combat" or "common couple violence" (Johnson, 1995) works to shift the blame, or part of it, to the victim, and dismisses the increased vulnerability faced by these victims.

> The underlying assumption of the violence between males and females is
> that the women are disproportionately on the worst receiving end when
> it happens. But I understand the research says they are not unwilling
> participants. Or indeed precipitators of the dynamics or the pressure that
> reaches a particular stage and I really think that rather than spend any
> time focussing on men perhaps there should be more focus on women
> to not push men too far (Magistrate 3 in Winter, 2011).

Such a storyline underestimates the impact of the violence on women and their
children, their vulnerability and ignores the dynamics of violent relationships in
addressing a specific incident rather than seeing the violence as part of a pattern
of power and control.

Many crimes against intimate partners are difficult to process through the court
system. A "genuine victim" discourse influences the way police manage the risks of
intimate partner violence, and commonly draws strongly on the value base of the
officers. Personal beliefs about individual or social group behaviours can influence
the way in which the assessment and monitoring processes are performed and the
ways protocols are actioned. The narratives around "genuine victimhood" subtly
influence what evidence is admitted or dismissed and what cases are pursued, or
dismissed. Circumstantial evidence, or witnesses judged to be unreliable by the
justice system, influence the practices of Safe at Home.

Among police and the legal fraternity, there is a tendency to accept a victim's
reluctance to resort to legal means as a sign that they are no longer vulnerable and
the situation is "under control". In addition, if a victim withdraws a complaint
and gives a plausible explanation for their injuries (for example, "I walked into
a door") and there are no other witnesses, the legal principle of proving "beyond
reasonable doubt" dominates proceedings. Even though Safe at Home provides
the prosecution with the power to continue even if the victim was unwilling, this
is rarely done. Almost all convictions under the *Family Violence Act* are the result
of guilty pleas (Urbis, 2008). The victim's reluctance to prosecute helps abus-
ers minimise victims' injuries and persuade legal officials that the violence does
not merit serious consideration. It also fosters a perception among police that
some women too readily mobilise the system despite a lack of serious danger to
themselves or their children.

In this sense, those that subscribe to a "genuine victim" discourse are in effect
colluding with perpetrators. It is well documented that perpetrators often blame
victims or find reasons to support or minimise their use of violence; in fact, many
perpetrators possess considerable charm and ability to convince both police,
and often the victim, that the incident was minor (Dobash and Dobash, 1992).
Even though research overwhelmingly shows that women minimise their abuse
(Anderson et al, 2003), police, lawyers and others in the criminal justice system
share a belief that a large proportion of women most likely fabricate or embellish
their vulnerability to violence.

In addition to discourses about genuine victims, there was a strong narrative circulating amongst operational police about the inability of the system to protect victims unless the perpetrator was detained or imprisoned. These officers regarded family violence orders as ineffectual against a perpetrator that was determined to do harm. These mixed messages about the lived experiences of family violence reinforce the fact that the phenomenon is indeed heterogeneous. Organisations and individuals that construct victims as "pure" will have difficulty in reconciling their clients with this kind of ideal behaviour. This (together with the lack of resources and increased accountability around police treatment of intimate partner violence), creates cynicism amongst officers. However, rather than focussing on an overt institutional culture around the difficulties inherent in policing family violence, the rhetoric turns on victims.

In this way, the "genuine victim" discourse gains purchase on institutional patterns. Sometimes the impact of the discourse on behaviour might be in terms of treating the dubious victim more harshly (for example, more rigid or overzealous following of rules and protocols). One third of all arrests made under Safe at Home in the first five years have been dual, where both parties have been arrested (Success Works, 2009). It is possible that in other cases, police might proceed more slowly in dealing with this group of victims or not act at all because of a perception of it being a waste of time and resources. Police managers argued that these behind-the-scenes attitudes did not affect police adherence to due process in dealing with family violence incidents and denied police practicing "postcode justice" (Winter, 2011). However, attitudes act as powerful filters and may translate into an unconscious strategy to manage workloads, by triaging incidents depending on the likelihood of incidents proceeding to prosecution. Safe at Home is a top down policy that suffers from limited resources and limited training. Designed to be a community response to intimate partner violence, in implementation it works better for those *perceived* to be vulnerable because of entrenched attitudes by police to families from broadacre estates.

Conclusion

Community policing programs that have police as the dominant agency – over communities and community organisations – are problematic, as differences in levels of organisation, coordination and clarity of mission can lead to program failure (Hughes and Rowe, 2007; Innes and Roberts, 2008; Pruegger, 2003). In many community-based programs there is a tendency of police to focus on their roles as problem solvers or community mobilisers. This is a "top down" mind-set, with police determining the strategy's objectives. Further, within policing, Chappell (2009) argues that often executive policing adopts the philosophy of community-based approaches and imposes these strategies onto to operational policing, without adequately considering the competencies, training and resources required to undertake these approaches. Both case studies presented in this chapter epitomise this problem with community policing in vulnerable communities such as broadacre public housing estates. As with other community policing programs in Australia they are dependent on officers taking ownership of a particular area and assuming responsibility for increasing the flow of information to police, and increasing trust in local operational police. However, the communication and trust is most commonly one-way. With or without high visibility policing strategies, two-way communication with residents of broadacre public housing estates is essential if community-based approaches are to succeed in addressing vulnerability, reducing fear of crime, and increasing trust in policing services. It is not enough to increase the visibility of policing in these communities. To address the vulnerabilities experienced by public housing residents, frontline officers and policing organisations need to be more aware of the economic, social and cultural barriers to "co-production" of security. To do this, they need to *dynamically* engage with these communities in ways that build capacities rather than in ways that are likely to increase vulnerability.

Endnotes

1   The review of the Officer Next Door program is a product of the contributions from Housing Tasmania residents, Housing Tasmania staff and management and Tasmania Police, and funding provided by Housing Tasmania.

2   The name of this suburb has been changed.

References

Family Violence Act 2004 (Tas).

Anderson, M, Gillig, P, Sitaker, M, McCloskey, K, Malloy, K, and Grigsby, N, 2003. "'Why Doesn't She Just Leave?': A Descriptive Study of Victim Reported Impediments to Her Safety" 18 *Journal of Family Violence* 151.

Asquith, N L, Eckhardt, M, Winter, R and Campbell, D, 2009, *Review and Evaluation of the Officer Next Door Program*, Tasmania Police & Housing Tasmania, Hobart.

Australian Bureau of Statistics, 2005, *Crime and Safety, Australia*, 4509, ABS, Canberra.

Bennett, T, 1989, "The neighbourhood watch experiment", *Coming to Terms with Policing; Perspectives on Policy* (Eds R Morgan and DJ Smith), Routledge, London.

Blokland, T, 2008, "Facing Violence: Everyday Risks in an American Housing Project" 42 *Sociology* 601.

Campbell, J, Webster, D, Koziol-McLean, J, Block, C, Campbell, D, Curry, MA, et al, 2003, "Risk Factors for Femicide in Abusive Relationships: Results from a multi-site Case Control Study" 93 *American Journal of Public Health* 1089.

Chappell, A T, 2009, "The Philosophical Versus Actual Adoption of Community Policing: A Case Study" 34 *Criminal Justice Review* 5.

Dobash, R E and Dobash, R P, 1992, *Women, Violence and Social Change*, Routledge, London.

Duffee, D E, Fluellen, R and Renauer, B C, 1999, "Community Variables in Community Policing" 2 *Police Quarterly* 5.

Fleming, J, 2005, "'Working Together': Neighbourhood Watch, Reassurance Policing and the Potential of Partnerships", *Trends & Issues in Crime and Criminal Justice*, 303, Australian Institute of Criminology, Canberra.

Hajer, M, 1995, *The Politics of Environmental Discourse: Ecological Modernization and the Policy Process*, Oxford University Press, New York.

Hughes, G and Rowe, M, 2007, "Neighbourhood Policing and Community Safety: Researching the instabilities of the local governance of crime, disorder and security in contemporary UK" 7 *Criminology and Criminal Justice* 317.

Innes, M, 2005, "Why 'soft' policing is hard: On the curious development of reassurance policing, how it became neighbourhood policing and what this signifies about the politics of police reform" 15 *Journal of Community & Applied Social Psychology* 156.

Innes, M, 2004, "Reinventing Tradition? Reassurance, Neighbourhood Security and Policing" 4 *Criminology and Criminal Justice* 151.

Innes, M and Roberts, C, 2008, "Reassurance Policing, Community Intelligence and the Co-Production of Neighbourhood Order", *The Handbook of Knowledge-Based Policing: Current Conceptions and Future Directions* (Eds T Williamson), Wiley, Chichester, USA.

Johnson, MP, 1995, "Patriarchal Terrorism and Common Couple Violence: Two forms of violence against women" 57 *Journal of Marriage and the Family* 283.

Long, J, Wells, W and de Leon-Grandos, W, 2002, "Implementation Issues in a Community Police Partnership in Law Enforcement Space: Lessons from a case Study of a Community Policing Approach to Domestic Violence" 3 *Police Practice and Research* 231.

Mama, A, 1989, "Violence against Black Women: Gender, Race and State Responses" 32 *Feminist Review* 30.

Pruegger, V, 2003, *Community and Policing in Partnership*. Viewed on 12 March 2012, <www.canadianheritage. gc.ca/progs/multi/pubs/police/partner_e.cfm>.

Reisig, MD and Parks, RB, 2004, "Can Community Policing Help the Truly Disadvantaged?" 50 *Crime and Delinquency* 139.

Schneider, SR, 1999, "Overcoming Barriers to Communication between Police and Social Disadvantaged Neighbourhoods: A Critical Theory of Community Policing" 30 *Crime, Law and Social Change* 347.

Success Works, 2009, *Review of the Integrated Response to Family Violence: Final Report*, Department of Justice, Tasmania.

Tasmania Police, 2006, *Police and the Community*, Department of Police and Emergency Management, Hobart.

Urbis, 2008, *Review of the Family Violence Act 2004*, Department of Justice, Hobart.

Vitale, A S, 2005, "Innovation and Institutionalization: Factors in the Development of 'Quality of Life' Policing in New York City" 15 *Policing and Society* 99.

Wilson, JQ and Kelling, GL, 1982, "Broken Windows: The Police and Neighbourhood Safety" March *Atlantic Monthly* 29.

Wilson, JQ and Kelling, GL, 2006, "A Quarter Century of Broken Windows" II *American Interest* 168.

Winter, RE, 2011, *Intimate Partner Violence: The Impact of Discourse on a Coordinated Response*, PhD dissertation, Tasmanian Institute of Law Enforcement Studies, University of Tasmania, Hobart.

Chapter 6

Reaching Out to Vulnerable People: The Work of Police Liaison Officers

Isabelle Bartkowiak-Théron

Inquiries into police services such as the Scarman and Macpherson reports (1982 and 1999, UK) and the Wood Reports (Australia) have revealed to the public an uncomfortable reality of policing. In response, police organisations worldwide have attempted to address criticisms of institutional racial prejudice, unethical conduct and community disengagement. First, they have aimed to recruit a force that is more representative of the diverse communities they serve; second, police organisations have tried to reach out to community groups (especially those known for having difficult relationships with the police, as well as those that are over-represented in the criminal justice system); and third, they have made efforts to adopt more inclusive policies and practices through collaborative work with community groups, associations and specialised agencies. At the very least, this is the official version of developments. The actual situation is more complicated than it appears on paper.

There is little doubt that police organisations have put considerable effort into addressing mistakes of the past and enhancing not only their community "representativity" but also their work with social groups that had formerly been the target of over-policing, mistrust and institutional racism. Recruitment practices have aimed to enrol more members from racial and ethnic communities. Training is now inclusive of cultural awareness curricula. Some police roles have been created or redesigned to focus on the needs of specific communities. Designated officers are now trained to reach out to these communities, and/or to act as advocates for vulnerable groups. Importantly, these officers often have specific problem-solving and diversion dimensions attached to their portfolio. This chapter develops on such roles, by studying what police liaison officers do. The rationale for police liaison officers is initially reviewed, followed by a brief typology of each liaison "profile". The realities of everyday tasks for these officers are examined, as well as the complexities of choosing this career path. This chapter concludes by considering the strategic and operational necessity of the police liaison officer in dealing with vulnerable people, and makes some observations on the political positioning of the role in policing generally.

The Genesis of Police Liaison Roles

The 1980s and 1990s were fraught with violent police encounters with vulnerable populations; commonly, riots involving youth or racial minorities, or violent episodes with people who behaved in ways that appeared to be suspicious. Many subsequent reports highlighted the dysfunction of police services in relation to their dealings with visible (usually ethnic) minorities. These reports documented "institutional and individual police behaviours that served to discriminate against minorities" (Casey, 2000: 167; see also Chan, 1997) and identified the institutionalisation of racism in police organisations:

> It must be recognised that racial discrimination, both direct and indirect, and harassment are endemic within our society and the police service is no exception (HMIC, 1997: 2).

In the overall context of higher incarceration rates for ethnic minorities (Ward, 2006; Yarwood, 2007; Barcham, 2010; Bartels, 2011; see also Henning, in this collection, Ch 14), the reports indicated that new mechanisms of control had to be created to re-establish the sovereignty of police and mend relationships with hard to reach communities. Police liaison officers seemed particularly suited to this task, considering that:

> At the heart of the liaison officer role is an effort to build bridges between two groups whose relations, historically and contemporaneously, have often been fractious and marked by power imbalances and distrust (Willis, 2010: 43).

There were three ways to build these bridges. First, police organisations could have a more diverse profile. They would increase recruitment from minority groups and select suitable candidates (that is, those who best fit the institutional mould or best meet selection criteria[1]) to be sent to police academies. The second strategy was to train existing police officers in cultural and social issues so that they could become more effective and proactive in addressing minority-related matters. Some police officers, in addition to receiving basic cultural awareness training (see Bartkowiak-Théron and Layton, in this collection, Ch 4) could also opt for additional professional development and become police liaison officers for their organisation in a particular locality. The final option was to appeal to hard to reach communities, and ask them to work hand in hand with local officers, through dedicated community liaison persons. These people would come from community "ranks", but would be part of the police organisation in a problem-solving and advisory role. They would remain unsworn, in a lay capacity (although sometimes remunerated).

Over recent years, police scholars have observed a multiplication of this latter outsourcing of liaison roles and an "extension of the policing family" (Johnston, 2005), with an increasing use of civilians and the creation of auxiliary roles (Yarwood, 2007). This has fuelled modern theories of policing revolving around concepts such as the pluralisation of policing, new governance of crime and partnership policing (Bartkowiak-Théron, 2011). It also strengthened arguments that police organisations were striving to create more diverse and inclusive forms of policing, by increasing their community representativity or the diversification of the organisation (Johnston, 2007), the representation of communities in policing initiatives (Crawford, 1997) and by engaging more police in community initiatives (Bartels, 2011). In time, in Australia, police liaison officers became part of a "concerted strategy to improve cultural competency of Australian police services" (Cherney and Chui, 2010: 281).

As evidenced in police annual reports, there is undeniable, albeit small, progress in police organisations becoming more representative of the communities they serve through recruitment of ethno-religious minorities (see also Ward, 2006). According to Casey, this is part of the normalisation of multicultural reality (Casey, 2000: 165). What is interesting, though, is how police liaison officers provide an added, highly visible option for police to show their interest in social diversity, and their wish to develop more culturally appropriate forms of policing (Barcham, 2010: 50).

Police-youth liaison schemes are also a good example of how police have tried to close the gap with "misunderstood" social groups. Youth or juvenile liaison schemes are not new, with programs going back as far as the 1940s in the United Kingdom (Mack, 1963) or as early as the 1910s for the United States, with special responsibilities of liaison with schools, monitoring playgrounds and behaviour supervision. Social control theorists (Hirschi, 1969)[2] have supported such schemes by acknowledging that schools play a central role in crime prevention, by identifying problem youth and providing early intervention pathways (Herrington and Bartkowiak-Théron, 2007).

This approach revolves around the articulation of partnerships between various agencies, usually police, schools, courts, community leaders and welfare agencies (Scheffer, 1987; Shaw, 2004). In the case of juvenile justice, the United States' *Omnibus Crime Control and Safe Streets Act 1968* formally defined the role of School Resources Officers (SROs) as:

> A career law enforcement officer, with sworn authority, deployed in community-oriented policing and assigned by the employing police department or agency to work in collaboration with school and community-based organisations (Part Q, Title 1).

For Scheffer (1987), SROs are a prime example of "knowledge-based policing" (see Williamson, 2008), which leads to a form of problem-solving built from the ground up. Based on reassurance, community engagement and high visibility principles, and directed at mainstream young people as well as at risk youths, SROs help deliver informed responses within the local community. They provide an early intervention mechanism that prevents a drift towards serious misbehaviour, and enables pathways for a quicker, more comprehensive police response to offending.

Liaison schemes therefore aim at an improved understanding of vulnerable groups to help police identify ways to decrease criminality (as well as victimisation, especially for sexual minorities and in the case of domestic violence) by way of community engagement (Nihart et al, 2005). The latter is an important strategic point for police organisations, and is stressed in many police public documentation. For example, it is the Australia New Zealand Policing Advisory Agency's (ANZPAA) first priority, under the generic umbrella of community policing (ANZPAA, 2010: 13)[3] to:

> [E]nhance police understanding of community needs and expectations [and develop] responsive policies and policing strategies to improve community engagement, particularly with youth and Indigenous communities.

At this juncture it is important to stress that liaison roles are *specifically* directed at vulnerable populations. Put bluntly, if legislation or policy does not indicate that "you" are part of a vulnerable group, then "you" do not have the support of a specialised liaison officer; except, sometimes, a "community liaison officer", who is commonly a general duties officer bearing the portfolio of community engagement. So how do specialised liaison roles work? What are they intended to achieve?

Police-Community Liaison Roles

The role of liaison officers is by no means straightforward, and goes beyond that of maintaining a two-way communication between police and the community. Furthermore, the more complex the problems they address, the more policy-driven their responsibilities become. They provide a contextual interface (Barcham, 2010) between the community and the police. Their core role is to build trust with those who have had historically tense relationships with police, who are the most at risk to offend, to not report crime, and those who are the most at risk to fall prey to offenders. In a nutshell, they deal with vulnerable people, as defined by legislation and policy (see also Asquith and Bartkowiak-Théron, Bartkowiak-Théron and Corbo Crehan, and Stanford, this collection, Chs 1, 3 and 2). Liaison officers have a wide range of core functions, and depending on their status in the police (sworn or unsworn), they may play a specific part in the investigation of criminal matters.

The best way to depict the work of police liaison officers is to describe it according to the officer's status within the police organisation.

There are three types of liaison portfolio: police auxiliaries, specialised police liaison officers, and police spokespersons. These liaison roles are all directed at vulnerable groups and follow the list (although not the full list) of vulnerable populations as featured in legislation and policies (see Bartkowiak-Théron and Corbo Crehan, and Henning, in this collection, Chs 3 and 14). It therefore seems that the liaison portfolio is *specifically* designed for police to work with vulnerable groups. Establishing a brief typology of liaison roles helps indicate the ways in which police do so (though, the author recognises that these might slightly differ with jurisdictions).

Police Auxiliaries

Police auxiliaries are adult members of the public who become non-sworn police personnel (hereafter "community liaison officers"). They participate in policing by way of support to police organisations and communities. To use an expression of Bayley and Shearing (1996: 592), they fulfil a role of "anticipatory regulation and amelioration" rather than the traditional law enforcement role of a police officer. The most prominent and well-known example of police auxiliary in Australia is the Aboriginal Community Liaison Officer (ACLO). ACLOs are civilian employees ("quasi-police personnel", Cherney and Chui, 2010: 280) working for police organisations throughout Australia. Willis describes the core functions of ACLOs as:

1. building good communication and relations between police and Indigenous communities;
2. resolving disputes between police and Indigenous people;
3. improving understanding within communities about the role of police and encouraging Indigenous people to discuss crime problems with police;
4. helping police and Indigenous communities work together on crime prevention solutions;
5. identifying local crime problems and other issues impacting on police relations with the community; and
6. educating police to increase cultural awareness (2010: 42).

The duties of ACLOs therefore focus on encouraging Indigenous Australians to discuss their main safety concerns, crime and violence with police, along with fostering better collaborative work, and developing dialogue and mutual understanding (culturally and operationally) with police. Their work parallels that of Volunteers in Policing, who are trained for specific support duties to help the police and the community, and support victims of crime during the investigation process with information and referrals. These roles are also similar to Multicultural Community Liaison Officers (MCLOs)[4] who provide a link between police and members of the

88

public who are from culturally and linguistically diverse backgrounds. They may provide language assistance, and may also work with local ethnic communities. None of these support persons wear a police uniform (although they might wear *a* uniform), nor do they carry a gun or drive a police vehicle. Depending on jurisdictions, they may sometimes exercise some powers, such as perform traffic duties in emergency situations, photograph prisoners, act as mediators between police and communities (like the Squamish Nation North Shore peacekeepers in Canada), or undertake patrol duties (like Community Support Officers in London) (Johnston, 2006; Willis, 2010; Barcham, 2010).

Community liaison officers have the added benefit of being more familiar with the community than sworn members of the police force. They are, by nature, more aware of local communities' traditions and customs, and of such things as community members' body language. Their local knowledge also allows them to play the community's "rules of the game". Ideally, they should also be less inclined to stereotyping (although research has documented the impact of indoctrination or programming of police auxiliaries through training; Casey, 2000; see also endnote 1).

Police Liaison Officers

The most prominent form of police liaison is probably that of sworn specialised frontline police liaison officers (hereafter, "police liaison officers"). After being allocated a geographical area as their zone of operation, they become the first port of call and the "friendly face" of the police for pre-determined social groups. Such groups include youth (either in the community[5] or specifically those at school[6]), and sexually and gender diverse communities.[7] As police liaison officers allocated with the responsibility of bridging the gap between hard to reach groups and the police organisation, their everyday duties include a careful balance of community engagement activities and police work. From a community point of view, police liaison officers have to make themselves visible and available to community members, build trust, network with related agencies and associations, provide information sessions about crime-related issues, and engage in real time problem solving in the case of minor matters. From a policing point of view, their role is fundamentally strategic. Nicely positioned at the centre or near a vulnerability nucleus, they are a precious source of information for the police organisation. Having access to community resources implies that they have access to local knowledge and can play a pivotal role in negotiating local strategies or in advising the hierarchy about local circumstances and the best means of solving problems.

The work of *sworn* police liaison officers differs vastly from that of *unsworn* community liaison officers though, due to the various duties held by police officers, and their possible involvement with investigation matters. To take the example of New South Wales, the portfolio of police liaison officers, as per their specialisation, is depicted in Table 1 (*see over page*).[8]

**Table 1: Specialised Police Liaison Officers in New South Wales
(modified from Attorney General's Victims Services, 2012)**

	TRAINING	ROLE	LOCATION
Domestic Violence Liaison Officer DVLO	Domestic and family violence, child protection issues	• advice and support to victims • help with Apprehended Violence Order court process • referral to support agencies (such as refuges) • monitoring of repeat victims and perpetrators	Throughout NSW, in major police stations
Gay and Lesbian Liaison Officer GLLO	Specially trained to address sexual and gender diversity issues	• sensitive to the law enforcement and safety needs of gay men and lesbians • recognise the disproportionate level of violence perpetrated against the gay and lesbian community • assist gay and lesbian victims of crime • work to reduce violence related to homophobic attitudes in the community	Throughout NSW. In 2012, there were more than 100 Gay and Lesbian Liaison Officers throughout the State
Youth Liaison Officer YLO	Youth issues, youth legislation, principles of restorative justice and conferencing	• deliver cautions to young people • make the final decision about referring them to a Youth Justice Conference as per the *Young Offenders Act 1997* • development of crime prevention programs to reduce youth crime and victimisation	One Youth Liaison Officer in every Local Area Command
School Liaison Police Officer SLP	Youth issues, legislation, crime prevention and school policies	• provide police presence and high visibility in NSW schools, by way of regular visits • support victims of crime • develop mentoring schemes • develop innovative ways to prevent youth crime • deliver crime prevention workshops in the classroom	Although not based directly in schools, they visit public, Catholic and independent high schools throughout New South Wales, in their allocated Local Area Command(s)

Police Spokespersons

Many police organisations throughout the world have allocated the role of "liaison" to senior members of the organisation. Endowed with a more strategic responsibility in dealing with vulnerability issues, their role lies at policy and public communication levels. These spokespersons are the first port of call for the media when a police organisation is involved in dealing with vulnerability matters. They also sit on a number of strategic committees that decide or advise on policy and implementation. Their role at corporate level is thus often that of management of initiatives and implementation strategies in collaboration with partner agencies (for example, the Department of Education or Youth Services for youth matters, and Anti-Discrimination offices for ethno-cultural issues).

The Tasmania Aboriginal Strategic Plan provides an illustration of such a portfolio, with the description of the Corporate Spokesperson for Aboriginal issues. The functions of the District and Assistant Aboriginal Liaison Officers focus on the coordination of partnerships with local associations (specifically the Aboriginal community, organisations, groups and individuals, any organisation representative of Aboriginal people, local government, government and non-government organisations representing indigenous persons), proactive problem-solving, advice, development and delivery of cross-cultural awareness training and policy development (Tasmania Police, 2012). The document is also one of the most descriptive of its genre, by allocating specific accountability duties to these officers. These include the development and maintenance of a corporate knowledge of Aboriginal issues, liaison with Aboriginal communities, advice in relation to Tasmania Police practices and procedures, advice to Police Commanders on local Aboriginal issues, maintenance of a database on Tasmania Police/Aboriginal interaction, and dissemination of information to Aboriginal people (Tasmania Police, 2012).

This position description is quite similar to (although more specific than) that of the Corporate Spokesperson for Aboriginal Issues in the New South Wales Police Force, who is:

> [A]n Assistant Commissioner level officer and is one of many corporate spokespersons within NSW Police Force. The Spokesperson Program gives nominated senior officers the corporate responsibility to develop an overview of strategy, policy and operational practice in a particular portfolio; to maintain the corporate profile for the portfolio and to be an advocate for the area when required. The Corporate Spokesperson chairs the Aboriginal Strategic Direction Steering Committee (NSWPF, 2006).

Aboriginality is not the only area in which police spokespersons are designated to work on policy in advisory and implementation capacities. The NSWPF also has spokespersons on a variety of domains including domestic and family violence, mental health, victims of crime, and youth.

More generally, police liaison *schemes* throughout Australia govern how police articulate their services with vulnerable groups, specialist agencies and courts. In Western Australia, for example, the Police Service and the Mental Health Division of the Health Department have developed a protocol that focuses on the statutory protection of patients' rights and placement of greater emphasis on community care and treatment options. This protocol allows for the creation of an Executive Liaison Committee, which ensures collaboration of police with Health services and also establishes the appointment of liaison persons and their responsibilities:

> The Police Service (Office of the Police Commissioner) and the Mental Health Division (Office of the Chief Psychiatrist) will facilitate greater communication and responsiveness to any urgent operational issues by the appointment of a liaison officer from each agency. The liaison officers will meet on a regular basis and progress any recommendations from the Executive Liaison Committee. They will also refer matters that require follow-up investigation and will report on any complaints/issues received relating to either agency to the relevant Local Liaison Committee (WA Health, 2012: 5).

Being a Liaison Officer and Being a Liaison Officer for Vulnerable People

Police liaison officers have not always enjoyed a respected status within police organisations. Initially, their portfolios were not perceived as "real police work", and police youth liaison officers were often referred to as "kiddies cops", "surrogate teachers" or "soft cops" by their colleagues (Bartkowiak-Théron and Herrington, 2008). In such circumstances, skills were wasted and officers were under-utilised for the intelligence gathering and networking potential they possessed. It was often thought that their duties were an inappropriate extension of police work, with police officers "pushed into little more than a public relations role" (CEPS, 2010: 36), especially in relation to cultural diversity. Also, it was thought that a lack of training resulted in a failure to prepare police liaison officers adequately (Johnston, 2005). Police officers who had formed this opinion thought that it was "unfair to petty offenders to deprive them of the opportunity to be given adequate attention and treatment" (Mack, 1963). This fostered a lack of credibility within police ranks.

However, various political and governance dynamics, whole-of-government approaches to crime and delinquency, the understanding of "wicked issues" and the need for better police performance have encouraged the development of highly sophisticated and knowledge-driven police practices (Williamson, 2008) inclusive of specific roles and portfolios. These are the outcome of highly specialised professional development (often driven by research), with police officers sometimes attending week-long training in age, health, sexuality and other vulnerability, social or community topics. Provided by specialists from the field (practicing academics, psychologists, social workers), this training is designed to enhance police work by providing specialised officers with the skills to deal with the vulnerabilities of their target groups. The training of youth liaison officers therefore includes lectures and seminars on bullying issues (including cyber-bullying), school disciplinary procedures and crime prevention (NSW DET, 2006).

This proficiency in specialised matters has contributed to recognition among the profession of police liaison officers as experts on specific issues, and, to some extent, to a form of leadership in the field. Approached from a tactical point of view, a police liaison officer has the potential for acute intelligence gathering, community reassurance (Johnston, 2006) and establishing strong relationships with professional networks and agencies locally. Although they have a role to play in improving reporting rates through their reassurance role in their allocated community, they may also listen to some individual concerns in confidence, which contributes to the building of trust with community members.

So if the role of frontline police liaison officer is currently supported at political and organisational levels, and offers positive professional interaction with the community, then, why do we not see hundreds of police officers take up the offer of specialised training and why do so few of them apply for frontline police liaison roles? Several hurdles need highlighting.

The main impediment here might be the most pragmatic one. Although the role is, by no means, intended to be a "career parenthesis", the liaison portfolio is by no means a springboard for promotion. The lack of career advancement opportunities has been flagged in the literature as a hindrance to police specialisation (Cherney and Chui, 2010; Bartkowiak-Théron and Herrington, 2008). This in turn impacts on job satisfaction, where some police officers sometimes feel that they are going nowhere, that their position is undervalued and not given due credit.

The fact that most liaison roles are directed at social groups known for their difficult relationships with police does not make the role attractive either. It may be branded with the idea that officers will have to engage in useless efforts in helpless situations. Police liaison officers are indeed heavily involved in the organisation of "bridging" activities (mostly social ones, like social soccer games, cultural awareness days) that are intended to promote understanding and cross-cultural awareness between groups that may be at odds with each other (CEPS, 2010). These efforts, which research has shown to be essential and undeniable, may nonetheless produce rather invisible effects in terms of performance measurement. Not having their efforts recognised by key performance indicators, in key *foci* of policy, may therefore be discouraging. Measuring the success of their strategies is the recurrent criticism towards community policing initiatives; so it is not surprising to see the issue resurface here. Obviously, further institutional benchmarking reform is needed here before the contributions of liaison officers are accurately measured and rewarded.

Institutional stability is also a problem. The concept of "filling in" which is part and parcel of police work, therefore bears significant tactical and operational problems for specialised liaison officers in the short term. For some, the liaison responsibility remains, fundamentally, a vocational one. Many police officers shoulder it as a way to express their passion for youth or community issues, or to provide relief and expertise for members of the community in a professional carers' role. However, the policing occupation is impacted by such things as illnesses, injuries and accidents. In such cases, some police officers are taken "off the field" to recover, or may be reallocated to less stressful positions. It therefore comes a time when, unavoidably, the police organisation will "tap into its resources", take a police officer off an area of specialisation and reallocate him or her to more general, first response duties. This is not well-appreciated by those who have dedicated themselves to an area of specialty. It is perceived (by officers or by community members) as a desertion of their post, with the "familiar face" of policing going "missing in action" for a while. It also counteracts the necessary criterion of geographic stability, which is the crux of trust building, and essential for communities to relate to the police officers they have come to know through community interactions. The mobility of police rosters and the reallocation of some officers elsewhere can be to the detriment of relationship building with groups with whom relationships are already stretched. This was particularly highlighted in the evaluation of projects targeting young Muslim communities:

> The Attarwon project ... was originally submitted by a senior sergeant who was the officer-in-charge of the police station and who held the community engagement portfolio. It was envisaged that the senior sergeant, the community liaison officer and the youth resource officer would run the project. However, the senior sergeant was transferred and the community liaison officer resigned, which left only one person (the youth resource officer) to take on the project and manage it along with other professional responsibilities (CEPS, 2012: 33).

Budget cuts also impact the viability of police liaison schemes. If a police organisa-tion is subject to large budget cuts (as in the case of Tasmania in 2010), the pressure of emergency response will take precedence over proactive work, and police liaison roles will either be combined with other duties or will be left on hold until the financial situation improves. In the case of police auxiliaries, it also means that positions are advertised, if at all, on a contractual basis (usually six months), which is neither conducive to operational stability, nor leading to protocol expertise.

There are also difficulties associated with the liaison position narrative. The in-between or bridging positioning of specialist police creates unique challenges for officers (Willis, 2010). People in charge of the liaison portfolio may feel ostracised from both the community and the police, as their role can be perceived in terms of allegiance ("working for the other") by both parties. Isolation, which ironically contradicts the terms of the position, may therefore well be a negative consequence of the portfolio.

Conclusion

There is a myriad of factors that contribute to the multiplication of specialised police liaison roles targeting vulnerable populations in the western world. These have been influenced by political comments and socio-legal change, as well as the regular feature of vulnerable groups in crime-related news. Although such factors vary from country to country, there is sufficient literature on the topic to make a number of generalisations about police liaison roles.

First, the rationale for police liaison portfolios is mostly influenced by a government and corporate desire to make up for past mistakes. These roles help address past and present public dissatisfaction with the police, although these may not be effective at all times (see the 2011-2012 riots in England). Secondly, a better documentation of "wicked" issues helped establish ways to enhance the work of police, and give it more directionality. Then, police organisations started to look at more inclusive forms of doing police business. This meant encouraging more involvement and active community participation in the design and implementation of community initiatives. Aside from recruiting a diverse police force, this meant that other ways had to be found to meet the needs of vulnerable groups. By "extending the police family" according to the modern, pragmatic acknowledgment of the pluralisation of policing, through the recruitment of police auxiliaries, the training and deployment of specialised officers and the creation of corporate liaison roles dedicated to vulnerable populations, the police seem to have found a way to progressively do this. Police liaison roles are as much a symbolic positioning at the political level as they are a public demonstration from police organisations that there exists a corporate will to do business better in relation to vulnerable groups. But if the role of liaison officers is to synchronise police services with the reality of local vulnerabilities, then police and policy makers can do better. Here are areas that warrant further policy and operational scrutiny.

First, we can but regret that liaison roles do not span the full gamut of vulnerable populations as featured in this collection, especially when these are a key focus of policy. It is even more regrettable when the proactive work of liaison officers seems to positively impact on police performance *in general*, on public satisfaction with police *as a whole*, in addition to bridging relationships with minorities and contributing to crime reduction and real time intervention.

Importantly though, we should reflect on the siloed responsibilities of liaison officers. If the coexistence of multiple vulnerabilities is acknowledged as a possibility by all, then specialist training for liaison officers needs to address more complex problems than they currently target. But there are several impediments to this. The first one is a lack of policing resources in an economic context where police are always asked to do more with less. It is therefore unlikely to see liaison roles multiply within the policing landscape. More provocatively though, the lack of liaison roles for *some* vulnerable groups or for groups experiencing multiple vulnerabilities can also be explained by those groups not being sufficiently problematic *yet*, at risk *yet*, large enough *yet* or vulnerable *overall* to warrant a specialised police resource. While cynical in nature, this is nothing but a neo-liberal explanation to such a deficiency, where liaison roles are created according to highly visible needs (and some chapters in this collection highlight that some vulnerabilities tend to be invisible or, rather, hidden; see Herrington and Clifford, and Asquith, Chs 8 and 10) and as matters of priority or urgency, as opposed to higher-order sociological considerations. This also supports the argument of non-interference advanced by Bartkowiak-Théron and Corbo Crehan in their chapter (Ch 3) within this collection.

The second obstacle is the (understandable) wish to avoid the particularisation of policing services. Complex, multiple vulnerability cases are known, but they remain more of an exception rather than a rule. Then, resources can realistically not be directed at services that will rarely be used. However, in the current circumstances, there is no evidence that suggests that the training of liaison officers systematically caters for complex vulnerabilities, due to the specific directionality of liaison schemes. Some empirical literature actually points at liaison officers asking for additional training on complex matters and especially in areas of cross-sectional vulnerability. Attention to a broader understanding of vulnerability, culture and to wicked issues needs embedding in liaison syllabus, for proficiency to be acquired across the board. This situation thus supports the point of this collection, which advocates cultural competency for all officers, in all, even the most complex vulnerabilities. The Queensland Police Service Vulnerable Persons Policy (2012) is indicative of police organisations adopting "broader lenses" to identify, assess and address vulnerabilities and expand competency in such matter. It is hoped, then, that if the liaison role is as much "the policing *of* communities as it is the policing *with* communities" (Willis, 2010: 47, italics in original), it is strengthened in the future in national and local policies, performance management guidelines and operational protocols.

Endnotes

1 See Bartkowiak-Théron and Jaccoud, 2008 for a critique of the pre-institution-alisation of recruitment, training and coaching.

2 Hirschi insisted that schools create a social bond that helped shield young people from the likelihood of delinquent involvement. This is reiterated in more recent literature, considering (1) that young people spend 18% of waking hours in school for 12 years (Gottfredson, 2001), and (2) the relationship between the likelihood of anti-social behaviour and truancy/absenteeism.

3 According to the ANZPAA *Strategic and Business Plan 2011-2012* a future action item for ANZPAA is to "Support the review of policing programs available for Culturally and Linguistically Diverse communities in partnership with the Centre of Excellence in Policing and Security" (ANZPAA, 2011: 2).

4 A multicultural liaison officer can be a sworn officer. In that case, the role is more policy driven and includes more operational duties than described here. This is the case, for example, in Tasmania, where the MCLO is an Inspector in charge of policy advice and implementation, education at recruit and corporate levels, and networking with diversity and cultural advocacy groups.

5 Such as "Youth Liaison Officers" (YLOs) or "Youth Specialised Officers" (YSOs) in New South Wales.

6 "School-Liaison Police Officers" or "Police-School Liaison Officers". These are also known as "Police Resource Officers" or "Police-School Resource Officers" in the United States.

7 "Gay and Lesbians Liaison Officers" (GLLOs) in New South Wales, or "LGBTI (Lesbian, Gay, Bisexual, Transgender and Intersex) Liaison Officers" in Tasmania, for example.

8 We use NSW terminology throughout this chapter for consistency. While roles would be similar, role titles might differ across States and Territories, with expressions such as Multicultural Liaison officers (MLOs), Ethnic Liaison Officers (ELOs); Lesbian, Gay, Bisexual, Transgender and Intersex Liaison officers (LGBTIs).

References

Omnibus Crime Control and Safe Streets Act 1968 (USA).

Young Offenders Act 1997 (NSW).

Australia New Zealand Policing Advisory Agency, 2010, *Annual Report 2009-2010*, ANZPAA, Adelaide.

Australia New Zealand Policing Advisory Agency, 2011, *Annual Report 2010-2011*, ANZPAA, Adeliade.

Barcham, M, 2010, "Indigenous Community Policing: Building Strength from Within", *Community Policing: Current and Future Directions for Australia – Research and Public Policy* (Ed J Putt) Canberra: Australian Institute of Criminology.

Bartels, L, 2011, "Crime Prevention Programs for Culturally and Linguistically Diverse Communities in Australia", AIC Reports, *Research in Practice*, 18, Australian Institute of Criminology, Canberra.

Bartkowiak-Théron, I and Herrington, V, 2008, "Picturing the School Liaison Police Role: Phase Two Report", *The School Liaison Police Initiative. A Multi-faceted Evaluation in New South Wales*, Charles Sturt University and New South Wales Police Force, Goulburn, Australia.

Bartkowiak-Théron, I and Jaccoud, M, 2008, "New Directions in Justice in Canada: From Top-down to Community 'Representatives'", *Justice and Community and Civil Society: A Contested Terrain* (Ed J Shapland), Willan Publishing, London.

Bartkowiak-Théron, I, 2011, "Partnership Policing for Police Organisations", *Policing in Practice* (Eds P Birch and V Herrington), Palgrave Macmillan, South Yarra.

Bayley, DH and Shearing, C, 1996, "The Future of Policing" 3 *Law and Society Review* 30.

Casey, J, 2000, "International Experiences in Policing Multicultural Societies" 2 *International Journal of Police Science and Management* 3.

Centre of Excellence in Policing and Security, 2010, Building Trust. *Working with Muslim Communities in Australia: a review of the Community Policing Partnership Project*, Canberra.

Chan, J, 1997, *Changing Police Culture: Policing in a Multicultural Society*, Cambridge University Press, Cambridge, UK.

Cherney, A and Chui, WH, 2010, "Police Auxiliaries in Australia: Police Liaison Officers and the Dilemmas of Being Part of the Extended Family" 3 *Policing and Society* 20.

Crawford, A, 1997, *The Local Governance of Crime: Appeals to Partnerships*, Clarendon Press, London.

Gottfredson, D C, 2001, *Schools and Delinquency*, Cambridge University Press, Cambridge, UK.

Her Majesty's Inspectorate of Constabulary, 1999, *Winning the Race Revisited*, Home Office, London.

Her Majesty's Inspectorate of Constabulary, 1997, *Winning the Race: Policing Plural Communities, Home Office*, London.

Herrington, V and Bartkowiak-Théron, I, 2007, "Tracking the Initial Stages of the Scheme: Phase One Report", *The School Liaison Police Initiative: A*

Multi-faceted Evaluation in New South Wales, Charles Sturt University and NSW Police Force, Goulburn, Australia.

Hirschi, T, 1969, Causes of Delinquency, California University Press, Berkeley, CA.

Johnston, L, 2005, "From 'Community' to 'Neighbourhood' Policing: Police Community Support Officers and the 'Police Extended Family' in London" 15 *Journal of Community and Applied Social Psychology* 14.

Johnston, L, 2006, "Diversifying Police Recruitment? The Deployment of Police Community Support Officers in London" 4 *The Howard Journal* 45.

Mack, JA, 1963, "Police Juvenile Liaison Schemes" 3 *British Journal of Criminology* 14.

Macpherson, W, 1999, *The Stephen Lawrence Inquiry*, Home Office, London.

New South Wales Department of Education and Training, 2006, Crime Prevention Workshops for Secondary Schools, NSW Government, Sydney.

New South Wales Police Force, 2006, *Aboriginal Strategic Direction 2007-2011*. Viewed on 23 March 2012, <www.police.nsw.gov.au/__data/assets/pdf_file/0015/105180/asd_pocket_guide.pdf>.

Nihart, T, Lersch, K M, Sellers, C S and Mieczkowski, T, 2005, "Kids, Cops, Parents and Teachers: Exploring Juvenile Attitudes Toward Authority Figures" 6 *Western Criminology Review* 79.

NSW Attorney General's Victim Services, 2012, *People in Policing*. Viewed on 23 March 2012, <www.lawlink.nsw.gov.au/lawlink/victimsservices/ll_vs.nsf/pages/VS_peopleinpolicing#dv>.

Queensland Police Service, 2012, *Queensland Police Service Vulnerable Persons Policy*. Viewed on April 24 2012, <www.police.qld.gov.au/Resources/Internet/rti/policies/documents/QPSVulnerablePersonsPolicy.pdf>.

Scarman, L G, 1982, *The Scarman report – The Brixton Disorders: Report of an Inquiry*, Penguin, London.

Scheffer, M W, 1987, *Policing from the Schoolhouse: Police-School Liaison and Resource Officer Programs – A Case Study*, C.C. Thomas Publisher, Springfield, IL.

Shaw, M, 2004, *Police, Schools and Crime Prevention: A Preliminary Review of Current Practices, International Centre for the Prevention of Crime*, Montreal, USA.

Tasmania Police, 2012, *Aboriginal Strategic Plan*, DPEM, Hobart.

Western Australia Department of Health, nd, *Protocol Between the Western Australia Police Service and the Mental Health Division of the Health Department of Western Australia*. Viewed on 23 March 2012, <www.chief psychiatrist.health.wa.gov.au/docs/guides/Protocol_Between_WA_Police_Mental_Health_Division.pdf>.

Williamson, T, Ed, 2008, *The Handbook of Knowledge-Based Policing: Current Conceptions and Future Directions*, John Wiley and Sons Ltd, Chichester.

Willis, M, 2010, "Aboriginal Liaison Officers in Community Policing", *Community Policing: Current and Future Directions for Australia – Research and Public Policy* (Ed J Putt), Australian Institute of Criminology, Canberra.

Wood, J, 2008, *Report of the Special Commission of Inquiry into Child Protection Services in NSW, State of New South Wales*, Sydney.

Yarwood, R, 2007, "Getting Just Deserts? Policing, Governance and Rurality in Western Australia" 38 *Geoforum* 13.

Chapter 7

The Vulnerable Thin Blue Line: Representations of Police Use of Force in the Media

Katrina Clifford

Police are often thought of as the "protectors of society", so it is understandable that when those considered amongst society's most vulnerable are killed by the fatal discharge of a police firearm, the public response is invariably complex. In most instances, the contacts police have with people with a mental illness are resolved safely and without incident (Queensland Office of the Public Advocate, 2005). However, in a small number of cases, these encounters may involve levels of hostility that heighten the resistance of a mentally ill individual towards attempts at negotiation by police officers, creating a situation that is beyond the point of de-escalation (Kerr, Morabito and Watson, 2010). This can precipitate a high-risk scenario that requires the police use of force (Coleman and Cotton, 2010). In these situations:

> The person with a mental illness will most likely be highly distressed and fearful of their own safety, may be experiencing paranoia or delusions involving police... Combined with this is the response of the police officer – an officer who may have received only cursory mental health training, who may be fearful for their own safety and that of others on the scene, and who is acutely aware of the potential for violence that exists in dealing with situations of behavioural disturbance (Queensland Office of the Public Advocate, 2005: 1).

These infrequent police interventions are distinguished from the numerous other, less precarious, everyday encounters between vulnerable individuals and frontline police officers (some of which are detailed in other chapters of this collection, and particularly the proceeding chapter) by a number of elements, including "the presence of or potential for violence or self-harm, the presence of firearms or other weapons, and the degree of distress experienced by the individual" (Queensland Office of the Public Advocate, 2005: 15). On rare occasions, these crisis situations may result in severe injury to, or the death of, attending police officers, or even family members or mental health workers. But they may also result in the death of the individual in psychiatric crisis, sometimes by police-involved shooting. These critical incidents can have "devastating and long-term consequences – not only for the person's family and loved ones, but also for the police officer involved and for community attitudes and perceptions" (Queensland Office of the Public Advocate, 2005: 1). Many police officers "never recover from such circumstances and themselves suffer severe psychological problems after such incidents – often for the rest of their lives" (Carroll, 2005: 22).

In Australia, the evidence base for the overall incidence of fatal mental health crisis interventions is limited. Figures from a seminal report on police-involved shootings indicate that, between 1 January 1990 and 30 June 1997, Australian police fatally shot 41 people (Dalton, 1998). At least one-third had a known psychiatric history or had experienced depression prior to police-involved crisis intervention (Dalton, 1998). A more recent, albeit localised, study of 48 police-involved shootings in the Australian state of Victoria, between November 1982 and February 2007, found that 87 per cent of individuals in reported fatalities during this period were known in some capacity to either mental health services or police, prior to their deaths (Kesic, Thomas and Ogloff, 2010). Obviously, even one fatal mental health crisis intervention is a death too many, especially in light of the possibilities for prevention (see Herrington and Clifford, in this collection, Ch 8). However, it is important to note that frontline police officers respond to a significant number of mental health events each year. For example, in 2009, police in New South Wales (NSW) attended 34,000 mental health-related incidents (Donohue, 2010). This was almost double the number of mental health events that required NSW police resources five years earlier. While it is accepted, therefore, that some frontline police officers "use force unjustly, this appears to be the exception rather than the rule" (McElvain and Kposowa, 2008: 506). On the whole, the majority of police officers "do a difficult and stressful job in a professional and humane manner" (Chappell, 2008: 39). In Australia, fatal mental health crisis interventions remain relatively uncommon (Clifford, 2010). However, the public could be forgiven for thinking otherwise, given the salience news media attribute to critical incidents of this kind.

By virtue of their circumstances, these incidents are both highly visible and contentious, and are often the subject of widely divergent perspectives, particularly between key stakeholders (that is, the police, and bereaved family and friends of the deceased). The inherent struggle that often ensues between these stakeholders to define the ways in which a fatal mental health crisis intervention is viewed and interpreted can be characterised in two ways. Primarily, it reflects a conflict between the institutional (official) discourse of the police, on the one hand, and the (non-official) lay discourse of bereaved individuals, on the other. This conflict – often related to attributions of culpability – is a form of "risk communication" where each stakeholder attempts to persuade others of the validity of their assessment of the principal risk (Blood et al, 2000; 2004). These conflicts between institutional and lay discourses, identifiable in the immediate aftermath of such critical incidents, can be traced to fundamental differences in the interpretive frameworks adopted by key stakeholders. For example, police organisations tend to evaluate the "reasonableness" of police use of deadly force according to the technical assessments and management of risks specified within the formal protocols and standard operating procedures of contemporary policing. In contrast, the critical perspectives of family and friends of the deceased are more often guided by subjective measures that are influenced by emotive responses to the death of a loved one. While no one position is necessarily more right or wrong than the other, the inherent conflict between the two appeals directly to the "values" of news, and its attraction to the controversial.

It is therefore of little surprise that fatal mental health crisis interventions are often prominently reported in news media; certainly more than mental health crises that have been successfully de-escalated and resolved by police using non-lethal means. As previously illustrated, for every critical incident, there are many more mental health crises in the community involving the same potential for fatal outcomes that are effectively resolved without the need for police use of deadly force. It is rare, however, for these incidents to be as regularly or extensively reported in news media. When they do appear, the column inches or broadcast time apportioned to such news stories are negligible in comparison to those of fatal mental health crisis interventions. Additionally, the circumstances related to these incidents need to be exceptional as to warrant being reported (for example, the mentally ill individual has to have armed themselves with an edged weapon or firearm).

This raises a particular set of questions about "news values" and editorial decisions about "newsworthiness" in relation to the construction of public risk knowledge and (mis)conceptions about the relationship between contemporary policing and mental illness. Apart from the psychological distress that fatal mental health crisis interventions can cause for the individuals involved, strong negative community sentiment towards such adverse incidents can threaten the credibility of police to the potential detriment of subsequent interactions between police and mental health consumers (Queensland Office of the Public Advocate, 2005). This highlights a number of issues about the ways in which police use of force is typically framed in news media coverage of fatal mental health crisis interventions, and the implications of this for police agencies in terms of how they approach their interactions with vulnerable people in the community while being in the media spotlight. It is these issues that form the focus of this chapter, drawing on a critical analysis of the news frames of a selection of stories about fatal mental health crisis interventions reported in Australian print and online news media between 1997 and 2009.

The Police-Media Relationship

Conflicting interpretations of "risk", "responsibility" and "vulnerability", as they relate to critical incidents such as fatal mental health crisis interventions, are primarily played out in two different arenas: the coronial (and sometimes criminal justice) system and the news media. It is principally through the latter that the story of a fatal mental health crisis intervention publicly unfolds and assumes narrative form. Public knowledge of these critical incidents is most often derived from news media reports; firstly of the fatal police-involved shooting, and then later in relation to the coronial inquest and any associated legal proceedings. It is within this news reporting that contested values of civil society are re-energised, emotions are galvanised and significant public debate is generated, particularly in relation to the moral authority of frontline police officers in their interactions with vulnerable people. More than simply "bearing witness" to these events, news media reports play a fundamental and influential role in shaping public understandings and interpretations of fatal mental health crisis interventions and the responsibility and vulnerability of the individuals involved.

As such, news media professionals serve as moral arbiters of the public discourse and socio-political environment that frames these critical incidents. The power of the news media to contribute to the process of where and how social problems are defined is significant. The way in which a story is told, to quote Tiegreen and Newman (2008), may "greatly affect the way media consumers perceive events in the world". Every journalistic choice – from the types of sources used to the perspective taken – helps determine the "prominent themes or meanings within or perceived from a news story as a whole" (Dorfman, Thorson and Stevens, 2001 cited in Tiegreen and Newman, 2008). This is not to say that media audiences cannot contest these dominant news frames. The idea that editors and journalists "frame news in particular or characteristic ways" therefore inevitably leads to questions about "the consequences of those framing decisions" (Blood and Holland, 2004: 326).

Previous research suggests that "vicarious experiences of policing have a substantial impact on perceptions of and confidence in police" (Herrington et al, 2009: 35). In particular, news depictions of controversial police use of deadly force responses to individuals in psychiatric crisis have important implications for how the public views police culture and mental illness more generally, and whether these critical incidents are considered typical or aberrations of contemporary policing practices (Hazelton, 1997). This, in turn, has significant implications for not only public trust in police, but also the perceived legitimacy of police and the public's general willingness to co-operate and collaborate with them (Herrington et al, 2009; Myhill and Beak, 2008; Novak, 2009). The impact and influence of news media reports on high-profile incidents involving police use of deadly force is therefore a legitimate concern and ongoing consideration for police agencies, especially since news media coverage of police use of force incidents has previously been found to increase negative attitudes toward the police (Kaminski and Jefferis, 1998; Weitzer, 2002).

This is neither an emerging realisation, nor a concern isolated to police use of deadly force. Previous research has left us in little doubt that media coverage "plays a significant role in the ways in which the community frames and views issues of crime, law and order, and social control" (McGovern and Lee, 2010: 445). This has previously led to criticisms about "moral panics" and the overstatement of the public's fear of crime in relation to the reality of crime statistics (Altheide, 2002; Blood, Tulloch and Enders, 2000; Farrall and Lee, 2008; Furedi, 2006). The role of police agencies in the media's dissemination of information about crime and law enforcement cannot be discounted, although police and media coopera-tion is not a new phenomenon. As Dowler (2002) points out, news media have often relied heavily on police agencies for information. In some countries, like Australia, this has led to the development of resources designed to support police in their encounters with the media, particularly around the accurate, responsible and sensitive communication of issues related to vulnerable people policing. The *Mindframe* National Media Initiative, for example, has issued pocket guides to help police officers manage their interactions with media at incidents involving mental illness or a suspected suicide. This follows research that shows that the information collected by journalists on these matters from the police and courts is often some of the most problematic in terms of reinforcing negative stereotypes about suicide and mental illness, and vulnerable individuals (*Mindframe* National Media Initiative, 2011).

Contemporary pressures on journalistic staffing levels, resources and time have exacerbated the media's reliance on police as "primary definers" (Hall et al, 1978) of news stories, raising concerns about the capacity of police to "control much of the flow of information" about crime and criminality, and "frame a great percent-age of narratives about law and order and policing" (McGovern and Lee, 2010: 459). This has reinforced the persistent view that police are the dominant party in the police-media relationship. However, as Mawby (1999: 267) explains, "the media context in which both parties operate is now infinitely more complex and accordingly more difficult for an agency such as the police to control". It follows that, if police are able to contribute to definitions of crime and social problems in news media coverage, then community perceptions of police effectiveness and legitimacy may be influenced by the higher visibility of police and their portrayals in the media. Dowler and Zawilski (2007) point to two contradictory observations: some research reveals a favourable disposition towards mediated representations of policing, while other research implies that the police are more often negatively portrayed, particularly in news media. In the latter instance, public information can function as "a crucial first line of defense and offense" for police agencies (Chermak and Weiss, 2005: 503).

The rise of police media units or public relations branches reflects this, as well as the increased recognition that police agencies need to proactively manage their visibility by promoting and preserving a positive public image (Mawby, 2001; Thompson, 1995). This may partially explain the favourable representations of police often associated with jointly-produced reality television programs (Dowler and Zawilski, 2007), such as *COPS, The First 48, Police Interceptors, The Force: Behind the Line, Recruits, Crash Investigation Unit* and *Missing Persons Unit*. The management of the police-media relationship and the mediated image of policing have become even more vital within the contemporary managerialist environment in which police operate, and in light of widespread concerns about police perform-ance and misconduct (Mawby, 2001). Technological advances in the media have also had an impact (Mawby, 2001), with police officers subjected to increasing levels of scrutiny and public accountability as a result of surveillance technologies, including in-car video camera systems and audio-video recording devices on Tasers. Likewise, media audiences are no longer seen as passive consumers, often serving as sources of news in the mediation of crime narratives (McGovern and Lee, 2010) through the use of amateur footage in news stories about policing (for example, the Rodney King beating by LAPD officers). Police agencies now also regularly use social networking and video-sharing sites, like Facebook, Twitter and YouTube, to appeal for public information about crime and to provide updates on the status of investigations, often bypassing traditional news media to communicate directly with the community (Dick, 2011).

Mediated Images of Police Use of Force

All of these issues serve to complicate the orthodox view that police maintain the balance of power in the police-media relationship, and demonstrates that there is no longer a simple two-way communications process between news media organisations and police agencies (Mawby, 1999), or between news consumers and the media. It also raises the prospect that police can find themselves as *vulnerable* to news media representation as they can be benefited by it. This is especially the case where there is a clear disjuncture between mediated images of contemporary policing and the realities of police work (Christensen, Schmidt, and Henderson, 1982). In Australia, for instance, the contentious issue of the use of lethal or deadly force against mentally ill individuals is often portrayed in media commentary and public debate as being indicative of, or revealing much about, a police officer's (lack of) "commitment to the upholding of the civil liberties of the citizens they are required to protect" (Chappell, 2008: 40).

However, there are numerous mitigating factors that can influence the necessity for, and a police officer's decision to use, coercive force. Police have the power to use force in certain circumstances as is necessary to effectively work with the community to reduce violence, crime and fear (NSW Ombudsman, 2008). There is obviously "significant interest in ensuring that when force is used, this occurs in a way that is reasonable and proportionate" (NSW Ombudsman, 2008). While national guidelines have previously established clear parameters for its application, the use of deadly force still ultimately remains *the discretion of the police officers involved*. As Teplin and Pruett (1992: 140) explain, "[w]hile the law provides the legal structure and decrees the police officer's power to intervene, it cannot dictate the police officer's response to that situation". In the case of fatal mental health crisis interventions, an individual police officer's perceptions of threat are often dictated by a strange convolution of perceptual distortions (Klinger and Brunson, 2009) and technical and subjective risk rationalities – in other words, the negotiation of rulebook instruction with personal discretion. This tension is most evident in the conflicts of interpretation identifiable between the lived experiences of frontline police officers and public discourse about the intentionality of police use of deadly force.

News media coverage of police use of force incidents is typically framed in terms of two distinct sets of causal claims, which Lawrence (2000) distinguishes as the "individualising" claims of institutional discourse and the "systemic" claims of non-officials and lay discourse. She explains:

> Officials generally try to control the news by "individualizing" these incidents, claiming that those subjected to police use of force brought that force on themselves with their deviant, violent behaviour; occasionally, when an incident looks particularly bad for the officer(s) involved, officials describe excessive force as a problem of a few rogue cops. These individualizing claims contrast with "systemic" claims about police brutality [or unreasonable excessive force], which are typically made by nonofficials. These claims cast brutality [or unreasonable excessive force] as an endemic and patterned problem arising from poor police management, inadequate police accountability, a hostile police subculture, or a racist culture more generally (Lawrence, 2000: 14-15).

On the one hand, the individualising news frames of police officials serve to normalise the necessity for police use of deadly force; portraying it as "consistent with departmental policies and with public expectations of how officers should behave in dangerous situations" (Lawrence, 2000: 37). This is often supported by references to the fatal police-involved shooting as "a last resort" and an amplification of the "the dangers police face daily". These individualising news frames impart political legitimacy to the police use of deadly force, portraying it as a sensible and an officially sanctioned response to a violent world (Lawrence, 2000). In doing so, it is typical for official police responses to fatal mental health crisis interventions to publicly demonstrate support towards the police officers involved, and a justification for the necessity of use of deadly force by these individuals – even before an investigation into the fatal shooting has commenced. This has repeatedly caused community disquiet about the perceived insensitivity of such official police responses in view of the fact that police "have already publicly committed themselves to a position" immediately after the fatal shooting (Walters, 2005). This can be seen to compromise the integrity of their involvement in the critical incident investigation (Walters, 2005).

The public discourse of family and friends of the deceased often highlights this incongruity and, in contrast, remains predisposed towards criticism of the police actions, with culpability for the death of their loved one directed towards the individual police officers involved, and police culture and management more broadly. This rush to attribute blame in the aftermath of a fatal mental health crisis intervention is not entirely unexpected, and reflects the fact that while police are expected to work in the public's interest "they are also accountable to many publics and political agents with conflicting interests and goals" (Chermak and Weiss, 2005: 502). For their part, news narratives often reflect this ebb and flow rather than present "a steady or independent discussion of the issues over which… [these] power struggles are waged" (Bennett, 2009: 106).

The Realities of Police Work vs Public Perceptions

In the context of news media coverage of fatal mental health crisis interventions, inferences of a causal link between mental illness and violence are not always restricted to erroneous assumptions and allegations about the "violent tendencies" inherent to mentally ill individuals in crisis. They can also extend to value judgments about the necessity for police use of deadly force against such individuals or, more broadly, to allusions of a systemic tendency among frontline police officers to routinely resort to unjustifiable displays of coercive force (over less excessive measures) in their everyday policing and as part of police culture more broadly. This is the outworn notion that all police officers are "trigger happy cops" (Kaba cited in Stephey, 2007). The perpetuation of such stereotypes in the press bears some correlation to, if it is not defined by, the temporal proximity of news media coverage to the critical incident. Often, these constructions of police subjectivity are most explicit where the lay discourse of bereaved family members has been given prominence within the news media coverage. However, these claims are often made without any requisite contextualisation of the circumstances leading to the police use of deadly force or the complexities of interactions between police and mentally ill individuals in crisis more generally (Clifford, 2010). Writes Lawrence (2000: 49):

> police often view the media with suspicion and express frustration and bitterness over what they see as the media's willingness to sensationalize the use of force without making the public aware of the difficulties and dangers faced by police officers.

The police response to such identity constructions highlights the fact that, despite the trend towards the predominance of official police voices as "primary definers" of the news agenda, not all police officers believe the media always fairly represents them. While police media operations may have become "more co-ordinated and better prepared", as Mawby (1999: 267) points out, tensions remain within police circles about "the media and openness". These concerns are not unfounded.

According to the police officers consulted as part of my research, these tensions are particularly obvious where use of deadly force involving firearms is repeatedly framed as the by-product of a calculated "shoot to kill" policy or "shoot first" culture within the police force. In this context, the discretionary decision by police to discharge their firearms is framed as entirely incommensurate with both the reality and level of risk posed by a mentally ill individual in crisis who is, more often than not, armed with only an edged weapon rather than a firearm. The difficulties often expressed by the public in reconciling the need for police use of deadly force against a person in possession of what is perceived to be a less-lethal weapon are well recognised by police officers themselves, albeit rarely contextualised within news media coverage. As one police officer told me:

> I understand what you're saying and... [m]y response to them would be, "well, you stand where I stood, put my boots on, and you show me how brave you are. You go in and wrestle him for the knife"... I can understand, you know, people [saying]... "Why didn't the police tackle him from behind?" I mean, you just can't afford to put yourself in danger and, if you put yourself in danger with something like that, you're putting your workmates in danger, because all of a sudden, you're on the ground, and he's on the ground, and you haven't effectively disarmed him, and they can no longer shoot him, because he's in a wrestle with you and he's got knives... But I can understand how, yes, somebody's got a knife, but the police shot him, well, it doesn't make sense.

Often family and friends of the deceased and other mental health advocates, after a fatal mental health crisis intervention, hold fast to the notion that police officers could have availed themselves of other less-lethal tactical measures in place of the decision to shoot. Regularly, this includes the argument that, where it was necessary to shoot, police officers should have aimed for the individual's leg or arm, rather than the torso. These sentiments are frequently foregrounded in news media coverage of fatal mental health crisis interventions where the voices of bereaved family members predominate (see, for example, Dundas cited in "Lethal Force", 2009).

Bearing in mind that the specialist weapons training provided to frontline police officers instructs them to aim for centre body mass in the discharge of firearms, the likelihood of lethal force as the outcome of a decision to shoot is not implausible. But it is not always the case that death is the motive and/or intent when a police officer determines to discharge their firearm. The intentionality of a fatal police-involved shooting is, however, only ever debatable after the event, at which point it is regularly demonstrated that police officers, as Van Maanen (1980) contends, do not often regard shooting and killing as tightly coupled. Instead, fatal police-involved shootings are "more attuned to the fearful particulars of one's own safety than to a logic of deadly offense" (Van Maanen, 1980: 149). This is borne out by the following comments from a police officer who was previously involved in a fatal mental health crisis intervention. He suggested that a police officer's intention in discharging their firearm is more often related, in operational circumstances, to *stopping* a perceived threat (usually an individual with a weapon), rather than *killing* them:

> If he gets to a particular spot and I don't shoot him and stop him – and it's not about shooting him to kill him; it's about stopping him – either my offsider next to me is going to potentially get killed or I am… people see firearms and death; that's all they see… We are trained to shoot centre body mass, which likely is going to result in somebody's death, but we don't shoot to kill people. We shoot to stop.

Conclusion

There has previously been much criticism directed towards news media for its general resistance towards the construction of thematic news frames, which would otherwise provide broader context for media consumers in relation to traumatic events. Traditionally, the news media coverage of fatal mental health crisis interventions has not been an exception to this. The lack of context, in these cases, has predominantly been attributable to the general absence of lay discourse and lived experience, as expressed by the voices of those involved in and impacted by fatal mental health crisis interventions – namely, the individual police officers responsible for the discharge of firearms and the family members of the deceased. Media reports of more recent fatal mental health crisis interventions have sought to redress this with a more central focus on bereaved family members as "primary definers" of these news events. This is especially true of circumstances where family and friends of the deceased have been proactive in their use of news media as a platform for their criticisms of the police operational response. In many cases, these individuals have also used the opportunity to (re)define the subjectivity of their loved one in terms of shared memories of the life they lived, rather than the circumstances by which they died.

There is undoubtedly an intrinsic value to the inclusion of these often marginalised voices in terms of the sharing of lived experience and their contribution to sense-making in relation to controversial and traumatic events. But while attempts to redress the imbalance of "voice" that has traditionally been identifiable within news media coverage of fatal mental health crisis interventions has served to provide some balance to news frames, the trend towards decontextualised reporting of these critical incidents continues. The result is that often the individual police officers involved in the incident are held accountable in the court of public opinion for the fatal outcomes to mental health crises whose tragedies are, more often than not, attributable to broader deficiencies in the mental health system, and the care and treatment of mentally ill individuals in the community. These systemic failures regularly precede the need for police-involved crisis intervention.

This is not to broadly excuse the police use of deadly force against mentally ill individuals in crisis, but to suggest that, in perpetuating the idea of vulnerability and responsibility as incompatible binaries (that is, that there are always "victims" and "villains" in these incidents), news media coverage continues to ignore the complexities of these events. It also neglects the traumatic effects of these critical incidents on the police officers involved, and continues to perpetuate the more provocative or salient aspects of a fatal mental health crisis intervention, without the requisite contextualisation of these events and their associated issues. This style of journalistic reporting has broad and serious implications for contemporary policing, not only in terms of reputational damage and the management of its public image, but more practically in terms of its relationship and interactions with mental health consumers in the community. News stories of police use of force resonate strongly with media audiences (Lawrence, 2000; Dowler and Zawilski, 2007), and stereotypes of frontline police officers as "gung ho" and "trigger happy" can have negative framing effects in terms of public confidence and willingness to cooperate with police, and the levels of fear and stigma associated with police contact by mental health consumers. It is important therefore that police agencies recognise (and respond to) the fact that their interactions with news media reflect a complex set of relations that may not always produce favourable outcomes for the organisation. These interactions with news media can leave police officers vulnerable to harmful constructions of risk-based identities with real-world implications for frontline policing and crisis encounters with vulnerable people in the community.

References

ABC TV, 2009, "Lethal Force", *Four Corners*, 26 October [Transcript of television broadcast], ABC TV, Sydney. Viewed 16 August 2010, <www.abc.net. au/4corners/content/2009/s2722195.htm>.

Altheide, D, 2002, *Creating Fear: News and the Construction of Crisis*, Aldine De Gruyter, New York.

Bennett, W L, 2009, "The Press, Power and Public Accountability", *Routledge Companion to News and Journalism* (Ed S Allan), Routledge, London and New York.

Blood, R W, Pirkis, J and Francis, C, 2004, "News and Social Policy: Reporting of Suicide and Mental Illness" 11 *Agenda* 273.

Blood, R W, Tulloch, J and Enders, M, 2000, "Communication and Reflexivity: Conversations about Fear of Crime" 27 *Australian Journal of Communication* 15.

Blood, W and Holland, K, 2004, "Risky News, Madness and Public Crisis: A case study of the reporting and portrayal of mental health and illness in the Australian press" 5 *Journalism* 323.

Carroll, M, 2005, "Mental-health System Overburdening Police" December *Police Journal* 18.

Chappell, D, 2008, "Policing and Emotionally Disturbed Persons: Disseminating knowledge, removing stigma and enhancing performance" 40 *Australian Journal of Forensic Services* 37.

Chermak, S and Weiss, A, 2005, "Maintaining Legitimacy using External Communication Strategies: An analysis of police-media relations" 33 *Journal of Criminal Justice* 501.

Christensen, J, Schmidt, J and Henderson, J, 1982, "The Selling of the Police: Media, Ideology, and Crime Control" 6 *Contemporary Crises* 227.

Clifford, K, 2010, "The Thin Blue Line of Mental Health in Australia" 11 *Police Practice and Research* 355.

Coleman, TG and Cotton, DH, 2010, "Reducing Risk and Improving Outcomes of Police Interactions with People with Mental Illness" 10 *Journal of Police Crisis Negotiations* 39.

Dalton, V, 1998, *Police Shootings 1990-1997*, Australian Institute of Criminology, Canberra.

Dick, T, 2011, "Reality TV the New Frontline for Police", *The Sydney Morning Herald*, 9 September. Viewed 23 May 2012, <www.smh.com.au/business/media-and-marketing/reality-tv-the-new-frontline-for-police-20110908-1jzm7.html>.

Donohue, D, 2010, *NSW Police Force Mental Health Intervention Team Corporate Spokesperson's Message*. Viewed 2 September 2010, <www.police.nsw.gov.au/community_issues/mental_health>.

Dowler, K, 2002, "Media Influence on Citizen Attitudes toward Police Effectiveness" 12 *Policing and Society* 227.

Dowler, K, and Zawilski, V, 2007, "Public Perceptions of Police Misconduct and Discrimination: Examining the impact of media consumption" 35 *Journal of Criminal Justice* 193.

Farrall, S, and Lee, M, 2008, *Fear of Crime: Critical Voices in an Age of Anxiety*, Routledge-Cavendish, London and New York.

Furedi, F, 2006, *Culture of Fear Revisited*, Continuum, London and New York.

Hall, S, Critcher, C, Jefferson, T, Clarke, J and Roberts, B, 1978, *Policing the Crisis: Mugging, the State, and Law and Order*, MacMillan, London.

Hazelton, M, 1997, "Reporting Mental Health: A discourse analysis of mental health-related news in two Australian newspapers" 6 *Australian and New Zealand Journal of Mental Health Nursing* 73.

Herrington, V, Clifford, K, Lawrence, P F, Ryle, S and Pope, R, 2009, *The Impact of the NSW Police Force Mental Health Intervention Team: Final Evaluation Report*, Charles Sturt University Centre for Inland Health and Australian Graduate School of Policing, Sydney, Viewed 27 May 2010, <www.police. nsw.gov.au/__data/ assets/pdf_file/0006/174246/MHIT_Evaluation_Final_ Report_241209.pdf>

Kaminski, R and Jefferis, E, 1998, "The effect of a violent televised arrest on public perceptions of the police" 21 *Policing* 683.

Kerr, A N, Morabito, M and Watson, A C, 2010, "Police Encounters, Mental Illness, and Injury: An Exploratory Investigation" 10 *Journal of Police Crisis Negotiations* 116.

Kesic, D, Thomas, S D M and Ogloff, J R P, 2010, "Mental Illness among Police Fatalities in Victoria 1982-2007: Case linkage study" 44 *Australian and New Zealand Journal of Psychiatry* 463.

Klinger, D A and Brunson, R K, 2009, "Police Officers' Perceptual Distortions during Lethal Force Situations: Informing the reasonableness standard" 8 *Criminology & Public Policy* 117.

Lawrence, R G, 2000, *The Politics of Force: Media and the Construction of Police Brutality*, University of California Press, Berkeley and Los Angeles.

Mawby, R C, 1999, "Visibility, Transparency and Police-media Relations" 9 *Policing and Society: An International Journal of Research and Policy* 263.

Mawby, R C, 2001, "Promoting the Police? The Rise of Police Image Work" 43 *Criminal Justice Matters* 44.

McElvain, J P and Kposowa, A J, 2008, "Police Officer Characteristics and the Likelihood of Using Deadly Force" 35 *Criminal Justice and Behavior* 505.

McGovern, A and Lee, M, 2010, "'Cop[ying] it Sweet': Police Media Units and the Making of News" 43 *Australian & New Zealand Journal of Criminology* 444.

Mindframe National Media Initiative, 2011, *New Mindframe Media Guide for all Frontline Police*, Hunter Institute of Mental Health, Newcastle. Viewed 25 May 2012, <www.mindframe-media.info/client_images/1002046.pdf>.

Myhill, A and Beak, K, 2008, *Public Confidence in Police*, National Policing Improvement Agency, London.

Novak, K J, 2009, "Reasonable Officers, Public Perceptions, and Policy Challenges" 8 *Criminology and Public Policy* 153.

NSW Ombudsman, 2008, *The Use of Taser Weapons by New South Wales Police Force: A special report to Parliament under section 31 of the Ombudsman Act 1974*, NSW Ombudsman, Sydney.

Queensland Office of the Public Advocate, 2005, *Preserving Life and Dignity in Distress: Responding to critical mental health incidents*, Department of Justice and Attorney-General, Queensland Government, Brisbane.

Stephey, M J, 2007, "De-criminalizing mental illness" *Time Magazine*, 8 August. Viewed 1 February 2010, <www.time.com/time/health/article/0,8599,1651002,00.htm>.

Teplin, L A and Pruett, N S, 1992, "Police as Streetcorner Psychiatrist: Managing the mentally ill" 15 *International Journal of Law and Psychiatry* 139.

Thompson, J B, 1995, *The Media and Modernity: A Social Theory of the Media*, Polity Press, Cambridge, UK.

Tiegreen, S and Newman, E, 2008, *The Effects of News "Frames"*, Dart Center for Journalism and Trauma. Viewed 25 May 2012, <dartcenter.org/content/effect-news-frames>.

Van Maanen, J, 1980, "Beyond Account: The Personal Impact of Police Shootings" 452 *Annals of the American Academy of Political and Social Science* 145.

Walters, B, 2005, "Accounting for the Lethal Force" *The Age*, 8 April. Viewed 16 May 2009, <www.theage.com.au/news/Opinion/Accounting-for-the-lethal-force/2005/04/07/1112815666095.html>

Weitzer, R, 2002, "Incidents of Police Misconduct and Public Opinion" 20 *Journal of Criminal Justice* 397.

Part Three

Police Response to Incidents Involving Vulnerable People

Chapter 8

Policing Mental Illness: Examining the Police Role in Addressing Mental Ill-health

Victoria Herrington and Katrina Clifford

> People affected by mental illness are one of the most vulnerable and disadvantaged in our communities. They suffer from widespread, systematic discrimination and are consistently denied the rights and services to which they are entitled. The stigma and suspicion directed at people affected by mental illness is a major barrier to their full and equal enjoyment of life – creating fear and isolation when people are most in need of tolerance and understanding. The level of ignorance and discrimination still associated with mental illness and psychiatric disability in the 1990's is completely unacceptable and must be addressed (Burdekin, 1993).

Despite being said almost two decades ago, the above excerpt from a speech given by then Federal Human Rights Commissioner, Brian Burdekin, at the launch of the *Report of the National Inquiry into the Human Rights of People with Mental Illness* continues to ring true today. Compared to then, there is undoubtedly now a greater awareness of mental ill-health. National awareness campaigns have successfully reminded us that mental ill-health can affect anyone – one in five Australians to be exact – and that those with a mental illness should not be stigmatised and incarcerated in institutions away from their communities. This was the philosophy behind the deinstitutionalisation policies of the 1980s, which transferred the care and treatment of many people with a mental disorder to community-based services. Of course, the level of funding provided to support psychiatric care in the community has not always met demand and, for a range of reasons, some individuals remain unable to access the support services they need. Many in this already vulnerable group have found themselves unable to manage the demands of day-to-day life, leading to broader problems with health, housing and employment. In some cases, these factors have converged to lead to contact with the criminal justice system. In other cases, the criminal justice system itself has formed a viable route to accessing psychiatric care. Statistics from the Australian prison system suggest that nearly 30 per cent of the inmate population has a diagnosed mental illness (Australian Institute of Health and Welfare, 2011).

Major mental illnesses, such as schizophrenia and depression, are thought to be between three and five times more prevalent among Australian prisoners than in the general community (Ogloff et al, 2007), with the rate of undiagnosed disorders likely much higher (Herrington, 2011). This is a pattern replicated across the world (Fazel and Danesh, 2002).

While the psychiatric institutions of days gone by may have been replaced with community care, there remain a large number of people with a mental disorder who find themselves incarcerated, stigmatised and, as such, vulnerable in other ways. In this chapter, we explore the relationship between policing and mental illness in the community. Police are often referred to as the *gatekeepers to the criminal justice system*, and they play a significant, albeit often unrecognised, role in facilitating access to social and public health services too. This, very often, includes mental health services. To this end, we examine the police role and response in relation to two groups of people with a mental illness: those who come in contact with the police by virtue of their offending and those who are in contact with the police by virtue of their mental illness. This chapter contributes to the growing debate on policing and mental health around the world by first considering the legislative imperatives governing the police response to mental illness, and the translation of this into policy. The link between policy and practice is then considered and implications for police practice are drawn out.

Current Legislative Imperatives

We have noted that the promise of community care enshrined in the deinstitutionalisation approach did not eventuate. As outlined in Australia's *Report of the National Inquiry into the Human Rights of People with Mental Illness* – The Burdekin Report (1993) – and other formal inquiries, and as experienced across the world, the savings resulting from deinstitutionalisation did not equate to funds being redirected into community-based services. Research suggests that, in Australia, somewhere between an estimated 60 to 65 per cent of individuals experiencing chronic mental illness are still unable to access the care they need (Mental Health Council of Australia and the Brain and Mind Research Institute, 2005; National Health and Hospitals Reform Commission, 2009; Rosenberg et al, 2009). Barriers also still exist "between services provided for different illnesses and different population groups" (Senate Select Committee on Mental Health, 2006: 7). This predicament is clearly exacerbated for those experiencing comorbid conditions in that the separation of (or barriers between) alcohol and other drug services and mental health services negates the prospect of holistic health treatment. The consequence is that a troubling proportion of mentally ill individuals continue to end up "falling through the cracks", while many more find themselves the subject of what is often referred to as the "revolving door syndrome" of repeat acute care admissions. Others will come in contact with the law and be incarcerated. While a historical and strongly hypothesised link between mental illness and criminality has been influential in the development of public policy for individuals with a mental illness, it is important to note that perceptions of normality, sanity, madness and deviance change over time (Foucault, 1967; Seddon, 2007). This can be observed in changes to legislation and public policy, as we turn to below. Importantly, this shift augurs a shift too in organisational responses to mentally ill individuals.

International Conventions

The changes in public policy governing mental illness – from a historic one of confinement to one of holistic community care – have borne implications for all agencies working in the community, including police. There is compelling evidence to suggest that, in Australia, police resources have been left to shoulder the burden of the inadequacies of deinstitutionalisation, and as such are critical to the success (or not) of legislative reforms and policies. As Teplin and Pruett (1992) point out, police officers are typically the first, and often the only, responders to mental health crises; by virtue of the 24/7 nature of their work, and often as a consequence of community stereotypes, which view mentally ill individuals – particularly those who do not meet socially accepted behavioural norms – as 'criminal' and danger-ous (Teller et al, 2006; Klein, 2010). Similar trends have been noted across the world. These trends can be particularly disconcerting for police operating in a managerialist environment, as acting as a gatekeeper to mental health services can be burdensome, and public sector organisations are being asked to do more with less. This is compounded when the control of crime, as opposed to providing a gatekeeper service to persons with a mental illness, is one of the key ways in which the effectiveness of policing is measured.

Overarching the care and treatment of individuals with a mental illness – and therefore governing policy development and the practical police response to this group – are two United Nations documents: the *Principles for the Protection of Persons with Mental Illness and the Improvement of Mental Health Care* (United Nations, 1991) and the *United Nations Convention on the Rights of Persons with Disabilities* (United Nations, 2006) ("The Convention"). In Australia, The Convention is operationalised through the *Disability Discrimination Act 1992* (last amended 2011), which defines disability, amongst other things, as "a disorder, illness or disease that affects a person's thought processes, perception of reality, emotions or judgment or that results in disturbed behaviour" (Part 1, s 4(1)(g)). This clearly includes mental illness. Central to The Convention is the principle of "respect for difference and acceptance of persons with disabilities [and long-term mental illness] as part of human diversity and humanity" (United Nations, 2006: Article 3d). This is an important point within the context of this volume, which has at its core the argument that policing and other aspects of the criminal justice system should understand and accept community diversity – in this case, the diversity of vulnerable groups. To say the same thing another way, the central thrust of this collection – that there is a need to recognise the nuances involved in policing vulnerability – builds on The Convention, and is, or should be, then central to public policy. With this in mind, it is perhaps surprising that the notion of police adopting particular processes and protocols when dealing with people with a mental illness still meets with resistance in some quarters and is in its relative infancy.

Mental Health Policy – The Australian Context

In all jurisdictions across Australia, "police are given wide-ranging power to intervene in the lives of the mentally ill and mentally disordered by virtue of the respective Mental Health Acts" (Police Federation of Australia, 2005: 4). These legislative instruments also set out the circumstances and processes involved for involuntary detention of individuals with a mental illness (or suspected mental illness) when they come to the attention of police by virtue of their offending, or their mental illness alone. These legislative instruments draw deliberately or otherwise on the aforementioned *Principles for the Protection of Persons with Mental Illness and the Improvement of Mental Health Care* (United Nations, 1991) and, in particular, the notion of *least restriction* (enshrined in Principle 7, promoting care in the community where possible). Drawing these legislative imperatives together in Australia is the *National Mental Health Strategy* (Department of Health and Ageing (DHA), 2009), which "provides a framework for national reform from an institutionally based mental health system to one that is consumer focused with an emphasis on supporting the individual in their community" (DHA, 2009). The strategy argues that a collaborative approach is required, with joined-up working between police, courts, mental health services, and emergency department staff having the potential to make a significant difference to the immediate and longer-term outcomes for the person involved (DHA, 2009: 68). Three points of particular note for police are made in the strategy:

1. The need for mental health to be considered and addressed in areas outside of its traditional health care realm, including (among others) police, courts and correctional services;
2. The need for education and training to be provided about mental health to frontline workers in emergency, welfare and associated sectors (including police). By ensuring that this group is better able to recognise, appreciate and understand mental illness, it is anticipated that early intervention will be improved, and better outcomes for the person with a mental illness will be assured; and

3. The need for emergency and community services to develop joined-up protocols to guide and support the transition of people with a mental illness between service sectors (DHA, 2009).

While the *National Mental Health Strategy* calls for shared responsibility and a clear understanding of organisational roles, it notes that this may be particularly difficult where the legislative frameworks guiding service protocols differ and, in some cases, conflict with each other. Transition between services is a time of increased risk for mentally ill individuals in terms of falling through the gaps in service provision (Groom, Hickie and Davenport, 2003), and joined-up working between agencies is one way of minimising this risk. But doing this effectively may require legislative, structural, and organisational change, and in some cases, the development of protocols specific to dealing with this vulnerable group. The implications for police are discussed in the following section.

The Police Role in Addressing Mental Illness

Research suggests that police interactions with people with a mental illness are on the rise. In 2003, for example, Queensland police responded to some 17,000 call-outs across the state relating to people with a mental illness; a 17 per cent increase from 2001 (Office of the Public Advocate – Queensland, 2005). By comparison, in 2004, NSW Police responded to around 18,000 calls involving individuals with a mental disorder (Donohue et al, 2008). By 2009, NSW police officers were responding to 34,000 mental health-related incidents (Donohue, 2010). In some jurisdictions, up to 30 per cent of all calls for service involve this group (Coleman and Cotton, 2010). It is unclear whether these figures include both groups of interest to this chapter: that is, those who come into contact with the police by virtue of their offending, and those who are in contact with the police by virtue of their mental illness.

Police Responses to Offenders with a Mental Illness

Regarding the first of these groups – offenders with a mental illness – it has been mooted that one consequence of the shift to community-based models of care has been the exposure of more people with a mental illness to the risk of offending (Reed, 1992) and, consequently, a rise in the number of people with a mental illness in prison. Before an individual ends up in prison, he or she will have passed through other stages of the criminal justice system where mechanisms exist to divert those who cannot be held accountable for their actions. The principles underwriting the aforementioned anti-discrimination and human rights legislation protect against unfair treatment of an individual by virtue of their mental illness, and many scholars believe that the criminal justice system is doubly punishing for those with a mental illness (Glaser and Deane, 1999). English and Australian law, of course, requires an offender to have the intent to commit an unlawful act (*mens rea*). Without this, their behaviour cannot be considered criminal. Such intent, it is argued, is contentious for many with a mental illness, and there is considerable evidence from the analogous field of intellectual disabilities that service providers may label otherwise criminal behaviour *challenging* (denoting a service rather than a sanction response) rather than report such offending to police (McBrien and Murphy, 2006). This illustrates that the transformation of *behaviour* into *crime* depends on a number of complex decisions and the perceptions of those making those decisions.[1]

In the UK, Lord Bradley's review of people with mental health problems or learning disabilities in the criminal justice system (Bradley, 2009) noted that available mental health legislation may not always be evoked when there is a suspicion of mental health needs, and that a decision to remand an individual to custody is possible where police determine that a suspect needs to be detained for their own protection. He assessed there was a heavy reliance on the use of remand as such a *place of safety* for vulnerable individuals presenting at court:

> Quite often the police, the Probation Service and the courts are unclear what other alternatives are readily available, and will default to the prison option (Bradley, 2009: 62).

Cavadino similarly concluded that, "courts were using remand prisons as social and psychiatric assessment and referral centres" (1999: 58). On the one hand, this may be a positive trend, with remand offering the possibility that mental health issues will be identified and the individual diverted from the criminal justice system and into appropriate care, although this hardly constitutes a *least restrictive approach* advocated by the legislative framework detailed above. Moreover, in practice, this approach is not as effective as it might be, with identification of mental illness occurring only where an individual has an obvious, severe and enduring mental health need (Herrington et al, 2004), and the continuing high numbers of people in prison with a mental illness are testament to this (see, for example, Fazel and Danesh, 2002; Singleton et al, 1997). Of course, diversion from the criminal justice system does not necessarily ensure psychiatric care:

> Of the patients diverted to inpatient services from the courts, at least one third had lost contact with psychiatric services at 12 months follow-up. For patients referred from the courts to psychiatric community teams or outpatient clinics, less than one third attended their first appointment and of those, almost one third had become disengaged from services before the follow-up 12 months later (Shaw et al, 2001: 203).

When we ask what becomes of these "missing" patients, and the potential for this group to be trapped in the "revolving door" of repeat acute care admissions described above, the implication for frontline policing – and in particular the resources required by police to respond to the crisis needs of this vulnerable group in the community – is clear. Of particular interest to this collection and the arguments made in this chapter, Coid et al (2002) suggest that decisions about access to mental health services may be based on the decision-making of "gatekeepers", rather than dependent on need. In the context of the criminal justice system, police are the primary gatekeepers, which gives rise to the important question of what criteria they use to make their determinations. Police awareness about mental illness and the availability of mental health services, and their attitudes to those who are mentally ill, are therefore key to ensuring a police response that is in line with the humanising and least restrictive intent of current legislative and policy frameworks.

Police Responses to Non-offenders with a Mental Illness

Police also come into contact with mentally ill individuals by virtue of their mental illness, rather than through their involvement in criminal activity. In such interactions, the police role is to protect the safety of the person with a mental illness and other members of the public, to ascertain identifying details, and ensure the individual is passed swiftly to services to address their needs. Some people who come into contact with the police in this way will be experiencing their first mental health crisis, or the first that has attracted service attention, while others will be well known to both police and mental health services and might be regarded as *frequent presenters*. Dealing with these non-offending groups has proven most challenging to police organisations, representing as it does the tension between the police role in crime control and its broader public service function (Reiner, 2001; Birch, 2011). A broadening of their function has not always been welcomed by police, who without an accompanying justification of such change might be forgiven for perceiving their role morph unacceptably into that of a "streetcorner psychiatrist" (Teplin and Pruett, 1992).

Of course, we can debate the boundaries of what *actually* constitutes a core policing public safety role and one that encroaches on their ability to do this. Arguably, policing has evolved beyond simply *crime fighting* so that mental health and other traditionally non-core activities are, in fact, part of their *raison d'être* (Senate Select Committee on Mental Health, 2006). The importance of frontline services – including police – in acting as effective gatekeepers to mental health services is exactly the role highlighted by the *National Mental Health Strategy* discussed above; emphasising the need for effective linkages to be formed between different sectors for the proposed holistic response to mental health care to work. Add to this the obligation for governments and organisations under the aforementioned *United Nations Convention on the Rights of Persons with Disabilities* (United

Nations, 2006), and the associated localised obligations through the *Disability Discrimination Act 1992* to "take all appropriate measures, including legislation, to modify or abolish existing laws, regulations, customs and practices that constitute discrimination against persons with disabilities" (Article 4b). We can conclude that whether regarded as a core aspect of police work or not, providing a gatekeeper function when people with a mental illness come to their attention, is an important function for police. This is all well and good, but it begs the question as to how an effective police response to persons with a mental illness might be best achieved whilst balancing legislative and policy imperatives and the practical (resource) reality of policing.

In most instances, the interactions police have with people with a mental illness are resolved safely and without incident (Office of the Public Advocate – Queensland, 2005). However, in a small number of cases, these encounters involve levels of hostility that serve to heighten the resistance of a mentally ill individual towards attempts at negotiation by police officers; creating a situation that is beyond the point of de-escalation (Kerr et al, 2010) and which may result in tragic consequences (see Clifford, 2010 for further discussion). Notwithstanding stigmatising stereotypes that correlate mental illness with an inherent propensity for violence (Corrigan et al, 2003; Kimhi et al, 1998; Lipson, Turner, and Kasper, 2010; Monahan and Steadman, 1994; Monahan et al, 2001; Ruiz and Miller, 2004), the disturbed behaviour of individuals experiencing irrational thoughts and delusional beliefs associated with acute psychosis (which is frequently accompanied by some form of paranoia about police) can precipitate high-risk situations that require police use of force (Coleman and Cotton, 2010).

On the other side, personal experience of mental health problems – be it through one's own direct experience as a mental health consumer or as a carer to family or friends – can predispose police involved in a mental health crisis intervention towards being "more informed and sensitive towards mental health issues than those without an appreciation of the actual reality of these experiences" (Morris, 2006: 7). Personal experience has also been shown to have a strong association with the adoption of "help-centred outcomes" as opposed to more restrictive options for dealing with mentally ill individuals in crisis (Godfredson et al, 2011). Training in mental health, too, has proven an effective mediating factor, influencing police responses to mental health.

Nationally and internationally, a number of police organisations have introduced specialised Crisis Intervention Team (CIT) training programs to "promote officer safety, safe and respectful interactions between police and individuals with a mental illness, and diversion to mental health services in lieu of criminal justice system processing" (Canada et al, 2010: 87). Specialised programs such as these involve three core components: intense training; partnership with community resources; and the adoption of the new role that CIT officers must play within their police organisation (Canada et al, 2010). Individual police training of this kind provides officers with "skills and knowledge that can be applied to assist officers in making crucial decisions and maintaining safety during first-responder circumstances" (Canada et al, 2010: 87). The specialised training, particularly in the framework of building a crisis response team, has the potential to improve the use of body language, active listening and communication skills among police officers (McMains, 2002).

In Australia, an independent evaluation of the NSW Police Force CIT-like Mental Health Intervention Team (MHIT), found training to result in a significant and sustained increase in self-reported levels of confidence in dealing with mentally ill individuals (Herrington et al, 2009). Over half of the MHIT-trained officers surveyed post-training indicated that being able to recognise the signs (as a result of the training) that a person might be mentally ill and being able to deliver an immediate response to their crisis had improved their ability to engage with the person and often proved an effective intervention and de-escalation technique (Herrington et al, 2009). Importantly, in the context of this collection, officers who were trained also reported greater confidence in administering disposals other than involuntary detention for psychiatric assessment for persons with a mental illness that they came across (Herrington et al, 2009). Thus, awareness about mental illness, and about alternative ways to address it, by engaging with services in the community, seems to support the overarching policy and legislative intent of providing the *least restrictive* response. Favourable results, such as these, are consistent with international studies, which have supported the hypothesis that an educational campaign for police officers may reduce stigmatising attitudes towards mentally ill individuals and enhance a police officer's response to those in crisis, thereby reducing the need for more costly interventions and/or incarceration (Compton et al, 2006).

Conclusion

If the vision of joined-up working and enhanced coordination of service responses to individuals with a mental illness set out under the *National Mental Health Strategy* is to be achieved, and an acceptance of community diversity embraced – such as that set out in the various international and national legislative instruments discussed – there is a need for police to tackle their role as gatekeepers to care systems for both offenders and non-offenders at two levels: organisationally and individually. At an organisational level, there is a need for the broader public health role of police to be recognised, and valued. Acting as gatekeepers to mental health services to assist people with a mental illness to receive appropriate care is – we would argue – fundamental to public safety (certainly as far as the individuals involved are concerned). To wit, there is a need for this activity to be seen as part of, rather than detracting from, the police role. Of course, few officers join the police specifically to deal with mentally unwell members of the community, and *selling* this function to the police at the frontline, on which the success of the approach depends, may be hard. This might be partly assisted by incorporating police involvement in addressing, holistically and in a joined-up way, mental health as part of strategic policing plans. Aligning meaningful key performance indicators around police involvement in mental health may also assist acceptance and associated cultural change. Organisations also need to work together more closely, in meaningful partnerships that identify complementary rather than competitive organisational goals. Partnerships are not without their difficulties, which include a mismatch of resources, skills, culture, processes, expectations, professional identity, and competing demands from one's own organisational structure, and organisational protectionism (Evans and Forbes, 2009; Joint Improvement Team, nd; Skinns, 2008; Wood et al, 2011). Police need to work with the services to which they pass people with a mental illness, to ensure a less resource-intensive and truly joined-up response.

At the individual level, the provision of mental health training for frontline police officers has proven successful on several of these fronts. Within many police organisations, the introduction of CIT-like responses has legitimised the important gatekeeper role frontline police play in the community. It has also improved relationships between police officers and other agencies, especially emergency department staff (see Herrington et al, 2009). Evaluative research has indicated that the introduction of specialised training programs leads to a reduction in the unnecessary arrest of mentally ill individuals and/or use of police force; more effective liaison and information-sharing between mental health service providers and police officers; and increased referral rates to emergency and community-based mental health care (Compton et al, 2006; Herrington et al, 2009; Sced, 2006). The aims of CIT responses are, therefore, in keeping with the need for a broad acceptance by police officers that responding to mental health is central to their role, that CIT programs are core to community policing initiatives and understandings of cultural diversity within policing (Steadman et al, 2000). Such approaches have an obvious resource implication for police (Sced, 2006), particularly across rural and remote areas (Herrington et al, 2009), necessitating the conceptualisation of policing as central to such a public health response and the allocation of resources accordingly.

While we have argued that police organisations have an obligation under the legislative and policy frameworks governing responses to individuals with a mental illness, this does not absolve or minimise similar requirements of other stakeholder organisations. Improvements in police response to mental health crises in the community cannot substitute the addressing of systemic problems in the mental health system, nor the development of preventive measures. The commitment demonstrated by an increasing number of police organisations towards joined-up working with other agencies (formalised through Memorandums of Understanding) and specialised mental health training of frontline police officers is to be commended. But this should not be viewed as an "alternative to filling service gaps within the health and disability support service systems" (Victoria Police, 2008: 1).

Endnote

1   Of course, even when events are reported to the police and a suspect is identified and charged, there remains considerable room for discretion throughout the criminal justice system. Not all offences have a *mens rea* component, including many (summary) offences tried at Magistrate courts, which are regarded as crimes of liability (Baroff et al, 2004). In cases where *mens rea* is required (including murder, rape, violence against another person and theft), this may lead to a defence of insanity. (Where there is a charge of murder, insanity cannot be used as a defence, and instead a defendant may claim diminished responsibility. This reduces the charge of murder to manslaughter and increases the range of sentencing options available to the judge). In the UK, a defence of insanity requires that a defendant prove the following points, set out by the House of Lords in response to the finding of not guilty by reason of insanity in the M'Naghten case in 1843, namely that: "at the time of committing the act, the party accused was labouring under such a defect of the reason, from disease of the mind, as not to know the nature and quality of the act he was doing, or, if he did know it, that he did not know he was doing what was wrong" (*R v M'Naghten*, cited in Baroff et al, 2004). If an individual is found not guilty by reason of insanity, or is found unfit to plead, or on coming into contact with the criminal justice system is regarded as having a mental health concern of such severity that it requires assessment and treatment in a hospital, the (UK) *Mental Health Act 2007* offers a means of diversion.

References

Disability Discrimination Act 1992 (Cth).

Australian Institute of Health and Welfare, 2011, *The Health of Australia's Prisoners 2010*, 149, Australian Institute of Health and Welfare, Canberra. Viewed 11 December 2011, <www.aihw.gov.au/publication-detail/?id=10737420111&tab=2>.

Baroff, G, Gunn, M and Hayes, S, 2004, "Legal Issues", *Offenders With Development Disabilities* (Eds W Lindsay, J Taylor and P Sturmey), John Wiley & Sons Ltd, Chichester, UK.

Birch, P, 2011, "Working with Communities: Social Inclusion and Policing Practice", *Policing in Practice* (Eds P Birch and V Herrington), Palgrave Macmillan, Melbourne.

Bradley, K, 2009, *The Bradley Report: Lord Bradley's Review of People with Mental Health Problems or Learning Disabilities in the Criminal Justice System*, Department of Health, London.

Burdekin, B, 1993, Speech given at the launch of the *Report of the National Inquiry into the Human Rights of People with Mental Illness*. Viewed 13 February 2012, <www.hreoc.gov.au/disability_rights/speeches/mii93.htm>.

Canada, K E, Angell, B and Watson, A C, 2010, "Crisis Intervention Teams in Chicago: Successes on the Ground" 10 *Journal of Police Crisis Negotiations* 86.

Cavadino, P, 1999, "Diverting Mentally Disordered From Custody", *Mentally Disordered Offenders: Managing People Nobody Owns* (Eds D Webb and R Harris), Routledge, London.

Clifford, K, 2010, "The Thin Blue Line of Mental Health in Australia" 11 *Police Practice and Research* 355.

Coid, J, Petruckevitch, A, Bebbington, P, Brugha, T, Bhugra, D, Jenkins, R, Farrell, M, Lewis, G and Singleton, N, 2002, "Ethnic Differences in Prisoners 1: Criminality And Psychiatric Morbidity" 181 *British Journal of Psychiatry* 473.

Coleman, TG and Cotton, DH, 2010, "Reducing Risk and Improving Outcomes of Police Interactions with People with Mental Illness" 10 *Journal of Police Crisis Negotiations* 39.

Compton, MT, Esterberg, ML, McGee, R, Kotwicki, RJ and Oliva, JR, 2006, "Crisis Intervention Team Training: Changes in Knowledge, Attitudes, and Stigma Related to Schizophrenia" 57 *Psychiatric Services* 1199.

Corrigan, PW, Markowitz, FE, Watson, AC, Rowan, D and Kubiak, MA, 2003, "An Attribution Model of Public Discrimination towards Persons with Mental Illness" 44 *Journal of Health and Social Behavior* 162.

Department of Health and Ageing, 2009, *National Mental Health Strategy*. Viewed 17 February 2012, <www.health.gov.au/internet/main/publishing.nsf/Content/360EB322114EC906CA2576700014A817/$File/plan09v2.pdf>.

Donohue, D, 2010, "Corporate Spokespersons Message" *NSW Police Force: Mental Health*. Viewed 10 October 2011, <www.police.nsw.gov.au/community_issues/mental_health>.

Donohue, D, Cashin, A, Laing, R, Newman, C and Halsey, R, 2008, "Mental Health Intervention" *Police News* 24. Viewed 16 September 2008, <www.pansw.org.au/PolNews/Police_News_May24-28.pdf>.

Evans, D and Forbes, T, 2009, "Partnerships in Heath and Social Care: England and Scotland Compared" 24 *Public Policy and Administration* 67.

Fazel, S and Danesh, J, 2002, "Serious Mental Disorder in 23000 Prisoners: A Systematic Review of 62 Surveys" 359 *The Lancet* 545.

Foucault, M, 1967, *Madness and civilization. A History of Insanity in an Age of Reason*, Routledge, London.

Glaser, W and Deane, K, 1999, "Normalisation in an Abnormal World: A Study of Prisoners With an Intellectual Disability" 43 *International Journal of Offender Therapy and Comparative Criminology* 338.

Godfredson, JW, Thomas, SDM, Ogloff, JRP and Luebbers, S, 2011, "Police Perceptions of their Encounters with Individuals Experiencing Mental Illness: A Victorian Survey" 44 *Australian & New Zealand Journal of Criminology* 180.

Groom, G, Hickie, I and Davenport, T, 2003, *"OUT OF HOSPITAL, OUT OF MIND!" A Report Detailing Mental Health Services in Australia in 2002 and Community Priorities for National Mental Health Policy for 2003-2008*, Mental Health Council of Australia, Canberra.

Herrington, V, 2011, *The In-betweeners: Exploring the Prevalence, Nature and Implications of Borderline Intellectual Disability among Young Adult Male Prisoners*, Unpublished PhD Thesis, King's College, London.

Herrington, V, Hunter, G, Curran, K and Hough, M, 2004, *The Feasibility of Assessing Learning Disabilities among Young Offenders*, Hounslow Primary Care Trust, London.

Herrington, V, Clifford, K, Lawrence PF, Ryle, S and Pope, R, 2009, *The Impact of the NSW Police Force Mental Health Intervention Team: Final Evaluation Report*, Charles Sturt University Centre for Inland Health and Australian Graduate School of Policing, Sydney. Viewed 27 May 2010, <www.police.nsw. gov.au/community_issues/mental_health>.

Joint Improvement Team, nd, *Barriers to Partnership Working. Briefing Notes for Practitioners and Managers*. Viewed 23 December 2011, <www.jitscotland. org.uk>.

Kerr, AN, Morabito, M and Watson, AC, 2010, "Police Encounters, Mental Illness, and Injury: An Exploratory Investigation" 10 *Journal of Police Crisis Negotiations* 116.

Kimhi, R, Barak, Y, Gutman, J, Melamed, Y, Zohar, M and Barak, I, 1998, "Police Attitudes toward Mental Illness and Psychiatric Patients in Israel" 4 *Journal of the American Academy of Psychiatry and the Law* 625.

Klein, G, 2010, "Negotiating the Fate of People with Mental Illness: The Police and the Hospital Emergency Room" 10 *Journal of Police Crisis Negotiations* 205.

Lipson, GS, Turner, JT and Kasper, R, 2010, "A Strategic Approach to Police Interactions Involving Persons with Mental Illness" 10 *Journal of Police Crisis Negotiations* 30.

McBrien, J and Murphy, G, 2006, "Police and Carers' Views on Reporting Alleged Offences by People with Intellectual Disabilities" 12 *Psychology, Crime & Law* 127.

McMains, MJ, 2002, "Developing Teams for Crisis Negotiation" 2 *Journal of Police Crisis Negotiations* 43.

Mental Health Council of Australia & the Brain and Mind Research Institute, 2005, *Not for Service: Experiences of Injustice and Despair in Mental Health Care in Australia*, Mental Health Council of Australia, Canberra.

Monahan, J and Steadman, H, 1994, *Violence and Mental Disorder: Developments in Risk Assessment*, The University of Chicago Press, Chicago.

Monahan, J, Steadman, HJ, Silver, E, Appelbaum, PS, Robbins, PC, Mulvey, EP, Roth, LH, Grisso, T and Banks, S, 2001, *Rethinking Risk Assessment: The MacArthur Study of Mental Disorder and Violence*, Oxford University Press, Oxford, UK.

Morris, G, 2006, *Mental Health Issues and the Media: An Introduction for Health Professionals*, Routledge, London and New York.

National Health and Hospitals Reform Commission, 2009, *A Healthier Future for all Australians – Interim Report December 2008*, Commonwealth of Australia, Canberra.

Office of the Public Advocate – Queensland, 2005, *Preserving Life and Dignity in Distress: Responding to Critical Mental Health Incidents*, Department of Justice and Attorney-General, Queensland Government, Brisbane.

Ogloff, JRP, Davis, MR, Rivers, G and Ross, S, 2007, "The Identification of Mental Disorders in the Criminal Justice System", *Trends & Issues in Crime and Criminal Justice Series*, 334, Australian Institute of Criminology, Canberra.

Police Federation of Australia, 2005, *Submission to Senate Select Committee on Mental Health*, 10 May, Police Federation of Australia, Canberra.

Reed, J, 1992, *Review of Health and Social Services for Mentally Disordered Offenders*, DOH/Home Office, London.

Reiner, R, 2001, *The Politics of the Police*, Oxford University Press, Oxford.

Rosenberg, S, Hickie, I and Mendoza, J, 2009, "National Mental Health Reform: Less Talk, More Action" 190 *The Medical Journal of Australia* 193.

Ruiz, J and Miller, C, 2004, "An Exploratory Study of Pennsylvania Police Officers' Perceptions of Dangerousness and their Ability to Manage Persons with Mental Illness" 7 *Police Quarterly* 359.

Sced, M, 2006, "Mental Illness in the Community: The Role of Police", ACPR Issues, 3, *Australasian Centre for Policing Research*, Adelaide.

Seddon, T, 2007, *Punishment and Madness: Governing Prisoners with Mental Health Problems*, Routledge-Cavendish, Abingdon, UK.

Senate Select Committee on Mental Health, 2006, *A National Approach to Mental Health – From Crisis to Community (First Report)*, Commonwealth of Australia, Canberra.

Shaw, J, Tomenson, B, Creed, F and Perry, A, 2001, "Loss of Contact with Psychiatric Services in People Diverted from the Criminal Justice System" 12 *Journal of Forensic Psychiatry & Psychology* 203.

Singleton, N, Meltzer, H, Gatward, R, Coid, J and Deasy, D, 1997, *Psychiatric Morbidity among Prisoners: Summary Report, Office for National Statistics*, London.

Skinns, L, 2008, "A Prominent Participant? The Role of the State in Police Partnerships" 18 *Policing & Society* 311.

Steadman, H, Deane, MW, Borum, R and Morrissey, JP, 2000, "Comparing Outcomes of Major Models of Police Responses to Mental Health Emergencies" 51 *Psychiatric Services* 10.

Teller, J, Munetz, MR, Gil, K and Ritter, C, 2006, "Crisis Intervention Team Training for Police Officers Responding to Mental Disturbance Calls" 57 *Psychiatric Services* 6.

Teplin, LA and Pruett, NS, 1992, "Police as Streetcorner Psychiatrist: Managing the Mentally Ill" 15 *International Journal of Law and Psychiatry* 139.

United Nations, 1991, *Principles for The Protection of Persons with Mental Illness and the Improvement of Mental Health Care*. Viewed 17 February 2012, <www. un.org/documents/ga/res/46/a46r119.htm>.

United Nations, 2006, *Convention on the Rights of Persons with Disabilities*. Viewed 17 February, <www.un.org/disabilities/default.asp?navid=14&pid=150>.

Victoria Police, 2008, *Victoria Police Submission on the Green Paper: Because Mental Health Matters*, Victoria Police Centre, Melbourne. Viewed 6 May 2009, <www.health.vic.gov.au/mentalhealth/mhactreview/submissions.htm>.

Wood, J, Swanson, J, Burris, S and Gilbert, A, 2011, *Police Interventions with Persons Affected by Mental Illnesses: A Critical Review of Global Thinking and Practice*, Center for Behavioral Health Services & Criminal Justice Research, Rutgers University.

Chapter 9

Policing Vulnerable Offenders: Police Early Encounters with Refugees

Penny Egan-Vine and

Katie Fraser

The arrival of refugees from a wide range of ethnic backgrounds is a relatively new experience for Australians. While migration has always been one of the defining characteristics of the human race, global forces have increased that mobility recently. Uprooted from their homes by conflict and by change, people are establishing new lives in new places (Castles and Davidson, 2000: 24). Of particular relevance to policing practices is Castles' (2012) observation that "the impact of that increase in mobility is experienced at the local level, as the arrival of new settlers impacts on those already resident. The newcomers bring cultural difference and the culture of the host country is changed". Skilled migrants, students and temporary work-visa holders, as well as refugees, come to Australia for the short or long-term. Community harmony, compliance with the law and management of difference are all aspects of the interface of new and existing communities and each arriving individual is vulnerable to stereotyping, ignorance and resistance to change.

Refugees, as a particular section of Australia's new arrivals, face multiple tasks in settling in a new country. The challenge is compounded by their experiences prior to arrival. They are vulnerable to entrenched disadvantage and their interaction with police can be a crucial factor in determining whether they have a smooth or problematic settlement experience. This chapter outlines some common legal and policing problems encountered by refugees, the causes and the consequences. Case studies illustrate the possible conflicts and misunderstandings that can arise when police have contact with newly arrived refugees. Strategies to engage refugees will also be provided. While the refugee situation will necessarily be discussed in general terms, there is no homogeneity within the refugee community: rather, there are individuals with different coping skills for different situations (see Bartkowiak-Théron and Corbo Crehan, in this collection, Ch 3).

Australia's Recent Experience of Refugees

A "refugee", as defined under the Refugee Convention, is

> [a] person who, owing to a well-founded fear of being persecuted on account of race, religion, nationality, membership of a particular social group or political opinion, is outside the country of their nationality and is unable to avail himself of the protection of that country (United Nations, 1951: 5).

Australia has been resettling people since soon after the initial British settlement in 1788 and the White Australia Policy was the cornerstone of who was welcome. Changes in the Immigration Policy in 1975 brought people from South-East Asia and intake continued to change, in keeping with areas of crisis throughout the world. Currently settlers on humanitarian visas are coming from Africa, Asia, and the Middle East (Refugee Council of Australia, 2012).

For 2012, Australia has set a quota of 13,750 visas for people who are refugees or in refugee-like situations. Approximately 7000 people, mostly long term-residents of refugee camps, are given humanitarian visas before they arrive in Australia (offshore processing). In addition, every year several thousand people who are already in Australia (arriving by boat or plane) apply for refugee status (onshore processing). About 4,000 of these "onshore" applicants were granted refugee status in 2009-2010 (DIAC, 2011). The remainder of the intake consists of people sponsored by an Australian resident. While not necessarily registered as refugees, sponsored people must be able to show that they are "subject to substantial discrimination amounting to gross violation of their human rights in their home country" (DIAC, 2011).

Over the past ten years, refugees have often been front-page news: boats arriving or sinking, or politicians proclaiming about "stopping the boats" or "being tough on refugees". The media focus is on the boat journey, the arrival and the detention process. However, onshore asylum-seekers are only a small proportion of the total number of people who are finding refuge in Australia. Other aspects of the refugee experience are essentially ignored. This media preoccupation is not without consequences. When the dominant perception is that refugees are illegal, not deserving and/or criminal, the concept of their vulnerability can be met with incredulity. Many refugees are young and male; they look fit and able, and are more likely to be perceived as perpetrators than victims (Muncie, 2009 cited in Walklate, 2011: 183). Sometimes, their vulnerability or the way their situation places them at a disadvantage is not fully comprehended, as shown in Case Study One (*see over page*).

The Refugee Experience: Between Vulnerability and Resilience

Becoming a refugee is an evolving process. Before becoming refugees, these people had a life with family, community and social structure, a sense of identity and a future. Mostly people are forced to seek refuge because of significant and prolonged disturbances of public order and they then live in a protracted situation of waiting to return home. They may be able to find refuge in refugee camps or can find themselves in the difficult situation of being non-citizens in another country, without any legal status and vulnerable to abuse. Only when a return home proves impossible do they seek resettlement elsewhere.

Table 1: Case Study One: First Contact with Police

CASE	ANALYSIS
James is a fourteen-year old refugee from Sudan. His travel documentation stated the wrong birth-date, indicating that he is only eleven years old. James and his mother have been trying for several months to get the mistake corrected. The complex administrative process has been made more difficult by the absence of a birth certificate from Sudan.	In this case, James was obeying the law and gave a truthful explanation of his situation, which related directly to his refugee experience. He was not believed, and was charged. The subsequent withdrawal of the charges indicates the validity of the explanation. However, both the transport officer and police officer had the opportunity to use discretion, and chose not to do so. This may have an impact on the perception of those initially involved.
One day, James was asked to provide proof of concession when travelling on the train. His concession card showed the incorrect birth date. The public transport officer decided that it was a fake, and confiscated James' ticket. Uniformed officers took James off the train. At the police station he was charged with travelling without a concession card and with giving police a false name and address.	
Both charges were withdrawn and James was issued with two warnings after a lawyer wrote to the Department of Transport and police explaining the circumstances.	Here the behaviour of the uniformed people involved – both public transport officials and police – will influence whether this was a teaching or traumatic experience for James. His experience with uniformed personnel also has the potential to affect the attitudes of his peers, his family, and his community.

Transition

According to the UNHCR,

> [r]efugees are often in a long-lasting state of limbo. Their lives may not be so much at risk, but their basic rights and essential economic, social and psychological needs remain unfulfilled over years in exile. A refugee in this situation is often unable to break free from enforced reliance on external assistance (2004:1).

As such, they are denied the chance to develop conventional pathways to positions of influence and authority (Pittaway and Muli, 2009). Decades in refugee camps are added to exposure to home invasion, torture, rape, arbitrary arrest, beatings, kidnappings of family members and deprivation of essentials, including food and housing. Flight from conflict usually has meant more conflict, injustice, deprivation and death. Many young people, born in a refugee camp, know no other life. After they have settled safely in the new country, some find the impact of their experiences can surface with nightmares, heightened anxiety and flashbacks (Post-Traumatic Stress Disorder, PTSD). Disturbed sleep, avoidance of anything that may provoke the distressing memory and "freezing" in the presence of certain triggers can create behaviour that may seem irrational to an outsider. Increased irritability, especially evident in close relationships, can heighten the risk of family violence, or involvement in physical fights.

Refugee camps (in theory safer than the situations that people have fled) are actually places of hardship. Thousands of people live in close quarters, and with minimal policing. Violence, robbery and rape are ever-present risks. Food is basic and rationed. It is the currency of the camp, traded for essentials such as fuel and clothing, or access to electricity to charge mobile phones – which are important in maintaining contact with family separated by the conflict. Malnutrition is frequent and, with only basic health-care available, illness is a significant issue. Housing may not be safe, dry or secure, and there is little opportunity for education, employment or any other form of meaningful occupation. Survival in the camp environment necessitates acquisition of skills in working the system, networking with people in power, judicious bribery, and ignoring what is not relevant to basic life. The common experience of hardship can promote strong bonds amongst family members and within their communities, including shared care of children and shared ownership of property (Pittaway and Muli, 2009).

Arrival

Arrival in Australia promises security, a renewal of hope for a meaningful future and, for many, the opportunity to improve the lives of their friends and family, left behind in camps or other "hopeless" situations. Refugees usually have few possessions on arrival; commonly with no money or goods, and little knowledge of Australia. They leave behind a community and sense of belonging, usually having to adjust to a much lower social standing. As a consequence of their experiences, many refugees crave security. Having a home is incredibly important and maintaining family and culture is significant for social and individual well-being. People feel the need to take control of their own lives and to regain their dignity and freedom (Pittaway and Muli, 2009). Allocated a caseworker on arrival, they receive assistance in finding accommodation, and in connecting to Centrelink for initial financial support. They are offered 500 hours of English lessons and, for the first six months, guidance in learning their way through the new and complex systems that constitute "normal life" in Australia.

In the long-term, there is the chance to be finally settled and to be contributing to their new country. Life is "normal" again after the trauma. They bring their identity, culture, language, fears, hopes, attitudes and skills to bear in reconstructing their life. Becoming Australian citizens brings a sense of belonging and real excitement about exercising rights with freedom. However, not all experiences after arrival are positive. While they share many aspects of adjustment with other people who have migrated to a new country, there are additional factors that can create a sense of disempowerment. Their departures from their homes were often hurried and unplanned, and they have little say as to which country grants them residency. The Victorian Foundation for Survivors of Torture argues that:

> As well as the grief of leaving behind their own culture and friends, there are the tasks of learning a new culture and way of life and gaining mastery over a host of practical tasks from acquiring a new language and using public transport to negotiating new and complex education, income support and health systems. They tend to be over-represented among the poor, experiencing relatively high rates of unemployment and underemployment (2007: 16).

New arrivals experience serious problems accessing appropriate employment, housing, education and health services (Pittaway and Muli, 2009: 11-12). Their backgrounds can range from illiterate farming communities to sophisticated professional environments in modern cities. Their education may have been severely disrupted. For people transplanted from familiar environments, uncertainty, insecurity and absence of forward planning through lack of knowledge, are common experiences (Shroder-Butterfill and Marianti, 2006: 14). Many new arrivals, particularly those from non-urban areas, are poorly equipped to deal with Australian systems and regulations. In particular, refugees may not understand the law, the role of police, and the fact that laws are enforced.

Some adjustments, normal and essential in the camp, may bring people into conflict with the law in Australia. For example, it is very common in the camp to leave young children with siblings or watched by neighbours while women queue for rations. In Australia, a woman going shopping for an hour and leaving her five-year old to look after the six-month old baby may be seen as neglectful, and attract the attention of police or child protection agencies.

Barriers to communication can be multiple. As well as an uncertain knowledge of legal matters, skills in oral and written English may vary considerably. Some refugees are very skilled in English. Others, possibly fluent in several languages, may have only a basic competency in English. Despite the useful Translation and Interpreting Service (TIS), accessing an interpreter may not solve all communication difficulties, as the translator may be the wrong gender, speak a different dialect or belong to a cultural group at odds with the person requiring their services. Many agencies in the community tend to muddle along, without accessing an interpreter, hoping that polite nods and smiles imply understanding.

Policing Refugees

The first year or two in a refugee's life in Australia can have a massive effect on their future and that of their children. If things go well, refugees will avoid major legal problems, gain skills in English, find employment, and contribute to Australia's economy, culture and society. If things go badly, refugees can find themselves in debt, without a driver's licence and hence with limited options for work, with a criminal record, and with a sense of futility. The interaction between refugees and police has the potential to weigh the odds one way or another.

Refugees' attitudes to police can be coloured by their prior experience. Refugee-police interaction is particularly complex for refugees who have experienced high levels of trauma. If they have been subject to government-sanctioned persecution or passed through countries where harassment of non-citizens is frequent and bribery is commonplace, they may carry an understandable fear of uniformed people (Nyaoro, 2010). When contact with police occurs in Australia (especially around an incident), the issues and the complexity of these situations are difficult for both the refugee (whether victim or accused) and for the police involved (Campbell and Julian, 2009). The contact will inform their understanding of Australian policing and their attitude to the rule of law. Additionally, word-of-mouth is a significant factor in close-knit refugee communities. The story of one person's encounter may be shared with an entire community (see Asquith, in this collection, Ch 10, about the ripple effect of messages and degrees of separation in vulnerable communities).

Refugee Education about Police and the Law in Australia

Refugees' prior experience will have involved a different culture, with different laws based on different social norms and values. Their existing knowledge of legal matters may vary considerably. In recognition of this, refugees are provided with some formal education about the law and police as part of the settlement process, even before they arrive in Australia. The Department of Immigration and Citizenship (DIAC) funds an "Australian Cultural Orientation" program (known as "AUSCO"), to provide some orientation to refugees shortly before they leave refugee camps for Australia. Developed in Australia, the three to five day program is delivered to small groups of refugees by locally engaged staff. Although a valuable introduction to Australian society and culture, the focus is mainly on preparing people for the journey, with information about plane travel, western-style toilets, or use of disposable nappies. While they can only give basic information about Australian law, trainers emphasise important aspects such as the separation between police and the military (DIAC, 2010).

A second orientation delivered in the first six months after arrival by DIAC-funded agencies covers money management, health and emergency services, with a short section on law. The presentation includes:

- child protection, domestic violence laws and their impact on family relationships,
- Australian culture and laws, and culturally appropriate behaviours (for example, politeness and punctuality),
- the role of police.

More information is given in the DIAC-funded English classes where some lessons discuss settlement issues, including the role of police. Recognising that refugees can experience information overload and may not absorb much initially, many of the programs are repetitive. Legal matters may seem abstract and confusing, and the real learning often happens some time after the initial orientation. Understanding how to avoid a legal problem may only come with real-life experience.

Australia's legal system is complicated. The difference between civil law and criminal law can be hard for an educated, middle-class Australian to understand, let alone a recently arrived refugee. As trainers may not have a detailed or accurate understanding of the law, some resources have been developed. National Legal Aid created a legal resource for use by AMEP teachers, and the Australian Securities and Investments Commission developed an information package about money management and credit for use in the settlement orientation (Fraser, 2009).

Despite the orientation, refugees may still develop one or more legal problems. The legal system can be bewilderingly complex and arbitrary to those caught up in it. Some may not identify that the problem is a legal one, or know that a lawyer could assist them. For some, seeking help with a personal problem involving money or family is culturally foreign and extremely difficult. Most do not know of the free legal help available from a community legal centre, or of legal aid. Interpreters may not have the language to express some of the policing or judicial concepts, and a person may not seek advice until after the legal proceedings are complete, as demonstrated in Case Study Two.

Common Legal Issues Experienced by Refugees

In 2007, the Footscray Community Legal Centre (FCLC) in Melbourne established a free legal service to provide legal assistance to African refugees. In her report of this initiative, Fraser (2009) documented the common legal issues experienced by their clients, and the underlying causes of their legal problems. While most of the clients were from large refugee camps, there was nothing particularly special or unique about these legal problems, as they were like many of the legal problems experienced by other vulnerable, low-income Australians. Analysis of approximately 450 client files showed that many people developed legal problems in the first five years after arrival in Australia and most were struggling with more than one problem. Driving-related fines, issues with housing or family law and disputes with Centrelink or with utility providers about large bills were frequent concerns, as seen in Case Study Three (*see over page*).

Generally, the problems dealt with at the legal centre related to cars and driving. There were many cases of multiple fines associated with driving an unregistered vehicle or with only a Learner's permit. Many clients, without third party insurance, owed money to insurance companies because of a car accident. Other problems were related to repayments on loans taken out to buy a car. In some cases, clients had continued to make payments after the car had been repossessed, or had been written off in an accident.

There are several reasons why people accumulated so many driving-related legal problems. For many new arrivals, a car was essential to their successful settlement. Affordable accommodation tends to be on the city's fringes, where public transport is poor. Lacking professional skills, and with limited English, people find shift work in factories which again tend to have restricted public transport (Case Study Four *see page 141*). In addition, their experience of the use of cars is usually limited and they are unaware of the complexity of the issues involved (Case Study Five *see page 141*).

Table 2: Case Study Two: "I Don't Understand What Has Happened"

CASE	ANALYSIS
Desmond assaulted his wife during a domestic argument. After she called the police, an intervention order (IVO) against Desmond was taken out on her behalf. At court, Desmond undertook to not fight with his wife nor harm her in any way. Later, when charged with the assault, Desmond was ordered to perform one year of community work. He did not understand the distinction between the IVO proceeding and the criminal proceedings for assault, believing that the court appearance and good behaviour commitment had been punishment enough.	The case illustrates the complexity issue. At no point had Desmond understood what the court processes meant, and what the implications were for him personally. The lawyer's explanation helped him to understand how the system worked and that his treatment had been prescribed and fair.
Desmond sought legal assistance after the criminal hearing when he had already started to perform his community service. When a lawyer explained the difference between the proceedings and the different purposes they served, Desmond was content to continue the community work.	

Table 3: Case Study Three: "I Didn't Understand I Could Lose My License"

CASE	ANALYSIS
Gebre said he had drunk two or three beers one afternoon, and had been stopped by police for a breath test that evening. The test showed the presence of some alcohol and he agreed to accompany police to the police station. There, he answered questions with the assistance of a phone interpreter. Via the interpreter, the police officer asked Gebre to take a blood test, and explained that the interpreter needed to be physically present during the test. The interpreter told Gebre that he lived some distance away and so it would take a few hours to get to the police station. Gebre informed the police officer that, as he had an early work shift, he needed to go home. Through the interpreter, he was advised about the consequences of refusing to take a blood test. The warning given stated:	There are several issues at play here. He did not understand the consequences of his refusal to take a blood test, possibly because the complex language was not easily translated. The police officer was not aware that the interpreter had effectively discouraged Gebre from taking a test by telling him of the long wait. As Gebre did not seek legal help until the day of the case, an interpreter was not available and so he was not able to give full instructions to the duty lawyer. The outcome for him was a sense that the whole process had been "unfair".
In the circumstances, it is compulsory for you to remain here for the purpose of providing a sample of your blood for analysis by an approved blood analysing instrument. If you refuse to remain here for the purpose of the blood test, you may be charged with this offence. If convicted, you may be fined and will lose your licence for the prescribed period. Are you prepared to remain here?	
Gebre claims he did not understand the meaning or consequences of the warning. He decided not to wait for the interpreter and to go home instead. He then received a charge and summons for his refusal to take a blood test. At court he saw a duty lawyer and was not assisted by an interpreter. He was advised to plead guilty and his driver's licence was suspended for two years. Dismayed at losing his licence, Gebre then sought additional legal advice from a Community Legal Centre where he learnt that it would be almost impossible to successfully appeal the decision.	

Table 4: Case Study Four: "I Need to Drive to the Meat Works"

CASE	ANALYSIS
Within six months of arriving in Australia from Africa, Thomas had found work so he could send money back to his immediate family, still in a refugee camp. The abattoir was in an industrial suburb of Melbourne where there is no public transport to the job. His shifts finish at midnight. Thomas acquired a Learner's permit, bought a car and started driving to work. After a car accident that led to a letter of demand from an insurer for $2000, he sought legal advice. He was told that he should not drive until he had passed a driving test and had his P-plates, and that an insurer would not provide cover if he was driving illegally on his L-plates. Thomas replied that he had to work and so would continue driving.	Disquiet about his family who remain in danger adds to Thomas's desire to take control of his life. Previous experiences of an obstructionist and corrupt state, where survival necessitated ignoring regulations designed to benefit a few elite, may also influence his decisions.

Table 5: Case Study Five: "The Police Are Always Picking on Me"

CASE	ANALYSIS
Moses presented with three charges relating to driving with a Learner's permit without a fully licensed driver in the car with him. The first charge arose from a "random" stop on the freeway. Moses was not speeding or driving erratically, was not given any reason for the stop, and believed he was stopped because he was a young African man. The second charge arose from police patrolling Moses' public housing block, where he was driving around the car park. A few weeks later, the same police, at the same location, issued the third charge. Moses was sitting at the wheel of a car in the public housing car park. With the motor running, he was waiting for his friend (a fully licensed driver) to come and give him a driving lesson. He was again charged with driving without a licence. He believed that the police were targeting him. Lawyers attended court with Moses who was fined a total of $600 and given a good behaviour bond. He now has his P-plates and is completing an apprentice-ship in mechanics.	It emerged that so many refugees in the local community were driving without a licence that there had ceased to be any stigma attached to this unlawful behaviour. Coming from experiences where people died on a daily basis, refugees can find some rules and regulations in Australia (for example, those around child seats or bike helmets) unbelievable or ridiculous. Also the newly arrived settlers had not been privy to the safety public health messages witnessed by those living here for longer periods.

**Table 6: Case Study Six: "In My Culture It is Not Appropriate to
Ask My Friend to Pay the Fines"**

CASE	ANALYSIS
Achol is 21, disabled, and a single mother to a six-year old. She has limited English and is not literate in English or in her native tongue. In buying her first car (before she had her driver's licence), she was helped by her friend Matthew, who witnessed her signature for a loan from the bank. She mistakenly believed that Matthew had co-signed the loan. Achol drove her car for a few weeks, but after being fined for driving an unregistered car without a licence, and receiving many parking fines (she was unaware that she needed to display a disabled sticker in a disabled parking space), she decided to stop driving until she got her licence. She lent her car to Matthew who then accumulated thousands of dollars in fines. Unable to pay the fines, Achol felt it would be impolite to ask Matthew to pay them as the car was on loan. She also feared that he could negatively influence the bank regarding her loan.	Here are several legal issues at play. Achol bought a car because she is disabled and wanted to get around more comfortably. As she had been pressured to buy beyond her means she was instantly in financial stress. Achol did not understand Matthew's role in her car purchase, and believed that she owed him a favour. Achol did not see the difficulties as "legal" problems nor understand that a lawyer could create a better outcome for her. A Legal Centre lawyer assisted Achol to write and explain the circumstances, but the police required Matthew's full details before they would withdraw any of the fines. Achol reluctantly agreed to provide the information required but remained deeply concerned how that action would be perceived in the community.

According to Fraser's study (2009), when police became aware that recently arrived refugees from Africa were driving unsupervised while still on their Learner's Permit, they were, not surprisingly, more likely to stop drivers of African appearance. The recipients of this action interpreted it as racial profiling and discrimination. Meanwhile, magistrates, acknowledging the refugees' recently arrived status and their general financial hardship, were giving relatively small fines. Police were frustrated and refugees were tempted to continue driving while unlicensed. When unlicensed drivers had car accidents, drivers, passengers or onlookers were injured or killed and insurers sought overwhelmingly large sums of money, the consequences were seen to be more serious. Interestingly, the problem of unlicensed driving decreased significantly when the practice of issuing summons was changed to "on-the-spot" fines.

There are some lessons here with regard to policing vulnerable people. First, police have an important role in educating people about the law and about the role of police. Every traffic stop is an opportunity to provide information about traffic laws, a police officer's powers of discretion, and the ability of individual police officers to make fully-informed and fair decisions. A traffic stop may be a refugee's first contact with police but will inform lifelong opinions about the law for that person and for many in their community. A traffic stop that is perceived as arbitrary, disproportionate and unfair is a poor outcome. When a refugee understands that he or she has broken the law, that police have discretion to enforce the law, and that there are consequences for breaking the law, this can lead to a good outcome. This delicate balancing act depends on goodwill and a lack of stereotyping on both sides.

Second, refugees may be experiencing all kinds of unseen pressures that affect their behaviours. Refugees may be driving because they need to work, and are responsible for supporting immediate and extended family in refugee camps. The pressure to continue the sharing practices developed in the camps may be significant. Family breakdown, housing stress, and financial hardship (as displayed in Case Study Six) are all increased in new settler communities. Direct experience of torture or difficulties with PTSD can lead to apparently irrational defensiveness and irritability. While not excusing unlawful behaviour, these possibilities need to be considered in exercising discretion, particularly for a first offence.

Finally, the way in which the law is enforced can have a significant effect on behaviour. The change from issuing a summons for unsupervised driving on Learner's Permits, to giving an immediate and substantial fine, may have reduced unlawful behaviour. Some well-publicised car accidents, in which people were injured by learner drivers, may also have influenced the community's awareness of road safety. Moreover, as settlement progressed, more refugees from African countries gained their driver's licence and so there were fewer L-Platers around.

The Albury-Wodonga Experience

In Albury-Wodonga, a project was developed to address similar concerns to those raised in Melbourne. This project aims to promote a two-way dialogue between newly arrived settlers and police. In the regional community of Albury-Wodonga, with a population of just under 90,000, the recent arrival of 500 refugees should have little impact and for many people, the disruption of new arrivals can be acceptable as long as they fit in well. However, these new arrivals, from refugee camps in Africa and Nepal are highly visible in a way previous arrivals have not been. Secondary movement from the larger cities and the arrival of skilled migrants from India, Sri Lanka, and Africa have added to the number of new settlers in the region.

While there had been little negative interaction between police and the new arrivals, a proactive approach was deemed appropriate (Bartkowiak-Théron, 2010). Discussions with both the police and refugees revealed a strong interest in building a culture of understanding and reliance. A program was initiated working towards developing a better understanding of the refugees' journeys for the police and developing a better understanding of legal issues, peacekeeping and law enforcement functions for the refugees. Raising the profile of interagency collaboration on such issues was another goal.

The concept of facilitating a peaceful community while promoting a successful settlement was developed in discussion with senior police. As Albury-Wodonga is on the border of the States of Victoria and NSW, two separate jurisdictions were involved and two programs were developed. Collaborations developed as part of this project led to:

- Consultation sessions with leaders of the new settlers in the community and senior police were arranged to plan the steps for the project. Albury and Wodonga Police invited speakers from the African and Bhutanese communities to present background information about their communities to the regular training session held at each station.
- The Family Violence Network held a forum where leaders of the Bhutanese and African communities presented information about the background of their arrival in the area and the usual ways conflict was resolved in their communities. Police and workers from child protection, domestic violence, Legal Aid and sexual assault services attended.
- Police met students in the special English classes in Albury and Wodonga, introducing themselves and their roles in the community.
- Wodonga Police held a football match between a team of refugees and police.
- Regular information sessions are held by the migrant settlement officers at the Wodonga Council on topics that relate to legal matters (including road rules and rental issues)

Meet and greet events were planned but have not eventuated for a variety of reasons, with difficulty obtaining funding being a significant factor. There is still a lot more to do and there is a risk that the parties involved will become complacent about the success so far. Interestingly, through the process of teaching police, members of both communities of new arrivals have remarked that their understanding of the Australian policing systems has been greatly enhanced. In teaching about their culture, they have also learnt a lot about Australian and police culture. The senior police continue to express enthusiasm for the project and cite instances where the information has been of use in refugee/police interactions.

Further Comments and Conclusion

A major attribute of refugees generally is their resilience and adaptability. Despite experiences of persecution, violence, forced migration, loss of family, home, and cultural identity, many refugees are settling successfully and working, not only for themselves, but to assist their communities both here and in their country of origin. There are, however, some who are facing significant challenges in the process of settling into a vastly different country and culture (Pittaway and Muli, 2010). While a person's refugee status may not be evident at first glance, evidence of vulnerability can become rapidly apparent. Awareness of issues that can be pertinent to a refugee background is important with respect to the ultimate outcome. The impact of well-informed police cannot be emphasised enough. Ignorance of the complex issues can have long-term implications for the life of the refugee and for future interactions with the community. Police have a valuable role in educating refugees about the role of police and establishing the important place of law in our community. As the source of new arrivals is constantly changing, so does the information about their background need to be updated at all levels of the police workforce. Promoting resilience and recognising their role in successful settlement are powerful aspects of policing that deserve recognition.

Australia is known for its policies underpinned by multiculturalism. New arrivals have contributed significantly to the development of Australia and yet the settlement process can involve disruption and distress both for the new arrivals and the host community. The role of police in managing and minimising the negative impacts is vitally important to successful settlement. Many guidelines already exist but the lived experience illustrated in the above examples indicates that the process is far from easy.

References

Australian Bureau of Statistics, *2006 Census of Population and Housing*, ABS, Canberra.

Australian Bureau of Statistics, *2001 Census of Population and Housing*, ABS, Canberra.

Bartkowiak-Théron, I, 2010, *Bridging the Gap between the Police and Refugee Communities: Project Brief*, Tasmanian Institute of Law Enforcement Studies, Hobart.

Ben-Porat, G and Yuval, F, 2011, "Minorities in Democracy and Policing Policy: From Alienation to Cooperation" iFirst, *Policing and Society* 1.

Campbell, D and Julian, R, 2009, *A Conversation on Trust: Community Policing and Refugee Settlement in Regional Australia*, Tasmanian Institute of law Enforcement Studies, University of Tasmania, Hobart.

Castles, S, 2012, "Resettling Visible Migrants", *A Long Way from Home? The Rural and Regional Resettlement Experiences of Visible Migrants and Refugees Conference*, University Melbourne, Melbourne, February 2012.

Castles, S and Davidson, A, 2000, *Citizenship and Migration: Globalisation and the Politics of Belonging*, Macmillan, London.

Department of Immigration and Citizenship, 2010, The Australian Cultural Orientation (AUSCO) Program – Fact Sheet 67. Viewed 07/05/12 <www.immi. gov.au/media/fact-sheets/67ausco.htm>.

Fraser, K, 2009, *Out of Africa and Into Court: The Legal Problems of African Refugees*, Footscray Community Legal Centre, Melbourne.

Muncie, J, 2009, *Youth and Crime*, Open University Press, Maidenhead, UK.

Nyaoro, D, 2010, "Policing with Prejudice: How Policing Exacerbates Poverty among Urban Refugees" 14 *International Journal of Human Rights* 126.

Pittaway, E and Muli, C, 2009, *We have a Voice: Hear Us. Settlement Experiences of Refugees and Migrants from the Horn of Africa* Centre for Refugee Research, University of NSW, Sydney.

Refugee Council of Australia, 2012, *History of Australia's Refugee Program*. Viewed on 23 April 2012, <staging.refugeecouncil.org.au/resources/history. php>.

Shroder-Butterfill, E and Marianti, R, 2006 "A Framework for Understanding Old-Age Vulnerabilities" 26 *Aging and Society* 9.

UNHCR, 2004, "Protracted Refugee Situations", *Thirtieth Executive Committee of the High Commissioner's Programme* (Standing committee), EC/54/SC/ CRP/14, 10 June, United Nations, Geneva.

Victorian Foundation for Survivors of Torture Inc., 2007, *Refugee Health and General Practice*, Western Melbourne Division of General Practice, Melbourne.

Walklate, S, 2011, "Reframing Criminal Victimization: Finding a Place for Vulnerability and Resilience" 15 *Theoretical Criminology* 179.

Chapter 10

Vulnerability and the Art of Complaint Making

Nicole L Asquith

Considerable research, in recent times, has been devoted to some of the experiences of increased vulnerability in victimisation, especially those victims of sexual assault and domestic violence (see for example, Heenan and Murray, 2006; Lievore 2003; Taylor and Gassner, 2010). Other vulnerable victims[1] remain under-represented in the research, and few resources have been allocated to investigate their specific experiences. In particular, the victimisation experiences of elder abuse and hate crime continue to be marginal to both research and policy development in policing. In this chapter, the experiences of gay men and lesbians are deployed to illustrate some of the extreme victimisation processes faced by hate crime victims. Importantly, these are not necessarily unique to this vulnerable population; apart from similarities with other victims of hate crime (especially, the elderly and disabled), the issues raised in this chapter can, at times, present themselves in crimes without a "hate" motivation, and thus provide a resource for policing other vulnerable groups.

Most people experience vulnerability as part of the victimisation process; though, the nature and severity of this victimisation varies considerably, especially in relation to the type of crime, level of violence, length of victimisation, and the individual characteristics of the "victim". Some victims, however, are more vulnerable to the consequences of victimisation; more vulnerable because of who they are (as individuals and as members of specific social groups), but also more vulnerable because of the social contexts of their victimisation. While the legislative frameworks guiding how police respond to "hate" crimes (or "prejudice-related" or "bias" crimes) vary between jurisdictions, the policies and practices necessary to manage these unique forms of interpersonal violence remain the same. This chapter addresses some of the unique characteristics of hate crimes, the additional barriers faced by gay men and lesbians in reporting hate crimes, and the wider consequences for policing hate crime. Using case studies from New South Wales Police, the London Metropolitan Police Service, the West Yorkshire Police, True Vision and the Lesbian and Gay Anti-Violence Project (AVP), this chapter highlights the "art" of complaint-making and outlines what has become best practice for policing services responding to this form of hate violence.

Sexuality and Vulnerability

Some victims of hate crime encounter difficulties in approaching policing organisations to make a report of violence because of a pre-existing relationship marked by animus, distrust in their policing services, and/or fear of the consequences of making a report. Repealing sodomy laws and decriminalising homosexuality are relatively recent transitions for most countries; as such, some in the GLBTIQ (gay, lesbian, bisexual, transgender, intersex and queer) communities have recent experiences of being treated as criminals simply because of their sexual and/or gender identity. For gay men and lesbians, as with some other vulnerable groups, making a complaint of hate violence brings with it additional barriers. Most uniquely, in homophobic/ heterosexist hate violence is the need for the victim to "out" themselves in order for the complaint to be considered a hate crime. In turn, coming out can lead gay men and lesbians to be more vulnerable to losing their jobs, families, and friends, and to additional hate crime victimisation.

Hate crimes, in addition to the primary offence (whether this is homicide, assault, vandalism or, in some cases, robbery), contain an additional "offence". The latter is constituted most commonly as a motive of "hatred" of, or bias or prejudice against, the perceived characteristics of a social group (Hall, 2010: 153). In this sense, the individual victim is often irrelevant to the perpetrator, as they are simply a representative of the victim's social group. Each member of this group therefore becomes vulnerable, in the sense that they represent a possible (and easy) target for the perpetrator. McDevitt et al (2001: 698) call this the "interchangeability" of hate crimes, as "any individual who possesses, or is perceived to possess, a specific trait could be selected as a target". In most policing jurisdictions, the focus was initially on crimes motivated by racism, antisemitism and/or xenophobia, and laws, policies and practices often developed in response to a critical incident (such as the murder of Stephen Lawrence in the UK, or James Byrd Jr in the US) (Chakraborti and Garland, 2009). Over the last twenty years, the social categories recognised under hate crime legislation have been extended to include, in most jurisdictions, sexuality, religion and disability. Other jurisdictions have expanded the list of specific hate crime victims to include sex/gender/transgender, some forms of elder abuse, and homelessness (Jenness and Grattet, 2001).

The recognition of sexual and gender minorities as a vulnerable group, and hate crimes as unique criminal encounters, is a relatively new exercise on part of governments and their policing services (Jenness and Grattet, 2001). Legislation recognising the specific offence of a hate crime have been in place in the UK and US since the late 1980s, and by 2010, over 55 countries (including some states of Australia) had enacted legislation to respond to the unique circumstances of hate crimes (OSCE cited in Hall, 2010: 149). However, the legislative and policy "career" (Jenness and Grattet, 2001) of hate crime provisions in some Australian jurisdictions lags behind that developed in the USA and the UK. Australian jurisdictions are in the early stages of criminalising these as specific offences, and creating the policing capacity to respond to this unique form of victimisation.

Hate Crimes as Message Crimes

As many scholars and practitioners have pointed out, hate crimes are message crimes (Perry, 2001; Levin and McDevitt, 2002; Lim, 2009). Immediate messages to the victim declare they are unwanted, distrusted, despised and less-than human. However, there are also the additional messages sent to an "audience" well beyond the original victim; whether these are the victim's families and communities, or onlookers and witnesses. These secondary victims receive a version of the statement of hatred, but unlike the immediate trauma experienced by the primary victim, the consequences can vary from behavioural change to increased conflict between marginalised and dominant communities, or, in the case of the dominant community, a "dog-whistle" or permission to hate (Perry, 2001; Asquith and Poynting, 2011). Walters (2006) even suggests that the consequences of the initial act of hate could extend beyond the immediate primary and secondary victims to include all citizens, as it puts at risk the very viability of an engaged democracy and citizenry.

The more marginalised the community, the smaller the degrees of separation, and thus the greater the risk that these messages ripple out to the wider community (Noelle, 2002; Lim, 2009). In a study undertaken by the NSW government in 2003, 86% of gay men and lesbians reported that they knew another person who had been attacked because of their sexuality or gender identity (NSW Attorney General's Department – Crime Prevention Division, 2003). The US Bureau of Justice argues that a bias-motivated incident (or hate crime) "...can cause a broad ripple of discomfiture among members of a targeted group, and a violent hate crime can act like a virus, quickly spreading feelings of terror and loathing across an entire community" (cited in Iganski , 2002: 25). The ripple effect can constrain the actions of the community, including limiting where and when individuals go, and how they act in public (such as gay men or lesbians holding hands with their partners). As such, while a victim must face the individual consequences of hate violence, their experiences inform the actions of many more people in their communities.

Further, beyond the initial act of hatred, victims also receive complementary, often symbolic, messages created in response to the hatred. Just as the primary and secondary victims receive a message from the perpetrator, they also receive multiple – sometimes contradictory – messages from their governments, police, courts, prison, and probation systems, and the media. A message of homophobic or heterosexist hate is measured by victims against and/or with the messages received from their government and community about their sexual and/or gender identity. When same-sex relationships remain unrecognised by the Federal government (including same-sex marriage and adoption), the measures taken at a state level (such as increased police services) appear, and are lived, as a contradiction. Based on comments by politicians, public servants, and the media over the last twenty years, most gay men and lesbians could easily be mistaken for believing that the perpetrators of hate violence share a social vision with many in the government and the police.

Barriers to Complaint-Making

The act of making a complaint to police contains all the power imbalances present in the wider society, yet focused upon the request (at times, demand) for justice. For an individual to feel capable of making a complaint, they must first feel they are entitled to full social and political citizenship. Yet, as Phelan (2001) argues, gay men and lesbians are "passport citizens" as they are "not currently citizens in the full political sense"; in part, due to the limited rights they hold under Australian law, including the failure of Australian governments to recognise same-sex relationships (and the rights attached to those relationships). A complainant must also believe that they will be taken seriously, and that the information they provide will not be used against them (Christmann and Wong, 2010). However, systems of complaint making are built into systems of political and structural inequalities – some so extreme that they constitute a denial of citizenship. The tragedy of seeking justice is that it is a culturally and historically defined moment of "truth" telling and one that is inherently social; yet it is, conversely, an inherently individual act, requiring the resources of a single person to make a complaint.

Making a complaint, therefore, comes at a very high cost for some gay men and lesbians, as the very act of reporting violence requires an individual to "out" themselves to a stranger. Yet, at the same time they must assess this against the understanding that being "completely out" most commonly leads to hate crimes (Faulkner, 2009), and serious and traumatic injury (Samis, 1995 cited in Faulkner, 2009: 129). In Comstock's early research, they found that 40 per cent of gay men and lesbians were fearful that reporting homophobic violence would result in public disclosure of their sexuality (cited in Herek and Berrill, 1992: 294). Further, unlike most forms of hate crime, gay men and lesbians must also negotiate difficult family contexts; either estranged relationships with family members or family members and friends who are perpetrators of the hate violence against them (approximately 15% of known perpetrators of hate crime; Asquith, 2009: 33). Managing the disclosure of their sexuality, and the absence of familial support in reporting incidents to police, increases both the invisibility and vulnerability of gay men and lesbians in the criminal justice system.

As with sexual assault and domestic violence, in complaint making, these barriers often lead to an absence or a failure to make a complaint of hate violence, or a failure to recognise the violence as a crime at all (Herek and Berrill, 1992a; Lievore, 2003; Asquith, 2009; Taylor and Gassner, 2010). Jill Tregor, a Client Advocate with Community United against Violence (an American community-based anti-violence project), argues that

> [t]he denial among lesbians and gay men about the extent of the problem is amazing. I know it's a coping mechanism but it's scary to know just how many people think, "Oh, that doesn't happen ... here" [or] that "violence is so much a part of my life that I don't even need help dealing with it" (cited in Herek, 1992a: 243).

Apart from not recognising the violence as something to complain about, the primary reason that gay men and lesbians under-report hate violence is fear of secondary victimisation (Berrill and Herek, 1992). Comstock found that over two-thirds of US gay men and lesbians who had experienced hate violence declined to report the incident to the police because they perceived the police to be homophobic/heterosexist, and feared abuse from the police (cited in Berrill and Herek, 1992: 293). In Faulkner's (2009: 132) comparative hate crime research, she found that between 11.5 per cent and 14 per cent of Canadian, American and British respondents (between 1999 and 2004) had been harassed by the police, and 2.5 per cent been beaten or assaulted by police because of their sexuality. When these experiences of secondary victimisation are considered in light of the historically hostile relationship between the police and GLBTIQ communities – especially, in relation to the criminalisation of homosexuality (which was only fully decriminalised in Australia in the late 1990s and even later in some US states) – it is unsurprising that hate crime incidents are not consistently reported to the police.

In addition to these social factors limiting gay men and lesbians' reporting of hate violence, community organisations and the police must also manage the psychological barriers encountered in extreme violence. Memories of traumatic events are central to complaint-making. Yet memory is an act of constructing a knowable truth out of a past already gone. We cannot recreate the moment exactly, but complaint-making requires a sequential narrative of these experiences (Brison, 1999: 42). What is traumatic today may not be so tomorrow, and vice versa. Given that memory is active rather than a frozen moment, the "truth", as required in formal complaint-making procedures requires complainants to fix their stories, usually before a full understanding of the sequence of events has been achieved by the complainant (Van Alphen, 1999: 24).

Institutional Responses to Hate Crime

As "gatekeepers" to the criminal justice system, police officers – especially front-line officers – are often required to make decisions about "whether and how to enforce the law" (Hall, 2010: 155). Hall (2010) suggests that police discretion and decision-making are central to the success of hate crime laws and policies, as it is they who have the power to apply the label of "hate crime". The level of discretion afforded to frontline officers by their Standard Operating Procedures (SOPs), strongly shapes the approach taken to evaluating and investigating hate crimes, and even if an incident is defined as a hate crime at all. Given this gate-keeping role of frontline officers, it is important that a right mix of police education and training is matched with appropriate institutional measures and symbolic support from executive policing and the government.

Education and Training

As with many other areas of vulnerable people policing, the policy and practice debate is divided over whether policing services aim for a broad-based practical understanding of hate crime policing (such as the integration of hate crimes into police training) or specialist understanding of hate crimes with a dedicated unit within the police service (staffed with officers and support staff with extensive knowledge of hate crimes, and the power to shepherd any particular hate crime case from victim reporting through to offender prosecution). In some jurisdictions, policing organisation have adopted both responses in order to tackle hate crime; others, with fewer resources (or less symbolic and financial support from executive policing and government) are forced to "make do" with the issues being raised as part of a short silo workshop aimed at specific social groups (Parker, 2009) (such as the workshop provided to Tasmania Police by Working It Out on sexuality and gender diversity, or the SpeakOut Panel that was added to the recruit training in NSW in the early 1990s). In siloed training, hate crime is only one of many crime-related topics addressed.[2] These silo workshops also aim to promote critical reflection and behavioural change on the part of police officers in relation to sexuality and gender identity (Parker, 2009). Given the breadth of material required to be covered in these limited workshops, the significant specialist knowledge required for policing hate crimes is often not adequately acquired by students.

If a silo workshop is provided *in tandem* with the integration of hate crimes into the wider curricula (and the introduction of a specialised module on hate crimes), police officers are provided with the basic cultural knowledge about the unique circumstances of GLBTIQ communities, whilst also being provided with the skills and competencies to employ this knowledge to a range of vulnerable victimisations (Parker, 2009; Nolan et al, 2009). In practice, this type of hate crime education and training (including SOPs) would result in the acquisition of specialised knowledge (as with sexual assault and family violence training) and as a consequence, would require students to demonstrate high-level critical thinking and assessment skills (such as discussed in Bartkowiak-Théron and Layton, in this collection, Ch 4). Reading hate crime across the victimised communities (rather than within victimised communities) enables police officers to acquire a wider cultural competency than is traditionally developed in training. In this type of specialised hate crime training, in addition to the specific SOPs relating to hate crime policing, students learn to be critically aware of:

- the multiple layers of cultural diversity (between and across the race/ethnicity, sex and sexuality and religious lines – to name a few), and the common experiences of hate-related violence,
- their own personal perceptions about victimised communities, and the impact these have on decision-making and use of discretion, and
- the consequences of both of these for operational policing and policy development.

Further, officers acquire competencies in recognising the signs of hate motivation, including the collection of linguistic forensic evidence in order to assess the "motive" from the verbal and/or textual hostility (hate speech) employed before, during or after an incident (Nolan et al, 2009; Asquith, 2009; Parker, 2009). Finally, specialist training would also, necessarily, contain additional skills development in the area of community policing and liaison. This is a critical competency required for addressing the issues of under-reporting of hate crimes, and the lack of trust between the police and vulnerable communities who experience hate crimes.

Specialist Units

While an institution-wide response such as education and training is essential, in the short term, the police may find that the increased time required in policing hate crimes (as with sexual assault and family violence) may necessitate the creation of a specialist unit and/or a network of specialist liaison officers (see Bartkowiak-Théron, in this collection, Ch 6, for a more detailed discussion of liaison officers). The form and function of specialists units, their power to shape frontline, as well as executive, policing and their mission in relation to research and data collection all contribute to a wide variety of institutional structures. As an interim measure, these specialist units provide frontline officers and commanders with a deeper understanding of the characteristics of hate crimes, best practices in operationalising policies, and access to community networks for referral and support to the victim. When specialist units are also tasked with policy development and research, and play an integral role in training and education, they are more capable of transforming day-to-day policing practices.

Over the last twenty years, policing services in the UK have employed a range of strategies to manage and respond to hate crimes. These strategies have been guided by the recommendations stemming from the *Stephen Lawrence Inquiry* (Macpherson, 1999). Legislative changes recognising and responding to hate crimes (such as the *Crime and Disorder Act 1998* (UK)) have led to multiple service enhancements to victims, along with a comprehensive re-organisation of policing organisations' SOPs and reporting techniques (see Nolan et al, 2009, for a detailed discussion of the International Association of Chiefs of Police best practice model). The Violent Crime Directorate of the London Metropolitan Police Service (MPS) includes a specific Hate Crime Unit, with over seven sworn and unsworn officers taking primary responsibility for each recognised victim community ("Black and Minority Ethnic", Jewish, Muslim, GLBTIQ, disabled, elderly). They act as a "one stop shop" for frontline officers and commanders, and are tasked with reviewing all cases identified as a hate crime in the service's computer operating system.

Importantly, in the UK, any participant (including the responding officer) can identify an incident as a hate crime. This has led to an increase in the number of cases reported to the MPS.[3] In reporting such an incident as a hate crime, the responding officer will be prompted to complete additional variables in the crime report, and under SOPs will be required to initiate follow-up contact with the victim within 24 hours, seven days, and one month of the incident. Most commonly, this additional contact is *mandated* as part the victim's enrolment on VIVID (Vulnerable and Intimidated Victims Database). Senior officers in each borough command are responsible for oversight of these additional reporting and contact mechanisms, and tasked with bringing to the attention of the Hate Crime Unit any hate crime recidivism, and recognisable pattern in hate crime victimisation or offending (especially as it relates to organised hate groups such as the British National Party and the English Defence League). These enhanced contact and reporting procedures are believed necessary if police are to secure a formal complaint, retrieve important forensic evidence, and support victims through to prosecution. It also provides a strong symbolic gesture to victims that their experiences have been acknowledged as a hate crime, and that the police take their complaint seriously. In the longer term, this also bolsters the victims' and communities' trust in the police.

In addition to this increased operational policing, the MPS is also subject to a range of oversight and research processes in relation to hate crime. Over the last eight years, the London Metropolitan Police Authority (MPA) has been conducting a borough-by-borough review of policing and social service responses to hate crime. Each borough was required to report to the MPA in relation to the *Stephen Lawrence Inquiry* recommendations, and was assessed independently by a panel of specialists including criminal justice experts and members of victimised communities (Iganski, 2007). The London Metropolitan Police Service also has at its disposal one of the most productive criminal research departments resourced and housed within a policing service. The Strategy, Research and Analysis Unit – independently, or collaboratively with external academics – have produced a series of research reports looking at specific and more general forms of hate crime (see for example, Mason, 2005; Stanko et al, 2003; Iganski, Kielinger and Patterson, 2005; Asquith, 2009). This research is generated from the MPS' own hate crime data, and as such, serves as a means through which more critical policing practices can emerge from within the service.

Further, each of the UK's 43 policing services is required to create local Hate Crime Scrutiny Panels, which are tasked with reviewing a random sample of hate crimes reported to an area command during a monthly or tri-monthly period. Scrutiny Panels consist of specialists (sworn and unsworn) working with volunteer members of the victim communities. Depending on the size of the policing organisation, the scrutiny panels can be generalist (looking at all forms of hate crime) or specialist (such as the West Yorkshire Police's Race Hate Crime Scrutiny Panel, and Sexuality Hate Crime Scrutiny Panel). The scrutiny of hate crime files usually involves a detailed outline of the case, procedures taken by responding officers and commanders, and a critical discussion of the problems encountered in operationalising the hate crime policies and SOPs. Importantly, specialists officers participating in these panels are not required to defend specific officers' (in)actions. Rather, the panel as a whole, asks for clarification from, and makes recommendations to, responding officers and area commanders; at times this takes the form of an official recommendation to be included in individual officer's file for outstanding service delivery. Community oversight of policing practices of hate crimes through these scrutiny panels, as with the additional contact with victims, enhances the trust between victim communities and the police, which has a flow-on effect of increasing the willingness of vulnerable victims to report crimes to the police.

Third-Party Reporting

While developing enhanced training and case management processes can greatly assist in increasing the reporting, investigation and prosecution of hate crimes, in the short term, these measures may not increase vulnerable communities' trust in their policing services. The divide between GLBTIQ communities and the police is not just the result of discrimination and violence but also in many cases, a deep distrust stemming from the criminalisation of sexual and gender diversity. Less than 50 per cent of hate crimes against gay men and as few as 15 per cent of hate crimes against lesbians are reported to the police (Herek and Berrill, 1992; Von Schulthess, 1992; Asquith, 2008). As a result of a range of institutional, social and individual factors, victims of heterosexist hate violence have not consistently reported their experiences to police; preferring instead to report to community organisations (such as the Lesbian and Gay Anti-Violence Project (AVP) in Sydney, Community United against Violence in San Francisco, the New York Anti-Violence Project, or GALOP in the UK).

In the absence of a trusting relationship with their policing services, GLBTIQ communities have developed their own responses to hate violence, which, in many cases, has led to the creation of anti-violence projects (Herek, 1992). The goals and practices of these community organisations vary considerably, though most collect (or have collected) reports of hate violence. In addition to this central task of "third party reporting", these organisations are also responsible for (re)building a relationship of trust between their communities and the policing service, and working with police to improve service delivery for GLBTIQ victims and offenders, and victims of hate crime. This work has led to increasingly strong collaborations between the police and the GLBTIQ communities, and the development of more effective community and problem-oriented strategies, including the creation of liaison officers; all of which has contributed to better hate crime policing and increased reporting of hate crime.

Third party reporting offers a link between policing services and vulnerable communities. When distrust is too high, community organisations act as facilitators and negotiators between the two. Third party reporting practices vary depending on the resourcing of organisations. In this final section, a case study of the NSW Police and the Lesbian and Gay Anti-Violence Project (AVP) is used to illustrate the different third-party options available to monitor hate crime in the context of under-reporting to the police. In its most basic form, third-party reporting can be achieved through an *ad hoc* survey of the communities' experiences of hate crime, which is converted into a research report to be distributed to key stakeholders, including the police. In its most advanced form, such as True Vision in the UK, individuals who do not wish to contact their police directly, can report an incident via an online portal, with the data then transmitted to the relevant policing service (True Vision, 2012).

Since 1989, gay men and lesbians in New South Wales have been assisted in their relationship with policing services by the advocacy, representational and community education work of the Lesbian and Gay Anti-Violence Project (AVP). As with its international counterparts, the AVP began as a project of the Gay and Lesbian Rights Lobby, resourced from within the gay and lesbian communities. Since its creation, the AVP has been on the leading edge of hate crime data collection in Australia. Once data were collected, the AVP was able to secure financial support from the government. The AVP was also instrumental in changing the relationship between gay and lesbian communities and their policing services, including advocating on behalf of victims to ensure increased reporting of violence, and better crime prevention outcomes (Asquith, 2008). The central task for which the AVP was established was hate violence mapping. In 1989, the Gay and Lesbian Rights Lobby surveyed communities' experiences of violence and the policing responses to these incidents of hate. The *Interim Report of the Streetwatch Advisory Committee* (Cox, 1990) was to be the first of many research reports generated – either as standalone documents on the hate violence data collected (for example, Cox, 1992, 1994), or in relation to specific crime issues faced by gay men and lesbians (such as their reviews of same-sex domestic violence, and the experiences of school bullying).

From the first days of its establishment in 1991, the AVP provided an ongoing reporting service for victims unwilling to contact NSW Police. The experiences documented in these reports of violence were instrumental in bringing the issue of hate violence against gay men and lesbians to the attention of the police. The AVP has advocated, represented and educated the community and the police about hate violence for twenty years. From a peak of 142 reports of violence in 1995 – of which, most complainants did not report to police – by 2001 reports of violence had dropped to an average of 30 – with most complainants reporting to the police prior to reporting to the AVP (Asquith, 2008). Apart from data collection and client advocacy, by the late 1990s, the Anti-Violence Project had also secured support from NSW Police to act as a third-party complainant on behalf of those clients who did not want to make a formal complaint. These data were entered into the NSW Police crime database as "for information only" files, and used to direct operational and hot-spot policing resources. This was especially the case in relation to the unreported hate violence experienced during the annual Mardi Gras parade, which is the single most dangerous night of the year for those perceived to be gay or lesbian (Cox, 1994; Asquith, 2008).

During this same period, NSW Police mainstreamed the network of Gay and Lesbian Liaison Officers, created the position of the Gay and Lesbian Client Consultant, established specific reporting mechanisms for hate violence, and authorised its officers to march in the Mardi Gras parade – in uniform and under the banner of the NSW Police. The last of these transformations, whilst symbolic, was also in many ways the most significant given the history of this event (as a protest rally against over-policing of sexuality and under-policing of hate crime), and the radical changes that have occurred since its creation in 1978.

Conclusion

When institutional arrangements are created without reference to the individual and social barriers to complaint-making, the results can be counter-productive, especially when the needs of victims of hate crime are not integrated into policing responses. The combination of generalised training, specialised units and community-based third-party reporting ensures that hate crimes are:

- more likely to be reported to the police,
- appropriately investigated by the police in a culturally competent manner,
- better monitored for trends in victimisation and offending, and that these trends are used in operational policing.

However, as with any policy or practice innovation, there will be a significant delay in service-wide implementation. These changes to the policing framework come at a time of increasing complexity for police officers and for policing services as organisations. Increased oversight and reporting mechanisms can lead to a range of "institutional pathologies" (Sheptycki, 2004), which reduce the advantages to be gained from intelligence-led policing models. Transforming policing services so they are more capable of managing the unique incident, victim and offender characteristics of hate crime requires a careful mix of zero-tolerance of hate crimes and community capacity building, including building trust between vulnerable communities and their police. There is an "art" to this process, which is necessarily embedded in the local contexts of law, policing and community relations. It is important, however, that we remain mindful of the common experiences that underlie hate crime victimisation and its associated vulnerability.

Endnotes

1 The term "victim" is used in this paper rather than "survivor"; not only to complement the academic and policy language but also to highlight the transitional processes that occurs between "victim" and "survivor". The success of this transition is, in large part, a product of effective criminal justice processes.

2 After all, gay men and lesbians can be victims of non-bias crimes, and offenders of any type of crime (the latter of which, brings with it another set of unique issues and concerns especially as it relates to custody arrangements).

3 An average of just under 20 000 incidents were reported to the MPS each year between 2003 and 2007(Asquith, 2009), which, despite difference in population size, is considerably more than is submitted to the FBI's Hate Crime database for the whole of the USA.

References

Crime and Disorder Act 1998, c37, UK Parliament, London.

Asquith, NL, 2009, *Understanding the Role of Verbal and Textual Hostility in Hate Crime Regulation: Interim Report*, London Metropolitan Police Service, London.

Asquith, NL, 2008, *Text and Context of Malediction: A Study of Antisemitic and Heterosexist Hate Violence in New South Wales (1995-2000)*, VDM Verlag, Saarbrücken, Germany.

Asquith, NL and Poynting, S, 2011, "Anti-Cosmopolitanism and 'Ethnic Cleansing' at Cronulla", *Between the Outback and the Sea: Cosmopolitanism and Anti-Cosmopolitanism in Contemporary Australia*, (Ed K Jacobs and J Malpas), UWA Press, Perth, 96.

Berrill, KT and Herek, GM, 1992, "Primary and Secondary Victimization in Anti-Gay Hate Crimes: Official Response and Public Policy", *Hate Crimes: Confronting Violence against Lesbians and Gay Men* (Eds GM Herek and KT Berrill), SAGE, Newbury Park, USA, 289.

Brison, SJ, 1999, "Trauma Narratives and the Remaking of the Self", *Acts of Memory: Cultural Recall in the Present* (Eds M Bal, J Crewe and L Spitzer), University Press of New England, Hanover.

Chakraborti, N and Garland, J, 2009, *Hate Crime: Impact, Causes and Responses*, SAGE, London.

Cox, G, 1990, *Interim Report of the Streetwatch Implementation Advisory Committee*, NSW Anti-Discrimination Board, Sydney.

Cox, G, 1992, *Off Our Backs*, Lesbian and Gay Anti-Violence Project, Sydney.

Cox, G, 1994, *Count and Counter*, Lesbian and Gay Anti-Violence Project, Sydney.

Faulker, ME, 2009, "Anti-Lesbian, Gay, Bisexual, and Transgendered Victimization in Canada and the United States: A Comparative Study", *Hate Crime: The Victims of Hate Crime*, Vol 3, (Ed B Perry), Praeger, Westport, 121.

Hall, N, 2010, "Law Enforcement and Hate Crime: Theoretical Perspectives on the Complexities of Policing 'Hatred'", *Hate Crime: Concepts, Policy, Future Directions* (Ed N Chakraborti), Willan, Cullompton, 149.

Heenan, M, and Murray, S, 2006, *Study of Reported Rapes in Victoria 2000-2003*. Office of Women's Policy, Department for Victorian Communities, Melbourne.

Herek, GM, 1992, "The Community Response to Violence in San Francisco: An Interview with Wenny Kusuma, Lester Olmstead-Rose and Jill Tregor", *Hate Crimes: Confronting Violence against Lesbians and Gay Men* (Eds, GM Herek and KT Berrill), SAGE, Newbury Park, USA, 241.

Herek, GM, and Berrill, KT, 1992, "Documenting the Victimization of Lesbians and Gay Men: Methodological Issues", *Hate Crimes: Confronting Violence against Lesbians and Gay Men* (Eds, GM Herek and KT Berrill), SAGE, Newbury Park, USA, 270.

Iganski, P, 2002, "How Hate Hurts", *Gyulolet es politika (Hate and Politics)* (Eds G Csepeli and A Orkeny), Friedrich Ebert Stiftung – Minoritas Alapitvany Kisebbsegkutato, Intezet, Budapest, Hungary, 25.

Iganski, P, 2007, *The London-Wide Race Hate Crime Forum: A Model of Good Practice for 'Third Tier' Multi-agency Partnerships against Race Hate Crime in Europe*, Metropolitan Police Authority, London.

Iganski, P, Kielinger, V and Paterson, S, 2005, *Hate Crimes Against London's Jews*, Institute for Jewish Policy Research, London.

Jenness, V and Grattet, R, 2001, *Making Hate a Crime: From Social Movement to Law Enforcement*, Russell Sage Foundation, New York.

Levin, J and McDevitt, J, 2002, *Hate Crimes Revisited: America's War on Those Who Are Different*, Westview Press, Boulder.

Lievore, D, 2003, *Non-reporting and Hidden Recording of Sexual Assault: An International Literature Review*, Commonwealth Office of the Status of Women, Canberra.

Lim, AH, 2009, "Beyond the Immediate Victim: Understanding Hate Crimes as Message Crimes", *Hate Crime: The Consequences of Hate Crime*, Vol 2, (Ed P Iganski), Praeger, Westport, 107.

McDevitt, J, Balboni, J, Garcia, L and Gu, J, 2001, "Consequences for Victims: A Comparison of Bias- and Non-Bias-Motivated Assaults" 45 *American Behavioral Scientist* 697.

Macpherson, W, 1999, *The Stephen Lawrence Inquiry*, Cm 4263, The Stationery Office, London.

Mason, G, 2005, "Can You Know a Stranger? Racist and Homophobic Harassment in the United Kingdom", 17 *Current Issues in Criminal Justice* 185.

New South Wales Attorney General's Department – Crime Prevention Division, 2003, *'You Shouldn't Have to Hide to be Safe': A Report on Homophobic Hostilities and Violence Against Gay Men and Lesbians in New South Wales*, Network of Government Agencies: Gay, Lesbian, Bisexual & Transgender Issues, Sydney.

Noelle, M, 2002, "The Ripple Effect of the Matthew Shepard Murder: Impact on the Assumptive Worlds of Members of the Targeted Group" 46 *American Behavioral Scientist* 27.

Nolan III, JJ, Bennett, S and Goldenberg, P, 2009, "Hate Crime Investigations", *Hate Crime: Responding to Hate Crime*, Vol 5, (Ed F Lawrence), Praeger, Westport, 71.

Parker, R, 2009, "Police Training", *Hate Crime: Responding to Hate Crime*, Vol 5, (Ed F Lawrence), Praeger, Westport, 51.

Perry, B, 2001, *In the Name of Hate: Understanding Hate Crimes*, Routledge, New York & London.

Phelan, S, 2001, *Sexual Strangers: Gays, Lesbians, and the Dilemmas of Citizenship*, Temple University Press, Philadelphia.

Stanko, E, Kielinger, V, Paterson, S, Richards, L, Crisp, D and Marsland, L, 2003, "Grounded Crime Prevention: Responding to and Understanding Hate Crime", *Crime Prevention: New Approaches*, (Eds H Kury and J Obergfell-Fuchs), Weisser Ring, Mainz, 5.

Taylor, SC and Gassner, L, 2010, "Stemming the Flow: Challenges for Policing Adult Sexual Assault with Regard to Attrition Rates and Under-Reporting of Sexual Offences" 11 *Police Practice and Research* 240.

True Vision, 2012, "Reporting Online". Viewed on 1 March 2012, <www.report-it.org.uk/your_police_force>.

Van Alphen, E, 1999, "Symptoms of Discursivity: Experience, Memory and Trauma", *Acts of Memory: Cultural Recall in the Present* (Eds M Bal, J Crewe and L Spitzer), University Press of New England, Hanover.

Von Schulthess, B, 1992, "Violence in the Streets: Anti-Lesbian Assault and Harassment in San Francisco", *Hate Crimes: Confronting Violence against Lesbians and Gay Men* (Eds, GM Herek and KT Berrill), SAGE Publications, Newbury Park, 65

Walters, M, 2006, "The Cronulla Riots: Exposing the Problem with Australia's Anti-Vilification Laws" 17 *Current Issues in Criminal Justice* 165.

Part Four

Vulnerable People and Custody

Chapter 11

Acquired Brain Injury and Vulnerability to the Criminal Justice System

James M Huntley

Bob was a thirty-four year old man arrested for sexual assault after "groping" a young woman at the supermarket check-out. He didn't say anything as the arresting officers brought him to the Police Station, where the Custody Manager read him the Caution and Summary of Part 9 of the (NSW) Law Enforcement (Powers and Responsibilities) Act (LEPRA). Bob said "Yes" when asked if he understood the charges. But no matter how hard the Senior Constable tried to impress upon him the seriousness of the issues, Bob's vacant grin remained.

Modern neuroscience is expanding upon our knowledge of the complexity of human brain function at unprecedented rates. Injuries can bring about the full range of change, from complete loss of function and need for support in breathing, to changes in understanding of social subtleties. Sizeable tissue damage in some regions of the brain may have comparatively little effect, or the most minor of damage indiscernible on scans may have catastrophic ramifications. In this chapter, I will briefly cover the incidence and prevalence of brain injury, and outline the common changes seen post-injury. I will look at some of the links made between focal brain lesions and violent or aggressive behaviour, and how that may lead to police attention following criminal-type behaviour. I will then suggest practical considerations police can take into account in managing this challenging population. The aim of this chapter is to provide information and understanding that may better inform police officers contending with a vulnerable person in their charge. Bob's story, introduced in the above vignette, is used throughout this chapter to illustrate some of the issues that arise for people with acquired brain injuries during their initial contact with the police chain of custody.

The Human Brain and its Vulnerability to Trauma

The brain functions, for the large part, consistently and reliably in an environment fraught with the dangers of trauma – from within in terms of the delicacy of arterial and venous supply, infections and disease processes, the balance of innumerable neurochemicals, hormones, and electrical impulses that all have their specific roles – and from such external factors as blunt impact, acceleration/deceleration forces, piercing objects, exposure to toxins, or cessation of oxygen supply. These vulnerabilities result in significant prevalence of people with brain trauma within our communities. While improvements in medical retrieval and procedures are saving lives, the consequences are that the person, their families, and the wider community deal with the sequelae of such trauma that would have been fatal not long ago.

There is general agreement in the Australian and international literature that Traumatic Brain Injury (TBI) is derived from externally inflicted trauma to the head, and excludes congenital or degenerative disorders and birth trauma , leading to significant impairment to physical, psychosocial, and/or cognitive functional abilities, and deterioration in functioning causing partial or total disability or psychosocial maladjustment. The broader term of Acquired Brain Injury (ABI) generally includes traumatic brain injury, in addition to aetiologies which involve medically acquired disease or pathology processes, as well as hypoxic or anoxic injuries such as follows cardiac arrests, near-drownings, or attempted hanging.

According to the U.S Center for Disease Control and Prevention (CDC), of all types of injury, those to the brain are most likely to result in death or permanent disability (CDC, 2011). Information published by the International Brain Injury Association (IBIA) states that ABI itself is the leading cause of death and disability worldwide, and TBI is the leading cause of seizure disorders (IBIA, 2011).

In Australia, the primary risk group for TBI is young males aged between 15 and 19. In this high-risk group, motor vehicle traffic accidents are the main cause of TBI. Falls are the main cause of TBI overall, most particularly in young children and the elderly. However, there are some grounds for optimism, with the incidence rate of new injuries each year declining by an average of 5% annually .

Change Following Brain Injury

Physical Mechanisms of Damage and Physical Changes

Closed head injury is the most common form of TBI, and is usually associated with transport accidents, assaults, or falls. The direct mechanical forces of acceleration and deceleration result in the soft tissue of the brain being thrown against the hard and craggy casing of the inside of the skull. The primary mechanisms of damage are the result of severance of neuronal connections, rupture of blood vessels and the death of nerve or glial cells, and consequent disruption of blood supply to other

Figure 1: The Lobes of the Human Brain

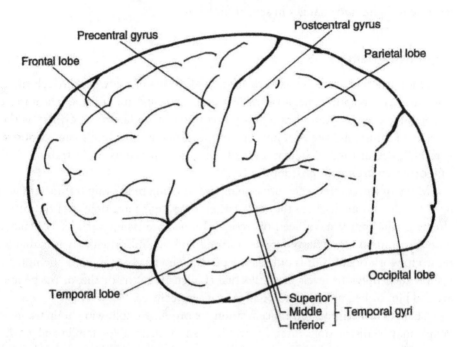

Source: Adapted from Darby and Walsh, 2005.

areas of the brain , which then die quite quickly. In high-speed impacts, shearing of brain tissue can occur between grey matter and the underlying white matter. This type of injury is widely believed to result in a worse outcome (Lezak et al, 2004).

Cerebro-circulatory changes are also implicated in the exacerbation of the effects of injury (Lishman, 1998), and are associated with poorer outcomes. Structural damage associated with vascular disorders of the brain may have an effect on a diverse range of functions. Nerve or glial cell function may be damaged by processes such as disruption of oxygen, glucose, or blood supply. Prolonged disruption to, or cessation of, these vital elements may cause cells in the affected area to die, resulting in irretrievable loss of function for that specific area (Kolb and Whishaw, 2009).

The physical effects of brain trauma are related to the size and location of damage. Small lesions in critical areas such as the brainstem or basal ganglia may result in profound deficits of basic functions, such as independent breathing, and temperature and appetite regulation. Large haematomas that are managed quickly, or contusions that are confined to one lobe, may not have consequences that are so severe. Some common physical effects of brain trauma include headaches, pain, and epilepsy; deficits of balance and gait; hemiplegia, or the loss or reduction of function of the upper, lower or both limbs on one side; changes in or loss of one or more of the five senses (sight, hearing, touch, taste and smell); hypersensitivity to noise or light; and changes in sexual function.

Cognitive Changes

Cognition is a wide-ranging term relating to all forms of knowing through functions such as perception, memory and learning, reasoning and judging. The impact of cognitive change after a brain injury is contingent on factors as diverse as the severity of injury, the site of injury or injuries, demographic and socio-economic variables, age at time of injury, level of education, previous brain trauma, and supportive environment post-injury.

Many of the common cognitive changes following mild brain trauma are not linked to the trauma itself, as they may become apparent some time after the initial effects of the injury have been overcome. Immediate issues such as headache, dizziness, and pain may have largely resolved and the individual may feel able to return to work or study. It is only as the person who has been injured attempts to resume their previous levels of intellectual challenge that he or she, or the people around him or her, notice that not all is as it was before.

Changes in attention and concentration are prominent following brain trauma. People may be distractible, often frustratingly so for themselves, family and work-mates. They may find it difficult to follow the plot of a movie or a book, and resort to only reading short articles in magazines that they can process more easily. They may have greater difficulty multi-tasking. They may also complain of not remembering the small day-to-day things that they took for granted previously. It is very common to hear the complaint that they never needed a diary or reminder notes before, but they rely on them more and more since injury, and this is a source of profound frustration. The person may complain of an ongoing sense of confusion and "muddle-headedness".

With more moderate to severe levels of brain trauma, cognitive problems become more pronounced. Temporal lobe impact may bring about problems with verbal or visual memory or both, and with difficulty learning new material. In some cases, the injured person may have trouble encoding or taking in information so as to remember it. In other cases, the information may be "in the system" but need prompts in order to be retrieved. Verbal material may be adequately processed and remembered, but spatial abilities or finding one's way may be significantly impaired. Changes in communication abilities may also be affected, with damage to specific language areas of the brain resulting in changed ability to understand what is said, or to express one's own speech, or both. Visual construction skills may be impacted by trauma to yet other areas of the brain, which can then lead to problems with sequencing tasks or putting together items. Indeed, specific deficits can be seen even in the severe range without other cognitive abilities necessarily being affected.

Cognitive fatigue is almost universal following brain injury of any severity and often severely impacts a person's daily routine. The most common person seen in brain injury rehabilitation units is the young male. The all-encompassing fatigue that they very typically experience is all the more mystifying to them and very often self-mislabelled as a sign of weakness. The fact that they must take rests through the day is often distressing to them and they will sometimes fight this need with all their remaining energy – of course, exhausting themselves all the more and exponentially affecting their cognitive decline, including reasoning and insight.

Executive function deficits are those often associated with involvement of the frontal lobes of the brain, and can have an especially devastating effect. This affects a range of functions such as problem-solving and concept formation (Baldo, Delis, Wilkins, and Shimamura, 2004), processing abstract information, initiating activity, switching between tasks , inhibiting previous responses in learning new rules, or generating words according to rule. A person's self-control, self-correction, or flexibility in thinking and responding laterally or "outside the square" can be affected. Planning and organising activities in correct sequence is a complex task that most people do to some degree every day, but can be severely disrupted following damage to executive areas of the brain. Moreover, the person may be able to verbalise the difficulties he or she is having, yet not be able to initiate an adaptive response to correct the problem. Impact on insight, or accurate self-monitoring and awareness, is particularly troublesome as it may well impede the rehabilitation effort or lead to an inability to adopt corrective behaviour in the face of a problem.

Behaviour and Personality Changes

Changes in behaviour arising from brain trauma can range from an amotivational or laissez faire-type presentation, to disinhibition, depression and anxiety, puerile actions and interactions, impulsivity, frustration intolerance and anger outbursts (Tranel, 2002; Goldberg, 2001; Gainotti, 2003; Ponsford, Olver, Ponsford and Nelms, 2003). The fatigue mentioned earlier often serves to heighten the behavioural problems, as the individual with a brain injury calls upon ever-depleting cognitive resources through the day to meet the challenges of tasks they took for granted prior to injury. Changes to sexual health and behaviour have also been noted following brain injury. Frustration at not being able to return to work, changed tolerance for, and professional advice against, alcohol consumption, suspension of their drivers licence and restricted freedom following injury, often leads young men to feel that they are being punished for events that were often not their fault. In many cases the individual with the brain injury is prescribed medication for the first time – sometimes quite substantial quantities of it – and compliance is either erratic because of memory issues, or objected to as "pill-popping". Even enjoyment of food can change with damage to specific areas affecting taste and leading to frustratingly boring meals.

However, the psychological effects of the profound trauma of brain injury also must be taken into account: the loss of independence, income, work, relationships, and lifestyle. The pain often associated with physical injury, as well as the stigma attached to brain injury, would affect most people to some degree. The cognitive challenges borne of organic injury mentioned above, as well as a profoundly changed environment, means that the person with a brain injury may indeed choose to withdraw from society and take comfort in whatever he or she can manage, what Prigatano calls "a safer milieu" (1987: 41). Research has also provided evidence that boredom is more frustrating and stressful than overwork (Damrad-Frye and Laird, 1989).

Mesulam (2003) described another frequently found type of behavioural disturbance, the frontal disinhibition syndrome, in which the person exhibits a lack of judgment, insight, and difficulty in learning from experiences, even very poignant ones. For example, an attractive young woman, who sustained very severe frontal injury in a fall, lost all ability to judge appropriate versus inappropriate sexual behaviour and was unremittingly exploited by malevolent men in the community. Fights broke out at her apartment between men trying to "claim" her, to which police constantly attended. Her distraught parents contacted police on numerous occasions to help extricate their daughter from horrendously abusive situations. Initially, police mislabelled the nature of her behaviour, but soon became aware of the vulnerability of the young woman, and became a key element in enhancing her security as much as they were able.

Prefrontal cortex areas are thought to be responsible for emotions around complex moral and social nuance behaviour. Damage to these, and predominantly orbital and medial aspects of the frontal lobes bilaterally, result in emotional shallowness and stimulus-bound emotional outbursts. This is the type of behaviour that finds young people with such injury in trouble at social events, thereby accentuating the risk of at least increased isolation as people give him or her a wide berth, or at worst, further injury through assault.

Epilepsy following brain trauma can be a major contributor to behavioural disturbance (Pincus and Tucker, 2003). Some of the common changes associated with seizures in the temporal lobes may appear as sudden-onset irrational, agitated or combative behaviour typical of that which draws police attention. This behaviour can last from seconds to minutes, usually terminating as rapidly as it began, with no recollection of the event by the person experiencing the seizure. It may then result in confusion at the negative responses from those who have been subject to or witnessed the event. The person who develops a seizure disorder as a result of traumatic brain injury may experience additional distress in their fear of further seizures, limitations on activities such as driving and sport, and emotional reactions to the stigma of epilepsy, which may in turn significantly impact on quality of life. Moreover, the risk of seizure is prevalent even years after TBI (Lishman, 1997), with up to 20% of people suffering their first seizure four years post-injury. These late-onset seizures are more likely to occur more frequently and have a poorer chance of resolution.

Pre-existing or co-existing psychiatric disturbances also need to be taken into account in behavioural changes following brain injury (Cantagallo and Dimarco, 2002; Evans et al, 2005; Anson and Ponsford, 2006; Draper, Ponsford and Schonberger, 2007) with symptoms of mild ABI being potentially exacerbated by a pre-existing psychological disorder, increased stress, and higher rates of anxiety and depression symptoms after mild ABI (although this could also be organically mediated). These authors concluded that brain injury is a risk factor for subsequent psychiatric disabilities, and highlighted the need for proactive psychiatric assessment and interventions.

> Bob was questioned about his medical history, including medication, as standard procedure during custody processing. He told of sustaining severe brain injury in a 60-metre cliff-fall fourteen years prior. The custody manager suggested he contact a supportive person. His father then attended the police station and provided further history of injury, hospitalisation, rehabilitation, and finally community integration. "When he arrived home after months in hospital units around the State, everyone was overjoyed! But he wasn't the same as before".

Social Adjustment and Isolation

The changes in social circumstances for the injured person have been described by numerous authors (see, for example, Draper et al, 2007; Huntley and Perlesz, 2008). Given the extent of cognitive and behavioural changes described earlier, one can see how these factors would negatively influence social adjustment, ability to return to work, social contact, and participation in leisure activities. Most of the research in this area describes how the person with a brain injury very often experiences a significant decline in social attachments , as well as reduced employment prospects, both of which preface an ever-greater reliance on family for support.

Many authors have identified the isolation that sets in for those people who have suffered a brain injury and their family members (Winstanley et al, 2006; Farmer, Clark, and Sherman, 2003). The cognitive demands of social interaction can impede effective communication with others. Such problems may include difficulty processing the language being spoken and needing repetition from those speaking to them, poor memory for what had been said, problem-solving difficulties, and understanding nuance and communication subtleties. As mentioned, behavioural changes also make for difficult social interaction leading to social withdrawal (Wood, 2005). Problems with behaviour regulation and control, anger management, problems with initiation (which is often labelled as laziness or lack of motivation), paranoid or delusional thinking, along with psychological effects of anxiety and depression, compounded by lack of insight, can all lead to friends and relatives finding it too difficult to manage the demands of social interaction with the person who has been injured.

> Bob had been a very popular young man in his small rural community. His passion was cricket, where he had achieved prowess at the State level. He was being groomed for top-level representation in the sport. Following injury, he could no longer play cricket and his team-mates and friends stopped visiting after a while. His girlfriend left him. He could not manage his own finances as he was too impulsive with his spending. This impulsivity drew the attention of unsavoury characters in the community who exploited his vulnerability until there was nothing left of his savings. He remained living with his father who quit his job to care for him. His father managed the day-to-day spending, organised routines, and tried endless strategies to involve his son in community activities with people his own age. Invariably though, the only people Bob really socialised with were his father's friends.

The Link between Brain Trauma and Criminal Activity

In the above, we have seen how the physical, cognitive, psychological, and social effects of brain trauma can change behaviour. I now turn to the evidence of the direct impact of brain trauma to behaviour that lends itself to police attention. There is a significant body of research that examines the effects of brain trauma and subsequent violent behaviour.

In an interesting birth cohort study conducted in northern Finland, almost 11,000 people were followed up prospectively to the age of 31 (Timonen et al, 2002). They found that traumatic brain injury (TBI) during childhood and early adolescence substantially elevated the risk of criminal offenses being committed, with age of onset of criminal behaviour being earlier in those who sustained TBI before aged 12. In a Spanish study, Leon-Carrion and Ramos (2003) found that sustaining a brain injury greatly accentuates the possibility of criminal or violent behaviour in young people who already have a history of learning disability or school behavioural problems. It is compounded again in those whose brain injury or injuries go untreated, which is the case particularly for those who sustain mild TBI, or cumulative TBI, or in poorer socioeconomic circumstances, where they may not seek medical attention post-injury.

Moreover, the effects of brain injury are compounding. The risk of second brain injury exacerbating the effects of the initial injury are threefold; the risk of yet further brain injury increases exponentially after that, compounded by the effects mentioned above of ever-increasing psychological isolation, social vulnerability, dependence on others, abuse of alcohol and other drugs, deteriorating ability to manage cognitive challenge, and reactive psychological adjustment issues surrounding brain injury and criminal background.

In an American study, Turkstra, Jones and Toler (2003), examined the risk of domestic violence and brain injury, and speculated on TBI being just one factor in a complex interaction between genetic predisposition to violent behaviour, emotional stress, poverty, substance abuse, and child abuse. They felt that TBI status alone was insufficient to manifest as violent and aggressive behaviour. Perhaps though, more severe TBI may impair the ability to inhibit violent impulses. A joint Australian and New Zealand study (Marsh and Martinovich, 2006) discussed the impact of executive dysfunction on domestic violence, with damage to prefrontal regions of the brain reducing the ability to manage situations that are stressful, frustrating, or provocative. They found higher prevalence of TBI, particularly severe TBI, in partner-abusive men than in the general population. This is in keeping with the findings of other researchers who have examined criminal or violent behaviour following focal brain lesions. In a more recent review, Batts (2009) outlined research demonstrating that damage to the ventromedial area of the frontal lobes significantly increased the risk of aggression and violence (Brower and Price, 2001). Pillman, Rohde et al, (1999) found compromised behavioural skills in people with left hemisphere focal injury affecting language processing competency and the ability of "inner speech" to ameliorate behaviour, resorting to developmentally immature response strategies.

> As much as Bob tried, his tactics for meeting people and making friends only achieved at best mockery, at worst scorn and abject hostility. When he visited the pub hoping to strike up camaraderie, soda in hand, he was either plied with alcohol unwittingly for someone's entertainment, or openly rejected, sometimes violently. He couldn't understand why a "funny, good-looking bloke" should be without a girlfriend, so he particularly focused on women. On an ordinary afternoon he strove to prove his friendliness and approachability to a young woman in the supermarket line ahead of him by urging her ahead of him. Somehow it went terribly wrong.

The Prevalence of Brain Trauma in Prison Populations

The unfortunate end-point for those surviving all the effects of brain trauma described so far is sometimes imprisonment. There is little doubt that people with brain injury, and other vulnerabilities described in this volume, are over-represented in the prison statistics. Reported prevalence of people with history of brain trauma in prison populations range from 23 per cent in one Canadian study (Colantonio et al, 2007) to about 80 percent in a series of Australian studies (Schofield et al, 2006a; Schofield et al, 2006b); differences between these results stem from the criteria adopted for inclusion in studies. Perron and Howard (2008) found that nearly one in five incarcerated youths reported a lifetime TBI. Their respondents were more likely to be male, with a psychiatric diagnosis, be the victim of criminal behaviour themselves, have substance abuse problems, profess an external locus of control, and report lifetime suicidality.

In a recent study of self-reported brain injury in juvenile justice system in the UK, Williams et al, (2010) found a high level of multiple mild TBIs and a high number of moderate to severe injuries, with a greater incidence of high velocity mechanisms, such as violence. They felt that offenders with TBI may therefore have a neurogenic basis for behavioural problems, with neuropsychological deficits in executive function and attention, potentially leading to irritability and disinhibited behaviour. They further postulated that repeat offending may suggest that neuro-cognitive deficits limit the ability to change behaviour within custodial systems. Moreover, the risk of further brain injury while incarcerated is significantly greater, with assault in prison being the second most prominent medical condition reported to prison authorities.

There is universal agreement among the authors cited, and others (for example, Chan, Hudson and Parmenter, 2004) about the need to advocate for consideration of neuropsychological factors in better understanding the roots of violent behaviour, and in devising effective strategies to manage it in the criminal justice system. In a comprehensive review of people with ABI in the criminal justice system, Nick Rushworth of Brain Injury Australia, an advocacy group for people with ABI, recommended that criminal justice system personnel undergo a nationally consistent curriculum of training in ABI in order to provide "more effective responses from the criminal justice system to people with disability who have complex needs or heightened vulnerabilities" (Rushworth, 2010: 3).

Some Practical Steps in Police Intervention

I have detailed the effects of changes in physical, cognitive, psychological and psychosocial abilities following brain injury as an indication that brain injury affects all of these domains to some extent. For many people, and their families, these changes will prove all-encompassing, and life-altering. Police officers in the field will rarely be in a position to alter the course of these changes, and it is not the intention of this all-too-brief chapter to pretend otherwise. At the same time though, having some level of understanding of these concepts can make it easier to deal with circumstances in which officers and vulnerable persons find themselves. When witnessing, or dealing with, aberrant behaviour, it is quite natural for someone to ask "Why is this person behaving like that?". It is hoped that this chapter may go a little way towards providing a better understanding of that "why".

Notwithstanding the constraints imposed by specific Police Standard Operating Procedures, the following practical considerations may assist. Police in NSW, and elsewhere, have access to automated data base systems that have the potential to record and subsequently alert officers to potential risks. In NSW, the Computerised Operating Policing Systems (COPS) is used by officers to record crime information, intelligence and legal proceedings. Using COPS, the radio operator can advise the officer that the person in front of them has issues that they should be aware of. This is used routinely for people with intellectual disability, but it is not widely utilised for people with ABI. Examples of warnings that may be useful include "Acquired Brain Injury: May require slow, short sentences, repeated often, to understand"; or "Acquired Brain Injury: May say inappropriate verbal responses". There are no doubt many other warning phrases that may be useful for specific people. This alerts the officer to acknowledge the cognitive or behavioural challenges that may impact on their responses to police.

Table 1: Common Problems and Solutions

ISSUE	PROBLEM	SOLUTION
Cognitive Issues	The vulnerable person is likely to have substantial difficulty processing or remembering what is being said to him or her. This is all the more so in stressful circumstances such as an arrest	He or she will need constant repetition of information in order to process it. This will need to be broken down into simple one- or two-sentence chunks, repeated often, that will be integrated slowly. Alternatively, it can help to write the salient points down in simple block-sentences and post it where they can see it. This can help save time and stress for the officers in not having to constantly repeat information
	Inflexibility of thinking and difficulty solving problems can lead to "broken record"-type behaviour	In a calm, steady tone, talk the person through changes in routine. Try to explain things in basic terms, using familiar language
Behavioural Issues	Agitated inappropriate verbal outbursts	Ignore inappropriate behaviour where possible. Any response may act as a "reward". When calmer, let them know that you are willing to engage when they are acting in an appropriate manner. People will usually respond better to a non-confrontational, calm, minimalist approach. Remember, the officer's need to get a point across is not enhanced by yelling at the individual. It may seem initially counter-intuitive to adopt these approaches in terms of saving time, but that is indeed likely to be the case
Psychological Issues	Contacting a support person can provide further information, as well as help calm an agitated vulnerable person. Taking a medical history is often a SOP in many police jurisdictions. This may identify an agency such as a brain injury unit or mental health program involved in the person's care, which can provide information and support.	

Conclusion

Batts (2009) and others warn against being overly simplistic in linking brain lesions to violence and criminal behaviour. They argue that "we must resist the urge to be entirely deterministic" in applying moral reasoning to any one area of the brain (2009: 270). There are many people with similar lesions in similar areas who do not engage in criminal or violent behaviour. Rather, it seems reasonable to suggest that brain trauma in specific areas of the brain may predispose an individual to the greater risk of problematic behaviour, taking into account a multitude of factors including, but not necessarily limited to:

- pre-injury disposition,
- alcohol or illicit substance intake,
- environmental or adjustment-related stress,
- family dynamics and level of support,
- psychosocial demographics
- a background of poor education,
- engagement in meaningful activity.

Nonetheless, an appreciation of the cognitive, behavioural, psychological, and psychosocial impact of brain trauma can, and should, be part of a comprehensive assessment in police procedures. This can make it easier for police to understand the basis for aberrant behaviour, and lead to more effective management of this vulnerable population.

> The Custody Manager decided that it would not be in the public interest to charge Bob with the offence, and that he would be at greater risk in custody. Bob was released into the care of his father, who then contacted the Brain Injury Rehabilitation Unit. A review of behaviour was arranged at the inpatient unit, and liaison made with community agencies in his own town. No one was under the illusion that this was a panacea, but few were under the illusion that Bob would be better managed in custody. Mindful of the young woman who was the victim of the assault, Bob's father undertook to provide closer supervision of Bob's whereabouts, and accompany him to areas of potential risk.

References

Anson, K and Ponsford, J, 2006, "Evaluation of a coping skills group following traumatic brain injury" 20 *Brain Injury* 167.

Baldo, JV, Delis, DC, Wilkins, DP and Shimamura, AP, 2004, "Is it bigger than a breadbox? Performance of patients with prefrontal lesions on a new executive function test" 19 *Archives of Clinical Neuropsychology* 407.

Batts, S, 2009, "Brain lesions and their implications in criminal responsibility" 27 *Behavioral Sciences and the Law* 261.

Brower, MC and Price, BH, 2001, "Neuropsychiatry of Frontal Lobe Dysfunction in Violent and Criminal Behaviour: A Critical Review" 71 *Journal of Neurology, Neurosurgery and Psychiatry* 720.

Cantagallo, A and Dimarco, F, 2002, "Prevalence of neuropsychiatric disorders in traumatic brain injury patients" 38 *Europa Medicophysica* 167.

Chan, J, Hudson, C and Parmenter, T, 2004, "An Exploratory Study of Crime and Brain Injury: Implications for Mental Health Management" 3 *Australian e-Journal for the Advancement of Mental Health* 1.

Colantonio, A, Stamenova, V, Abramowitz,C, Clarke, D and Christensen, B, 2007, "Brain Injury in a Forensic Psychiatry Population" 21 *Brain Injury* 1353.

Damrad-Frye, R and Laird, JD, 1989, "The Experience of Boredom: The Role of the Self-perception of Attention" 57 *Journal of Personality and Social Psychology* 315.

Darby, D and Walsh, K, 2005, *Walsh's Neuropsychology: A Clinical Approach*, Elsevier, London.

Draper, K, Ponsford, J and Schonberger, M, 2007, "Psychosocial and emotional outcomes 10 years following traumatic brain injury" 22 *Journal of Head Trauma Rehabilitation* 278.

Evans, CC, Sherer, M, Nick, TG, Nakase-Richardson, R and Yablon, SA, 2005, "Early Impaired Self-awareness, Depresison, and Subjective Well-being Following Traumatic Brain Injury" 20 *Journal of Head Trauma Rehabilitation* 488.

Farmer, JE, Clark, MJ and Sherman, AK, 2003, "Rural Versus Urban Social Support Seeking as a Moderating Variable in Traumatic Brain Injury Outcome" 18 *Journal of Head Trauma Rehabilitation* 116.

Fortune, N and Wen, X, 1999, *The Definition, Incidence, and Prevalence of Acquired Brain Injury in Australia*, AIHW, Canberra.

Gainotti, G, 2003, "Emotional Disorders in Relation to Unilateral Brain Damage", *Behavioural Neurology and Neuropsychology* (Eds, TE Feinberg and MJ Farah), McGraw Hill, New York.

Huntley, J and Perlesz, A, 2008, "Rurability: Community Support for Rural Families Managing Acquired Brain Injury" 16 *Australian Journal of Rural Health* 319.

International Brain Injury Organisation (IBIO), 2011, *Brain Injury Facts*. Viewed on 12 January 2012, <www.internationalbrain.org/?q=Brain-Injury-Facts>.

Kolb, B and Whishaw, IQ, 2009, *Fundamentals of Human Neuropsychology*, 6th ed, Freeman, New York.

Langlois, JA, Rutland-Brown, W and Wald, MM, 2006, "The Epidemiology and Impact of Traumatic Brain Injury: A Brief Overview" 21 *Journal of Head Trauma Rehabilitation* 375.

Lezak, MD, Howieson, DB and Loring, DW, 2004, *Neuropsychological Assessment*, Oxford University Press, New York.

Lishman, WA, 1998, *Organic Psychiatry*, 3rd ed, Blackwell Scientific, Oxford, UK.

Marion, DW, 1996, "Pathophysiology and Initial Neurosurgical Care: Future Directions", *Medical Rehabilitation of Traumatic Brain Injury* (Eds, LJ Horn and ND Zasler), Hanley and Belfus, Pennsylvania, USA.

Marsh, NV and Martinovich, WM, 2006, "Executive Dysfunction and Domestic Violence" 20 *Brain Injury* 61.

Mesulam, M-M, 2003, "Some Anatomic Principles Related to Behavioural Neurology and Neuropsychology", *Behavioural Neurology and Neuropsychology* (Eds, TE Feinberg and MJ Farah), McGraw Hill, New York.

O'Connor, P, 2002, "Hospitalisation Due to Traumatic Brain Injury (TBI), Australia 1997-8", *Injury Research and Statistics Series*, Australian Institute of Health and Welfare, Adelaide.

Perron, BE and Howard, MO, 2008, "Prevalence and Correlates of Traumatic Brain Injury among Delinquent Youths" 18 *Criminal Behaviour and Mental Health* 243.

Pillman, F, Rohde, A, Ullrich, S, Draba, S, Sannemuller, U and Marneros, A, 1999, "Violence, Criminal Behaviour and the EEG: Significance of Left Hemispheric Focal Abnormalities" 11 *Journal of Neuropsychiatry and Clinical Neurosciences* 454.

Pincus, JH and Tucker, GJ, 2003, *Behavioral Neurology*, 4th ed, Oxford University Press, New York.

Ponsford, JL, Olver, JH and Curran, C, 1995, "A Profile of Outcome: 2 Years after Traumatic Brain Injury" 9 *Brain Injury* 1.

Ponsford, J, Oliver, J, Ponsford, M and Nelms, R, 2003, "Long-term Adjustment of Families Following Traumatic Brain Injury where Comprehensive Rehabilitation has been Provided" 17 *Brain Injury* 453.

Prigatano, GP, 1987, *Neuropsychological Rehabilitation after Brain Injury*, John Hopkins, Baltimore.

Rauch, RJ and Ferry, SM, 2001, "Social Networks as Support Interventions Following Traumatic Brain Injury" 16 *Neurorehabilitation* 11.

Rushworth, N, 2011, *Out of Sight, Out of Mind: People with an Acquired Brain Injury and the Criminal Justice System*, Brain Injury Australia, Sydney.

Schofield, PW, Butler, TG, Hollis, SJ, Smith, NE, Lee, SJ and Kelso, WM, 2006a, "Neuropsychiatric Correlates of Traumatic Brain Injury (TBI) among Australian Prison Entrants" 20 *Brain Injury* 1409.

Schofield, PW, Butler, TG, Hollis, SJ, Smith, NE, Lee, SJ and Kelso, WM, 2006b, "Traumatic Brain Injury among Australian Prisoners: Rates, Recurrence and Sequelae" 20 *Brain Injury* 499.

Strettles, B, Bush, M, Simpson, G and Gillett, L, 2005, *Accommodation in New South Wales for Adults with High Care Needs after Traumatic Brain Injury*, Motor Accidents Authority, Sydney.

Timonen, M, Miettunen, J, Hakko, H, Zitting, P, Veijola, J, von Wendt, L and Rasanen, P, 2002, "The Association of Preceding Traumatic Brain Injury with Mental Disorders, Alcoholism and Criminality: The Northern Finland 1966 Birth Cohort Study" 113 *Psychiatry Research* 217.

Tranel, D, 2002, "Emotion, Decision Making, and the Ventromedial Prefrontal Cortex", *Principles of Frontal Lobe Function* (Eds, DT Stuss and RT Knight), Oxford University Press, New York.

Turkstra, L, Jones, D and Toler, H, 2003, "Brain Injury and Violent Crime" 17 *Brain Injury* 39.

US Center for Disease Control and Prevention, 2011, *Injury Prevention and Control: Traumatic Brain Injury*. Viewed on 12 January 2012, <www.cdc.gov/ncipc/tbi/TBI.htm>.

Von Cramon, DY and Matthes-von Cramon, G, 1994, "Frontal Lobe Dysfunctions in Patients: Therapeutical Approaches", *Cognitive Rehabilitation in Perspective* (Eds, RL Wood and I Fussey), Lawrence Erlbaum, Hove, UK.

Williams, WH, Cordan, G, Mewse, AJ, Tonks, J and Burgess, CNW, 2010, "Self-Reported Traumatic Brain Injury in Male Young Offenders: A Risk Factor for Re-offending, Poor Mental Health and Violence?" 20 *Neuropsychological Rehabilitation* 801.

Winstanley, J, Simpson, G, Tate, R and Myles, B, 2006, "Early Indicators and Contributors to Psychological Distress in Relatives during Rehabilitation Following Severe Traumatic Brain Injury" 21 *Journal of Head Trauma Rehabilitation* 453.

Wood, RL, 2005, "Waking up Next to a Stranger" 18 *The Psychologist* 138.

World Health Organization (WHO), 2005, *World Health Assembly Commits to Strengthen Rehabilitation Services for People with Disabilities*, World Health Organization, Geneva, Switzerland.

Chapter 12

Twenty Years On: Indigenous Deaths in Police Custody and Lessons From the Frontline

Lorana Bartels

The Royal Commission into Aboriginal Deaths in Custody (RCIADIC) was established in 1987 in response to concern over the number of deaths of Aboriginal and Torres Strait Islander (ATSI) people in custody[1] and is "widely acknowledged as the most thorough legal inquiry ever conducted into the lives of Indigenous Australians" (Marchetti, 2005: 104). The Commission examined the circumstances in which 99 Indigenous people died in custody between 1 January 1980 and 31 May 1989. The majority of these deaths (63 of these deaths) occurred in police custody and involved hanging in the first few hours of custody. Governments were required to report on the RCIADIC recommendations until 1997 (Allison and Cunneen, 2010) and committed to a number of reforms following the *Indigenous and Ministerial Summits on Deaths in Custody* in 1997 (Cunneen, 2007c). Now, 20 years after the RCIADIC, it is timely to review the ongoing police response to the recommendations.

Indigenous Australians continue to be arrested and imprisoned at high rates. In spite of comprising only 2.3 per cent of the total Australian population, Indigenous people accounted for 33 per cent of people involved in police custody incidents in 2007, and were 22 times more likely to be arrested or detained by police than non-Indigenous people (Williams et al, forthcoming, cited in Lyneham, Joudo Larsen and Beacroft, 2010). The national average daily Indigenous imprisonment rate in the March 2012 quarter was 2,247 per 100,000, compared with 166 prisoners for the general adult population, while the age-standardised Indigenous imprisonment rate was 14 times higher than the non-Indigenous rate (Australian Bureau of Statistics (ABS), 2012; see also Henning, in this collection, Ch 14).

This chapter outlines the key findings of the RCIADIC report relevant to policing operations. The chapter then presents the most recent data available on Indigenous deaths in police custody and, on the basis of publicly available information, considers some of the steps state and territory police have taken to implement the RCIADIC recommendations. Due to space constraints, the specific needs of

Indigenous women and young people are not discussed in detail, but these clearly remain issues of particular concern. In addition, the chapter does not consider in any depth the issues which may arise from some apparently positive initiatives, for example, the challenges associated with Indigenous police liaison officers, including the difficulties attracting candidates, inadequate training and conflicts inherent in the role (see Cunneen, 2007a; McRae and Nettheim, 2009; Office of Police Integrity (OPI), 2011).

Key Findings from the RCIADIC Relevant to Police

In its *National Report*, the RCIADIC (1991) did not find any instances of unlawful, deliberate killing of Indigenous people by police officers, but nevertheless found there was a poor understanding of police accountability for the care of prisoners, coupled with a lack of understanding of the standard of care required and an absence of commitment to care in general. Criticisms of the standard of care were particularly prominent in the context of police, rather than prison, cells. The Commission identified numerous failings and called for improvements in the recruitment, training and placement of police officers. In addition, as inadequacies tended not to be revealed or rectified as a result of incomplete police investigations, the need to make inquiries more independent and transparent was identified.

In its examination of why Indigenous people were placed in custody, the RCIADIC found that they were much more likely than non-Indigenous people to be placed in custody because of public intoxication (57 v 27 per cent) and Cunneen (2008: 7) has suggested that "[p]ublic order offences and police powers to intervene in public places remain among the most contentious issues". The RCIADIC also considered historic colonial relations between Indigenous people and police, which continues to be a subject of ongoing debate in the academic literature (see Behrendt, Cunneen and Libesman, 2009; Cunneen, 2007b; Keenan, 2009; McRae and Nettheim, 2009). The RCIADIC found that "far too much police intervention in the lives of Aboriginal people throughout Australia has been arbitrary, discriminatory, racist and violent" (1991: Vol 2: 13.2.3). This background was found to have resulted in significant mistrust between police and Indigenous people, although there were some examples of positive initiatives to improve relations, including the establishment of community patrols and community justice panels and the appointment of Indigenous liaison officers.

In total, the RCIADIC made 339 recommendations, including the following needs most relevant to police: independent investigation of deaths in custody; improved data on police detainees; measures to reduce racism and violence by police officers; alternatives to police detention for intoxication; reduced use of arrest for minor offences and the development of policies and programs relating to Indigenous people and recruitment of Indigenous police officers.

Recent Data on Indigenous Deaths in Police Custody

As a result of the RCIADIC recommendations, the Australian Institute of Criminology (AIC) publishes annual data on two forms of deaths in custody: prison custody and "police custody and custody-related operations". Unfortunately, police custody death rates are not available, due to a lack of reliable data for the total number of people placed into police custody each year.

The most recent report (Lyneham, Joudo Larsen and Beacroft, 2010) covered deaths for 1980-2008 and found that, as was the case at the time of the RCIADIC, Indigenous people were no more likely to die in custody than non-Indigenous people, but remained significantly overrepresented throughout the criminal justice system. Notwithstanding this, Indigenous deaths in custody had in fact been decreasing for the past decade. In 2007 and 2008, there were four Indigenous deaths in police custody, the second-lowest number on record. Given there were five such deaths in 1990 and 1991, and the Indigenous population is estimated to have increased by approximately 71 per cent between 1991 and 2006 (ABS, 2003, 2010), these findings are cause for some cautious optimism. The data also indicated that Indigenous deaths accounted for one in eight deaths in police custody in 2008, the lowest rate since 2001, and down from one in three in 2005.

Progress and Future Directions of Policing

This section examines the extent to which police agencies around Australia appear to have implemented the RCIADIC recommendations.[2] In 2001, for the tenth anniversary of the RCIADIC, the *Indigenous Law Bulletin* (ILB) published progress reports on each state and territory, generally prepared by representatives of Indigenous justice organisations. In 2007, the ILB contacted police forces in Australia, seeking to determine how they had responded to the RCIADIC recommendations. The findings from this review (Houston, 2007) were less than encouraging: of the eight services contacted, only six responded, and of these, only two provided substantive responses. Although it cannot be inferred that the other police agencies had not, at that stage, taken any steps to implement the RCIADIC recommendations, it is somewhat telling that they were unable or unwilling to provide evidence of such measures to the ILB.

The following section draws on the 2001 and 2007 ILB reports and other commentary, supplemented by information from each state and territory police agency's most recent annual report and website, as well as relevant documents referred to in those sources. It is not suggested that these sources represent the entirety of each jurisdiction's policing response to the RCIADIC, nor that the annual reports present police actions in an impartial light (Allison and Cunneen, 2010), but this approach nevertheless provides a snapshot of how police agencies represent themselves publicly in relation to Indigenous issues. For the purposes of brevity, examples of community crime prevention activities, such as sporting events, are not described here, although they may help improve relations between police and Indigenous people.

New South Wales

In 2001, NSW was reported to have "successfully implemented a number of recommendations of the Royal Commission that relate to the upgrading of police cells" but "[o]ver-policing [was] still a very real issue, particularly in small country towns with high Aboriginal populations" (Kelly, 2001: 8), with no improvement in the attitudes among police officers. In addition, Kelly considered that there had not been any coordinated effort by the NSW Government to address the core RCIADIC recommendations.

In 2000, the NSW Aboriginal Justice Advisory Council (NSWAJAC) released *RCIADIC: Review of NSW Government Implementation of Recommendations*, in which it found that a number of policing recommendations had not been implemented (NSWAJAC, 2000). In 2003, the NSWAJAC released the *NSW Aboriginal Justice Plan: Beyond Justice 2004-2014* (NSW AJA), which included a number of items relevant to police, such as establishing "responsive policing that meet[s] Aboriginal community's crime concerns" (NSWAJAC 2003: 20).

NSW was one of the two jurisdictions which provided a response to the 2007 ILB request, in which it suggested significant steps had been taken. Specifically, the Police Commissioner had endorsed the *Aboriginal Strategic Direction (ASD) 2007-2011*, which was underpinned by the premise that "Aboriginal people know their problems and want to be part of the solution" (Houston, 2007: 22). The ASD "makes clear links to RCIADIC and recognises the importance of this historical document" (Houston, 2007: 23) and, by 2007, the NSW Police Force (NSWPF) had reportedly implemented 82 RCIADIC recommendations.

The ASD is a lengthy document (currently available on the NSWPF website) in which the NSWPF has committed to "continu[ing] to link our work to and implement[ing] the Recommendations from the Royal Commission into Aboriginal Deaths in Custody (RCIADIC)" (NSWPF, 2007: 24). The ASD includes seven objectives, such as reducing overrepresentation of Aboriginal people in the criminal justice system. These objectives are linked to specific RCIADIC recommendations and aspects of the NSW AJA and are accompanied by strategies (for example, "Develop and implement a model of Aboriginal community policing"), actions ("Establish pilot in Aboriginal community"), accountability, indicators ("Reduction in summary offences by 10% during trial period") and timeframes ("Review and evaluation by March 2010"). The ASD also sets out the principles underpinning the

ASD, details of who bears responsibility for implementing the ASD and the means of measuring performance, including specific quarterly reporting requirements.

In the ASD, the NSWAJAC commended NSWPF for "producing a focused blueprint which guides the way in which Police will deliver their services to Aboriginal people", noting that this was:

> the first time that an organisation as large as NSW Police Force has included links to the Royal Commission into Aboriginal Deaths in Custody (RCIADIC) indicating the purpose for the implementation of the strategy outlined, providing Police with the historical reasons to pursue the goals of the ASD (NSWPF, 2007: 9)

Finally, it should be noted that the NSWPF *Aboriginal Issues* webpage includes a number of brochures on Indigenous issues, a description of Aboriginal community patrols and a link to the (regrettably now defunct) NSWAJAC. The latest NSWPF annual report also indicated that just under 2 per cent of the probationary constables appointed in 2010-11 were Indigenous, with a strategy in place for increasing Indigenous representation to 4 per cent.

In spite of the difficult circumstances surrounding and following the 2004 death of TJ Hickey (see Cunneen, 2006), overall, it would appear that the NSWPF has come some considerable way in seeking to act on the RCIADIC recommendations. A 2005 review by the NSW Ombudsman indicated that the NSWPF had "shown a commitment to delivering practical solutions to the seemingly intractable problems" (NSW Ombudsman, 2005: 28). It would now be of benefit to see independent evaluation of any further developments.

Victoria

The 2001 ILB report on Victoria was positive, heralding as a "landmark" (Bitsis, 2001: 13) the 2000 Aboriginal Justice Agreement. In 2003, Victoria Police (VicPol) developed the *Aboriginal Strategic Plan 2003-2008*, which referenced the RCIADIC and set out 10 goals and seven key objectives. A recent review of the plan by the OPI found that although some of its strategies had had an adverse impact, there had "been significant improvements in some areas" (2011: 13).

In 2005, the *Victorian Implementation Review of the Recommendations from the Royal Commission into Aboriginal Deaths in Custody* (Victorian Department of Justice, 2005) was finalised, which has been described as a "model example of the method by which the Recommendations of the RCIADIC should be assessed" (Edney, 2006: 19), as well as the Government's response to the review, which in turn led to the development of the *Victorian Aboriginal Justice Agreement Phase 2* (VAJA2). The VAJA2 explicitly referred to the RCIADIC and includes strategies such as "[i]ncreas[ing] the rate at which Koories are diverted from more serious contact with Victoria Police" (Victorian Department of Justice, 2006: 32).

It was against this background that VicPol indicated in 2007 that "RCIADIC is the key driver for most of our activities" (Houston, 2007: 23), adding that it had

> prepared an Action Report [the *Aboriginal Strategic Plan 2003-2008*] against the Victorian Review where we have identified the policies, procedures and activities that directly link to the RCIADIC and Review recommendations.

VicPol also indicated that it had implemented the *Koori Action Plan*, which was directly linked to VAJA2 and "enables us to measure our performance against the activities of the [V]AJA2 directed at police". The plan was overseen by a reference group which included Indigenous representatives and was reviewed quarterly. In addition, VicPol had developed a *Reconciliation Action Plan*, which included details of programs to improve justice outcomes for Indigenous people. Finally, VicPol asserted that it "engage[d] in a highly transparent process in regard to Aboriginal justice issues which has been and remains the catalyst for a great deal of change within the organisation" (Houston, 2007: 23).

Currently, the VicPol website includes information on the Aboriginal Advisory Unit, as well as details of Aboriginal Community Justice Panels (ACJPs) operating in regional Victoria (VicPol, 2011a). According to the 2010-11 VicPol annual report, the evaluation of the Aboriginal Community Liaison Officer (ACLO) program has found that it is "creating a mutual trust and respect created between police and the Aboriginal community that is directly linked to the program" (VicPol, 2011b: 42). Other initiatives included cultural awareness training programs delivered to police in partnership with local Aboriginal communities, appointment of an Indigenous officer to oversee the progress of statewide cultural awareness training, community awareness campaigns, improving police responses to family violence in Indigenous communities and supporting Indigenous staff, as well as discussion of the role of ACJPs. Although the recent OPI report (2011) referred to above casts doubt on the adequacy of some of these initiatives, Victoria remains something of a leader, albeit in a poor field, in responding to the RCIADIC recommendations.

Queensland

In 1994, the Queensland Government's response to some of the RCIADIC recommendations was described as "empty words" (Lavery, 1994: 11). By 2001, the situation was more positive, with the ILB report commenting that the Queensland Aboriginal and Torres Strait Islander Justice Agreement (QATSIJA) aimed to "have a demonstrated continuing reduction by 50% of Aboriginal and Torres Strait Islander peoples coming into contact with the Queensland criminal justice system and to achieve at least parity with the non-Indigenous rate by the year 2011" (Neliman, 2001: 10). Unlike most jurisdictions, the QATSIJA was independently reviewed (Cunneen, Collings and Ralph, 2005); the review found progress toward meeting the aims of the QATSIJA, although there was a need to resource and expand initiatives. In particular, although the Queensland Police Service (QPS) had introduced some innovative programs, one of the main failings identified was the inequitable use of alternatives to arrest for Indigenous people. The review recommended that a strategy be developed and implemented to replace Indigenous community police with Queensland Aboriginal and Torres Strait Islander Police (QATSIP), but this recommendation was rejected by the Queensland Government (Cunneen, 2007a).

In 2004, Queensland saw the highly publicised and politicised death of Cameron Doomadgee (referred to as Mulrunji) on Palm Island (see McRae and Nettheim, 2009, for discussion) and the 2006 coronial inquiry found a lack of compliance with the RCIADIC recommendations. In 2009, however, the Crime and Misconduct Commission reported on policing in Indigenous communities, stating that police practices had "clearly changed for the better" since RCIADIC, "particularly in terms of care for Indigenous people in watch-house detention", but acknowledged that the relationship between police and Queensland's Indigenous communities "remain[ed] delicately balanced" (CMC, 2009: v).

Currently, the QPS website includes details on *Aboriginal and Torres Strait Islander Action Plan 2011-12* (QPS, 2011a) and the *Indigenous Community/Police Consultative Groups* (QPS, 2011c). Both of these initiatives were referred to in the most recent annual report (QPS, 2011b), which also reported on the Indigenous employment plan and the commitment of the Queensland Government to work with Indigenous people in relation to early childhood, schooling, housing, health and economic participation issues. In addition, the report referred to initiatives in relation to family violence and measures taken by the Indigenous Police Reference Group to "ensure appropriate focus is maintained on relevant Indigenous/police issues" (QPS, 2011c: 145). Although much has been done in Queensland, there is clearly much more to do, especially in light of the sequelae of Mulrunji's death.

South Australia

In 2001, it was suggested that "things are not changing for the better" in South Australia (Sansbury, 2001: 10). Sansbury did not specifically consider the role of police, but was critical of the fact that there had been no consultation with Indigenous people when planning the drug diversionary court. A decade later, there is still room for considerable improvement. The link on the South Australia Police (SAPOL) website entitled *Aboriginal and Multicultural Unit* (AMU) notes SAPOL's involvement in "partnerships across government and with community groups on Aboriginal & Multicultural issues", and indicates that the AMU "develops policies and provides services to support policing which meets the expectations and needs of a diverse, open and cohesive South Australian community" (SAPOL, 2012).

However, no specific information is provided on the operation of the AMU, nor are any contact details listed.

The most recent annual report (SAPOL, 2011) referred to the *SAPOL Strategy for Engaging Aboriginal Communities 2011-2014*, which "was developed in a planned approach to engagement between police and Aboriginal communities to aid reconciliation and reduce Aboriginal involvement in the criminal justice system" (SAPOL, 2011: 29). This engagement was to be achieved in part through the deployment of community constables, who were described as "an integral and essential component in enhancing communication, trust and shared knowledge between the Aboriginal community and police in South Australia". The report also included a one page appendix on "Aboriginal Reconciliation", which included details about the AMU and Aboriginal and Multicultural Coordination Committee and provided details about sporting events and activities around NAIDOC (National Aborigines and Islanders Day Observance Committee) Week and Reconciliation Week.

The report included data on the number of Indigenous staff at different pay scales, which indicated SAPOL had 54 Aboriginal staff members, but it was only close to reaching its 2 per cent target at the $50,400 - $64,099 level. However, it was reported that "the 2010-12 Aboriginal Employment and Retention Strategy continues to identify strategies to enable SAPOL to work towards achieving the target" (2011: 57).There had also been measures to transition staff from community constables to mainstream policing.

These initiatives are welcome, but they do not provide any clear link to the RCIADIC recommendations, and suggest more needs to be done in South Australia to ensure the recommendations are not only implemented (such as in relation to the recruitment of Indigenous officers), but are also seen to be implemented.

Western Australia

In 2001, Mallott stated that "very little has been achieved toward the effective implementation of the 339 recommendations handed down by the RCIADIC" (2001: 14). Eggington and Allingham (2007: 6) later described WA Police complaint mechanisms described as "woefully inadequate" and contrary to recommendations from the RCIADIC and the WA Ombudsman. More recently, there appears to have been some progress, with the WA Police *Indigenous Communities* webpage commencing with the acknowledgment that "historically there have been areas of inequity in the protection and services provided to Aboriginal people" (WA Police, 2011b). The webpage includes a link to the *Strategic Policy on Service Delivery to Aboriginal People* (WA Police, 2011a), the role of and details for the Aboriginal Corporate Development Unit, as well as contact details for relevant support agencies, such as the Aboriginal Legal Service of WA, and reporting racially motivated crimes.

The Strategic Policy is a one-page statement in which WA Police

> acknowledges that its past relationship with Aboriginal people has suffered from a legacy of harsh policy and enforcement practices, and commits to building and maintaining a new relationship with Aboriginal people based on mutual respect and a commitment to the principles of justice (WA Police, nd: 4).

Under the policy, police will "respect local cultural traditions" and "take responsibility for … engaging with Aboriginal people in the delivery of services". The policy is contained in a 13-page document, which considers such issues as accessibility of services, cultural respect and communication with police. The document also sets out the rationale for the policy and refers to the inquiries and policy documents underpinning it, including the WA AJA, which was developed in 2004. Interestingly, though, there is no mention of the RCIADIC in the strategic policy; there are also no details for procedures for implementation or evaluation (Allison and Cunneen, 2010).

There was little consideration of Indigenous issues in the most recent WA Police annual report, although it was asserted that "WA Police continues to work towards forming more positive partnerships with Indigenous and Culturally and Linguistically Diverse (CaLD) communities" (WA Police, 2011b: 19). Somewhat perturbingly, however, the resourcing information indicates that the number of Aboriginal Police Liaison Officers had fallen steadily from 59 in 2007 to 16 in 2011. There is clearly a need to increase these numbers if WA Police is to deliver on its stated intentions for improving relationships with Indigenous communities.

Tasmania

In 2001, Mansell noted that the Tasmanian government "no longer bothers to report on its progress in implementing the recommendations of the Deaths in Custody Inquiry" (2001: 11). In addition, although legislative amendments had eliminated drunkenness as a criminal offence, the police retained the power to take a person considered to be drunk into custody, which still enabled them to charge intoxicated persons "with the old trifecta – offensive language, obstruction and resist arrest" (Mansell, 2001: 11), thereby frustrating the intentions of the RCIADIC. Mansell also referred to anecdotal feedback that "nothing ha[d] changed" in relation to police attitudes to refusing bail. Mansell was critical of expansion of police powers to search, detain and interrogate suspects, especially in relation to young people, and asserted that the Government continued to "balk [sic] at imposing a legislative direction on both police and the courts to increase the granting of bail to Aborigines as a means of diverting them from [prison]".

Fortunately, there have since been some indications of progress. The Tasmania Police (TasPol, 2011) *Aboriginal Liaison* webpage refers to cross-cultural training to ensure TasPol are "aware of their obligations to people in custody and, in particular, the duty of care to those Aboriginal people who are considered to be at greater risk" and the commitment "to ensuring that indigenous members of the community are appropriately represented in recruiting and welfare requirements". The website includes a link to the *Aboriginal Strategic Plan* (TasPol, 2008), a 16-page document which sets out, in addition to generic personal values and business principles:

- *guiding principles*, including that racist and discriminatory behaviour will not be tolerated within Tasmania Police, police use of discretion "is central to improving the relationship Aboriginal people have with Tasmania Police and the criminal justice system" (TasPol, 2008: 5) and Indigenous people will be consulted and involved in all issues affecting the development of community safety;
- details of the roles of the State Aboriginal Liaison Coordinator and District and Assistant Aboriginal Liaison Officers;
- *key objectives* of the plan, such as identifying the ways in which TasPol can support the Aboriginal community in enhancing recognition of Indigenous rights; and
- five *key result areas*. Each area lists specific objectives, strategies and key performance indicators. As an example, the objective of "reduc[ing] the number of Aboriginal people who are detained in custody and provide a safe environment for those for whom a viable alternative is not readily available" (TasPol, 2008: 9) is to be achieved by, *inter alia*, promoting the preferred practice of not incarcerating people in cells. Performance indicators include an increase in the use of alternatives to arrest and a decrease in the number of people detained in custody.

The strategic plan offers a clear improvement from the position in 2001. Although not enshrined in legislation, the specific promotion of diversionary practices instead of police custody is to be commended. However, it would be desirable for the plan to explicitly acknowledge the RCIADIC and for TasPol to resume reporting against the RCIADIC recommendations.

Northern Territory

The 2001 ILB report on the Northern Territory (NT) was overwhelmingly critical of their response to the RCIADIC. There was no specific mention of policing in the report, which related to correctional practices, but the NT Government was accused of being "hypocritical" and having "ridden roughshod" over recommendations it said it supported (Howse, 2001: 9). Unfortunately, there is little to suggest that NT Police has taken significant steps to improve its response since. Even though Indigenous people represent the majority of people involved in the NT criminal justice system, there is no information on the NT Police website about culturally responsive policing practices. One positive development, however, is the *Indigenous Employment and Career Development Strategy [IECDS] 2010-2012*, which focuses on increasing the representation of Indigenous Australians in the NT Police, Fire and Emergency Services (NTPFES, nd). The IECDS lists tasks, key performance indicators and responsibilities for its initiatives, which include "providing a supportive and culturally inclusive workplace environment for all employees and volunteers" (NTPFES, nd: 6). Details of the Indigenous Policing Development Division (IPDD) (which was established in 2007, developed the IECDS and manages the recruitment and training of Indigenous police officers) are also set out on the NT Police website (NT Police, 2011).

The 2010-11 NTPFES annual report referred to the IECDS and the review of police selection processes to increase the number of Indigenous officers, as well as the appointment of an Indigenous community liaison representative in a remote area. The report also noted four staff members' participation in Indigenous leadership staff development programs. Other initiatives by the IPDD included developing the Indigenous employees' network, and securing external funding to support and develop Indigenous employees and developing and delivering cross-cultural awareness training to all inductees. The report also indicated that 94 per cent of persons taken into police protective custody over the previous year were Indigenous. Undoubtedly, more could be done to reduce Indigenous over-representation in this regard (see Behrendt, Cunneen and Libesman, 2009; McRae and Nettheim, 2009, for discussion).

Australian Capital Territory

The 2001 review of the ACT's response to RCIADIC was relatively positive, but indicated that police appeared to still be choosing custody over the "sobering-up shelter" option and there was low participation by Indigenous people in diversion-ary conferences. Drumgold (2001) concluded that further education to promote the appropriate use of police discretion was required.

The ACT Policing webpage for *Indigenous Persons* (ACT Policing, 2011c) provides fairly generic "safety advice for the Indigenous community" and the phone numbers for the Aboriginal Legal Service and local Indigenous support agencies. The page also describes and provides a link to the page for the *Indigenous Community Liaison Program* (ACT Policing, 2011b), which sets out the role and contact details for officers in the program.

As set out in the ACT Policing 2010-11 annual report, the *ACT Aboriginal and Torres Strait Islander Justice Agreement 2010-2013* (ACTATSIJA), a partnership agreement between the ACT Government and the Indigenous elected body, came into effect on 1 July 2010. ACT Policing is the lead agency for the agreement and listed "tak[ing] a leadership role ... in realising the vision and objectives" of the agreement as a goal for 2011-12 (ACT Policing, 2011a: 55). The agreement is underpinned by five objectives, including:

- reducing the overrepresentation of ATSI people in the criminal justice system;
- improving collaboration between stakeholders to improve justice outcomes and service delivery for ATSI people; and
- facilitating ATSI people taking a leadership role in addressing their community justice concerns (ACT Justice and Community Safety (ACTJACS), 2010).

The 52-page agreement is available on the ACT Justice and Community Safety website, but not on the ACT Policing website. The agreement includes 105 action items, with clear allocation of responsibility and reporting dates. ACT Policing has responsibility for 19 action items, including ensuring that "the philosophy flowing from the Royal Commission into Aboriginal Deaths in Custody (1991) recommendations are embedded into strategic policy and contemporary practice" (ACTJACS, 2010: 30). Specifically, ACT Policing is to review the RCIADIC recommendations to "ensure that contemporary practice is consistent with the aspirations and philosophy of the Royal Commission which advocated systemic reforms to improve outcomes and overcome poverty and disadvantage in a range of areas". Other policing actions include increasing the number of ATSI people referred to the restorative justice program and increasing the diversion of intoxicated Indigenous people to appropriate shelters.

Other developments referred to in the 2010-11 ACT Policing annual report included:

- training 15 Indigenous contact officers;
- establishing the Front-Up Program, whereby Indigenous people subject to an arrest warrant or in breach of their bail conditions can voluntarily surrender themselves to the court, to avoid being taken into police custody; and
- involvement in the MPower program, an inter-agency program designed to provide services to assist disadvantaged Indigenous people; the Aboriginal Interview Friends Program; and the Pathways Program, which "focuses on re-empowering Indigenous people who have become entrenched within the judicial system" (ACT Policing, 2011a: 159).

The most recent data indicated that 9 per cent of people taken into custody by ACT Policing reported as Indigenous, down from 16 per cent in 2009-10. However, 17 per cent of people arrested were Indigenous, as were 11 per cent of people taken into protective custody for intoxication, suggesting there is still some way to go in promoting diversionary practices. Notwithstanding this ongoing overrepresentation, the foregoing suggests that the ACT has recently made significant effort to act on the RCIADIC recommendations.

Conclusion

Lamentably, "the over-policing and imprisonment of indigenous Australians is an integral part of today's Australia" (Keenan, 2009: 249) and more is required in relation to police discretion, especially for minor offences (see McRae and Nettheim, 2009). This chapter has provided a brief overview of the key findings and recommendations of the RCIADIC relevant to police. Examination of policing responses to the RCIADIC in each state and territory, as identified by ILB reports, relevant commentary and policing agencies' websites and annual reports, revealed some positive initiatives, especially from Victoria, NSW and the ACT, while the responses of other jurisdictions, especially South Australia and the Northern Territory, left much to be desired.

In 2010, the Standing Committee of Attorneys-General endorsed the *National Indigenous Law and Justice Framework 2009-2015*, which contains a number of strategies and actions relevant to police and acknowledges the RCIADIC as "a foundation document guiding the work of governments" (Commonwealth of Australia, 2010: 5). This goes some way to ensuring, as Edney (2004: 22) suggested, that the RCIADIC "remains a living document". Although it would be naïve to suggest that the development of Indigenous justice agreements and policing policy documents alone will overcome so many years of police injustices, Allison and Cunneen (2010: 645) concluded that "quality Indigenous-justice related strategic planning does have a positive impact" and that the development by agencies (such as police) of their own specific strategic framework brings particular benefits. The potential remains, however, for such measures to simply continue the experience of the RCIADIC, which "showed that governments can say a great deal about what they are doing in regard to implementing recommendations, while at the same time achieving very little in tangible outcomes" (Cunneen, 2007a: 21). Accordingly, there is a critical need for ongoing *independent* evaluation of policing agencies to ensure more than mere lip service to the RCIADIC recommendations and contribute towards lasting improvements by police in relation to Indigenous people.

Endnotes

1 Throughout this chapter, the terms "Indigenous", "Aboriginal and Torres Strait Islander" and "ATSI" are used interchangeably. Where the term "Aboriginal" is used, this reflects the terminology in the source document.

2 As policing is primarily a concern for the states and territories, the Federal response to the RCIADIC is not examined here.

References

ACT Justice and Community Safety, 2010, *ACT Aboriginal and Torres Strait Islander Justice Agreement 2010-2013*, Canberra.

ACT Policing, 2011a, Annual Report 2010-11, ACT Police, Canberra.

ACT Policing, 2011b, "Indigenous Community Liaison". Viewed on 1 December 2011, <www.police.act.gov.au/community-safety/programs/indigenous-community-liaison.aspx>.

ACT Policing, 2011c, "Indigenous Persons". Viewed on 1 December 2011, <www.police.act.gov.au/community-safety/for-other-community-groups/indigenous-people.aspx>.

Allison, F and Cunneen, C, 2010, "The Role of Indigenous Justice Agreements in Improving Legal and Social Outcomes for Indigenous People" 32 *Sydney Law Review* 645.

Australian Bureau of Statistics, 2003, Population Characteristics, Aboriginal and Torres Strait Islander Australians, 2001, 4713.0, ABS, Canberra.

Australian Bureau of Statistics, 2010, Population Characteristics, Aboriginal and Torres Strait Islander Australians, 2006, 4713.0, ABS, Canberra.

Australian Bureau of Statistics, 2012, Corrective Services, 4512.0, ABS, Canberra.

Behrendt, L, Cunneen, C and Libesman, T, 2009, *Indigenous Legal Relations in Australia*, Oxford University Press, Melbourne.

Commonwealth of Australia, 2010, *National Indigenous Law and Justice Framework 2009–2015*, AGPS, Canberra.

Crime and Misconduct Commission, 2009, *Restoring Order: Crime Prevention, Policing and Local Justice in Queensland's Indigenous Communities*, CMC, Brisbane.

Cunneen, C, 2006, "Aboriginal Deaths in Custody: A Continuing Systematic Abuse" 33 *Social Justice* 37.

Cunneen, C, 2007a, "Justice Agreements, Strategic Plans and Indigenous/Police Relations" 6 *Indigenous Law Bulletin* 19.

Cunneen, C, 2007b, "Policing in Indigenous Communities", *Police Leadership and Management*, (Eds M Mitchell and J Casey), Federation Press, Sydney.

Cunneen, C, 2008, "Reflections in Criminal Justice Policy since the Royal Commission into Aboriginal Deaths in Custody", *University of New South Wales Law Research Series*, No 7, Sydney.

Edney, R, 2004, "R v Scobie: Finally Taking the Royal Commission into Aboriginal Deaths in Custody Seriously?" 6 *Indigenous Law Bulletin* 20.

Edney, R, 2006, "The Importance of Indigenous Stories: The Victorian Implementation Review of the Recommendations from the Royal Commission into Aboriginal Deaths in Custody" 6 *Indigenous Law Bulletin* 17.

Eggington, D and Allingham, K, 2007, "Police Investigating Police Complaints: An Urgent Need for Change in Western Australia" 6 *Indigenous Law Bulletin* 6.

Houston, J, 2007, "Policing Around Australia: How Have Police Responded to the Royal Commission's Recommendations" 28 *Indigenous Law Bulletin* 22.

Howse, C, 2001, "State and Territory Implementation of the Recommendations of the Royal Commission – Northern Territory" 5 *Indigenous Law Bulletin* 9.

Keenan, S, 2009, "A Blue Wristband View of History? The Death of Mulrunji Doomadgee and the Illusion of Postcolonial Australia" 34 *Alternative Law Journal* 248.

Kelly, L, 2001, "State and Territory Implementation of the Recommendations of the Royal Commission – New South Wales" 5 *Indigenous Law Bulletin* 8.

Lavery, D, 1994, "Empty Words – Queensland's Response to RCIADIC Recommendations 6 to 40" 3 *Aboriginal Law Bulletin* 11.

Lyneham, M, Joudo Larsen, J and Beacroft, L, 2010, *Deaths in Custody in Australia: National Deaths in Custody Program 2008, Monitoring Report 10*, Australian Institute of Criminology, Canberra.

McRae, H and Nettheim, G, 2009, *Indigenous Legal Issues, Commentary and Materials*, 4th ed, Lawbook Co, Sydney.

Mallott, K, 2001, "State and Territory Implementation of the Recommendations of the Royal Commission: Western Australia" 5 *Indigenous Law Bulletin* 14.

Mansell, M, 2001, "State and Territory Implementation of the Recommendations of the Royal Commission – Tasmania" 5 *Indigenous Law Bulletin* 11.

Marchetti, E, 2005, "Critical Reflections upon Australia's Royal Commission into Aboriginal Deaths in Custody" 5 *Macquarie Law Journal* 103.

Neliman, B, 2001, "State and Territory Implementation of the Recommendations of the Royal Commission: Queensland" 5 *Indigenous Law Bulletin* 10.

NSW Aboriginal Justice Advisory Council, 2000, RCIADIC: Review of NSW Government Implementation of Recommendations, NSW Attorney-General's Department, Sydney.

NSW Aboriginal Justice Advisory Council, 2003, NSW Aboriginal Justice Plan: Beyond Justice 2004-2014, NSW Attorney-General's Department, Sydney.

NSW Ombudsman, 2005, Working with Local Aboriginal Communities: Audit of the implementation of the NSW Police Aboriginal Strategic Direction (2003-2006), Sydney.

NSW Police Force, 2011, *Annual Report 2010-2011*, NSWPF, Sydney.

NT Police, 2011, "Indigenous Development Division – Yidiyu Initiative". Viewed on 1 December 2011, <www.pfes.nt.gov.au/Police/Careers-in-policing/Indigenous-Development-Division-Yidiyu-Initiative.aspx>.

NT Police, Fire and Emergency Services, nd, Indigenous Employment and Career Development Strategy 2010-2012, Darwin.

NT Police, Fire and Emergency Services, 2011, *Annual Report 2010-2011*, Darwin.

Office of Police Integrity, 2011, *Talking Together – Relations Between Police and Aboriginal and Torres Strait Islanders in Victoria: A Review of the Victoria Police Aboriginal Strategic Plan 2003-2008*, Melbourne.

Queensland Police Service, 2011a, Aboriginal and Torres Strait Islander Action Plan 2011-12, QPS, Brisbane.

Queensland Police Service, 2011b, Annual Report 2010-11, QPS, Brisbane.

Queensland Police Service, 2011c, "Indigenous Community/Police Consultative Groups". Viewed on 6 December 2011, <www.police.qld.gov.au/programs/community/CulturalAdvisory/ indgnsCommPlcConsGrps.htm>.

Royal Commission into Aboriginal Deaths in Custody, 1991, National Report, Adelaide.

Sansbury, T, 2001, "State and Territory Implementation of the Recommendations of the Royal Commission: South Australia" 5 Indigenous Law Bulletin 10.

South Australia Police, 2011, *Annual Report 2010-2011*, Adelaide.

South Australia Police, 2012, "Aboriginal and Multicultural Unit".Viewed on 9 August 2012, <www.police.sa.gov.au/sapol/community_services/aboriginal_and_multicultural_unit.jsp>.

South Australia Police, 2012, *Annual Report 2010-11*, South Australia Police, Adelaide.

Tasmania Police, 2008, Aboriginal Strategic Plan, DPEM, Hobart.

Tasmania Police, 2011, "Aboriginal Liaison". Viewed on 1 December 2011, <www.police.tas.gov.au/what-we-do/aboriginal-liaison/>.

Victorian Department of Justice, 2006, Victorian Aboriginal Justice Agreement: Phase 2 (AJA2), Melbourne.

Victoria Police, 2011a, "Aboriginal Advisory Unit". Viewed on 1 December 2011, <www.police.vic.gov.au/content.asp?Document_ID=287>.

Victoria Police, 2011b, *Annual Report 2010-2011*, VP, Melbourne.

WA Police, 2011a, *Annual Report 2010-11*, WAP, Perth.

WA Police, 2011b, "Indigenous Communities". Viewed on 5 December 2011, <www.police.wa.gov.au/Ourservices/Indigenouscommunities/tabid/995/Default.aspx>.

WA Police, nd, Strategic Policy on Service Delivery to Aboriginal People, WAP, Perth.

Chapter 13

Detention and Investigation of Vulnerable Suspects

Karl Roberts and Victoria Herrington

The detention and investigation of individuals by police is the first stage of a journey through the criminal justice system for most suspects, and it is hard to overstate its importance. The procedures involved in detention, and the experience of the individual detained, set the stage of the police investigation. The police investigation provides the evidence for the subsequent trial and both of these activities underpin conviction and sentence if the individual is found guilty. There is, then, a lot resting on the procedures involved in this detention and investigation stage. The purpose of this chapter is to consider this with particular reference to the experience of suspects who are psychologically vulnerable. *Psychological vulnerability* (PV) is a term used to describe those who face additional cognitive challenges to most of the rest of the population. Typically, it has described the particular difficulties facing individuals with a mental illness or intellectual disability (Gudjonsson, 2010). Through this chapter, we will demonstrate that individuals with a PV are at an additional disadvantage during social interactions in general, and doubly so when those interactions involve police (Department of Health, 2009). This means that police handling of the detention and investigation of individuals with a PV is of paramount importance in ensuring that miscarriages of justice do not occur.

Defining Psychological Vulnerability

While a universally accepted definition of psychological vulnerability (PV) remains elusive, Gudjonsson (2006; 2010) noted the term has tended to describe the various psychological characteristics or mental states that are risk factors for problem behaviours across a range of circumstances. Problem behaviours in the context of police detention and interviewing are particularly the provision of inaccurate or unreliable information by an individual with a PV that may, in the case of suspects, lead to self-incrimination. Characteristically captured under a definition of PV are psychiatric disorders and intellectual disability. Given the manifestation of a PV, is dependent on the particular condition, it is important to briefly consider the characteristics of the various disorders. *Psychiatric disorders* are grouped under three key categories – schizophrenia, depression and anxiety:

- Schizophrenia is characterised by *positive* symptoms such as disordered thought (delusions), disordered perception (auditory hallucinations, typically hearing voices) and disorganised speech (jumbled speech and leaping from theme to theme), as well as *negative* symptoms such as lack of volition, situationally inappropriate emotions and catatonia.
- Depression is categorised by low self-esteem, negative thoughts, lack of volition and energy, disturbed sleep and feelings of sadness and emptiness.
- Anxiety disorders are characterised by feelings of fear, anxiety and panic which may be in response to specific objects or events (phobias), or generalised (APA, 2000).

Intellectual disability is a clinical condition characterised by intellectual impairment (a low IQ) and deficits in adaptive behaviour (difficulty achieving the day-to-day tasks required to take care of oneself independently) (AAIDD, 2010). This group often have pervasive difficulties with learning, including difficulty reading, writing and understanding verbal instructions (Carr and O'Reilly, 2007), and are susceptible to acquiesce, particularly with authority figures such as police (Milne and Bull, 2001).

For individuals with one of these mental disorders, vulnerability in an arrest or investigative setting emanates from their disordered thoughts and difficulty following a line of questioning. This affects both the quality and the reliability of the information that they are likely to provide. It also affects, as we discuss later in this chapter, their interaction with the police officer affecting the arrest or undertaking the investigation, and potentially also the disposition of the officer to the individual themselves.

Psychiatric disorders and intellectual disability are not always discreet categories, and comorbidity (where an individual experiences more than one condition at the same time) is frequently found in these vulnerable groups (Emerson and Hatton, 2007; Cooper et al, 2007). For example, individuals with an intellectual disability are also highly likely to suffer from depression and anxiety, and may have a lower personal resilience to these. Recent research has suggested the incidence of depression among prisoners with an intellectual disability was much higher than among the rest of the prison population (52 compared to 19 per cent respectively) as was anxiety (70 compared to 25 per cent respectively) (Talbot, 2008), and that prisoners with an intellectual disability are twice as likely to commit suicide (Shaw et al, 2003). Psychiatric and intellectual disorders are complex clinical phenomena, and as such it is neither desirable nor possible for frontline police to attempt diagnosis. The aim of this chapter is to raise awareness about such clinical disorders, and how these might manifest in an investigative setting, as well as provide tools to assist police when identifying and dealing with vulnerable suspects.

The Prevalence of Psychological Vulnerability

Population estimates for the prevalence of PV in the UK population suggest that approximately 25 per cent of the population experience mental disorder in a given year, most commonly depression 12 per cent, anxiety 9 per cent, and schizophrenia 2 per cent (Office of National Statistics, 2001), and 1-2 per cent are thought to have an intellectual disability (Department of Health, 2001). These figures are similar across most major Western nations. Importantly, the prevalence of both mental disorders and intellectual disability are much higher amongst those in contact with the criminal justice system, and particularly so at police custody, which is the first point of contact with the criminal justice system for suspected offenders, and therefore ahead of the impact that any diversionary measures (under mental health legislation, for example) may have.[1] One study found that 80 per cent of individuals in contact with an arrest referral link worker scheme had a severe mental health problem requiring psychiatric treatment (Finn et al, 2000), and more than 90 per cent of prisoners were found to suffer from at least one of five disorders including personality disorder, psychosis, neurosis, alcohol misuse, and drug dependence (Singleton et al, 1997). Another study found that at one police station 9 per cent of suspects had an IQ score in the intellectual disability range (IQ <70), with 42 per cent having an IQ in the borderline range (IQ between 70 and 79) (Gudjonsson et al, 1993). Similarly Barron et al (2002) found 45 per cent of suspects at a police station had learning difficulties, with 40 per cent having attended a special education school as a result. It is then fair to conclude that police come into regular contact with suspects who have a PV.

Legislative Provisions Governing Police Interactions with PV Suspects

The additional needs of individuals with a PV have been recognised by the legislature, and the importance of providing additional support for suspects with a PV has been enshrined in legislation across the world (see Bartels, 2011, for a summary of Australian state and territory legislation). Typically these legislative instruments incorporate PV, as well as broader vulnerabilities including those related to physical functioning, English language abilities, and membership of particular – specifically, Indigenous – groups. *Non-psychological vulnerabilities* such as these are clearly of importance to police in detention and investigative settings (see Bartels, in this collection, Ch 12, for a discussion of the latter of these), but unlike PV, they are much easier to identify – being largely related to the physical characteristics of individuals. As we discuss later in this chapter, the particular challenge for police in dealing with individuals with a PV are compounded by the fact that PV itself is a broad and multifaceted concept, and associated vulnerabilities can often be hard to identify.

In NSW, a list of vulnerable people is provided in cl 24 of the *Law Enforcement (Powers and Responsibilities) Regulation 2005* (NSW)[2] and supported by the NSW Police Code of Practice for CRIME (Custody, Rights, investigation, Management and Evidence) (NSW Police Force, 2012). Under this legislation a support person may accompany a vulnerable person when they are detained, and may be present during an investigative interview. The custody manager who, in the first instance, is requested to assist the suspect in locating their preferred choice of support, and if this person is deemed unsuitable (for example, they are a suspected accomplice) or unable to be located, the manager is responsible for locating another suitable support person (for example, a religious minister, or social worker (Del Monte, 2012). The role of the support person is set out under cl 30(1) of the *Law Enforcement (Powers and Responsibilities) Regulation 2005* (NSW) as being to: (a) assist and support the detained person, (b) observe whether or not the interview is being conducted properly and fairly, and (c) identify communication problems with the detained person.

Similar legislation is found in the UK, where the rights of vulnerable interviewees have been strengthened under the *Police and Criminal Evidence Act 1984* and best practice guidelines for interviewing vulnerable witnesses are set out in *Achieving Best Evidence in Criminal Proceedings* (ABE) (Home Office, 2007).[3] While there is no such guidance for interviewing vulnerable suspects, the principles contained within the ABE translate across both victim and suspect interviews. The *Police and Criminal Evidence Act 1984*, Code C provides that an Appropriate Adult (AA) be called to the police station whenever a mentally vulnerable person has been detained. The role of the AA is set out in Home Office guidance (2003) as to support, advise and assist the detained person; observe police are acting properly, fairly and with respect; assist with communication; and ensure that person understands their rights (Home Office, 2007).

But why is it important that individuals with a PV are catered for differently to others in contact with the police? The report of the Joint Committee on Human Rights (2008) in the UK concluded that suspects, detainees, defendants and prisoners are vulnerable to discrimination and breaches of human rights at all stages of the criminal justice system. Discrimination based on disability, which incorporates intellectual disability and mental disorder, is further legislated against through the United Nations' *Convention on the Rights of Persons with Disabilities* (United Nations, 2006), and specifically under Article 5, which sets out that signatories must ensure:

- equal protection and equal benefit of the law for all
- equal and effective legal protection against discrimination on all grounds
- reasonable accommodation is provided
- measures taken to accelerate or achieve de facto equality of persons with disabilities are not discriminatory (United Nations, 2006, Article 5, emphasis added).

The spirit of Article 5 of the Convention has been translated into local legislation across the world, including in Australia through the *Disability Discrimination Act 1992* (Cth) (DDA). In Part 1 (5, 2b) of the Act, *direct discrimination* is defined as a situation wherein, "the failure to make the reasonable adjustments has, or would have, the effect that the aggrieved person is, because of the disability, treated less favourably than a person without the disability would be treated in circumstances that are not materially different". This is of significant importance for the police officer faced with a suspect with a PV, who would be considered to fulfil the definition of disability under the UN Convention and the *DDA*. As such, failure to take special measures to ensure that a PV suspect is not discriminated against – by ensuring that their additional needs are accounted for throughout the investigative process – could be considered a breach. There is precedence for legal challenge on such grounds internationally (see, *Disability Discrimination Act (England and Wales) 1992*, and the case of *Gill v Secretary of State for Justice*; 2010 cited in Herrington, 2011).

Of course, in order for these special provisions for vulnerable suspects to be enacted, the identification of vulnerability in the first place is crucial. Sanders et al (1996) note that this is not always the case, with police having particular difficulty recognising cases of mild and borderline PV, and as a result not always applying the appropriate legislative safeguards and interviewing techniques. This is exacerbated by a tendency for those with mild and borderline PV to try and cloak their vulnerability (Edgerton, 1967), lest it be used against them in some way. Self-identification is therefore unlikely, and identification by other means is improbable at the police station, where impairment may be underestimated (Agnew et al, 2006). Talbot's (2008) UK research noted that less than a third of prisoners with intellectual disability had access to an Appropriate Adult during their interaction with the police, and Gudjonsson and MacKeith (1994) note that even when available, the choice of AA may not always be appropriate.[4] Legget et al (2007) similarly note the paucity of AAs in interviews with individuals with a PV and that when an AA was not present, that individuals more often reported the interview being a negative experience. So how can PV be identified?

Identifying Psychological Vulnerability

Diagnosis of specific mental disorders and intellectual disability requires detailed case formulation by appropriately qualified and experienced clinicians (APA, 2000; AAIDD, 2010). This is time consuming and involves consideration of a wide range of material from different sources (information from family and friends, detailed medical history, education, psychiatric and other records, in-depth clinical interviews with clients, and the use of standardised tests). Police have neither the time, nor expertise to diagnose specific psychological vulnerabilities. But it is incumbent on them to be sensitive to, and recognise the presence of, PV in its broadest sense. If this can be achieved, steps can be taken from an early stage to mitigate some of the risks to PV individuals and the integrity of police investigations, and miscarriages of justice can be avoided.

In the UK, the Association of Chief Police Officers (ACPO) has published a guide for police officers in dealing with PV (ACPO, 2010). The guide stresses the importance of early identification of PV and advises close liaison between police and stakeholders with expertise in PV. Where PV is suspected, the ACPO guide recommends that police officers collect as much detail as possible to aid in their decision making, and recommends that a medical assessment should be carried out to determine the suspect's fitness for interview. If deemed fit, an appropriate adult should be present throughout the interview. In the UK the responsibility for making decisions relating to a suspect with a PV rests with the custody officer who, ACPO advises, should be familiar with the characteristics of and risks associated with PV. The ACPO guide fails, however, to provide any guidance on *how* a police officer should identify PV in the first place, and simply lists signs and symptoms of PV without noting the relative importance of them in making judgments. The guide also makes little mention of best practice in interviewing PV suspects referring police instead to the ACPO Investigative Interviewing Strategy (ACPO, 2009), which in turn refers police to the Achieving Best Evidence (ABE) approach for PV witnesses, recommending caution in interviewing PV suspects.

In some circumstances, identification of PV may be very easy: bizarre behaviour or unusual speech would probably alert most police officers that the suspect may need referral for psychiatric assessment. Other symptoms of PV are more subtle, or transient, only becoming apparent over time, if at all. The time dependent nature of some symptoms flags the need for behavioural observations and judgments to be ongoing throughout detention and investigative interview, rather than based on one observation when a decision to detain is made.

There have been a number of formal screening tools developed for various forms of PV, designed specifically for police to use. These tools tend to be either very broad and rely on individual self-report (for example, they ask individuals to list their medical and psychological history; Jacobson, 2008; McBrien, 2003), or relate to specific conditions (for example, the Hayes Ability Screening Index which identifies those requiring additional testing for a suspected intellectual disability). The difficulty facing the former is its reliance on individuals to identify their vulnerabilities, which as we have indicated, may not be forthcoming (Perske, 2005; Edgerton, 1967; Herrington, 2011). The difficulty facing the latter is that while it may alert the police to the particular vulnerability it was designed to test – for example, intellectual disability – it is unlikely to highlight other types of vulnerability, such as anxiety or depression. Nonetheless, screening tests such as these are useful because they do not require lengthy observation and interaction with an individual to make a judgment about their PV status. However, until better assessment tools are designed, mitigation against the risks of PV relies upon police officers increasing their knowledge of the symptoms of PV and being sensitive to the presence of those symptoms throughout custody. Certainly, where there is any question about the vulnerability of an individual, professional clinical advice should be obtained as soon as possible (Milne et al, 2009).

The Challenges Facing Individuals with a PV in the Criminal Justice System

There is some evidence to suggest that the experience of individuals with a PV in the criminal justice system is largely dependent on who they encounter once in it (Cant and Standen, 2007; Talbot, 2008). For example, McAfee et al (2002) found police officers thought suspects with an intellectual disability were less believable, their crimes more serious, and that officers would more often take *drastic action* in such cases than those involving suspects without a PV – in this case, intellectual disability. Conversely, reluctance among police to formalise criminal proceedings involving offenders with an intellectual disability has also been reported and police disposals in such cases may be based on perceptions of motivation for offending:

> If you are talking about someone with some major learning difficulties, for instance someone with Down's syndrome, who you could blatantly tell was extremely upset and they had been and nicked a packet of Smarties because they didn't have any money and they were hungry, you would be taking them home, you know (Police Sergeant Interview, quoted in Gendel and Woodhams 2005: 76).

This being the case, identification of learning difficulties, mental illness and intellectual disability in the first place, as well as a clear understanding of the impact that PV has on an individual's behaviour and style of interaction is paramount. Training can be of benefit here, and can positively impact police officer awareness of mental illness and intellectual disability (ID), and can lead to attitudinal change and an increase in positive interactions (Herrington et al, 2009).

Mental disorders and intellectual disability are associated with biases in thinking, stereotypical thinking patterns and reduced mental capacity. In general, individuals with a PV are more uncertain about events they have witnessed or experienced and as a result, during interactions with the police are susceptible to providing misleading information and falsely confessing to offences (Gudjonsson and MacKeith, 1994; Perske, 1994). Individuals suffering positive symptoms of schizophrenia – delusions or hearing voices – may be so distracted that they are in no position to comprehend that they have been arrested or the implications of their behaviour. Suspects with an intellectual disability have been found to be highly likely to confess to offences in order to end the interview, in the mistaken beliefs that they could go home, or could retract their confession later (Gudjonsson, 2003). Perske (2005) reports on 38 cases in the United States in which individuals with an ID confessed to serious crimes (including murder, rape and robbery) and were later found innocent.

Individuals with a PV – particularly an intellectual disability – often have low self-efficacy and rely on cues from others to help make sense of their environment (Bybee and Zigler, 1992). There is a strong desire to provide socially desirable answers (individuals answer *yes* to questions about desirable behaviour, and *no* to undesirable behaviour, regardless of truth) (Shaw and Budd, 1982) and susceptibility to acquiescence response bias (where individuals answer *yes* regardless) (Siegelman et al, 1982; Ternes and Yuille, 2008). Everington and Fulero (1999) cite research by Siegelman et al (1981) which found 73 per cent of individuals with ID answered *yes* to the question *"Does it ever snow here in summer?"* and 44 per cent to the question *"Are you Chinese?"*. The research was conducted in the southern US state of Texas (where it does not snow) and none of the participants were Chinese. The authors also found that as the linguistic difficulty of the questioning increased, so did the tendency to acquiesce (Siegelman et al, 1981).

PV and the Investigative Interview

Increasingly, academic commentators and practitioners have voiced concerns about the impact of vulnerabilities in police interviews, particularly on the reliability of the information obtained (Gudjonsson, 2003). In any police investigation, the interview is one of the primary methods used to obtain information from suspects. With suspects with a PV there is a higher than normal risk of collecting unreliable and/or misleading information. This information has regrettably led to many miscarriages of justice across the world, with attendant damage to the public's perception of the integrity and reputation of the police and the broader criminal justice system (Gudjonsson, 2003).

It is fair to conclude that even where PV has been identified, and additional support safeguards are in place, police interviews are undoubtedly stressful, particularly for an individual suspected of committing a crime, where the stakes are high. Individuals with a PV may cope less well with this stress than others, may feel excessively anxious, with existing cognitive limitations exacerbated, contributing further to an inability to cope effectively with the interview (Roberts and Herrington, 2011; Herrington and Roberts, 2012). Susceptibility to poor – although legally acceptable – overly complex and leading questions may mean individuals struggle to maintain a coherent account, and the uncertainty they experience with their recall serves to increase doubt about the veracity of their account, for themselves as well as for the police interviewer (Roberts and Herrington, 2011; Kebbell et al, 2004). This group are particularly likely to struggle if faced with disapproval, anger or threats on the part of the interviewer (Fulero and Everington, 2004), which ironically are increasingly likely to be elicited from the investigating police officer as they become frustrated by the poor performance of the interviewee (Gudjonsson, 2003). Increased uncertainty raises the likelihood of contradiction, confabulation, suggestibility and, ultimately, false confession (Savage and Milne, 2007). Difficulties with understanding complex ideas and questions present problems for this group at the court stage of the criminal justice system too (Talbot, 2008) and for both witnesses and suspects with a PV there is concern that they may not "survive" cross examination (Kebbell et al, 2004).

We have already noted that there is limited guidance on how best to interact with suspects with a PV, and most of the internationally recognised best practice work has explored the interviewing of PV witnesses (Home Office, 2007). Recommendations for PV witness interviews can inform suspect interviews of course, although care must be taken given the different contexts in which these interviews take place. In particular, the personal implications for a suspect are significantly more threatening than for a witness. Broadly the PEACE model of investigative interviewing (see Savage and Milne, 2007; Roberts and Herrington, 2011) provides a useful structure for all suspect interviews. This is because it stresses the development and maintenance of rapport with the interviewee. In all interview scenarios – where information is being elicited – much depends on when and how questions are asked. This is doubly so for individuals with a PV. Where individuals with a PV perceive real or implied criticism, threat, or condescension in the tone of the questioner they are more likely to respond untruthfully, and cloak their needs (Clare, cited in McBrien, 2003). By developing rapport, trust is enhanced and serves to reduce uncertainty (Colquitt et al, 2012). This in turn increases the likelihood of honesty in answering questions, as well as reducing stress and risk of heightened emotional arousal on the part of the suspect (Ord et al, 2008). This is particularly important for PV suspects who have a lower resilience to stress and are more likely to experience increased emotional arousal, which can exacerbate symptoms, and increase the unreliability of information provided (Gudjonsson, 2003).

Conversation management (Shepherd, 1991) is complementary to PEACE and widely used to obtain accounts from interviewees. Key in this approach is that it is cognisant of human cognitive performance. Conversation management consists of three stages. First, the suspect presents an unchallenged account of events (the suspect agenda), which is then clarified through targeted questioning (police agenda), followed by a challenge of the account (challenge phase). For PV suspects, the sequence of these phases is particularly important because they are at greatest risk of confabulation – changing an account by incorporating information from other information that is presented within questions – when their account of events is directly challenged (Gudjonsson, 2003). This is because such a challenge implies that the PV suspect's account is false and they lack the cognitive skills or certainty about their experiences to maintain their account in the face of this. For similar reasons, constantly repeating a question can raise the risk of confabulation for PV suspects and should be avoided.

Suspects with a PV often have difficulty maintaining focussed attention (Kingdom and Turkington, 2005) and long interviews increase the likelihood of distraction, increase situational stress, which can increase the manifestation of the symptoms of a PV, with attendant risks to the reliability of information obtained. Reducing the length of an interview and providing frequent breaks is therefore good practice in interviewing PV individuals. Complex questions should also be avoided in all interviews, and particularly so when interviewing individuals with a PV. They are susceptible to recency bias and confusion. Short, simple, questions have been found to be most productive (Milne and Bull, 2001; Savage and Milne, 2007). For all interviews, open questions are considered best practice as they allow for more expansive answers and greater detail. However, for some PV suspects who might struggle to engage with the interviewer, carefully worded closed questions can obtain information that the suspect may be unable to provide in a more expansive way. Similarly, rapid questioning increases existing difficulties in processing information, recall and formulation of responses, increases situational stress and the likely manifestation of a PV. A slower pace is recommended (Milne and Bull, 2001).

In Their Own Words

There is little empirical work that has asked offenders with a PV about their experiences in the criminal justice system. One significant exception is the work of the UK's Prison Reform Trust's (PRT) *No One Knows* program. This program talked to prisoners with intellectual disabilities and learning difficulties about their experiences as they progressed through the criminal justice system. Talbot's (2008) report makes for uncomfortable reading, with prisoners reporting feeling excessively fearful when arrested and being (or at least perceiving to have been) handled roughly and even beaten by police. Prisoners also reported less explicitly brutal, but still intimidating, behaviour such as being told they would get 10 years in prison, or having "mad noises" made at them, or being generally "treated like shit" (Talbot, 2008: 20) during their interactions with the police. Not understanding what was going on and having difficulty expressing themselves clearly was another issue faced by those with a PV, compounded perhaps by their answering *yes* to questions to avoid looking "thick" (Talbot, 2008: 21). This notion of cloaking one's difficulties and masking a lack of understanding is reported across the PV literature, and is of significant importance to police who are charged with ensuring that those with a PV are appropriately treated.

It is important to acknowledge that the behaviour meted by some criminal justice staff and reported by Talbot (2008) cannot be verified, and given the difficulties faced by those with ID recalling information accurately (as we have noted above) there is a possibility that some of these experiences may have been confabulated or inadvertently influenced by the interviewers themselves. Equally it is important not to dismiss these accounts, which has itself been the experience of victims of crime with a PV (Milne and Bull, 2001; Ternes and Yuille, 2008), and they are certainly the salient experience for the individuals. The broader impact such negative experiences have is debated in the body of work discussing procedural justice,[5] and there is consensus that it risks little and offers much (in reduced re-offending and normative compliance with the law) if individuals in contact with the criminal justice system treated fairly and with respect (Hough, 2010). Certainly, Talbot (2008) notes that a seemingly small action – like being offered a cup for tea – had a lasting impression on those with a PV (a finding also reported by Leggett et al, 2007). The irony is that such actions may serve to increase compliance to such a degree that it also increases the likelihood of acquiescence or socially desirable responses (Gudjonsson, 2003). Improving awareness among criminal justice staff about the interpretation of interactions for this group seems a clear first-level implication for the criminal justice system from the literature.

Conclusion

In this chapter we have set out the importance of considering the particular needs of individuals with a PV in a detention and investigative setting. Without consideration of this group's additional needs they are highly susceptible to providing unreliable information, and may be particularly vulnerable to miscarriages of justice as a result. Moreover, there is considerable legislation that protects against the direct and inadvertent discrimination of individuals with a PV, including in relation to their involvement in the criminal justice system. To not account for these additional needs during detention and investigation is to breach these legislative instruments, which can undermine the legal process on both sides. While all are agreed that accounting for the vulnerabilities of suspects with a PV is important, there is little practical advice for police on how to identify PV and how to tailor the investigative process to account for such needs. We have addressed this gap in the literature by providing advice around the investigative interview, where the PEACE model of interviewing widely used across the UK and Australia can be specifically tailored to meet the needs of this group.

Endnotes

1 While there are diversionary provisions in place under most legislative systems to divert suspects who are too mentally unwell to cope in the criminal justice system for treatment or assessment in hospital, there remains debate about the efficacy of these (eg Shaw et al, 2001; Department of Health, 2009; Forrester et al, 2009; McKenzie and Sales, 2008), and a high proportion of acutely unwell individuals are continually found in offender (prison and probation) populations, either having been overlooked by such diversionary measures or with their mental state having deteriorated in the interim (Fazel and Danesh, 2002; Singleton et al, 1997; Harrington and Bailey, 2004).

2 Vulnerable people are listed under the *Law Enforcement (Powers and Responsibilities) Regulation 2005* (NSW) as: children, a person with impaired intellectual functioning, people who are Aboriginal or Torres Strait Islanders, people who are of a non-English speaking background.

3 Under section 16 (paragraph 2) of the *Youth Justice and Criminal Justice Act 1999*, a vulnerable witness is defined as: a person under the age of 17, or anyone whose quality of evidence is likely to be diminished because they i) suffer from a mental disorder as defined by the *Mental Health Act*, ii) have a significant impairment of intelligence and social functioning, or iii) have a physical disability or are suffering from a physical disorder.

4 Gudjonsson and MacKeith (1994) present the case of 'Z' who confessed falsely to the murder of a woman and her five year old child. The appropriate adult in this case was a relative of Z, who had a full scale IQ of 77, placing her in the borderline range of intellectual functioning. The AA was also unable to read.

5 Procedural justice can be simplistically defined as treating people in a fair, respectful and procedurally correct manner and in doing so influencing individual assessments of legitimacy (Murphy et al, 2008; Sunshine and Tyler, 2003).

References

Convention on the Rights of Persons with Disabilities 2006 (United Nations).

Disability Discrimination Act 1992 (Cth) (DDA).

Disability Discrimination Act 1992 (UK).

Law Enforcement (Powers and Responsibilities) Regulation 2005 (NSW).

NSW Police Code of Practice for CRIME (Custody, Rights, Investigation, Management and Evidence) 2012 (NSW).

Police and Criminal Evidence Act 1984 (UK).

Youth Justice and Criminal Justice Act 1999 (UK).

American Association of Intellectual and Developmental Disabilities (AAIDD), 2010, *Intellectual Disability: Definition, Classification and Systems of Support*, AAIDD, Washington.

Association of Chief of Police Officers, 2010, *Guidance on Interviewing Victims and Witnesses, and Using Special Measures*. ACPO, London.

Association of Chief of Police Officers, 2009, *National Investigative Interviewing Strategy*, NPIA, London.

American Psychological Association, 2000, *Diagnostic and Statistical Manual-IV-Text Revision (DSM-IV-TR)*. American Psychological Association, Washington DC, USA.

Barron, P, Hassiotis, A and Banes, J, 2004, "Offenders with Intellectual Disability: A Prospective Comparative Study" 48 *Journal of Intellectual Disability Research* 69.

Bartels, L, 2011, "Police Interviews with Vulnerable Adult Suspects", *Research Practice Report*, 21, Criminological Research Council, Canberra.

Cant, R and Standen, P, 2007, "What Professionals Think about Offenders with Learning Disabilities in the Criminal Justice System" 35 *British Journal of Learning Disabilities* 174.

Carr, A and O'Reilly, G, 2007, "Diagnosis, Classification and Epidemiology", *The Handbook of Intellectual Disability and Clinical Psychology Practice* (Eds A Carr, G O'Reilly, P Walsh and J McEvoy), Routledge, Hove.

Colquitt, J, LePine, J, Piccollo, R, Zapata, C and Rich, B, 2012, "Explaining the Justice–Performance Relationship: Trust as Exchange Deepener or Trust as Uncertainty Reducer?" 97 *Journal of Applied Psychology* 1.

Cooper, S, Smiley, E, Morrison, J, Williamson, A and Allan, L, 2007, "Mental Ill-Health in Adults with Intellectual Disabilities: Prevalence and Associated Factors" 190 *British Journal of Psychiatry* 27.

Del Monte, R, (2012) "Personal communication" [Superintendent Rick Del Monte and Victoria Herrington], 5 April 2012.

Department of Health, 2009, *Valuing People Now: A New Three-Year Strategy for Learning Disabilities*, Department of Health, London.

Department of Health, 2001, *Valuing People: A Strategy for Learning Disability for the 21st Century*, The Stationary Office, London.

Edgerton R, 1967, *The Cloak of Competence: Stigma in the Lives of the Mentally Retarded*, University of California Press, Berkeley, CA.

Emerson, E and Hatton, C, 2007, "Mental Health of Children and Adolescents with Intellectual Disabilities in Britain" 191 *British Journal of Psychiatry* 493.

Everington, C and Fulero, S, 1999, "Competence to Confess: Measuring Understanding and Suggestibility of Defendants with Mental Retardation" 37 *Mental Retardation* 212.

Fazel, S and Danesh, J, 2002, "Serious Mental Disorder in 23000 Prisoners: A Systematic Review of 62 Surveys" 359 *The Lancet* 545.

Finn, W, Hyslop, J and Truman, C, 2000, *Mental Health, Multiple Needs and the Police: Findings from the Link Worker Scheme, Revolving Doors Agency,* London.

Forrester, A, Henderson, C, Wilson, S, Cumming, I, Spyrou, M and Parrott, J, 2009, "A Suitable Waiting Room? Hospital Transfer Outcomes and Delays from Two London Prisons" 33 *Psychiatric Bulletin* 409.

Gendel, K and Woodhams, J, 2005, "Suspects who have a Learning Disability: Police Perceptions Toward the Client Group and their Knowledge about Learning Disabilities" 9 *Journal of Intellectual Disabilities* 70.

Gudjonsson, GH, 2010, "Psychological Vulnerabilities during Police Interviews: Why are they Important?" 15 *Legal and Criminological Psychology* 161.

Gudjonsson, GH, 2006, "The Psychological Vulnerabilities of Witnesses and the Risk of False Accusations and False Confessions", *Witness Testimony. Psychological, Investigative and Evidential Perspectives* (Eds A Heaton-Armstrong, E Shepherd, GH Gudjonsson and D Wolchover), Oxford University Press, Oxford, UK.

Gudjonsson, GH, 2003, *The Psychology of Interrogations and Confessions: A Handbook,* Wiley, Chichester, UK.

Gudjonsson, GH, 1984, "A New Scale of Interrogative Suggestibility" 5 *Personality and Individual Differences* 303.

Gudjonsson, GH, Clare, I and Rutter, S, 1994, "Psychological Characteristics of Suspects Interviewed at Police Stations: A Factor-Analytic Study" 5 *Journal of Forensic Psychiatry* 517.

Gudjonsson, GH, Clare, I, Rutter, S and Pearse, J, 1993, *Persons at Risk during Interviews in Police Custody: The Identification of Vulnerabilities. The Royal Commission on Criminal Justice,* HMSO, London.

Gudjonsson, GH, Hayes, G and Rowlands, P, 2000, "Fitness to be Interviewed and Psychological Vulnerability: The Views of Doctors, Lawyers and Police Officers" 11 *Journal of Forensic Psychiatry* 74.

Gudjonsson, GH and Mackeith, J, 1994, "Learning Disability and the Police and Criminal Evidence Act 1984. Protection During Investigative Interviewing" 5 *Journal Of Forensic Psychiatry* 35.

Harrington, R and Bailey, S, 2004, *The Mental Health Needs and Effectiveness of Provision for Young Offenders in Custody and in the Community*. The Youth Justice Board, London, United Kingdom.

Herrington, V, 2011, *The In-betweeners: Exploring the Prevalence, Nature and Implications of Borderline Intellectual Disability among Young Adult Male Prisoners*. Unpublished PhD thesis, King's College London, London.

Herrington, V, Clifford, K, Hatzopolous, P, Ryle, S and Pope, R, 2009, The NSW Police Force Mental Health Intervention Team: Evaluation Final Report. Viewed on 30 May 2010, <www.police.nsw.gov.au/__data/assets/pdf_file/0006/174246/MHIT_Evaluation_Final_Report_241209.pdf>.

Herrington, V and Roberts, K, 2012, "Addressing Psychological Vulnerability in the Police Suspect Interview" Policing, in press.

Home Office, UK, 2007, *Achieving Best Evidence in Criminal Proceedings: Guidance on Interviewing Victims and Witnesses, and Using Special Measures*. Viewed on 5 May 2010, <www.Cps.Gov.Uk/Publications/Docs/Achieving_Best_Evidence_Final.Pdf>.

Jacobson, J, 2008, *No One Knows: Police Responses to Suspects with Learning Disabilities and Learning Difficulties*. A Review of Policy and Practice, Prison Reform Trust, London.

Joint Committee On Human Rights, 2008, *A Life Like Any Other? Human Rights of Adults with Learning Disabilities: Seventh Report of Session 2007-08*, Volume I, Report and Formal Minutes, The Stationary Office, London.

Kebbell, M, Hatton, C and Johnson, S, 2004, "Witnesses with Intellectual Disabilities in Court: What Questions are Asked and What Influence do they Have?" 9 *Legal and Criminological Psychology* 23.

Kingdom, DG and Turkington, D, 2005, *Cognitive Therapy of Schizophrenia*, The Guildford Press, London.

Leggett, J, Goodman, W and Dinani, S, 2007, "People with Learning Disabilities' Experiences of Being Interviewed by the Police" 35 *British Journal of Learning Disabilities* 168.

McAfee, J, Cockram, J and Wolfe, P, 2002, "Police Reactions to Crimes Involving People with Mental Retardation" 36 *Education and Training in Mental Retardation and Developmental Disabilities* 160.

McBrien, J, 2003, "The Intellectually Disabled Offender: Methodological Problems in Identification" 16 *Journal of Applied Research in Intellectual Disabilities* 95.

McKenzie, N and Sales, B, 2008, "New Procedures to Cut Delays in Transfer of Mentally Ill Prisoners to Hospital" 32 *Psychiatric Bulletin* 20.

Milne, R and Bull, R, 2001, "Interviewing Witnesses with Learning Disability for Legal Purposes: A Review" 29 *British Journal of Learning Disabilities* 93.

Office for National Statistics, 2001, *Psychiatric Morbidity*, HMSO, London.

Ord, B, Shaw, G and Green, T, 2008, *Investigative Interviewing Explained*, 2nd ed, LexisNexis, Sydney, Australia.

Perske, R, 1994, "Thoughts on Police Interrogation of Individuals with Mental Retardation" 32 *Mental Retardation* 377.

Perske, R, 2005, "Search for Persons with Intellectual Disabilities who Confessed to Serious Crimes They did not Commit" 43 *Mental Retardation* 58.

Roberts, K and Herrington, V, 2011, "Police interviews with Suspects: International Perspectives", *Handbook of Police Psychology* (Ed J Kitaef), Routledge, New York.

Sanders, A, Creaton, J, Bird, S and Weber, L, 1996, "Witnesses with Learning Disabilities", *Research Findings*, 44, Home Office Research and Statistics Directorate, London.

Savage, S and Milne, R, 2007, "Miscarriages Of Justice – The Role of the Investigative Process", *Handbook of Criminal Investigation* (Eds T Newburn, T Williamson and A Wright), Willan, Cullompton.

Shaw, J, Appleby, L and Baker, D, 2003, *Safer Prisons – A National Study of Prison Suicides 1999-2000, The National Confidential Inquiry into Suicides and Homicides by People with Mental Illness*, London, United Kingdom.

Shaw, J and Budd, E, 1982, "Determinants of Acquiescence and Nay Saying of Mentally Retarded Persons" 87 *American Journal of Mental Deficiency* 108.

Shepherd, E, 1991, "Ethical Interviewing" 7 *Policing* 42.

Siegelman, C, Budd, E, Spanal, C and Shoenrock, C, 1981, "When in Doubt Say Yes: Acquiescence in Interviews with Mentally Retarded Persons" 19 *Mental Retardation* 53.

Singleton, N, Meltzer, H, Gatward, R, Coid, J and Deasy, D, 1997, *Psychiatric Morbidity among Prisoners: Summary Report*, Office for National Statistics, London.

Talbot, J, 2008, *Prisoner's Voices: Experiences of the Criminal Justice System by Prisoners with Learning Disabilities*, Prison Reform Trust, London.

Ternes, M and Yuille, JC, 2008, "Eyewitness Memory and Eyewitness Identification Performance in Adults with Intellectual Disabilities" 21 *Journal of Applied Research in Intellectual Disabilities* 519.

Chapter 14

Vulnerable Suspects and Arrest and Investigative Processes

Terese Henning

This chapter considers how Australian laws recognise and deal with the vulnerabilities of particular groups of suspects in encounters with the police during criminal investigations. The focus of this chapter is on juvenile suspects, Indigenous suspects and suspects with mental disorders or cognitive impairments. While this focus is narrower than the widely accepted definition[1] of vulnerable people in the criminal justice context, it is chosen because these groups are significantly overrepresented in criminal justice statistics.

Recognition of their particular vulnerability is manifested in stipulations in international human rights instruments that States Parties[2] implement special measures and protections for them during criminal investigations. Though usually couched in broad terms these provisions explicitly mandate the development of accommodations in the investigative stages of the criminal justice process to ensure the equal access to justice of these vulnerable groups. For example, Article 13 of the United Nations *Convention on the Rights of Persons with Disabilities* requires States Parties to make procedural and age-appropriate modifications to investigative procedures to ensure the effective participation in the justice process of people with disabilities. The implicit basis of this provision is an understanding of the power imbalance and potential comprehension and communication mismatches between law enforcement officials and suspects with disabilities. This understanding is seen too in Article 40 of the United Nations *Convention on the Rights of the Child*, which requires that children's encounters with law enforcement officials be mediated by parents or legal guardians and by laws and procedures specifically applicable to them.[3]

Communication and comprehension problems also make particular points in criminal investigations key sites of risk for these vulnerable groups, namely, the arrest process and police questioning. In these situations they are highly susceptible to inappropriate treatment with potentially unjust or even tragic consequences. Accordingly, the discussion in this chapter focuses on these points in the criminal process. It is divided into two main parts within which relevant fundamental legal and international human rights principles are identified and their realisation in domestic law and practice considered. Particular attention is given to the incidence of arrest for these vulnerable groups because this is both indicative and determinative of the adequacy for them of legal protections in the criminal justice system.

Arrest

In *Donaldson v Broomby* Deane J characterised arrest in the following terms:

> Arrest is the deprivation of freedom. The ultimate instrument of arrest is force. The customary companions of arrest are ignominy and fear. A police power of arrest is a negation of any true right to personal liberty.[4]

For this reason, international human rights instruments and Australian human rights legislation provide that no one shall be arbitrarily arrested or deprived of his or her liberty except on grounds and in accordance with procedures established by law.[5] According to international human rights jurisprudence, to avoid characterisation as arbitrary an arrest must not only be permitted by domestic law, but that law, too, must conform to international human rights standards.[6] Consequently, the law of arrest in any jurisdiction must comply with principles of justice and the dignity of the human person and be appropriate and predictable.[7]

Attempts to achieve greater certainty and predictability for Australian arrest laws have seen the removal, in many Australian jurisdictions, of the distinction between arrestable and non-arrestable offences, with a consequent extension of the police power to arrest for all offences rather than its restriction, as is the case at common law, to serious or indictable offences (felonies at common law). This expansion in arrest powers has been accompanied by legislated provisions that seek to control their exercise by requiring that arrest be treated as a measure of last resort, only to be utilised where proceeding by an alternative means would not secure specified ends, including the appearance in court of the alleged offender, the termination of the offending behaviour, prevention of the loss or destruction of evidence or preservation of the safety or welfare of members of the community or of the arrestee. Thus the police in most Australian jurisdictions have now been vested with a guided discretion to arrest for all offences.[8]

The treatment of arrest as a measure of last resort conforms to international human rights doctrines, which impose the principle of proportionality on the exercise of executive powers of detention. For an arrest to comply with these doctrines, it must be reasonable and necessary in all the circumstances of the particular case.[9] It also replicates Australian judicial statements in cases like *Fleet v District Court*,[10] *Director of Public Prosecutions (NSW) v CAD*,[11] *Director of Public Prosecutions v Carr*,[12] *Lake v Dobson*[13] and *Donaldson v Broomby*.[14] These cases tell us that arrest is unwarranted and may be judged unlawful where the offence is minor, the police know the suspect's name and address and there is no reason to believe that a summons will not be effective to ensure his or her appearance in court.

The requirements of lawfulness and non-arbitrariness are also reflected in statutory and common law restrictions on when and for what purpose an arrest may be made. So an arrest cannot be made in order to further police investigations, for example, to question a suspect to obtain evidence against him or her. An arrest can only be made when there is already sufficient evidence to provide reasonable grounds for a suspicion or belief that the arrestee has committed or is committing an arrestable offence. Then, the sole purpose of the arrest must be to bring the arrestee before a judicial officer to be dealt with according to the law, that is, to have the question of bail determined.[15] An arrest made for investigative purposes is unlawful.

Even with these generally applicable inhibitions on the exercise of arrest powers, the particular vulnerability of children, Indigenous Australians and suspects with mental or developmental impairments warrants extra vigilance in the enforcement of arrest minimisation principles. For the great majority of the community, arrest is recognised as being innately punitive.[16] It is unavoidably coercive, inherently humiliating and frightening. Additionally an arrest record can have repercussions beyond the criminal justice system. It can preclude certain types of employment and international travel. For Indigenous people arrest appears to have particularly invidious implications for their employment prospects. Research has shown that high arrest rates are a factor in low rates of employment for Indigenous people (Hunter and Borland, 1999; Blagg, Morgan, Cunneen and Ferrante, 2005; Lawrie, 2002).

Whether or not a person is arrested can also materially affect how he or she subsequently fares in the criminal justice system. Rates of detention on remand are higher for arrestees than for those summonsed for the same offence. This has implications for their ability to defend charges and avoid an ultimate custodial sentence (Hunter, Cameron and Henning, 2005). These problems appear to be exacerbated for detainees with a mental disability or cognitive impairment. For example, it has been found that people with an intellectual disability are less likely to be released on bail than other people, possibly because they cannot demonstrate an understanding of bail conditions or an ability to keep them or because they lack the type of support in the community that would enable them to do so (Grundseit, Forell and McCarron, 2008). For obvious reasons, detention in custody can be highly inimical to their best interests – they may be particularly susceptible to exploitation by others in custodial institutions or to physical harm if their behaviour is misunderstood.

It is an uncontroversial fact that children and young people are particularly vulnerable participants in the criminal justice process. It is also clear that the offending rates for 15-19 year-olds are four times those of adult offenders (Australian Institute of Criminology (AIC), 2010a). Because juvenile offenders generally "grow out of" crime, and stigmatisation is regarded as a determinative factor in children's and adolescents' criminal trajectories, the avoidance of stigmatisation is a key component of juvenile justice thinking in Australia (Richards, 2011: 5-6). Similarly, because formal intervention in the lives of juvenile offenders greatly increases the likelihood of adult offending, criminal justice authorities are encouraged to adopt the least intensive and intrusive interventions possible (Gatti, Tremblay and Vitaro, 2009; see also Robinson, Ch 16 and Graham, Ch 17, in this collection). This has clear implications for their arrest.

The *International Convention on the Rights of the Child* provides in Article 37 that the arrest of a child "shall be used only as a measure of last resort and for the shortest appropriate period of time". However, there is no similar separate provision in international human rights instruments for Indigenous people and people with mental and intellectual impairments. They are covered only by the generally applicable international human rights principles noted above. The same approach is evident in Australian legislation. While special provision is made in some jurisdictions for arrest powers to be used sparingly where children are concerned[17] there is no separate, specific provision in this regard for Indigenous people or people with mental and developmental impairments. They are covered merely by general inhibitions and directives on the use of arrest powers. Further, where children are concerned, in some legislative regimes, the need to treat arrest as a measure of last resort is a guiding principle rather than an obligation.[18] The same pattern can be observed in Australian Police Codes of Conduct and manuals. They set down the generally applicable principle that arrest is to be used as a matter of last resort and then separately re-emphasise this principle for children. But there is no separate restatement of this principle for Indigenous People or people with mental disabilities and developmental impairments.[19]

The failure to legislate specifically for arrest to be used as a measure of last resort in relation to Indigenous people and people with mental and developmental impairments is a distinct gap in Australia's protection of these vulnerable groups. Police owe a higher duty of care to vulnerable people because their particular characteristics place them at greater risk than other people during the arrest process and in custodial situations. Yet, as shown below, they are also at greater risk of being arrested than other people. For Indigenous people it is clear that systemic discrimination is an explanatory factor in their rates of arrest (Mahoney, 2005: 9.25; Law Reform Commission of Western Australia, 2006: 82; see also Bartels, in this collection, Ch 12). This underscores the toxicity of the criminal justice environment for them and emphasises the importance of ensuring that their arrest is genuinely treated as an exceptional measure.

While it is difficult to obtain a definitive picture of the arrest profiles of Indigenous people and people with mental impairments, available evidence indicates that both groups are overrepresented in arrest statistics. For example, Western Australian arrest statistics[20] published in 2007 show that from 1995 to

2005, Indigenous people were consistently overrepresented in arrest statistics in that State. That overrepresentation rose from a factor of 5.7 in 1995 to a factor of 8.1 in 2005. This means that in 2005, Indigenous people were over eight times more likely to be arrested in Western Australia than non-Indigenous people (Loh, Maller, Fernandez, Ferrante and Walsh, 2007: 44). The National Police Custody Survey in 2002 found that Indigenous people were 17 times more likely to be in police custody than non-Indigenous people (Taylor and Bareja, 2005). The 2009 Australian Bureau of Statistics NATSISS survey found that in 2008, 15% of Indigenous people aged 15 and over had been arrested once or more than once in the past five years (Australian Bureau of Statistics (ABS), 2009). For Aboriginal women, the statistics are even more disquieting.[21] For example, in 2002 Indigenous women accounted for 23% of police custody incidents compared with 14% of non-Indigenous police custody incidents (AIC, 2010b). An earlier study found that Indigenous women were 58% more likely to be held in police custody than non-Indigenous women (Carcach and McDonald, 1997: 10).

Imprisonment rates for Indigenous people also suggest that they are arrested at disproportionate rates. The Australian Bureau of Statistics reported that at 30 June 2011, 26% of the overall Australian prison population identified as Aboriginal or Torres Strait Islander and that the rate of imprisonment for Indigenous people was 14 times higher than for non-Indigenous people (ABS, 2011). As long ago as 1991 the Royal Commission into Aboriginal Deaths in Custody found Aboriginality to be a significant factor in the arrest rates of Indigenous people and therefore a major contributor to their disproportionate rates of death in custody (Royal Commission into Aboriginal Deaths in Custody, 1991). Consequently, the Commission identified minimising the use of arrest powers as fundamental to the reduction of Aboriginal and Torres Strait Islander deaths in custody. This is yet to achieve explicit recognition in Australian statutory regimes.

While there are no national data on the arrest rates of people with mental and intellectual impairments, it is nevertheless possible to achieve some understanding of their levels of police detention. If we can extrapolate from their incarceration rates, then they are significantly overrepresented in police arrests. This is certainly the inference Ogloff, Davis, Rivers and Ross drew in their study for the Criminology Research Council. They noted that the police have four options for dealing with people with a mental disorder and concluded that the prevalence of mental disorder in gaols suggested that arrest was the preferred choice (Ogloff et al, 2007: 3; see also Butler, Andrews, Allnutt, Sakashita, Smith and Basson, 2006, and Tye and Mullen, 2006).[22] The New South Wales Law Reform Commission has also reported on research showing that intellectual disability is significantly more common among prisoners than in the general population. The Commission estimates that approximately 20% of the adult prison population has an intellectual disability with approximately 10% to 13% of young people matching the criteria for intellectual disability (Kenny et al, 2006: 24 and Allerton et al, 2003:

21 cited in NSW Law Reform Commission, 2010: 1.37). Rates of mental illness have been found to be between three and five times higher in offender populations than those expected in the general community (Ogloff et al, 2007: 1-2; Butler et al, 2006; see also Herrington and Clifford, in this collection, Ch 8). The Drug Use Monitoring in Australia (2012) program regularly finds high rates of mental health problems reported by police detainees. For example, its 2009-2010 report states,

> two in five detainees (38%) reported having been previously diagnosed with a mental health related issue. Female detainees were more likely than male detainees to report having been previously diagnosed with a mental health related issue (51% cf 36%) (Sweeny and Payne, 2012: xiii).[23]

Police perceptions may help to explain the high rates of involvement in the criminal justice system of people with mental impairments. It appears that the police generally perceive the behaviour of people with mental disabilities and developmental impairments as unpredictable, uncontrollable, irrational and frequently violent and dangerous (Modell and Cropp, 2007: 60-3). The police may also feel pressured to arrest if they or members of the community perceive someone to be a public nuisance or a danger to him or herself. Further, there is evidence that the police are increasingly relied upon to manage mental illness in the community (Henderson, 2006):

> Police have become "de facto" ambulances transferring people from one hospital to another. Frequently failing to secure a hospital admission the police must "do something", and "arrest by default" (Davis, 1992 cited in Henderson, 2006).[24]

Their role in this regard has been attributed to the deinstitutionalisation of the mentally ill without adequate provision of supportive accommodation, an increase in drug and alcohol use by those with mental and cognitive problems and inadequate resourcing of community based mental health services (Ogloff et al, 2007: 2). However, it has been argued that the criminal justice system provides an opportunity to deliver treatment to people who have poor or no access to community support services (Ogloff, 2002; Ogloff, Lemphers, and Dwyer, 2004).

So would a special legislative direction not to arrest Indigenous suspects and suspects with mental disorders and developmental disabilities (unless specified criteria are met) be likely to have any impact on their arrest rates? Arguably the absence of provisions specific to these groups makes it easier for both the police and courts to ignore or overlook arrest minimisation principles where they are concerned. Certainly, generally applicable statutory provisions and guidelines in police manuals are insufficient to deter the police from making inappropriate arrests or the courts from condoning them. While occasionally judicial strictures and legislative attempts to minimise the use of arrest are observed and applied, the decisional law is patchy in this regard. Whereas in cases like *Director of Public*

Prosecutions v Carr[25] and *Donaldson v Broomby*[26] the courts gave teeth to the need to curtail unnecessary arrests, (in the former, excluding evidence of the offences charged obtained pursuant to an unnecessary arrest and, in the latter, holding police officers liable for assault) in other cases they have prioritised policing interests over the enforcement of arrest minimisation principles. For example, in cases like the *Director of Public Prosecutions v AM*,[27] *Ashley v Balchin*,[28] *Klewer v Fleming LCM*[29] and *Perrin v Jackson*[30] the courts upheld decisions to arrest where it was clearly open to the police to proceed by way of summons or infringement notice and, in some instances, where proceeding by way of arrest was acknowledged to have breached police guidelines. From these cases and arrest statistics it appears that specific statutory provisions may be required in each jurisdiction to give weight to the arrest minimisation principle. The Tasmanian Law Reform Institute (2011: 5.2.14) has additionally recommended that the police should be required to furnish written reasons for decisions to arrest. The need to supply explanations may discourage unwarranted arrests.

The arrest process itself is particularly dangerous for vulnerable adults and children. In 2009, the United Nations Human Rights Committee expressed concern about "reports of the excessive use of force by law enforcement officials against groups such as indigenous people, racial minorities, persons with disabilities as well as young people" (UN Human Rights Committee, 2009: para 59). The Committee made clear that Australian legislation and policies do not yet accord with the United Nations Basic Principles on the Use of Force and Firearms by Law Enforcement Officials. Those Principles include requirements that Governments implement rules that:

- Make clear that the intentional lethal use of firearms is only permissible when strictly unavoidable in order to protect life.
- Proscribe the use of firearms except in self-defence or defence of others against the imminent threat of death or serious injury or to prevent the perpetration of particularly serious crimes involving a grave threat to life, and only when less extreme means are insufficient to achieve these objectives.
- Require law enforcement officials to identify themselves and give a clear warning of their intent to use firearms, with sufficient time for the warning to be observed, unless to do so would unduly place the law enforcement officials at risk or would create a risk of death or serious harm to other persons.
- Ensure that relatives or close friends of persons injured or killed by the police force are notified at the earliest possible moment.
- Ensure that an effective independent review process is available in relation to all incidents involving law enforcement officials' use of firearms in the performance of their duty.

No Australian jurisdiction has enacted legislation that meets all these terms.

Further, it is apparent that Australian police resort to lethal force too readily, that they are inadequately skilled and lack the communication competencies to deal with people with mental health problems and apparently dangerous situations with minimum force (Office of Police Integrity Victoria, 2009). These deficiencies and the disturbing mismatch between Australian police practice and the United Nations Basic Principles on the Use of Force were starkly demonstrated in the case of Adam Salter, a young man who, in 2009 during a psychotic episode, was killed by police. The New South Wales Coroner's investigation of this case reveals that the police conduct failed against each of the standards outlined above. Alarmingly, the Coroner's Report also shows that the police involved and those who subsequently investigated the incident colluded in covering up the avoidability of and police responsibility for, Adam Salter's death. The Coroner described the police intervention as an "utter failure" and the subsequent police investigation as "a disgrace" and as so seriously flawed as to be incapable of persuading the community that the circumstances surrounding Adam Salter's death were investigated fairly and scrupulously.[31]

Various mechanisms have been suggested to de-escalate violent confrontations between the police and people who are mentally impaired. They include involving mental health clinicians in police responses. Different manifestations of this approach have been found to have differential success rates but generally to achieve an improvement on police only responses. In addition they may reduce unnecessary arrests.[32]

Questioning

Inescapably, the power imbalance inherent in situations of custodial questioning and the high likelihood of communication mismatches place vulnerable adult and juvenile suspects at a significant disadvantage in investigative interviews. People with cognitive and mental impairments may lack understanding of what is happening. Many may be overly trusting and agree with investigating officials' suggestions even when they are not correct (Ochoa and Rome, 2009: 133). Those questioning them may misinterpret their behaviour and/or have little understanding of how to communicate with them (Dixon and Travis, 2007). We know that particular kinds of questioning techniques (the use of leading questions for example) produce unreliable responses from children and people with mental impairments.[33] Similarly, language and cultural factors produce failures in communication between Indigenous people and the police and can lead them to give answers that are misleading or erroneously self-incriminating (Eades, 2010).

In Australia, recognition of these problems for Indigenous people, prompted decisional law[34] that established rules to be observed during investigative interviews – the so-called *Anunga* rules. They mandate the use of interpreters, require a "prisoner's friend" to be present during questioning and stipulate that particular care be taken in administering the caution and asking questions. In addition, in some Australian jurisdictions special protections have now been enacted for vulnerable adults and children who are in custody and are being questioned by the police.[35] These protections include shorter time limits on interviews than apply to other detainees,[36] requirements for a support person or "interview friend" to be present during the interview and the requirement to notify a parent or guardian (or in the case of Indigenous detainees, the Aboriginal Legal Service) of the person's arrest.[37] Provisions that apply to all detainees relating to the use of interpreters and enabling detainees to communicate with a relative, friend and/or legal representative are also relevant.[38] Yet, there remain significant gaps in the protections provided. For example, in Tasmania, there are no special provisions for any vulnerable detainees other than for the employment of an interpreter where a detainee's grasp of English is limited.[39] In South Australia and Victoria there are special provisions only for children and for the use of interpreters.[40] The Commonwealth legislative regime contains special protections for juvenile and Indigenous detainees only.[41] There are no special protections for detainees with cognitive or mental disabilities.

Police manuals may to some degree fill these deficiencies.[42] For instance, the Tasmanian Police Manual contains detailed guidelines for questioning children, Indigenous detainees and detainees with cognitive and mental impairments. These guidelines encompass such matters as information about disability service providers, the notification of relatives, friends and relevant legal advisory bodies (including the Aboriginal Legal Service) about interviewees' arrest, the attendance of an independent or support person and advice about modes of questioning and how to administer the caution (Tasmanian Department of Police and Emergency Management, 2010: 7.1, 7.1.2, 9.1, 9.1.14).[43] By their very nature, Police Guidelines cannot provide sufficient protection. They do not have the force of law. Accordingly, their breach may have limited impact on the outcome of any hearing or trial. While trial judges have a discretion[44] to exclude any evidence obtained in breach of police guidelines, there is no guarantee that they will exercise this discretion to do so. Further, such surveillance of police conduct can only occur in cases that proceed to trial. Thus, both the police guidelines and the judicial discretion to exclude improperly obtained evidence, provide only weak protection to vulnerable suspects. They, therefore, also constitute a weak disincentive to inappropriate treatment of vulnerable suspects. This is reinforced by Canadian and United States' research showing that exclusionary rules of evidence have minimal impact on police conduct. Where they operate on a discretionary basis the affect appears to be to encourage rather than deter improper conduct.[45]

Clearly there is a need for more comprehensive legislation to be enacted throughout Australia. Further, the legislated protections are limited in their conception of what can be done to protect vulnerable suspects during police interviews. While provision is made for interpreters and support people to be present, there is no provision for intermediaries to attend who can advise the police about the appropriate style of questioning to use to elicit reliable answers and intervene where the nature of the questioning is not appropriate. As noted earlier, inappropriate questioning styles and techniques can elicit unreliable responses from vulnerable interviewees and even result in their making untrue admissions. In two Australian jurisdictions, Western Australia and New South Wales,[46] there is statutory provision for children and people with mental impairments to be assisted in testifying by intermediaries with expertise in facilitating communication between them and the court. Under a similar United Kingdom model,[47] intermediaries may also assist the police in communicating with vulnerable witnesses during investigative interviews. This regime also makes provision for certain young and vulnerable defendants to be assisted by an intermediary, but only when they testify at trial.[48] While the statutory provision in this regard is yet to be implemented, the courts have nevertheless exercised their inherent jurisdiction to enable intermediaries to assist vulnerable defendants in giving evidence at trial.[49] Australian courts have not yet considered such an approach. Further, in Australia, there is no statutory provision for defendants to be assisted by an intermediary either at trial or during investigative interviews. The United Kingdom experience with the intermediary model for witnesses has prompted requests for its extension to defendants during investigative interviews (O'Mahoney, 2010). If such provision were to be made in Australia, then legislation imposing time limits on the questioning of suspects would need to be amended to ensure that obtaining the assistance of an intermediary could be accommodated without unduly extending detention times.

Summary

The overview provided in this chapter suggests that there are significant deficiencies in Australian legal protections for juveniles, Indigenous people and people with mental and cognitive impairments where arrest and investigative interviews are concerned. Australian legislation does not yet meet United Nations human rights guidelines and existing statutory protections have limited scope. The position is worst for people with mental impairments. They remain largely unrecognised in the protections provided by Australian legislation and yet they are massively over-represented in criminal justice statistics.

Endnotes

1 See for example cl 24(1) *Law Enforcement (Powers and Responsibilities) Regulation 2005* (NSW); Tasmania Law Reform Institute, *Consolidation of Arrest Laws in Tasmania*, Final Report No 15 (2011) at [5.2.1]; New South Wales Law Reform Commission, *Criminal Procedure, Police Powers of Arrest and Detention*, Report No 66, (1990) 131.

2 A 'State Party' to a treaty is a country that has ratified or acceded to that particular treaty and is therefore bound by the provisions in the instrument.

3 Similarly, special procedures for children are mandated by the *Charter of Human Rights and Responsibilities 2006* (Vic), ss 23 and 25(3) and the *Human Rights Act 2004* (ACT), ss 20 and 22(3).

4 (1982) 160 FLR 124 at 126.

5 Article 9, *International Covenant on Civil and Political Rights*, replicated in s 18(1) and (2) of the *Human Rights Act 2004* (ACT) and s 21 of the *Charter of Human Rights and Responsibilities 2006* (Vic).

6 *Shams v Australia* (UNHRC, Communication No 1288/2004, UN Doc CCPR/C/90/D/1255, 1256, 1259, 1260, 1268, 1270, 1288/2004, 2007); *Benjamin v Wilson* (2003) 36 EHRR 1.

7 *Hugo van Alpen v The Netherlands* (UNHRC, Communication No 305/1988, UN Doc CCPR/C/39/D/305/1988, 1990) analysed in Gans et al (2011).

8 *Crimes Act 1900* (ACT), s 212; *Crimes Act 1914* (Cth), s 3W(1); *Law Enforcement (Powers and Responsibilities) Act 2002* (NSW), s 99; *Police Administration Act* (NT), s 123; *Police Powers and Responsibilities Act 2000* (Qd), s 365(1); *Police Offences Act 1935* (Tas), s 55(2); *Crimes Act 1958* (Vic), s 458; *Criminal Investigation Act 2006* (WA), s 128.

9 *A v Australia* (UNHRC, Communication No 560/1993, UN Doc CCPR/C/59/D/560/1993); *Shams v Australia* (UNHRC, Communication No 1288/2004, UN Doc CCPR/C/90/D/1255, 1256, 1259, 1260, 1268, 1270, 1288/2004, 2007); *Danyal Shafiq v Australia* (UNHRC, Communication No 1324/2004, CCPR/C/88/D/1324/2004, 2006); *Hugo van Alpen v The Netherlands* (UNHRC, Communication No 305/1988, UN Doc CCPR/C/39/D/305/1988, 1990).

10 [1999] NSWCA 464 at 74.

11 [2003] NSWSC 193 at 7.

12 [2002] NSWSC 194.

13 (1981) 5 PS Rev 221 (unreported, NSWCA, 19 December 1980).

14 (1982) 60 FLR 124.

15 *Williams v R* (1986) 161 CLR 278; *R v Dungay* [2001] NSWCCA 443; *Woodley v Boyd* [2001] NSWCA 35; *Norton v R* (2001) 24 WAR 488; *Drymalik v Feldman* (1966) SASR 227 at 231.

16 *Director of Public Prosecutions v Carr* [2002] NSWSC 194 at [12]; *Fleet v District Court; Director of Public Prosecutions (NSW) v CAD* [2003] NSWSC 193 at [7]; *Zavarinos v New South Wales* (2004) 214 ALR 234 at [37]; *Donaldson v Broomby* (1982) 60 FLR 124 at 126; *Lake v Dobson* (1981) 5 PS Rev 221 (unreported, NSWCA, 19 December 1980).

17 For example, *Youth Justice Act 1997* (Tas), s 24; *Children, Youth and Families Act 2005* (Vic), s 345; *Youth Justice Act 1992* (Qd), ss 12 and 13; *Young Offenders Act 1994* (WA), ss 7(h) and 42; *Youth Justice Act* (NT), ss 4(c) and 22; *Children and Young People Act 2008* (ACT), s 94(1)(f); *Children (Criminal Proceedings) Act 1987* (NSW), s 8.

18 For example, *Children and Young People Act 2008* (ACT), s 94(1)(f); *Young Offenders Act 1994* (WA), s 7(h).

19 For example, the NSW Police Force, *Code of Practice for CRIME (Custody, Rights, Investigation, Management and Evidence)* (2012) and the Tasmania Department of Police and Emergency Management (TDPEM), *Tasmania Police Manual: Orders, Instructions and Operational Guidance for Members of Tasmania Police,* (2010).

20 Western Australia is the only jurisdiction for which arrest statistics have been consistently published. However, their publication appears to have been discontinued in 2007.

21 For a comprehensive literature review of Indigenous women's involvement in the criminal justice system, see Bartels (2010).

22 The other options are to attempt to resolve the issue informally, contact a crisis team, or take the person to a hospital.

23 For the higher prevalence for women prisoners, see Tye and Mullen, (2006) and Butler, T, et al, (2006).

24 See also Burgess, (2005) and Carroll, (2005).

25 [2002] NSWSC 194.

26 (1982) 60 FLR 124.

27 [2006] NSWSC 346.

28 [2006] NTSC 41.

29 [2005] NSWSC 1318.

30 [2008] WASC 77.

31 *Inquest into the Death of Adam Quddus Salter* findings of Magistrate Scott Mitchell, Deputy State Coroner, 14 October 2011, In the Local Court of New South Wales Coronial Jurisdiction, File Number 3333/09 at [128], [111] and [124].

32 For an overview of the different models see Ogloff, JRP, et al (nd).

33 See, for example, Bull (1995); Ceci and Friedman (2000); Milne and Bull (2003); Powell (2002); Bull (2010); Smith and Tilney (2007).

34 *R v Anunga* (1976) 11 ALR 412.

35 For a comprehensive analysis of provisions for vulnerable adult see, Bartels (2011).

36 For example, *Crimes Act 1914* (Cth), s 23C(4).

37 For example, *Crimes Act 1914* (Cth), Pt IC, Div 3; *Summary Offences Act 1953* (SA), ss 83A and 79A(1a) and (1b); *Law Enforcement (Powers and Responsibilities) Regulation 2005* (NSW), Pt 3, Div 3; *Police Powers and Responsibilities Act 2000* (Qd), Ch 15, Pt 3, Div 3; *Crimes Act 1958* (Vic), s 464E; *Young Offenders Act 1994* (WA), s 20.

38 *Criminal Law (Detention and Interrogation) Act 1995* (Tas), ss 5, 6 and 16; *Crimes Act 1958* (Vic), ss 464C and 464D; *Police Powers and Responsibilities Act 2000* (Qd), ss 418-419 and 433; *Law Enforcement (Powers and Responsibilities) Act 2002* (NSW), Pt 9, Div 3; *Criminal Investigation Act 2006* (WA), ss 10, 137 and 138.

39 *Criminal Law (Detention and Interrogation) Act 1995* (Tas), s 5.

40 *Summary Offences Act 1953* (SA), ss 83A and 79A(1a) and (1b); *Crimes Act 1958* (Vic), ss 464D and 464E.

41 *Crimes Act 1914* (Cth), Pt IC, Div 3.

42 or detailed analysis see Bartels (2011).

43 See also, Queensland Police Service (nd); Queensland Police Service (2010); Victoria Police (2011); WA Police (nd); NT Police (1998a); NT Police (1998b); NSW Police Force (2012).

44 Section 138 of the Commonwealth, New South Wales, Norfolk Island, Tasmanian and Victorian *Evidence Acts* and *Bunning v Cross* (1978) 141 CLR 54.

45 Stribopoulos, J 'In Search of Dialogue: the Supreme Court Police Powers and the *Charter*' (2005) 31 *Queen's Law Journal* 1 at 49-54.

46 *Evidence Act 1906* (WA), s 106F and *Criminal Procedure Act 1986* (NSW), s 306ZK.

47 *Youth Justice and Criminal Evidence Act 1999* (UK), s 29.

48 *Youth Justice and Criminal Evidence Act 1999* (UK) inserted by the *Coroners and Justice Act 2009* (UK), s 104 yet to be implemented.

49 *R (C) v Sevenoaks Youth Court* [2010] 1 All ER 735; *R (AS) v Great Yarmouth Youth Court* [2011] EWHC 2059 (Admin) and *R v Walls* [2011] EWCA Crim 443.

References

Australian Bureau of Statistics, 2011, *Prisoners in Australia*, 4517.0, ABS, Canberra. Viewed on 23 March 2012, <www.abs.gov.au/ausstats/abs@.nsf/mf/4517.0>.

Australian Bureau of Statistics, 2008, *National Aboriginal and Torres Strait Islander Social Survey*, 4714.0, ABS, Canberra.

Australian Institute of Criminology, 2010a, *Australian Crime: Facts & Figures 2009*, AIC, Canberra. Viewed on 23 March 2012, <www.aic.gov.au/publications/ current%20series/facts/1-20/2009.aspx>.

Australian Institute of Criminology, 2010b, *Data on Policing and Arrests*, AIC, Canberra.

Bartels, L, 2011, "Police Interviews with Vulnerable Adult Suspects", *Research in Practice*, 21, AIC, Canberra.

Bartels, L, 2010, "Indigenous Women's Offending Patterns: A Literature Review", *AIC Reports, Research and Public Policy Series*, 107, Australian Institute of Criminology, Canberra.

Blagg H, Morgan N, Cunneen, C and Ferrante, A, 2005, *Systemic Racism as a Factor in the Overrepresentation of Aboriginal People in the Victorian Criminal Justice System*, Report to the Equal Opportunity Commission and Aboriginal Justice Forum, Equal Opportunity Commission, Melbourne.

Bull, R, 2010, "The Investigative Interviewing of Children and Other Vulnerable Witnesses: Psychological Research and Working/Professional Practice" 15 *Legal and Criminological Psychology* 5.

Bull, R, 1995, "Interviewing Children in Legal Contexts", *Handbook of Psychology in Legal Contexts* (Eds R Bull and D Carson), John Wiley and Sons, Chichester, UK, 242.

Burgess, M, 2005, "Police: Working with Mental Health" 9 *Association News* 7.

Butler, T, Andrews, G, Allnutt, S, Sakashita, C, Smith, NE and Basson, J, 2006, "Mental Disorders in Australian Prisoners: A Comparison with a Community Sample" 40 *Australian and New Zealand Journal of Psychiatry* 272.

Carcach, C and McDonald, D, 1997, *National Police Custody Survey August 1995*, AIC, Canberra.

Carroll, M, 2005, "Mental Health System Overburdening Police" 86 *Police Journal* (South Australia) 18.

Ceci, SJ and Friedman, RD, 2000, "Suggestibility of Children: Scientific Research and Legal Implications" 86 *Cornell Law Review* 33.

Dixon, D and Travis, G, 2007, *Interrogating Images: Audio-visually Recorded Police Questioning of Suspects*, Institute of Criminology Press, Sydney.

Eades, D, 2010, *Sociolinguistics and the Legal Process*, Multilingual Matters, Bristol.

Gans, J, Henning, T, Hunter, J and Warner, K, 2011, *Criminal Process and Human Rights*, Federation Press, Sydney.

Gatti, U, Tremblay, R and Vitaro, F, 2009, "Iatrogenic Effect of Juvenile Justice" 50 *Journal of Child Psychology and Psychiatry* 991.

Grundseit, AS, Forell, S and McCarron, E, 2008, *Taking Justice into Custody: the Legal Needs of Prisoners*, Law and Justice Foundation of NSW, Sydney. Viewed on 23 March 2012, <www.lawfoundation.net.au/report/prisoners>.

Henderson, C, 2006, *Why People with a Mental Illness Are Over-represented in the Criminal Justice System*, Mental Health Coordinating Council, Sydney.

Hunter, B and Borland, J, 1999, "The Effect of Arrest on Indigenous Employment Prospects" 45 *Crime and Justice Bulletin* 4.

Hunter, J, Cameron, C and Henning, T, 2005, *Litigation II: Evidence and Criminal Process*, LexisNexis Butterworths, Sydney.

Law Reform Commission of Western Australia, 2006, *Aboriginal Customary Laws: the Interaction of Western Australian Law with Aboriginal Law and Culture, Final Report*, Government of Western Australia, Perth.

Lawrie, R, 2002, *Speak Out, Speak Strong: Researching the Needs of Aboriginal Women in Custody*, Aboriginal Justice Advisory Council, Sydney.

Loh, N, Maller, MG, Fernandez, JA, Ferrante, AM and Walsh, MRJ, 2007, *Crime and Justice Statistics for Western Australia, 2005*, Crime Research Centre, University of Western Australia, Perth.

Mahoney, D, 2005, *Inquiry into the Management of Offenders in Custody and the Community*, State Law Publisher, Perth.

Milne, R and Bull, R, 2003, "Interviewing by Police", *Handbook of Psychology in Legal Contexts*, 2d ed, (Eds D Carson and H Bull), John Wiley and Sons, Chichester, UK, 111.

Modell, SJ and Cropp, D, 2007, "Police Officers and Disability: Perceptions and Attitudes", 45 *Intellectual and Developmental Disabilities* 60.

New South Wales Law Reform Commission, 2010, *People with Cognitive and Mental Health Impairments in the Criminal Justice System: An Overview*, New South Wales Law Reform Commission, Sydney, 2010.

NSW Police Force, 2012, *Code of Practice for CRIME (Custody, Rights, Investigation, Management and Evidence)*, NSW Police, Sydney. Viewed on 23 March 2012, <www.police.nsw.gov.au/about_us/policies_and_procedures/legislation_list/code_of_practice_for_crime>.

NT Police, 1998a, *General Order Q1 – Questioning and Investigations*, NT Police, Darwin.

NT Police, 1998b, *General Order Q2 – Questioning People Who Have Difficulties with the English Language – The 'Anunga' Guidelines*, NT Police, Darwin.

Ochoa, T and Rome, J, 2009, "Considerations for Arrests and Interrogations of Suspects with Hearing, Cognitive and Behavioral Disorders" 9 *Law Enforcement Executive Forum Journal* 131.

Office of Police Integrity Victoria, 2009, *Review of the Use of Force by and against Victorian Police*, OPI, Melbourne.

Ogloff, JRP, 2002, "Identifying and Accommodating the Needs of Mentally Ill People in Gaols and Prisons" 9 *Psychiatry, Psychology, and Law* 1.

Ogloff, JRP, Lemphers, A, and Dwyer, C, 2004, "Dual Diagnosis in an Australian Forensic Psychiatric Hospital: Prevalence and Implications for Services" 22 *Behavioral Sciences and the Law* 543.

Ogloff, JRP, Davis, MR, Rivers, G and Ross, S, 2007, "The Identification of Mental Disorders in the Criminal Justice System", *Trends and Issues in Crime and Criminal Justice*, 334, AIC, Canberra.

Ogloff, JRP Davis, MR, Rivers, G and Ross, S, nd, *The Identification of Mental Disorders in the Criminal Justice System*, Monash University and Centre for Forensic Behavioural Science.

O'Mahoney, B, 2010, "The Emerging Role of the Registered Intermediary with the Vulnerable Witness and Offender: Facilitating Communication with the Police and the Members of the Judiciary" 38 *British Journal of Learning Disabilities* 232.

Powell, M, 2002, "Specialist Training in Investigative and Evidential Interviewing: Is It Having Any Effect on the Behaviour of Professionals in the Field?" 9 *Psychiatry, Psychology and Law* 44.

Queensland Police Service, 2010, *Operational Police Manual: Special Needs Groups*, QPS, Brisbane.

Queensland Police Service, nd, *Vulnerable Persons Policy*, QPS, Brisbane. Viewed on 23 March 2012, <www.police.qld.gov.au/Resources/Internet/rti/policies/documents/QPSVulnerablePersonsPolicy.pdf>.

Richards, K, 2011, "What Makes Juvenile Offenders Different from Adult Offenders?", *Trends and Issues in Crime and Criminal Justice*, 409, AIC, Canberra.

Royal Commission into Aboriginal Deaths in Custody, 1991, *National Report: Volumes 1- 5*, Australian Government Publishing Service, Canberra.

Smith, K and Tilney, S, 2007, *Vulnerable Adult and Child Witnesses*, Oxford University Press, Oxford.

Sweeney, J and Payne, J, 2012, *Drug Use Monitoring in Australia: 2009-2010: Report on Drug Use Among Police Detainees*, AIC, Canberra.

Taylor, N and Bareja, M, 2005, "National Police Custody Survey 2002", *Technical and Background Paper*, 13, Australian Institute of Criminology, Canberra.

Tasmania Law Reform Institute, 2011, *Consolidation of Arrest Laws in Tasmania, Final Report*, 15. Viewed on 23 March 2012, <www.law.utas.edu.au/reform/documents/Consolidation_of_Arrest_Laws_in_Tasmania.pdf>.

Tasmania Department of Police and Emergency Management (TDPEM), 2010, *Tasmania Police Manual: Orders, Instructions and Operational Guidance for Members of Tasmania Police*, TDPEM, Hobart. Viewed on 23 March 2012, <www.police.tas.gov.au/uploads/file/Right%20to%20Information%20Disclosures/TPM_RTI_Version_-_11_November_2010.pdf>.

Tye, CS and Mullen, PE, 2006, "Mental Disorders in Female Prisoners" 40 *Australian and New Zealand Journal of Psychiatry* 266.

United Nations Human Rights Committee, 2009, *Concluding Observations of the Human Rights Committee: Australia*, UN Doc CCPR/C/AUS/CO/5, Ninety-fifth session, Geneva, 16 March-3 April 2009. Viewed on 23 March 2012, <www2.ohchr.org/english/bodies/hrc/hrcs95.htm>.

Victoria Police, 2011, *Interviewing Specific Categories of Person*, Victoria Police, Melbourne.

WA Police, nd, *Questioning Children and People with Special Needs*, WA Police, Perth.

Part Five

Pathways to Sentencing and Punishment

Chapter 15

Vulnerabilities in the Courtroom

Lorana Bartels and Kelly Richards

Police deal with vulnerable people, including offenders, on a daily basis. Sentencing processes, including traditional courtroom processes and alternatives (such as therapeutic jurisprudence and restorative justice) give rise to particular vulnerabilities or place offenders into particular positions of vulnerability. In Australian criminal justice systems, a wide range of pathways to sentencing and punishment exist alongside traditional court processes. In particular, restorative justice and therapeutic jurisprudence processes have emerged during the last quarter of a century and now occupy a key position in the criminal justice landscape. Although there are significant differences between the two approaches, both "emphasise the need for more effective forms of communication in relation to and helping offenders desist from crime and reintegrate into a community" (Daly and Marchetti, 2012: 456). Both models also promote the involved parties' active participation in the processes that affect them, especially decision-making, as well as respectful dialogue and 'healing' (King, 2011).

This chapter presents an overview of restorative justice and therapeutic jurisprudence processes and considers how these alternative routes to sentencing and punishment respond to offenders with vulnerabilities. Using examples from the Australian and international literature, this chapter outlines key challenges to responding to vulnerable offenders under restorative justice and therapeutic jurisprudence paradigms. Finally, the chapter makes some observations about the need for language competence (for definitions, see Snow and Powell, 2012) among offenders who participate in restorative justice or therapeutic jurisprudence processes, the evidence about deficits in this regard, and the need for police to be aware of such issues.

Vulnerabilities in the Courtroom

Ross (2009: 44) has noted that "[r]elatively little is known about the problems and disadvantages associated with defendants at court. While the health and associated problems of custodial population have been extensively and systematically studied, information about court defendants is patchy". It is widely accepted, however, that vulnerabilities become more entrenched and more complex the further an individual progresses into the criminal justice system. It is perhaps unsurprising, therefore, that defendants in court often have multiple and multifaceted vulnerabilities. Recently, it was estimated by the Victorian Department of Justice that "approximately 55% of offenders at court suffer from some form of mental impairment" (Gray, 2011). In a recent review of 156 Supreme and District Court sentencing cases, the Law Reform Commission of Western Australia (LRCWA) found that in approximately 90 per cent of cases, there was evidence of at least one of the following: substance abuse, mental health, gambling, family violence and homelessness. The LRCWA noted that this would likely be an underrepresentation, as some offenders might not have disclosed certain issues to the court, or the sentencing judge might not have adverted to certain issues in his or her remarks (LRCWA, 2009; conversely, the rates might be different, likely lower, for those who are not convicted). Significantly, substance abuse was involved in 71 per cent of cases, while 19 per cent had both substance abuse and mental health issues. This latter figure is lower than one might expect, with some suggesting that in the criminal justice setting, comorbidity of this nature is "the rule, rather than the exception" (Ogloff et al, 2006: 17).

Notwithstanding the lack of more comprehensive data about the prevalence and incidence of problems experienced by defendants in court, the data on police detainees (see, for example, Gaffney et al, 2010) and prison populations (see, for example, Indig et al, 2010) would suggest that people who come before the criminal courts typically experience a number of vulnerabilities. In addition to the foregoing issues, other areas of vulnerability commonly experienced by people who come before the courts may include intellectual and/or physical disability, financial adversity, youth and Indigenous status. As King (2009: 13) noted in the *Solution-Focused Judging Bench Book* endorsed by the Chief Justice of Australia, Robert French, courts "often become the dumping ground for those with significant problems – problems society has otherwise been unable to resolve or that society has aggravated due to poorly conceived and/or executed policies". As shall be seen further below, defendants in court (and/or parallel processes such as restorative justice and therapeutic jurisprudence) can be considered to experience two types of vulnerabilities: those that characterise them personally (for example, mental health issues, alcohol and other drug problems), and those that occur as a corollary of participating in the sentencing process (for example, having to face victims and having to discuss their offending behaviour). After introducing restorative justice and therapeutic jurisprudence and discussing the vulnerabilities associated with these alternative pathways to sentencing, this chapter considers a vulnerability rarely considered in the relevant literature: the oral competence of defendants.

Restorative Justice

Restorative justice is notoriously difficult to define, and there are many competing definitions in the vast literature on this topic. One that "has come closest to general acceptance" (Strang, 2000: 23), however, is Marshall's (1996: 37) definition of restorative justice as "a process whereby all the parties with a stake in a particular offence come together to resolve collectively how to deal with the aftermath of the offence and its implications for the future". Although, in Australia at least, restorative justice processes are utilised primarily in cases of juvenile offending (Richards, 2010; Robinson, in this collection, Ch 16), forum sentencing and victim-offender mediation programs for adult offenders are also common.

Restorative justice has multiple and diverse antecedents, and consequently a range of aims, including:

- a less formal and more community-based response to offending;
- engaging and responding to victims of crime;
- making offenders aware of the consequences of their behaviour;
- responding to Indigenous offenders in a more culturally-appropriate way; and
- empowering victims, families and communities through communication.

As Sherman et al (2005: 367) argued, however, the primary objectives of restorative justice can be condensed to two: reducing recidivism better than traditional court processes, and repairing harm to victims better than traditional court processes. Restorative justice can be used at all stages in the criminal justice system, from pre-trial diversion to post-sentencing, albeit in most cases only after a person has admitted responsibility for an offence.

An enormous body of empirical research literature exists on restorative justice, and results vary according to a wide range of factors, including the demographic characteristics of the offender and the offence type. In relation to its two primary aims (reducing recidivism and repairing harm to crime victims), however, the evidence shows that in general, victims who participate in restorative justice are satisfied with the process (see, for example, Morris and Maxwell, 2000). Certainly, they are more satisfied with restorative justice than with traditional court procedures (Sherman and Strang, 2010). It appears, however, that victims are often less satisfied with restorative justice than other participants (such as offenders), and less satisfied with those who support victims and offenders (Braithwaite, 1995; Triggs, 2005). In relation to its capacity to reduce recidivism, Strang's (2010) review of the evidence found that while restorative justice can reduce recidivism in general, its impacts on recidivism are larger for adult offenders and in cases of violent crime.

Therapeutic Jurisprudence

The term "therapeutic jurisprudence" was first used in the United States in the late 1980s in the context of mental health cases, but has since been expanded into the domains of family and, significantly for the present text, criminal justice matters. Broadly speaking, therapeutic jurisprudence involves the "study of the role of the law as a therapeutic agent" (Wexler and Winick, 1996: xvii), which "focuses attention on the ...law's considerable impact on emotional life and psychological well-being" and sees the law as "a social force that can produce therapeutic or antitherapeutic consequences" (Winick and Wexler, 2003: 7; see also King, 2009). One of the key ways the criminal justice system has implemented therapeutic jurisprudence practices is through the development of *problem-oriented (or problem-solving) courts*, which aim to use the courts' authority and structure to further therapeutic goals (for example, dealing with an offender's anger management issues) and improve the performance of agencies involved in delivering court-mandated services (see Blagg, 2008; King, 2009, 2011 for discussion).

As discussed elsewhere (see Bartels, 2009; King, 2009, 2011; LRCWA, 2009), key features of therapeutic jurisprudence or problem-oriented justice, whether in specialist courts or the mainstream criminal justice system, include:

- *case outcomes* – working on tangible outcomes for offenders, victims and the community;
- *system change* – seeking to reorient how government systems respond to problems, such as substance abuse and mental illness;
- *judicial monitoring* – actively using judicial authority to solve problems and change offenders' behaviour;
- *collaboration* – engaging government and non-government partners to reduce the risks of reoffending. In particular, police often have an ongoing role in monitoring offenders' progress; and
- *non-traditional roles* – this involves changing aspects of the adversarial court process, such as the role of the judicial officer becoming more interventionist or police officers wearing suits instead of uniforms. In addition, offenders are required to play an active role in the process, for example, by being asked questions and being spoken to directly, as well as being required to contribute to the process by developing strategies and goals.

There are a number of court-intervention programs currently in operation, predominantly at the magistrates' court level, around Australia, which mainly deal with the specific issues of Indigenous offenders; offenders with mental health, drug and alcohol problems; and domestic violence offences. There are significant differences in how they operate (for example, whether they are underpinned by specific legislation), but most are premised on a therapeutic jurisprudence philosophy (although some also involve restorative justice principles) and many involve an active role for police.

A number of these programs have been evaluated, indicating, for example, that the NSW and South Australian Drug Court programs reduced reoffending rates among program completers, while the Perth Drug Court not only reduced offending, but was more cost-effective than prison and community corrections. Similarly, the NSW MERIT program and Collingwood Neighbourhood Justice centre have been found to reduce reoffending rates, while remaining cost-effective (see King, 2011; LRCWA, 2009, for a summary of evaluations). Other benefits that may flow from therapeutic jurisprudence processes include exposure to available treatment options and community support services, improved physical and mental wellbeing, increased employment opportunities, improved education and financial stability, and enhanced personal relationships and general life skills. For example, an evaluation of the Victorian Court Integrated Services Program (CISP) found that as well as having lower rates of offending than a comparison group, participants demonstrated improved mental health (Ross, 2009; Walsh, 2011).

Another positive outcome is increased confidence in the criminal justice system. Indeed, Daly and Marchetti (2012: 471) have asserted that a recurring finding of research on problem-oriented courts in Australia, especially drug courts, is that "participants say they are listened to and they perceive the process as being fair". In order for offenders to play an active role in the criminal justice process, and have the opportunity to be listened to, however, they must have adequate language skills. As will be discussed later in this chapter, there is an emerging body of research that suggests that some offenders display particular vulnerabilities in this regard.

Restorative Justice and Vulnerable Offenders

Like any sentencing forum, offenders in restorative justice processes often have a range of vulnerabilities that practitioners should take into account. In this section, three interrelated vulnerabilities that are somewhat specific to restorative justice are discussed. The first of these vulnerabilities is youth. As described above, in Australia, restorative justice is most commonly applied to juveniles (that is, 10 to 16-year-olds (inclusive) in Queensland and 10 to 17-year-olds (inclusive) in all other jurisdictions). By definition, juveniles in the criminal justice system are more vulnerable than adults, as they lack maturity and life experience. Research on adolescent brain development, for example, demonstrates that while the second decade of life is a period of rapid change, these changes often occur before juveniles develop competence in decision making (Steinberg, 2005). This disjuncture, it has been argued, is akin to 'starting an engine without yet having a skilled driver behind the wheel' (Steinberg, 2005: 70).

While the vulnerability of juveniles is widely recognised in Australia, with each jurisdiction having discrete legislation for dealing with young offenders, what is less recognised is that a number of other vulnerabilities, such as mental impairment, and drug and alcohol problems, can compound with youth to make juveniles particularly vulnerable in the criminal justice system, including in restorative justice. For example, intellectual disabilities are more common among juveniles than adults under the supervision of the criminal justice system or among the general Australian population. Three per cent of the Australian public has an intellectual disability and one per cent of adults incarcerated in New South Wales (NSW) prisons was found to have an IQ below 70 in a recent study (Frize, Kenny and Lennings, 2008). By comparison, 17 per cent of juveniles in detention in Australia have an IQ below 70 (Frize, Kenny and Lennings, 2008; see also HREOC, 2005). Mental illness is also over-represented among juveniles in detention compared with those in the community. The Young People in Custody Health Survey, conducted in NSW in 2005, found that 88 per cent of young people in custody reported symptoms consistent with a mild, moderate or severe psychiatric disorder (HREOC, 2005).

Indigenous status is another potential vulnerability of juveniles who participate in restorative justice. Although it is often argued that restorative justice has strong Indigenous roots (see, for example, Umbreit, 2001), this version of history has been contested (Richards, 2009), as has the appropriateness of restorative justice for Indigenous juveniles (Blagg, 2001). Research has shown paradoxically that restorative justice is offered to Indigenous juveniles *more* frequently than their non-Indigenous counterparts (Luke and Lind, 2002), and *less* frequently than their non-Indigenous counterparts (Allard et al, 2010). As discussed below, one issue for Indigenous youth who participate in restorative justice is oral competence and capacity to engage with the process.

Finally, having to face the victim(s) of an offence is a unique vulnerability that impacts offenders who participate in a restorative justice process. Although, for a variety of reasons, it is not always the case that a victim (or victim representative) will take part in a restorative justice process, having to make amends and repair harm caused to the victim(s) is a central tenet of restorative justice. This feature of restorative justice is undoubtedly often a nerve-wracking and confronting experience for offenders – particularly young offenders. Indeed, it could be argued that this is the very point of restorative justice. It is important for criminal justice practitioners to be aware, however, that in order for restorative processes to be successful (that is, to reduce recidivism), this aspect of restorative justice needs to occur in a constructive way.

Therapeutic Jurisprudence and Vulnerable Offenders

Therapeutic jurisprudence is underpinned by the premise that judicial officers can play a role in 'encourag[ing] offenders to confront and solve their problems' (Daly and Marchetti, 2012: 469). By definition, therapeutic jurisprudence models target offenders with one or more identified 'problems' that appear to have contributed to their offending behaviour and commonly constitute an area of vulnerability (although this may apply to a lesser extent in the context of domestic violence courts, which deal with a specific form of offending differently than the mainstream criminal justice system). In practice, these 'problems' or vulnerabilities may include mental illness, substance abuse, anger management, financial difficulties and homelessness. For example, in the recent Victorian (CISP) evaluation (Ross, 2009), 72 per cent of participants reported current drug use; one-third were alcohol dependent, with a further 31 per cent reporting alcohol abuse; 40 per cent were currently receiving mental health treatment; and 9 per cent had some form of acquired brain injury. Significantly, one third of participants were recorded as having more than one offending-related drug, alcohol or mental health problem.

Restorative Justice, Therapeutic Jurisprudence and Communication Skills

As the above sections demonstrate, alternative pathways to sentencing such as restorative justice and therapeutic jurisprudence not only respond to individuals with diverse and complex vulnerabilities, but the processes themselves can give rise to unique vulnerabilities. The remainder of this chapter discusses one of these, which is rarely considered in the mainstream literature on restorative justice and therapeutic jurisprudence: the communication skills required by participants in such processes.

In traditional court processes, little active engagement by offenders is expected – or even desired. restorative justice and therapeutic jurisprudence processes, by contrast, require offenders' active engagement. In fact, in restorative justice procedures, passive behaviour on the part of offenders is frowned upon: "the process is not restorative if key participants are required to remain silent or passive" (Davey, 2000: 25). Behaviours such as remaining silent and/or staring at the floor during a conference are deemed inappropriate and inimical to the purpose of restorative practices. In a pilot conferencing scheme in the Northern Territory, a "low level of interest in offence proceedings" (Fry, 1997: 68) on the part of offenders was even considered grounds to deny the offender a diversionary option and proceed directly to court . A review of the NSW conference convenor training program even highlights the importance of convenors learning to recognise "non-productive/

defensive/destructive behaviours" (NSW Department of Juvenile Justice, nd; Appenix 1, s 6.2) on the part of participants.

Offenders' lack of engagement with the criminal justice system is, in particular, constructed as problematic in a restorative justice setting. Stewart (1993: 45), for example, commended New Zealand's family group conferencing scheme on the grounds that young offenders are often so removed from court proceedings that "on enquiring from them what had happened [in court] we often received the information that they had been 'astonished and discharged' (admonished and discharged)". Indeed, Dittenhoffer and Ericson's (1983) report of early victim offender reconciliation programs revealed that staff in these programs excluded offenders from participating if deemed lacking in verbal skills.

Restorative justice has, however, been criticised by a number of scholars on the grounds that it assumes offenders will be intelligent, engaged and articulate enough to "tell their story" and "express their emotions" in a restorative justice setting (see, for example, Roche, 2004).

In addition, as has been noted in the therapeutic jurisprudence context,

> Participants are often highly stressed when they come to court ... Anxiety can compromise motivation and cognitive functioning, adversely affecting memory, the ability to express one's thoughts and feelings clearly and language skills (King, 2009: 123).

As King (2009) went on to identify, many of the vulnerabilities that people in court experience, such as mental health, substance abuse and family violence problems, as well as personality factors and cultural differences, may impact adversely on their communication abilities.

Offenders and Language Competence

The issue of offenders' language competence has received relatively little attention in the context of involvement in the criminal justice system, and appears to primarily consider young offenders. The limited evidence available suggests that offenders may perform significantly worse than their non-offending counterparts when it comes to language ability. Assessment of inmates in a health facility for adolescent males in the American juvenile corrections system found that the spoken language competence of the juveniles tested consistently fell in the bottom one per cent of the population at large (LaVigne and Van Rybroek, 2011). The authors noted that poverty, ADHD, learning disabilities, poor academic performance, substandard literacy, behaviour problems, and conduct disorders are not only the "the stock in trade for the juvenile and criminal justice systems", but are also closely associated with impaired language skills. As a result, the individuals most at risk for language deficit are the very same people who are regularly on the docket in criminal and juvenile court and on the rosters in correctional facilities ... The potential implications of language disorder within the juvenile and criminal justice systems seem infinite (LaVigne and Van Rybroek, 2011: 65).

In Australian research, Snow and Powell (2002) examined the language skills of a group of 30 young offenders completing community-based juvenile-justice orders, in comparison with a group of 50 males attending a local high school, and found that although the young offenders studied were an average of two years older than the comparison group, they performed significantly more poorly on almost all of the measures employed. In subsequent research, Snow and Powell (2008) found that over 50 per cent of a sample of young offenders on community orders could be classified as "language impaired". This was particularly the case where the measures of comprehension and verbal expression employed were related to the processing and manipulation of abstract language. Furthermore, there was negative correlation between offence severity and language skills in a sample of incarcerated young offenders (Snow and Powell, 2011).

Snow and Powell (2002: 5-6) noted that language abilities in young offenders had received "virtually no attention". This raises particular concerns, given that interventions delivered to such offenders (for example, drug treatment programs, which are a common feature of therapeutic jurisprudence approaches) are premised on the assumption that "language abilities in this population are 'normal', however there are strong grounds to suspect that this is not the case" (Snow and Powell, 2002: 6). In addition, they argued, interventions that seek to improve young offenders' social skills may fail, if they do not take into account offenders' difficulties with underlying language processing. Clearly, such concerns may also be relevant in the context of vulnerable adult offenders. It stands to reason that many will lack the verbal ability and/or intellectual capacity to participate in any meaningful way in a restorative justice conference or therapeutic jurisprudential court setting. Snow and Powell (2011) have suggested that where "linguistic competence is lacking, the young person is likely to revert to minimal responses such as 'yep', 'nup', 'dunno', and 'maybe'". In the context of an restorative justice conference, this may result in "excessive deferral to the mediator for communicative assistance and may create an impression of shallowness and low credibility on the part of the young offender" (Snow and Powell, 2012).

There is no reason to think that the complications arising in the restorative justice context would disappear upon an offender reaching adulthood; accordingly, undiagnosed language deficits may continue to adversely impact on offenders' ability to interact effectively in restorative justice conferences and the criminal justice system more broadly. Furthermore, concerns may also arise in the therapeutic jurisprudence setting, as offenders may be impaired when it comes to explaining their issues and communicating with judicial officers and other practitioners involved in their ongoing treatment.

Where practitioners involved in restorative justice conferences or court settings adopting a therapeutic jurisprudence approach (or, indeed, in any criminal justice context) suspect that they are dealing with someone experiencing deficits in language competence, it has been suggested (see LaVigne and Van Ryebroek, 2011; Snow and Powell, 2004; 2012) that:

- oral language problems may be difficult to identify, and may be misperceived as boredom, evasion, resistance, or, conversely, a desire to appear cooperative;
- people with language deficits may be able to engage in superficial discussion without any apparent difficulties, but will encounter problems in circumstances that require more sophisticated language skills. The genuine level of understanding should be ascertained by asking the same question in different ways and checking the consistency of responses;
- given the high correlation between ADHD or learning disorders and language deficits, evidence of such conditions may serve as a signal that language disorders may be present;
- practitioners should employ less complex language to ensure comprehension, for example, by using shorter and less complex sentences, or employing diagrams, story-telling or role-play, and allow more time for responses;
- judges and other practitioners should employ open-ended questioning and ask participants to paraphrase questions and explain themselves in their own words;
- especially in the therapeutic jurisprudence context, the legal system may play a crucial role in ensuring that the person gets the requisite assistance (for example, speech therapy and psychological support); and
- practitioners may benefit from specialised training on how to identify language impairment and employ strategies to maximise the reliability, detail, and accuracy of statements obtained.

Conclusion

Offenders who come before the courts may face a number of vulnerabilities, including youth, Indigenous status, mental and physical health and/or substance abuse issues. Traditionally, such issues were considered beyond the scope of the court's processes. Over the last two to three decades, however, restorative justice and therapeutic jurisprudence have emerged as influences on how justice is done and the latter in particular takes a more holistic view of offenders' vulnerabilities and envisages an active role for the court in ameliorating these issues.

This chapter has sought to give an overview of the key restorative justice and therapeutic jurisprudence principles as they operate in the Australian criminal justice system, before examining the under-researched issue of oral competence. As Daly and Marchetti (2012: 473) noted recently, both restorative justice and therapeutic jurisprudence emphasise improved communication between legal authorities, offenders, victims and community members, with advocates arguing that "justice practices ought to be more inclusive, dialogic, and participatory". Accordingly, both restorative justice and therapeutic jurisprudence require that the offender be engaged and "have a say", rather being than mere passive observers in the decisions made about them. Snow and Powell (2008: 24) have described linguistic competence as "fundamental to every interpersonal interaction ...in which a person engages", arguing that

> The notion of justice is predicated upon an assumption of a fair hearing. If a defendant has a real, but unidentified oral language impairment ...a fair hearing may be inadvertently denied (2004: 224).

LaVigne and Van Rybroek (2011: 44) have similarly suggested that "[w]idespread language and communication dysfunction among the individuals in our courts and in our correctional system presents urgent needs that are ignored at our peril". These concerns are particularly relevant in restorative justice and therapeutic jurisprudence settings, which require a more active role for offenders. Police officers and others involved in processes which seek to adopt a restorative or therapeutic framework – as well as those more broadly concerned with the administration of justice – should therefore be aware not only of the range of commonly recognised vulnerabilities discussed in this chapter, but also the linguistic issues many offenders face, and endeavour to take measures to remedy this under-recognised vulnerability.

References

Allard, T, et al, 2010, "Police diversion of young offenders and Indigenous over-representation", *Trends & Issues in Crime and Criminal Justice*, 390, Australian Institute of Criminology, Canberra.

Bartels, L, 2009, "Challenges in Mainstreaming Specialty Courts", *Trends & Issues in Crime and Criminal Justice*, 383, Australian Institute of Criminology, Canberra.

Blagg, H, 2008, *Problem-oriented Courts*, Law Reform Commission of Western Australia, Perth.

Blagg, H, 2001, "Aboriginal Youth and Restorative Justice: Critical Notes from the Australian Frontier", *Restorative Justice for Juveniles: Conferencing, Mediation and Circles* (Eds A Morris and G Maxwell), Hart Publishing, Oxford, UK, 227.

Braithwaite, J, 1995, "Resolving Crime In The Community: Restorative Justice Reforms In New Zealand And Australia" *Resolving Crime In The Community: Mediation in Criminal Justice* (Ed C, Martin), Institute for the Study and Treatment of Delinquency and the London Victim-Offender Mediation Network London, 5.

Daly, K and Marchetti, E, 2012, "Restorative Justice, Indigenous Justice, and Therapeutic Jurisprudence", *Crime and Justice: A Guide to Criminology* 4th Edition (Eds M Marmo, W De Lint and D Palmer), Thomson Reuters, Sydney, 455.

Davey, L, 2000, "Can Police Services Deliver Sound And Safe Restorative Practice?", *Second International Conference on Conferencing and Circles*, Toronto, CA.

Dittenhoffer, T and Ericson, R, 1983, "The Victim/Offender Reconciliation Program: A Message To Correctional Reformers" 33 *University of Toronto Law Journal* 315.

Frize, M, Kenny, D and Lennings, C, 2008, "The relationship between intellectual disability, Indigenous status and risk of reoffending in juvenile offenders on community orders" 52 *Journal of Intellectual Disability Research* 510.

Fry, D, 1997, *A Report on Community Justice Programme 'Diversionary Conferencing'*, Alice Springs, Northern Territory Police.

Gaffney, A, Jones, W, Sweeney, J and Payne, J, 2010, "Drug Use Monitoring in Australia: 2008 Annual Report on Drug Use Among Police Detainees", *Monitoring Report*, 9, Australian Institute of Criminology, Canberra.

Gray, I, 2011, *Submission from the Magistrates Court of Victoria to the Inquiry into Access to and Interaction with the Justice System by People with an Intellectual Disability and Their Families and Carers*, Melbourne.

Human Rights and Equal Opportunity Commission (HREOC), 2005, *Indigenous Young People with Cognitive Disabilities and Australian Juvenile Justice Systems: A Report*, HREOC, Sydney.

Indig, D, Tropp, L, Ross, B, Mamoon, H, Border, B, Kumar, S and McNamara, M, 2010, *2009 NSW Inmate Health Survey: Key Findings Report*, Justice Health, Sydney.

King, M, 2009, *Solution-Focused Judging Bench Book*, Australasian Institute of Judicial Administration, Melbourne.

King, M, 2011, "Therapeutic Jurisprudence Initiatives in Australia and New Zealand and the Overseas Experience" 21 *Journal of Judicial Administration* 19.

LaVigne, M and Van Ryebroek, G, 2011, "Breakdown in the Language Zone: The Prevalence of Language Impairments Among Juvenile and Adult Offenders and Why It Matters" 15 *UC Davis Journal of Juvenile Law and Policy* 37.

Law Reform Commission of Western Australia, 2009, *Court Intervention Programs, Final Report*, Project 96, Perth.

Luke, G and Lind, B, 2002, "Reducing Juvenile Crime: Conferencing Versus Court", *Contemporary Issues in Crime and Justice*, 69, NSW Bureau of Crime Statistics and Research, Sydney.

Marshall, T, 1996, "The Evolution of Restorative Justice in Britain" 4 *European Journal on Criminal Policy and Research* 21.

New South Wales Department of Juvenile Justice, nd, Conference Convenor Training Program Review. Viewed on 26 November 2003, <www.djj.nsw.gov. au/pdf_htm/publications/policies/CCTRPROG.pdf>.

Ogloff, J, Davis, M, Rivers, G and Ross, S, 2006, *The Identification of Mental Disorders in the Criminal Justice System*, Report to the Criminology Research Council, Melbourne.

Richards, K, 2010, "Police-referred restorative justice for juveniles in Australia", *Trends & Issues in Crime and Criminal Justice*, 398, Australian Institute of Criminology, Canberra. <www.aic.gov.au/publications/current series/tandi/381-400/tandi398.aspx>.

Richards, K, 2009, "Rewriting and reclaiming history: An analysis of the emergence of restorative justice in Western criminal justice systems" 5 *International Journal of Restorative Justice* 104.

Roche, D, (Ed), 2004, *Restorative Justice*, Ashgate Publishing, Aldershot, UK.

Ross, S, 2009, *Evaluation of the Court Integrated Services Program*, Final Report, University of Melbourne, Melbourne.

Sherman, L et al, 2005, "Effects of face-to-face restorative justice on victims of crime in four randomized, controlled trials" 1 *Journal of Experimental Criminology* 367.

Sherman, L, and Strang, H, 2010, "Restorative justice as a psychological treatment: Healing victims, reintegrating offenders", *Forensic Psychology* (Eds G Towl and D Crighton), BPS Blackwell, West Sussex, UK, 398.

Snow, P, and Powell, M, 2002, *The Language Processing and Production Skills of Young Offenders: Implications for Enhancing Prevention and Intervention Strategies*. Report to the Criminology Research Council, Melbourne.

Snow, P, and Powell, M, 2004, "Interviewing Juvenile Offenders: The Importance of Oral Language Competence" 16 *Current Issues in Criminal Justice* 220.

Snow, P, and Powell, M, 2008, "Oral Language Competence, Social Skills, and High Risk Boys: What Are Juvenile Offenders Trying to Tell Us?" 22 *Children and Society* 16.

Snow, P, and Powell, M, 2011, "Oral Language Competence in Incarcerated Young Offenders: Links with Offending Severity" 13 *International Journal of Speech Language Pathology* 480.

Snow, P, and Powell, M, 2012, "Youth (In)justice: Oral Language Competence in Early Life and Risk for Engagement in Antisocial Behaviour in Adolescence", *Trends & Issues in Crime and Criminal Justice*, 435, Australian Institute of Criminology, Canberra.

Steinberg, L, 2005, "Cognitive and affective development in adolescence", 9 *Trends in Cognitive Sciences* 69.

Stewart, T, 1993, "The Youth Justice Co-Ordinator's Role – A Personal Perspective Of The New Legislation In Action", *The Youth Court In New Zealand: A New Model Of Justice: Four Papers* (Eds B Brown and F McElrea), Legal Research Foundation, Auckland, NZ, 43.

Strang, H, 2000, "The Future of Restorative Justice", *Crime and the Criminal Justice System in Australia: 2000 and Beyond* (Eds D Chappell and P Wilson), Butterworths, Sydney, 22.

Strang, H, 2010, "Restorative Justice". Presentation to the Australian Institute of Criminology, Canberra.

Triggs, S, 2005, *A summary of: New Zealand court-referred restorative justice pilot: Evaluation* Ministry of Justice Wellington, NZ.

Umbreit, M, 2001, *The Handbook of Victim Offender Mediation: An Essential Guide to Practice and Research*, Jossey-Bass, San Francisco, USA.

Walsh, T, 2011, "Defendants' and Criminal Justice Professionals' Views on the Brisbane Special Circumstances Court" 21 *Journal of Judicial Administration* 93.

Wexler, D, and Winick, B, Eds, 1996, *Law in a Therapeutic Key: Developments in Therapeutic Jurisprudence*, Carolina Academic Press, Durham, UK.

Winick, B, and Wexler, D, Eds, 2003, *Judging in a Therapeutic Key: Therapeutic Jurisprudence and the Courts*, Carolina Academic Press, Durham, UK.

Chapter 16

The Relationship between Diversion, Restorative Justice and Vulnerability

Angela Robinson

In Tasmania, and similarly in other states, police officers are afforded different options for dealing with young offenders. More recently, specialist drug courts have also begun to receive acceptance by law enforcement agencies as an appropriate demonstration of therapeutic jurisprudence for vulnerable defendants. In addition to criminogenic issues, the compounding effect of the criminal justice system on offenders' already pronounced vulnerability(ies) warrants attention, particularly in the case of young people and those suffering substance abuse. The vulnerability suffered by these defendants can include, but is not limited to, unstable or no accommodation; poor financial, legal and emotional support as well as serious physical and mental health problems, particularly for drug abusing defendants (Rowe, 2005). Based on the professional experience of the author, this chapter provides a brief overview of Youth Justice restorative processes, as well as Court Mandated Drug Diversion programs – both of which offer appropriate, forward-focused options for criminal justice agencies and the wider community to address criminality.

Restorative Justice – Overview and Necessity

As discussed in other chapters (Bartels and Richards, Ch 15, and Graham, Ch 17, in this collection), restorative justice focuses on "righting the wrong" – with the criminal justice system, the offender and those affected by the offence working collaboratively to forge a resolution and to make restitution for previous actions. A simple example of this approach is a youth cleaning off the offensive graffiti they sprayed on a wall. Restorative justice differs from pure punishment however, as everyone involved (police, victim, offender and their parent or guardian) also examines what underlying issues created this offending activity. Those issues are then addressed in a positive way. In this scenario, the youth might then be encouraged to participate in community art projects to channel their energy and reduce their social isolation.

Although recently becoming popular, the philosophy of restorative justice is much older, and can be seen as the antecedent of rehabilitative approaches. Across Australia, legislation underlying criminal punishment in Australia demonstrated an ethos of rehabilitation and reform over 20 years ago, whereby the South Australian *Sentencing Act 1988* stated in Division 2, Section 10 that:

> (1) A court, in determining sentence for an offence, should have regard to such of the following matters as are relevant and known to the court:
>> (l) the character, antecedents, age, means and physical or mental condition of the defendant;
>> (m) the rehabilitation of the defendant.

Likewise in the Tasmanian *Sentencing Act 1997,* Section 3 states that the purpose of the Act is to:

> (e) help prevent crime and promote respect for the law by allowing courts to...
>> (ii) impose sentences aimed at the rehabilitation of offenders ...

It is interesting to note however, that Court Mandated Drug Diversion programs designed specifically to rehabilitate offenders did not come into effect in Tasmania until some ten years later. Restorative justice as a theory, as well as in practice for young offenders, has been in existence for quite some time. But the acceptance and implementation of this practice for offenders with substance abuse issues has only recently caught up with the theory of restorative justice.

Further, long before these laws were enacted, Indigenous communities used circle sentencing, community conferences, reintegrated shaming and similar restorative justice processes to discipline negative behaviour but, more importantly, to recognise the person can still make a contribution to society. These processes can help ensure the delinquent actions of a youth do not define them as a person and become their entire identity or a self-fulfilling prophecy. The Reintegrative Shaming Experiment undertaken in the Australian Capital Territory during the mid-1990s was particularly effective with regards to serious crimes committed by youth (Sherman and Strang, 2000, cited in Richards 2010:7).

Restorative justice, as practiced today, emerged during the 1990s. This was at a time when the financial strain on governments of imprisoning offenders, as well as the social and moral costs to the wider community of ineffective custodial processes, became increasingly problematic. A growing prison population with high recidivism rates, in conjunction with legislation that criminalised a widening net of behaviour, necessitated an examination of alternatives to detaining people in custodial facilities as a panacea for all criminal behaviour. Sentencing an offender to a period of custody some time after the incident occurred – which, considering lengthy court processes, can be up to a year or more – is arguably a backward looking process. Classical theorists such as Beccaria (1764) noted as early as the mid-eighteenth century that one of the three important elements for effective deterrence is swiftness. A lack of timely punishment could thus have little impact on future illicit behaviour by the offender or the wider community. As identified by Nicholas Cowdery (2002), another negative facet of an all-encompassing, punitive approach is the notion that prisons are "universities of crime". Custodial facilities for adults and youth alike enable networks of criminal associates to develop, as well as the transmission of knowledge and skills relating to crime. Further, recidivism rates demonstrate the shortcomings of custody as effective deterrence to offending (see Payne, 2007: 88). A number of prisoners also commit offences whilst in custody (such as assault on other detainees and staff, possession of contraband materials and other disciplinary offences) which could result in these people being released with a longer criminal record than when they were initially imprisoned and armed with better resources to commit crime when they are released.

The forward-focused perspective of restorative justice centring on rehabilitation and reform, in which punishment should be administered only when "it produces positive future consequences or outcomes for society", or to avoid unacceptable social ills (White and Perrone, 2010: 452), should therefore be considered. This is especially important when dealing with vulnerable persons such as impressionable youth and substance abusing offenders. These groups often have complex issues that need to be addressed in a positive way if a law-abiding future is the desired result. Utilising an approach of cultural competency, which seeks to understand the unique perspective and expectations of clients, as well as address both past and present circumstances of that particular person with sensitivity and culturally appropriate methods (Sue, 2006), is thus complimentary to notions of restorative justice.

Why Restorative Justice?

The chance of a young offender growing out of their criminal behaviour is "one of the most generally accepted tenets of criminology" (Fagan and Western, 2005 cited in Richards, 2011: 2). Therefore, placing them into custody unnecessarily could lead to future offending they might not otherwise be involved in if they remained out of custody. This may also outweigh any potential, perceived benefits to their imprisonment. A more effective method of reintegrating young offenders into the community is necessary in order to avoid leading them down the path of lifelong criminality. Sociological theory could help explain why this is the case.

Theories which seek to clarify the causes of criminal behaviour, such as differential association theory, indeed have merit. Yet, in regards to restorative justice for youth and substance abusing offenders, as well as the application of cultural competency practices to their rehabilitation, labelling theory provides a reasonable explanation specifically relating to these vulnerable people. Labelling theorists argue that the cause of crime is stigma, and the associated negative connotations that come with being labelled a "criminal" (White, Haines and Asquith, 2012: 97) by the police and courts, schools, family and friends as well as the wider community within which the youth interacts. Once treated or labelled as a "criminal", youth may take on that persona and continue to act in the illegal ways expected of them. The necessary response to crime as suggested by the labelling approach is diversion away from formal systems of courts and prisons, as well as the decriminalisation of various behaviour labelled as "criminal" in order to prevent further crime (White, Haines and Asquith, 2012: 75).

Labelling theories also apply to offenders addicted to drugs, as many of them will be imprisoned for their crimes and released into the community without any assistance with their addiction. The subsequent stigma and social problems of being an "ex-con" and "drug addict" breeds instability and unemployment. In the absence of treatment for their drug problem, along with lack of supervision whilst on probation or parole, these people can again find themselves committing crime in order to fund their addiction and thus the cycle begins again.

Considering these obvious difficulties that youth and substance-abusing offenders face, a criminal justice system that uses culturally competent methods, to consider their criminogenic needs and personal expectations to effectively rehabilitate them, is arguably more suitable than simply delaying the inevitable, through incarceration and youth detention.

Role of Police in Recommending Diversion Programs

Youth justice in Tasmania, as it does in other Australian states, operates as a means to keep vulnerable people and young people in particular, out of formal criminal justice system proceedings, and provide opportunities for positive future outcomes in their lives. Police officers dealing with an offender are afforded a procedure whereby youth can be informally cautioned, formally cautioned or referred to a community conference on the basis that they (1) accept their responsibility and involvement in the offence and (2) agree to this resolution. Should the youth deny their involvement in committing offences, they are referred for court proceedings and are unable to participate in the diversionary process as this goes against the premise of the *Youth Justice Act 1997* (Tas) as stated in section 5:

5. General principles of youth justice
(1) The powers conferred by this Act are to be directed towards the objectives mentioned in section 4 with proper regard to the following principles:

(a) that the youth is to be dealt with, either formally or informally, in a way that encourages the youth to accept responsibility for his or her behaviour.

Informal cautions refer to a situation when the offence committed is minor in nature, the offender has accepted responsibility for their involvement in the commission of that offence and there is no further need for formal criminal justice action. Police dealing with the incident may issue a warning to the offender with knowledge of parent/guardian about the matter and it is recorded that this has occurred, with no further penalty. Part of this process involves an assessment of the offender's own circumstances to ascertain the requirement for more formal disciplinary measures, as part of a culturally competent approach by police. Formal cautions are based on the same principles. However, a file is first submitted by the police officer for approval, to have the formal caution administered by an authorised police officer (Youth Justice trained) at a police station in the presence of a parent/guardian. This outcome is also recorded on the offender's file and formal cautions are generally deemed slightly more serious than an informal caution.

For a community conference to occur in Tasmania, the offender must admit their involvement in the offence, they are then referred for a conference by way of a police file (Tasmania Police, 2012). Although conferences are generally considered higher in severity than formal cautions as the offending may be more serious or the youth's behaviour requires stronger intervention, a community conference may also be the most appropriate means to address the offence. An example would be when victims are willing to participate and express the impact of the offence on them directly to the offender. The prevalence of youth engaging in riskier behaviour than adults has been identified (Boyer, 2006; Steinberg, 2005 cited in Richards, 2011: 4) and often youth do not consider the consequences of their actions at the time of offending. A community conference which facilitates the realisation of these effects could perhaps be sufficient for the youth to change their future behaviour.

Policies that apply to the use of restorative justice processes such as cautions and conferences are dependent upon various factors including the nature of the offence, the offender, and their current personal and legal situation. As per earlier suggestions that police act as "gate keepers" to restorative justice processes (see Bartels and Richards, in this collection, Ch 15), officers in Tasmania submit a file to the youth justice unit in their area making recommendations as to whether formal caution, community conference or court proceedings are the most appropriate avenue; they must also provide supporting evidence for this submission. Supporting evidence would address the circumstances of the offence(s); the offender's attitude, actions and level of involvement; any restitution made; the offender's family and personal situation; prior criminal history or currently processing criminal matters, including probation or court-issued good behaviour bonds. Arguably this is in line with a culturally competent approach, as the expectations and perceptions of all persons involved are considered (Sue, 2006: 238) and weighed accordingly against any determination for future action.

Serious matters are usually referred directly to the Youth Justice Division of Magistrates Courts. These courts also have a mandate to redirect young offenders to diversionary programs, or place them on probation with conditions to help address issues of education, drug or alcohol abuse, housing and employment. These procedures apply similarly in most other Australian states, albeit with some differing local processes. For example in Victoria, only the courts can refer youths to restorative justice processes, not the police (Richards, 2010:1) and the systems differ slightly. The fundamental philosophy is the same however, as the Victorian arrangement still intends to prevent juvenile recidivism by increasing youths' "understanding of the effects of their offending behaviour on victims and the community" (Richards, 2010:2).

Youth Justice workers, police, parents or guardians as well as relevant members of the community such as health professionals or educational staff are generally involved in dealing with these offenders throughout the offence resolution process. Through the application of a holistic approach such as the very successful U-Turn Program run in conjunction with Mission Australia, youth justice aims to identify the complex needs of youths within the criminal justice system. In doing so, we can implement appropriate assistance to resolve the issues behind their criminal behaviour, in an attempt to guide the young offender's future actions in a positive way.

Drug Courts in Tasmania

Another vulnerable group with complex needs is substance abusing offenders. There are separate schools of thought regarding the reasons for criminal punishment and how it should be administered. The model of "rehabilitation and reform" is perhaps the most appropriate in order to deal with offenders who repeatedly end up in court, mostly as a result of their drug use. The aim of this punishment model, as stated by White and Perrone is an:

> emphasis on correcting offender behaviour ...on 'therapeutic' programs focusing on reform, treatment and rehabilitation... tailored to the offender's needs... [in an] environment supportive to positive changes in [the] offender (2010: 453).

Magistrates, no doubt also frustrated by the revolving door of offenders in their courts, have also been willing to support rehabilitation-based court mandated drug treatment programs in Australia, which followed on from effective implementation of court mandated drug treatment programs overseas. The first drug courts in the United States began in 1989 in Florida and Miami Dade County Drug Court (2012) claims that "this effective alternative to prosecution has generated Drug Court activity in over 2000 communities nationwide" since that time. The United Kingdom underwent a similar process, employing specialised drug courts from 2005 (Ministry of Justice UK, 2008). Throughout Australia, drug courts were implemented more quickly than the UK, with the New South Wales Drug Court established in 1999 (Clarke, 2010: 15). In Tasmania, magistrates completed 95 per cent of the referrals to the Court Mandated Drug Diversion (CMD) program once operation began in 2007 and considered it "a useful alternative... illustrated by the fact that take up of the program in its first year... was almost 30% higher than its funded target" (Success Works, 2008).

Within the Tasmanian system, only Magistrates have the authority to refer offenders to CMD, however, as part of the overall process, police, prosecutors and defence counsel are able to make submissions in support or against the referral. CMD follows two main trajectories. The first includes offenders who are sentenced to the CMD program as part of a suspended jail term for offences they have been convicted of, knowing that breaches of the program may result in their immediate imprisonment. The second path sees offenders placed on a conditional bail-type program as part of a pre-sentencing arrangement, to ascertain their suitability for longer term CMD participation upon conviction.

The conditions of these programs include but are not limited to education and employment programs, urinalysis/drug screening and counselling, as well as no further involvement in serious criminal offending. From personal experience, the practical role of police within CMD in Tasmania is foremost as a prosecutor in the diversionary courts. Prosecutors aim to ensure the offender adheres to their conditions, that any relevant offences or breaches are brought to the courts attention and that the offender does not "use the system" simply to avoid incarceration when they are not appropriately placed to enter the CMD program. One major risk to the program's success, which has also fed criticism of CMD in the past, is instances whereby unsuitable defendants are placed into the program, as demonstrated in case study one (*see over page*).

Minimising Vulnerability in the Criminal Justice System

Sadly, the pathway of Defendant A in case study one is all too common. The Australian Institute of Health and Welfare's 2007 study found 5.1 per cent of people (aged 14 years and older) surveyed had perpetrated some form of norm violating behaviour whilst taking illegal substances. Although this may seem like a small amount, just one per cent of the Australian population in this age group

Case Study One – Defendant A[1]

DEFENDANT A
Defendant A had an extensive criminal record. Pleading guilty in court to a string of serious crimes such as motor vehicle theft, burglary, stealing, disqualified driving and other offences, Defendant A's lawyer argued that due to reported abuse of amphetamines, his client would be a candidate for the CMD program and requested Defendant A be sentenced accordingly. The magistrate agreed and suspended Defendant A's five month jail term, placing him on the CMD program instead.
A few months later, police had created a taskforce to specifically address the impact of crimes committed by prolific offenders such as Defendant A. Had this defendant abided by his CMD program conditions and ceased criminal behaviour, the public furore might have stopped there. However Defendant A continued to abuse drugs and commit further series of crimes, almost thumbing his nose at the program that had thus far kept him out of prison.
It was subsequently claimed within the community that the court drug scheme was a failure. Police prosecutors were stunned when on two further occasions the court allowed Defendant A to remain on the CMD program, in spite of the prosecution's strong objections and the defendant's non-compliant behaviour. Even after pleading guilty to two more episodes of serial offending, Defendant A had two further five month jail terms (fifteen months in total) suspended. Once arrested and charged with further crimes on the fourth occasion, Defendant A was finally remanded in custody and removed from the CMD program.
For those mandating a "tough on crime" stance, the case of Defendant A questioned whether these new court-initiated treatment schemes were an effective sentencing method for drug abusing recidivists, or simply a "get out of jail free card". Arguably, if Defendant A was remanded the first or second time he seriously breached the program as allowed for in legislation, the victims of his subsequent offending may not have been affected at all.

represents approximately 172,000 people (AIHW, 2008). In light of these results, the number of potentially vulnerable substance-abusing offenders within Australia in the future is concerning, and appropriate methods of dealing with them are thus important. Nearly three quarters of criminal offenders studied by Healthcare Management Advisors in 2008 admitted to cannabis addiction (cited in Success Works, 2008: 67). Considering two out of three prisoners in 2007 had previously been imprisoned and one in four prisoners were reconvicted within three months of their release from custody (Payne, 2007: xi), the effectiveness of custodial sentences as punishment for drug-dependent offenders is therefore also questionable.

A feature of "problem solving courts" such as CMD is the magistrate's ability to consider not only matters of law, guilt or innocence but also to address issues surrounding the offender's health, the risk they pose to the community and other social problems that may be a factor in the criminal behaviour (Success Works, 2008: 20). Another benefit of court mandated treatment programs is, as studies have shown, they have a positive impact on those who participate (Success Works, 2008; Willis and Ahmad, 2009).

The New South Wales program differs in operation to other states as it utilises an in-custody detoxification before being placed on the drug court program. As such, the encouraging results of their MERIT program should not necessarily be applied to other programs (Wundersitz, 2007: 11). Even so, results elsewhere demonstrate mandated drug treatment systems have a positive effect on reducing re-offending. As Makkal and Veraar (2003: 33) state, 52 per cent of the treatment group they studied in Queensland had not committed a new offence since entering the drug court program. In other states, re-offending occurred but the time taken for offenders to relapse was delayed, which was perhaps an unintended, but nonetheless, positive result (Success Works, 2008: 37). Results for South Australia were also encouraging for drug court participants (Success Works, 2008). It could thus be argued that any participation in a court mandated drug treatment program, whether completed or not, impacts favourably on the vulnerability of drug users, creates positive results for drug-using offenders and helps to reduce the amount of crime in society. It could also be argued that the use of CMD programs empowers substance abusing offenders, by overcoming their addictions, gaining employment, improving their education and contributing to the community. CMD thus seeks to minimise the vulnerability these people formerly experienced on a daily basis. In support of this, Birgden (2008: 3) states that even a reduction of five per cent in high risk offender recidivism is cost effective to both the government and the community. Given that across 56 studies the re-offending rates of drug court participants were shown to decline by as much as 10.7 per cent (Aos et al, cited in Birgden 2008: 3), the future of court mandated drug treatment programs, administered via a culturally competent focus on offender rehabilitation, appears positive.

Also central to minimising vulnerability experienced by substance abusing offenders, is the importance for police and other criminal justice professionals to appreciate that drug addiction is a serious and "chronic relapsing condition" (Makkal and Veraar, 2003: 35). As Makkal and Veraar argue, hurdles such as recidivism need to be considered not only as incidents of additional criminal behaviour but also in the context of the overall progress and long term treatment of an offender (2003: 35). It is suggested that relapses often occur in the initial stages of the program, when the offender is having the most difficulty adjusting their behaviour and personal situation (Makkal and Veraar, 2003:35). Persistent understanding and a demonstrated willingness from police and courts to be patient whilst dealing with offenders at this difficult time could ultimately result in highly positive outcomes in the longer term, as is examined in case study two.

Case Study Two – Defendant B

DEFENDANT B
Similar to Defendant A, Defendant B had an extensive prior conviction history upon his presentation to the courts for sentencing on numerous crimes. As an adult with ongoing substance abuse problems, the court reluctantly granted his lawyer's request for Defendant B's inclusion into CMD. This was at a time when the program was still in its infancy and suffering numerous "teething problems", as well as a general lack of acceptance and understanding.
It was a difficult process. Defendant B experienced some problems early in the program such as positive drug tests and failing to stick to scheduled appointments, for which he received sanctions. However, Defendant B was determined to comply with the demands of the program as he tried to forge a drug-free, law abiding life for himself. Defendant B became a regular participant in CMD court sittings as his progress was monitored by police prosecutors and the CMD program slowly began to show promise.
It was a momentous day for Defendant B when he finally finished the CMD program after two years warding off criminality, drug dependency, unemployment and numerous personal problems. When the Magistrate stepped down from his chair, walked across the courtroom and presented Defendant B with a CMD graduation certificate, tears welled up as prosecutors and defence lawyers alike watched something extremely notable – Defendant B's first achievement ever. Defendant B cried as the realisation slowly dawned upon him that not only had he completed a difficult, long term goal but had also set himself up for an increasingly positive future.

As Willis and Ahmad (2009: 6) claim in their review of court mandated drug treatments, and as demonstrated in Defendant B's case study, these programs have a role to play within the criminal justice system, and not solely in terms of punishment for criminal behaviour. Offenders who graduate from the programs experience other benefits from doing so (Willis and Ahmad, 2009: 6). They further advise that these effects are not only in relation to reduced criminal offending but also in areas whereby the offenders' "very poor health and social functioning" shows a notable improvement throughout the program duration (Willis and Ahmad, 2009: 6). It is imperative that criminal justice professionals and police also understand that offenders with substance abuse problems are vulnerable to other factors in their daily lives – such as chronic health problems, financial difficulties, lack of housing and support – which can influence their behaviour and lead to recidivism. Perhaps a suitable approach for these people would be to address the offence but also consider the needs of the offender.

Similarly for youth, it has been acknowledged that "young people are more at risk of a range of problems conducive to offending – including mental health problems, alcohol and other drug use and peer pressure" (Richards, 2011: 4). These factors can place youth in an extremely vulnerable position in regards to the authority of courts and police. Richards (2011: 5) argues that youth justice in

Western cultures is a mixture of welfare and justice models and that welfare models "consider the needs of the young offender and aim to rehabilitate the juvenile". Richards outlines measures within youth justice processes that are designed to reduce the stigmatisation of youthful offenders. These include the general prohibition of publicly naming offenders, differential recording of convictions in some jurisdictions (2011: 5-6) as well as closed courts. All these processes aim to avoid incidences of young offenders taking on the identity of criminal should they be labelled so, as well as reducing the vulnerability they endure within criminal justice proceedings. A requirement to address behaviour and underlying issues, instead of "pigeon-holing" or labelling the person, is therefore imperative to achieve a positive resolution for vulnerable offenders.

Police Contribution to Diversionary Outcomes

This examination of youth and substance abuse-related offending demonstrates the necessity to address vulnerable people with a criminal justice approach that encourages adherence to the law but more importantly, to assist offenders in resolving the complex issues underlying their criminal behaviour. For youth, community programs and local projects such as Tasmania Police's "U-Turn" initiative, as well as diversionary sporting programs Australia-wide, continue to have notable success in redirecting wayward youth (Cameron and MacDougall, 2000). In Tasmania, police have the opportunity to refer candidates they consider suitable for the U-Turn program as a means to address youth offending before it becomes dire and to teach participants important life skills. U-Turn has been run in partnership with Mission Australia since February 2003 and provides a Certificate 1 Automotive course over 10 weeks for youth who have or may be involved in stealing motor vehicles (U-Turn, 2010). More than 200 young people have participated in over 31 courses since 2003, learning not only automotive skills but undertaking training through a "cognitive behavioural approach to address young people's offending" (U-Turn, 2010) as well as accessing post-course support programs. Police can refer, at any time, a youth they consider suitable for the program, which can also provide transport and accommodation and usually operates four times per year (U-Turn, 2010).

In other areas of Australia and internationally, community sports programs have been highly successful in diverting youth away from criminal behaviour and police play a vital role in these projects. AusKick's "AusCop" program involves police officers taking on the role of coaching local Australian Rules Football teams in their area, which has led to increased trust, decreased anti-social behaviour and better relationships between police and community members, especially youth (Cameron and MacDougall, 2000: 3). Tatz's (1994) study "showed that consistency of sport programs was clearly correlated to reduced delinquency" (cited in Cameron and MacDougall, 2000: 3). Although research directly linking cultural and sporting activities with reduced crime levels is limited, the connection of *factors* for committing crime such as negative peer role models, low self-esteem and boredom are mitigated by the participation in physical activities (Quantum Consulting, 2008: 6). Cameron and MacDougall argue "recreational and sport-ing activities have potential to make crime prevention an unintended outcome" (2000: 3), demonstrating that these projects, which police utilise in a community policing approach, can be successful methods of addressing youth delinquency and diversion.

People who commit minor drug-related offences in Tasmania, and in other states of Australia, can also be diverted from formal charges prior to court proceedings. These diversion programs are often known as Drug Cautions or Drug Diversions and are applicable to minor offences such as possession or use of cannabis, possession or use of smoking devices and, on occasion, minor illicit drug possession or usage. There are varying levels of diversion available: from an informal caution notice that is recorded on the offender's file or provision of brochures on effects and risks of drug abuse, up to the requirement to contact a drug and alcohol service within a short timeframe to arrange a counselling session. Failure to comply with these measures can result in formal criminal charges in order to encourage offenders to seek assistance for their drug use as a first priority.

A recent evaluation of police drug diversions conducted by the Australian Institute of Criminology found that in all Australian jurisdictions examined, the majority of participants did not reoffend 12-18 months after the caution/diversion was issued (Ogilvie and Willis, 2009: 1). They also found that there was a high rate of offender compliance regardless of age, gender or Indigenous status (Ogilvie and Willis, 2009: 1), which demonstrates the widespread application of such police intervention in minor drug matters. The role of police in such interventions could be considered vital to the success of this diversion process. It is the officer's appre-ciation of the offender's circumstances, their suitability for a diversion and the officer's official discretion that designates whether cautioning or court is required for a resolution in these instances.

Conclusion

Throughout this chapter, the idea of restorative justice was developed, especially in regards to substance-abusing and youthful offenders. When the financial and social costs of sentencing offenders to custody as a "cure-all", as well as the associated high recidivism rates of released prisoners are examined, it becomes apparent that imprisonment is not as effective as once believed. The necessity to reduce the reliance upon this backward-looking custodial process and move towards a future-oriented rehabilitation and reform model was also demonstrated by the idea that prisons enhance criminal skills, knowledge and networks. Concepts of rehabilitation and reform are imperative in dealing with vulnerable populations such as youth and substance using offenders; both of whom experience complex problems that require holistic and culturally appropriate tactics to create a law abiding future consisting of improved health, education, employment and social outcomes.

Police dealing with offenders such as these can and do have an impact upon their criminal outcomes. When handling matters involving youths, the appropriate resolution through Youth Justice processes such as cautions or conferences as chosen by police could be the catalyst for law-abidance or law-breaking behaviour for the rest of that young person's life. Although crime reduction and community programs aimed at youth have not been directly evaluated, anecdotal evidence suggests these are effective and address the complex range of risk factors to youth offending.

Similarly, offenders with substance abuse issues who are afforded the opportunity and are referred into court mandated treatment programs may finally receive the support and discipline they need, to overcome their addictions and create a positive future. In these circumstances, a restorative justice model based on reform and rehabilitation is perhaps the most suitable method to resolve these vulnerable offender's complex issues and to avoid them repeatedly appearing in court as a result of their substance-related criminal offending. Treatment programs such as these have been successfully implemented overseas since the late 1980s and in Australia since the late 1990s and are finally proving their effectiveness to a wider audience. This could partially be due to the conditions they impose such as counselling, drug screening and not committing further offences. These programs achieve tangible results while also accepting that drug addiction is serious and difficult problem to overcome, usually with some minor hurdles along the way.

Restorative justice was considered as a process whereby all people affected by criminal offences collectively adopt a resolution to address crime and implement positive ways forward. In light of this, the evaluation and continuation of projects such as court mandated treatment, youth diversion and community programs can only serve to better provide just outcomes for victims, offenders and the wider community. In line with the reform and rehabilitation ethos of current legislation, and through a culturally appropriate and financially effective manner, these programs may provide positive resolutions to criminal activity.

Endnote

1   Case Studies 1 and 2 were taken from actual cases the author was involved in as a prosecutor within Court Mandated Drug Diversion courts. They have been de-identified to protect the identity of the defendants.

References

Sentencing Act 1988 (SA).

Sentencing Act 1997 (Tas).

Youth Justice Act 1997 (Tas).

Anglicare, 2010, Response to Department of Justice Discussion Paper, *Breaking the Cycle: Tasmania Corrections Plan 2010-2020*, DoJ, Hobart.

Australian Institute of Criminology, 2008, "Drug related crime: evidence from the National Drug Strategy Household Survey", *Crime Facts Info*, 172, Australian Institute of Criminology, Canberra.

Australian Institute of Health and Welfare, 2008, *2007 National Drug Strategy Household Survey: First Results*, AIHW, Canberra.

Beccaria, C, 1994[1764], "On Crimes and Punishments", *Classics of Criminology* (Ed J Jacoby), Waveland Press, Prospect Heights, 277.

Birgden, A, 2008, "A Compulsory Drug Treatment Program for Offenders in Australia: Therapeutic Jurisprudence Implications" 3 *Australasian Journal of Correctional Staff Development* 367.

Brown, D, 2010, "Youth Crime Tops the Nation", *The Mercury*, 19 March. Viewed on 27 January 2012, <www.themercury.com.au/article/2010/03/19/134881_ tasmania-news.html>.

Cameron, M and MacDougall, C, 2000, "Crime Prevention through Sport and Physical Activity", *Trends & Issues in Crime and Criminal Justice*, 165, Australian Institute of Criminology, Canberra.

Clarke, A, 2010, "Drug Courts: A New Direction" March *Police News* 15.

Cowdery, N, 2002, "Whose Sentences: The Judges, The Public or Alan Jones?" 34 *Australian Journal of Forensic Sciences* 49.

Makkal, T and Veraar, K, 2003, "Final Report on the South East Queensland Drug Court", *Technical and Background Paper Series*, 6, Australian Institute of Criminology, Canberra.

Marshall, T, 1996, "The Evolution of Restorative Justice in Britain' 4 *European Journal on Criminal Policy and Research* 21.

Miami Dade County Court, 2012, *Miami Dade County Drug Court*. Viewed on 20 January 2012, <www.miamidrugcourt.com>.

Ministry of Justice, 2008, "Dedicated Drug Court Pilots – A Process Report", *Ministry of Justice Research Series*, 7/08, Home Office, London. Viewed on 20 January 2012, <www.justice.gov.uk/publications/research010408.htm>.

Ogilvie J and Willis, K, 2009, "Police Drug Diversion in Australia", *Criminal Justice Bulletin*, 3, Australian Institute of Criminology, Canberra.

Payne, J, 2007, "Recidivism in Australia: Findings and Future Research", *Research and Public Policy Series*, 80, Australian Institute of Criminology, Canberra.

Quantum Consulting, 2008, *Indigenous Sport and Culture Plan*, Department of Sport and Recreation and Department of Indigenous Affairs, Perth.

Richards, K, 2010, "Police-referred Restorative Justice for Juveniles in Australia", *Trends & Issues Paper*, 398, Australian Institute of Criminology, Canberra.

Richards, K, 2011, "What Makes Juvenile Offenders Different from Adult Offenders?", *Trends and Issues Paper*, 409, Australian Institute of Criminology, Canberra.

Rowe, J, 2005, "Access Health: providing primary health care to vulnerable and marginalised populations – a practice paper" 11 *Australian Journal of Primary Health* 32.

Sue, S, 2006, "Cultural Competency: From Philosophy to Research and Practice" 34 *Journal of Community Psychology* 237.

Success Works, 2008, *Tasmania's Court Mandated Drug Diversion Program – Evaluation Report*, Success Works, Melbourne.

Tasmania Police, 2012, "Youth Justice", *Tasmania Police Manual*, DPEM, Hobart.

U-Turn, 2010, *U-Turn Newsletter*, 7, December. Viewed on 9 Feb 2012, <www.missionpromotion.com/uturn/index.html>.

White, R, Haines, F and Asquith, NL, 2012, *Crime and Criminology*, fifth ed, Oxford University Press, South Melbourne.

White, R and Perrone, S, 2010, *Crime, Criminality and Criminal Justice*, Oxford University Press, South Melbourne.

Willis, K and Ahmad, J, 2009, "Intermediate Court Based Diversion in Australia', *Criminal Justice Bulletin Series*, 4, Australian Institute of Criminology, Canberra.

Wundersitz, J, 2007, "Criminal Justice Responses to Drug and Drug-related Offending; Are they Working?", *Technical and Background Paper Series*, 25, Australian Institute of Criminology, Canberra.

Chapter 17

The Path Forward: Policing, Diversion and Desistance

Hannah Graham

Drugs and crime are complex issues that police face every day. The remit of reducing and preventing substance misuse and criminal activity, thus enforcing the law while working with those who break it, highlights risks, rights and responsibilities which can seemingly sit in tension, yet need to be balanced in equilibrium. Such work is quite visible, with the effectiveness and legitimacy of police responses to drug-related crime and disorder closely watched and publicly debated in the communities in which they occur.

Substance use is widespread in Western society, with Australia and New Zealand having the highest estimated rates of marijuana and amphetamine use in the world (Degenhardt and Hall, 2012). In discussions here, "drugs" refer to a broad range of stigmatised and celebrated substances, including licit substances (for example, alcohol, tobacco, caffeine, solvents, prescription drugs such as benzodiazepines), illicit substances (for example, cannabis, cocaine, amphetamines, heroin) and liminal or emerging substances (new synthetic drugs and precursor chemicals, for example, mephedrone). While the licit/illicit divide is quite pronounced in public perceptions (as the latter carries much more stigma), the divide between the two does not necessarily reflect what is more or less risky or harmful to individuals and societies. For example in Australia, the total cost of alcohol misuse is estimated to be $36 billion annually (Laslett et al, 2010), whereas the total cost of illicit drug misuse is estimated to be $6.7 billion (Collins, Lapsley and Marks, 2007). Furthermore, "drug-related crime" comprises a broad range of offences, ranging from many types of crimes that may be committed while under the influence, to acquisitive crimes funding the habit, through to drug possession, manufacture, dealing and trafficking as offences in and of themselves. Establishing whether the nature of the relationship between drugs and crime is causal, coincidental, or reciprocal is beyond the scope of analysis here, except to say that a relationship exists and the various complex links are well documented (see for example, Farrow, Kelly and Wilkinson, 2007; Hammersley, 2008).

The first half of this chapter explores the dynamic vulnerabilities and potential risks of substance misuse in custody and the community, along with the complex challenges that arise for practitioners charged with the care and control of drug-using offenders. The second half of the chapter considers two key questions:

1. Why and how do people stop offending?
2. What types of interventions and initiatives involving police best support desistance from drug-related offending?

Although often constructed as the problem, offenders and ex-offenders are key stakeholders in community safety and crime prevention as the choice to stop offending is theirs alone. These two questions and ensuing discussions of supporting desistance therefore have implications for the role of the police and relational dynamics with offenders, and the broad competencies, heightened professionalism and multi-tasking required of officers engaged in community policing and partnership working. Because this group of offenders often have complex needs underlying their substance misuse and offending, some of the most promising approaches involve police working closely with other stakeholders who are better placed to offer therapeutic interventions and practical supports. Examples are given to briefly illustrate the ways in which different types of partnerships can promote diversion and work towards supporting desistance.

The Marginalised Mainstream? Difficult Work and Contested Vulnerabilities

The starting point for this chapter is acknowledgement of the complexity and diversity inherent in any attempt to understand criminal offending, substance misuse and those involved with it. Applying notions of vulnerability to drug-using offenders and discussing them in a book on policing vulnerable people is itself debatable, with lack of consensus among stakeholders on the extent to which this diverse group can be considered 'vulnerable' or a minority in criminal justice, as well as the ways in which their human, health and citizenship rights are to be balanced with those of others.

While the chapter largely focuses on drug-using offenders, it needs to be acknowledged that policing this group can be complicated, stressful and risky work. Being first on the scene to the dead body of an overdose victim or substance-related homicide does not necessarily get easier with time. Responding to horrific drink driving car accidents or violent individuals "off their faces" on ice (methamphetamine) is not exactly enjoyable work. These first contacts, in times of crisis and conflict, can leave a lasting impression in the minds of officers of what alcohol and other drug users are like. The stakes are high; people – including police – can, and do, get hurt. Having to face the collateral damage and victims of alcohol and drug-related crime on a daily basis can breed cynicism and resentment about suggestions that this group are a vulnerable minority requiring special consideration.

The duty of care requirements expected of police in apprehending and working with this population are complex. If they use force in restraining alcohol-related violence at a nightspot or football game, their actions may be filmed by onlookers on mobile phones, attracting criticism or support in the local media and social media the next day. If police fail to detect serious mental health concerns or suicidality of an intoxicated individual in their care, they may be summoned to answer to a mental health ombudsman or deaths in custody inquiry. If they prioritise the interests of the individual drug user over public protection and law enforcement, they may attract criticism from colleagues and community members. Conversely, if they denigrate or ignore the interests and safety of an individual drug user, they may attract ethical and professional criticisms and complaints from human rights advocates, harm reduction services, individuals and families. Competing tensions between public interests, victim interests, institutional and union interests, personal practitioner interests and the individual interests of the offender have to be considered in tandem, along with the ethical, legal and operational difficulties that arise. It is not as easy as just dropping them off at the hospital or ringing social services, because a significant number of drug-using offenders experience multiple vulnerabilities, yet may pose risks of harm to themselves and/or others at the same time. Vulnerabilities associated with substance misuse and offending are dynamic and highly personalised. The potential exists for an individual to have multiple vulnerabilities across various domains (for example, co-existing health, welfare and social problems), becoming more or less vulnerable at different times or in different social, emotional or physical states (Graham, 2011). The stigma of substance misuse and commonly associated mental and physical health problems (for example, depression, post-traumatic stress disorder, or blood-borne viruses like hepatitis C), not to mention the criminalisation of illicit drug use and potential repercussions of disclosure, can hamper individuals' willingness to tell police about what is really going on, leaving hidden harms unidentified while police are liable for whatever happens on their watch.

On the other hand, people within the diverse categories of drug-users and drug-using offenders may resist or reject labels of "vulnerable population" or "vulnerable person" being applied for various reasons, including the fact that they do not consider themselves to be vulnerable, or they see this as a label not only of their past behaviour but of their whole identity as people; a negative label based on risks, deficits, and power inequalities (see Bartkowiak-Théron and Corbo

Crehan, this collection: 33, 39-40). The complexities of intervention, including protection without paternalism or pathologising, and choice of language remain a significant challenge in vulnerable people policing and community policing in general (see Bartkowiak-Théron and Corbo Crehan, 2011). It is important to stress that vulnerabilities here are considered as co-existent with capacity and agency. Criminogenic risks and harms coexist with strengths and protective factors, and are situated within discussions of the whole person and their social context, including available support and opportunities.

In Custody and Under the Influence

Public sensitivities and fears about disorder and the high visibility of people displaying uninhibited and unpredictable behaviour while under the influence of alcohol and other drugs have contributed to increasing expectations and calls for police to "do something" and take them off the streets and out of the public eye. It comes as no surprise that rates of substance misuse and other co-existing issues are high in criminal justice custody settings, with police lock-ups, remand centres and prisons full of drug users and drug-using offenders (for prevalence rates in prison custody, see Australian Institute of Health and Welfare, 2011). Recent findings from the Drug Use Monitoring in Australia (DUMA) program illustrate the extent of drug-related problems among police detainees. Investigations of alcohol consumption and assault on Friday and Saturday nights found that half of assault offenders charged on these nights consumed their last drink at a residential location, whereas 30% had been drinking at licensed premises (Sweeney and Payne, 2011a). It is not surprising that assault offenders charged on these nights were found to be highly intoxicated: "the median number of standard drinks consumed by assault offenders was 14, although this was higher for young males who had been mixing drinks on the last occasion they drank (22 drinks)" (Sweeney and Payne, 2011a: 1).

The other concern highlighted in DUMA research findings is the prevalence of polydrug use among Australian police detainees, and the mixed behaviours, symptoms and contra-indications associated with this. The research shows that use of more than one substance is common, with an estimated 65% of adult offenders in police custody testing positive to at least one drug in 2008 (Sweeney and Payne, 2011b). Table 1 illustrates some examples of socio-demographic and criminogenic factors that may be associated with polydrug use, although this list is not comprehensive.

Table 1: Socio-demographic and crime-related indicators, by polydrug user type (%)

	SINGLE DRUG USER	USER OF TWO DRUGS	USER OF THREE DRUGS	USER OF FOUR OR MORE DRUGS
Female	17%	17%	14%	21%
Aged under 30 years	57%	54%	62%	64%
Aboriginal/Torres Strait Islander	24%	19%	17%	16%
Unemployed	63%	64%	67%	75%
Gambling (past 30 days)	33%	41%	45%	46%
Charged (past 12 months)	57%	67%	64%	73%
Prison on sentence (past 12 months)	28%	35%	38%	47%

Source: Sweeney and Payne (2011b: 6)

In light of the vulnerabilities listed so far (and the complex links between risk factors), assessing and managing people in custody who are under the influence or in varying states of withdrawal can challenge even the most seasoned police practitioner. Someone under the influence may appear relatively coherent and fine one minute, seemingly obnoxious or aggressive soon after, and yet be facing life-threatening complications of toxicity (for example, alcohol poisoning, acute psychostimulant toxicity) or withdrawal within hours of being taken into custody. Knowing how to identify and manage these problems and vulnerabilities in police custody settings represents a major challenge, particularly in relation to the following areas and issues:

- *Interviewing* – intoxication and withdrawal symptoms affect the capacity and perceptions of vulnerable suspects in police interviews, with the potential for communication and social barriers leading vulnerable interviewees to provide information that is misleading, unreliable or self-incriminating (Powell, 2002 cited in Bartels, 2011);
- *Medical emergencies* – as has been highlighted, acute cases of intoxication and/or dependence have an increased potential for toxicity (alcohol poisoning, psychostimulant toxicity) and life-threatening complications in the early stages of being in custody, and symptoms and complications associated with unsupported detoxification may pose major threats to the health of chronically dependent substance users;

- *Other health and safety risks* – increased propensity for panic attacks, self-harming behaviours, and attempted suicide, as well as susceptibility to blood-borne viruses in the case of unsafe injecting practices; and
- *Antisocial behaviour risks* – increased propensity for violence and anti-social behaviour due to reduced inhibitions and increased impulsivity and volatility associated with intoxication.

Drug using offenders are usually omitted from guidelines on the policing and management of vulnerable populations, or discussed in passing as a subset of offenders with other coexisting vulnerabilities like mental illness (Bartels, 2011). There are some guidelines for police services in how to manage specific issues and populations, for example, policing licensed premises and alcohol-related violence or psychostimulant users and serious behavioural disturbances (see Baker, Whyte and Carr, 2004; Fleming, 2008). In the absence of detailed guidance and specialised training, discretionary case by case decision-making can raise difficulties in balancing risks, vulnerabilities, rights and needs. Every drug-using offender is different. Instead of continually seeing familiar faces on weekends and call outs, and the revolving door of the criminal justice system, something worthy of consideration is why people choose to give up drugs and crime, and what factors and pathways are associated with this behavioural change.

Understanding Desistance: Why and How do People Stop Offending?

Desistance is "a behavioural term meaning the absence of repeated behaviour among those who had established a pattern of such behaviour" (Maruna, 2012: 79), and it refers to ceasing and refraining from crime (Maruna, 2001) and/or substance misuse (Frisher and Beckett, 2006). Just as people use substances and commit crimes for different reasons, the "escape routes" and pathways to desistance and life after crime are diverse, non-linear and individualised (Farrall, Hough, Maruna and Sparks, 2011). Desistance is not an event, but a process; one that belongs to the desister themselves (McNeill, 2006). Some give up drugs and crime for a time, with lapses or relapses along the way, while others give up and never return. Two distinctions are made to describe these differences: *primary desistance* refers to ceasing offending, (that is, any lull or crime-free gap in the course of a criminal career), whereas *secondary desistance* is refraining from offending and sustained change, (that is, moving from the behaviour of not offending to adopting a new identity or role of a non-offender or "changed person") (Maruna and Farrall, 2004 in McNeill and Weaver, 2010: 53).

Table 2: Factors and Developments Associated with Desistance and Pro-Social Change

FACTORS	EXAMPLES
Age and Maturity	Getting older, growing up, the process of maturation, less risk taking
Roles and Responsibility	Social ties, increasing responsibilities and participation in socially and personally valued roles (for example, finding a partner, becoming a parent, getting a job)
Narrative and Identity	Changing self beliefs and how a person thinks about themself, a turning point toward new beginnings, moving on from the stigma and identity of being an offender/drug user
Welfare and Personal Security	Adequate provisions, basic human rights (for example, a roof over your head), personal safety
Human Capital and Capacity	Skills, competencies, personal strengths, the internal capacity to make positive contributions (for example, work, volunteering, learning)
Social Capital and Reciprocity	Positive relationships, social networks (for example, friends, family, colleagues) that model pro-social lifestyles
Motivation and Responsivity	Readiness to change, willingness, motivation to give up crime/drugs, responsiveness to rehabilitation
Hope and Possibility	Optimism, aspirations, seeing a different future, having someone believe the person is capable of changing for the better
Paying Back and Generativity	Giving in ways that focus on and benefit others, paying back, redeeming oneself through reparative activities
Opportunity and Mobility	Increasing social standing, de-labelling, moving past the past, changing from being stigmatised outsiders to citizens and stakeholders
Culture and Ethnicity	Being part of a supportive ethnic community that offers culturally sensitive means and opportunities for supporting change; tailored culturally competent supports and interventions
Religion and Spirituality	Participation in a supportive faith community that encourages positive change and pro-social beliefs and lifestyles; diversity-sensitive interventions
Recreation and Creativity	Creative expression, the arts, sports, positive recreational hobbies

Sources: Adapted from Bottoms and Shapland, 2011; Canton, 2011; Farrall, 2002; Farrall and Calverley, 2006; Farrall et al, 2011; Frisher and Beckett, 2006; Maruna, 2001, 2012; McNeill, 2009; McNeill and Weaver, 2010; McNeill and Whyte, 2007; Uggen et al, 2006; Weaver and McNeill, 2010.

A significant amount of research has been conducted examining why and how people stop offending and the dynamics of change (see Farrall, 2002; Maruna, 2001; McNeill, 2006, 2009, 2012a; McNeill and Weaver, 2010). Desistance literature highlights three key theoretical perspectives. 'Ontogenic theories' highlight how crime is disproportionately committed by young people under the age of 30, suggesting most people (even persistent offenders) grow out of crime and desist as a part of the maturation process (Maruna, 2001). 'Sociogenic theories' suggest desistance is associated with the changing social bonds and informal social controls related to adulthood, for example, 'securing meaningful employment, developing successful intimate relationships, investing in becoming a parent' (McNeill, 2012b). The third perspective, however, highlights the subjective dimensions of such developments and changes, focusing on the meaning and value of these to the individual and the effect on identity (a process of 'de-labelling' and adopting positive identities) (Farrall, 2002; Maruna and LeBel, 2010). While there are no neat formulas or universally causal correlations, Table 2 outlines factors and developments which may facilitate or assist people in the process of desistance and change.

Many of the things listed in Table 2 require opportunities in order for change to be fully realised. Ex-offenders' efforts to change and make positive contributions to the lives of others need to be recognised and reciprocated by communities, practitioners and societies willing to give them another chance (Weaver and McNeill, 2010).

All of this talk about positive new beginnings does not mean that risks and harms quickly disappear or should be naively ignored; doing nothing is not an option, as it would be too costly and leave too many victims in its wake (Maruna and LeBel, 2010). However, a central argument in the desistance literature is that criminal justice practitioners need to work *with* (not do to) offenders, which means adopting a relational and motivational approach to supervision and compliance because the threats of detection and sanction alone are not effective catalysts for lasting change (otherwise ex-prisoners would be the most likely to desist) (Canton, 2011). Although often constructed as the problem, offenders and ex-offenders are key stakeholders in community safety and crime prevention as the choice to desist is theirs alone.

In considering interventions and support of drug-using offenders, *who* is involved, *how* and *why* intervention takes place, and *where* (context) become just as important as *what* is being done. Police involvement cannot be based on punitive objectives of "toughening up" community interventions, but instead should rest on the ontological belief that people can and do change and that context and relationships matter in any rehabilitative and reintegrative endeavour. Assisting desistance involves engaging with a person to move past the vulnerabilities, risks and harms of offending and substance misuse, while supporting their capacity to progress towards a different and better future. This is a redemptive and reintegrative process harnessing their personal strengths, while drawing on social networks and available opportunities in the community. The final part of this chapter briefly canvasses examples of community partnerships and strategies that are suited to the aims of reducing reoffending and supporting desistance.

Pathways Out of Crime: Multi-Agency Partnerships, Policing and Diversion

The best setting for working with drug-using offenders is the community (Rumgay, 2004). Individuals, families, governments and communities cannot afford the human and economic costs of increasingly high rates of incarceration, and the risks and harms that are exacerbated in custody and upon release. The extent and nature of substance use and misuse is profoundly socially patterned, with the most public and harmful uses associated with various types of disadvantage and those with few social resources (White and Perrone, 2010). In light of this, incarceration should be used sparingly and as a last resort. Except in the minority of serious cases, the options of diversion or "constructive punishment" of drug-using offenders in the community are preferred (Duff, 2001 in Sparks and McNeill, 2009: 27).

Diversion can be used to mean two different things: (1) diversion at the front end of the criminal justice system into treatment and rehabilitation (particularly suited to first time or minor offenders), or (2) diversion where treatment and/or punishment in the community serve as alternatives to prison (intensive supervision and specialised interventions for those with prolific or serious offending histories). Strategies and initiatives falling under these umbrellas are highlighted in the following discussions for how police can partner with other stakeholders to support better outcomes for drug-using offenders, the agencies supporting them and the communities in which they live.

Multi-Agency Strategies and Initiatives

- *Diversion at the 'Front End' of Justice*: This can take different forms, for example, police diversion (in this case, referral and transport) of intoxicated people into "places of safety" such as sobering up facilities, rather than custodial responses to drunkenness (see Brady et al, 2006). Another prominent example is cannabis cautioning schemes, where police take a more educative role emphasising harm reduction. Early non-coercive diversion schemes such as these are showing promising results in Australia (see Ogilvie and Willis, 2009; Payne, Kwiatkowski, and Wundersitz, 2008).
- *Arrest Referral*: Relatively common in the UK, these multi-agency partnerships provide access to treatment for police detainees with the ultimate goal of reducing drug-related harm and drug-related offending (Seeling et

al, 2001; Hunter, McSweeney and Turnbull, 2005). Addiction specialists work in local police divisions to facilitate referral into drug and alcohol services, including detoxification. Such schemes require the cooperation and input of general duties policing staff.

- *Drug Courts and Therapeutic Jurisprudence*: Drug courts and diversion schemes exist in many jurisdictions, utilising legal orders and court-based supervision to divert defendants/offenders into treatment and rehabilitation to address the reasons underlying their offending (Centre for Court Innovation, 2012). Drug courts usually have specialist prosecutors and dedicated magistrates. Issues of non-compliance or reoffending discovered by frontline police in the community can be quickly referred to the drug court for follow up at the next supervision hearing. A necessary caution, however, concerns how and why drug courts compel compliance; procedural justice and the legitimate use of authority are integral to effectively reducing reoffending as well as supporting desistance and recovery.

- *Co-location and Community Justice*: For example, the North Liverpool Community Justice Centre in the UK where key justice, health and welfare stakeholders including police and probation services are co-located, retaining important boundaries in work roles, yet increasing interaction and referrals between agencies at a local level to achieve improved outcomes (see Mair and Millings, 2011). The Neighbourhood Justice Centre (2012) in Melbourne is similar. Community justice approaches tend to favour relational styles of diversion and supervision by mobilising local networks, services and resources to facilitate opportunities for reintegration and sustained desistance, while supervising the nature and level of risk and ensuring compliance.

- *Multi-Agency Integrated Offender Management*: Police involvement in offender management is increasingly common in the UK and the US (see Jannetta and Lachman, 2011). For example, Integrated Offender Management (IOM) initiatives in England and Wales see police working in teams with probation officers and health and welfare services to supervise (usually more persistent or serious) offenders, reduce recidivism and support desistance (see Frost, 2011; Dawson et al, 2011). Similar police-parole partnerships exist in Canada where officers work alongside each other to support the successful community reintegration of high-risk ex-prisoners. Increasing the interpersonal contact adds a relational dimension to managing compliance and engagement between offenders and officers, reducing breaches based on technicalities in the process (see Axford and Ruddell, 2010). Crucially, the legitimacy and strength of these types of initiatives and increased police involvement in offender supervision depend on how supervisory dynamics and matters of compliance are understood and overseen (see Robinson and McNeill, 2010; Tyler, 2004).

- *Cross-Fertilisation and Communities of Practice*: Developing interagency forums for knowledge exchange, particularly in partnership with alcohol and other drugs agencies, not focused around individual clients, but on regional service provision issues, opportunities for innovation, networking, harm reduction, crime prevention, and cross-sectoral workforce development.

- *Consultation and Coproduction*: If police are involved in local community building initiatives or forums (public forums, interagency panels, think tanks, committees, working groups), discussions may benefit from the involvement of ex-offender advocates (for example, groups like UserVoice or UNLOCK in the UK) to ensure service user perspectives are considered. Advocates and service users should also be meaningfully consulted in the design, implementation and evaluation of multi-agency initiatives, partnerships and programs. If something does not help or have legitimacy in their eyes, it is unlikely to foster compliance or desistance.

Traditional approaches to law enforcement involve isolated and privileged decision-making and reactive calls for service. Whereas community policing and partnership policing strategies like those mentioned above necessitate collaborative transparent decision-making and consideration of the interests of multiple stakeholders. Working more closely with drug-using offenders may spark concerns that police are being made to moonlight as social workers – an unpopular idea for offenders and police. Quite the opposite should be true, however, with the responsibilities for in-depth therapeutic engagement and addressing underlying health and welfare issues best left to others like probation officers and drug and alcohol workers – hence why they need to be involved. Supporting desistance does not mean police become personally involved in the running of offenders' lives, but that they are more relational and responsive in their encounters with this group, that they prioritise diversion where possible, and they work with other stakeholders to encourage offenders to pursue their own pathway out of drugs and crime.

Increasingly collaborative and relational approaches to policing, and the re-positioning of "vulnerable" (ex-)offenders as stakeholders integral to ending offending and community safety, have significant implications for how police understand and undertake their work. Yet diversionary options, including restorative justice and police-probation partnerships, do come with their own issues and considerations (for example, see Bartels and Richards, and Robinson in this collection, Chs 15 and 16). Embedding community policing partnership rhetoric into real world practice is easier said than done (see Bull, 2010; Fleming and O'Reilly, 2007). Regardless of the challenges, it represents the way forward, particularly in the context of disadvantaged neighbourhoods and members of marginalised groups (see for example, Winter and Asquith, in this collection, Ch 5), for a study of community policing in these circumstances; also Asquith et al, 2009). Responding to issues of substance misuse and drug-related offending forms a core component of frontline policing. It is not just something to be left solely to liaison officers or specialist workers in fragmented programs and one-off projects. Any new partnership initiatives need the buy-in and backing of all levels of policing as an institution, from the frontline to the executive. Achieving this takes time. Becoming more regularly and meaningfully involved in multi-agency partnerships focused around substance misuse and crime requires the resources, funding, training and time allocation to do so. What is done in these initiatives needs to be reflected in performance measures so that the work counts and is valued by policing organisations. Also, appropriate choice of lead agency and stakeholder role clarification is essential. Multi-agency collaborations must not be entered into for solely instrumental reasons, as other stakeholders may not be focussed explicitly on public protection and crime reduction, and may react to power inequalities between stakeholders and any expectation of becoming like an extension of the police. Healthy partnerships in multi-agency support of drug-using offenders "should allow agencies to maintain their uniqueness and should further the aims of all agencies rather than the most powerful" (Heath, 2010: 196). There is no point in building bridges if collaboration results in too many conflicts, culture clashes and, in the longer term, bridges burnt.

Conclusion

The proposal of collaborative offender management and community based justice initiatives is certainly not new, although expanding the focus in policing to emphasise desistance may be. Community policing has a long history of collaboration and partnership, as does community corrections. While working more closely together with each other and with health and welfare providers will involve implementation challenges and teething problems, the potential benefits of prioritising diversionary approaches and supporting desistance are manifold. As drug-using offenders are not exactly vote winning political priorities, the use of justice reinvestment principles (reducing prison numbers and costs and redirecting resources to local community justice initiatives) may help to win the favour of funding bodies, as diversion initiatives and alternatives to prison have the potential to realise major (human and economic) cost savings and provide realistic pathways out of mass incarceration (Lucken, 2011).

Police face the risks and harms associated with substance misuse and drug-related offending daily. Complex vulnerabilities and needs require responsive and coordinated interagency expertise (White and Graham, 2010). Working together to not only reduce risks and harms, but to support welfare and desistance is, arguably, in the best interests of all concerned. After all, the safest communities are those in which drug using offenders are supported to cease being just that; where even the labels of ex-drug-user and ex-offender have a use-by date and are subsumed by valued roles and identities of citizen, parent, colleague, neighbour. Focusing on diversion enables pathways out of the criminal justice system, and focusing on supporting desistance encourages those previously considered vulnerable to actively embark on pathways out of drugs and crime altogether.

References

Asquith, NL, Eckhardt, M, Winter, R and Campbell, D, 2009, *Review and Evaluation of the Officer Next Door Program*, Tasmania Police and Housing Tasmania, Hobart.

Australian Institute of Health and Welfare, 2011, *The Health of Australia's Prisoners 2010*, Australian Institute of Health and Welfare, AIHW, Canberra.

Axford, M and Ruddell, R, 2010, "Police-Parole Partnerships in Canada: A Review of a Promising Programme" 12 *International Journal of Police Science and Management* 274.

Baker, J, Whyte, I and Carr, V, 2004, *Psychostimulants – Management of Acute Behavioural Disturbances: Guidelines for Police Services*, Australian Government Department of Health and Ageing, Canberra.

Bartels, L, 2011, "Police Interviews with Vulnerable Adult Suspects" *Research into Practice Report*, 21, Australian Institute of Criminology, Canberra.

Bartkowiak-Théron, I and Corbo Crehan, A, 2011, "'A New Movement in Community Policing? From Community Policing to Vulnerable People Policing" *Community Policing in Australia* (Ed J Putt), Australian Institute of Criminology, Canberra.

Bottoms, A and Shapland, J, 2011, "Steps Towards Desistance Among Young Adult Recidivists" *Escape Routes: Contemporary Perspectives on Life After Punishment* (Eds S Farrall, M Hough, S Maruna and R Sparks), Routledge, Oxon, UK.

Bull, M, 2010, "Working with Others to Build Cooperation, Confidence and Trust" 4 *Policing* 282.

Canton, R., 2011, *Probation: Working with Offenders*, Routledge, Oxon, UK.

Centre for Court Innovation, 2012, *Drug Courts*. Viewed 10 February 2012, <www.courtinnovation.org/topic/drug-court>.

Collins, D, Lapsley, H and Marks, R, 2007, *The Three Billion $ Question for Australian Businesses*, Australian Drug Law Reform Foundation, New South Wales.

Dawson, P, Stanko, B, Higgins, A and Rehman, U, 2011, *An Evaluation of the Diamond Initiative: Year Two Findings*, Metropolitan Police Service and London Criminal Justice Partnership, London.

Degenhardt, L and Hall, W, 2012, "Extent of Illicit Drug Use and Dependence, and Their Contribution to the Global Burden of Disease" 379 *The Lancet* 55.

Farrall, S, 2002, *Rethinking What Works with Offenders: Probation, Social Context and Desistance from Crime*, Willan Publishing, Cullompton, UK.

Farrall, S and Calverley, A, 2006, *Understanding Desistance from Crime*, Open University Press, London.

Farrall, S, Hough, M, Maruna, S and Sparks, R, (Eds), 2011, *Escape Routes: Contemporary Perspectives on Life After Punishment*, Routledge, Oxon, UK.

Farrow, K, Kelly, G and Wilkinson, B, 2007, *Offenders in Focus: Risk, Responsivity and Diversity*, The Policy Press, Bristol, UK.

Fleming, J, 2008, *Rules of Engagement: Policing Anti-Social Behaviour and Alcohol-Related Violence In and Around Licensed Premises*, NSW Bureau of Crime Statistics and Research, Sydney.

Fleming, J and O'Reilly, J, 2007, "The 'Small-Scale Initiative': The Rhetoric and the Reality of Community Policing in Australia" 1 *Policing* 214.

Frisher, M and Beckett, H, 2006, "Drug Use Desistance" 6 *Criminology* and *Criminal Justice* 127.

Frost, T, 2011, "Hampshire's Integrated Offender Management Programme" 75 *The Journal of Criminal Law* 29.

Graham, H, 2011, "A Marriage of (In)Convenience? Navigating the Research Relationship between Ethical Regulators and Criminologists Researching 'Vulnerable Populations'", *Qualitative Criminology: Stories from the Field* (Eds L Bartels and K Richards), Hawkins Press, Sydney.

Hammersley, R, 2008, *Drugs and Crime: Theories and Practices*, Polity Press, Cambridge, UK.

Heath, B, 2010, "The Partnership Approach to Drug Misuse" *Multi-Agency Working in Criminal Justice: Control and Care in Contemporary Correctional Practice* (Eds A Pycroft and D Gough), The Policy Press, Bristol, UK.

Hunter, G, McSweeney, T and Turnbull, P, 2005, "The Introduction of Drug Arrest Referral Schemes in London: A Partnership Between Drug Services and the Police" 16 *International Journal of Drug Policy* 343.

Jannetta, J and Lachman, P, 2011, *Promoting Partnerships Between Police and Community Supervision Agencies* Office of Community Oriented Policing Services, US Department of Justice, Washington DC.

Laslett, A-M, Catalano, P, Chikritzhs, Y, Dale, C, Doran, C, Ferris, J, Jainullabudeen, T, Livingston, M, Matthews, S, Mugavin, J, Room, R, Schlotterlein, M and Wilkinson, C, 2010, *The Range and Magnitude of Alcohol's Harm to Others*, AER Centre for Alcohol Policy Research, Turning Point Alcohol and Drug Centre and Eastern Health, Melbourne.

Lucken, K, 2011, "Leaving Mass Incarceration: The Ways and Means of Penal Change" 10 *Criminology and Public Policy* 707.

Mair, G and Millings, M, 2011, *Doing Justice Locally: The North Liverpool Community Justice Centre*, Centre for Crime and Justice Studies, London.

Maruna, S, 2001, *Making Good: How Ex-Convicts Reform and Rebuild Their Lives*, American Psychological Association, Washington DC.

Maruna, S, 2012, "Elements of Successful Desistance Signaling" 11 *Criminology and Public Policy* 73.

Maruna, S and LeBel, T, 2010, "The Desistance Paradigm in Correctional Practice: From Programs to Lives" and, *Offender Supervision: New Directions in Theory, Research and Practice* (Eds F McNeill, FP Raynor, and C Trotter), Willan Publishing, Cullompton, UK.

McNeill, F, 2006, "A Desistance Paradigm of Offender Management" 6 *Criminology and Criminal Justice* 39.

McNeill, F, 2009, *Towards Effective Practice in Offender Supervision Report 01/2009*, The Scottish Centre for Crime and Justice Research, Glasgow.

McNeill, F, 2012a, "Four Forms of 'Offender' Rehabilitation: Towards an Interdisciplinary Perspective" 17 *Legal and Criminological Psychology* 18.

McNeill, F, 2012b, *Questions, questions, questions: Desistance and Probation*. Viewed 21/02/2012, <blogs.iriss.org.uk/discoveringdesistance/2012/02/21/questions-questions-questions-desistance-and-probation/>.

McNeill, F and Weaver, B, 2010, *Changing Lives? Desistance Research and Offender Management Report*, 03/2010, The Scottish Centre for Crime and Justice Research, Glasgow.

McNeill, F and Whyte, B, 2007, *Reducing Reoffending: Social Work and Community Justice in Scotland*, Willan Publishing, Cullompton, UK.

Neighbourhood Justice Centre, 2012, "Home Page". Viewed 28/03/2012, <www.neighbourhoodjustice.vic.gov.au>.

Ogilvie, J and Willis, K, 2009, "Police Drug Diversion in Australia", *Criminal Justice Bulletin Series 3*, March 2009, National Cannabis Prevention and Information Centre and the Australian Institute of Criminology, Canberra.

Payne, J, Kwiatkowski, M and Wundersitz, J, 2008, "Police Drug Diversion: A Study of Criminal Offending Outcomes", *Research and Public Policy Series*, 97, Australian Institute of Criminology, Canberra.

Robinson, G and McNeill, F, 2010, "The Dynamics of Compliance with Offender Supervision" *Offender Supervision: New Directions in Theory, Research and Practice* (Eds F McNeill, P Raynor and C Trotter), Willan Publishing, Cullompton, UK.

Rumgay, J, 2004, "Dealing with Substance-Misusing Offenders in the Community", *Alternatives to Prison: Options for an Insecure Society* (Eds A Bottoms, S Rex and G Robinson), Willan Publishing, Cullompton, UK.

Seeling, C, King, C, Metcalfe, E, Tober, G and Bates, S, 2001, "Arrest Referral: A Proactive Multi-Agency Approach" 8 *Drugs: Education, Prevention and Policy* 327.

Sparks, R and McNeill, F, 2009, *Incarceration, Social Control and Human Rights* Working Paper for the International Council on Human Rights Policy, Scottish Centre for Crime and Justice Research, Glasgow, UK.

Sweeney, J and Payne, J, 2011a, "Alcohol and Assault on Friday and Saturday Nights: Findings from the DUMA Program", *Research into Practice*, 14, Australian Institute of Criminology, Canberra.

Sweeney, J and Payne, J, 2011b, "Poly Drug Use Among Police Detainees", *Trends and Issues in Crime and Criminal Justice*, 425, Australian Institute of Criminology, Canberra.

Tyler, T, 2004, "Enhancing Police Legitimacy" 593 *Annals of the American Academy of Political and Social Science* 84.

Uggen, C, Manza, J and Thompson, M, 2006, "Citizenship, Democracy, and the Civic Reintegration of Criminal Offenders" 605 *Annals of the American Academy of Political and Social Science* 281.

Weaver, B and McNeill, F, 2010, "Travelling Hopefully: Desistance Theory and Probation Practice", *What Else Works? Creative Work with Offenders* (Eds J Brayford, F Cowe and J Deering), Willan Publishing, Cullompton, UK.

White, R and Graham, H, 2010, *Working with Offenders: A Guide to Concepts and Practices,* Willan Publishing, Cullompton, UK.

White, R and Perrone, S, 2010, *Crime, Criminality and Criminal Justice,* Oxford University Press, South Melbourne.

Chapter 18

Vulnerable People Policing: A Preparatory Framework for Operationalising Vulnerability

Isabelle Bartkowiak-Théron and Nicole L Asquith

Vulnerable People Policing: Emergence and Rationale

The contemporary work of police is increasingly multifaceted, and as a consequence is marked by intricacy. This intricacy has led, in recent years, to more structured results- and accountability-driven operations, often under the frameworks of problem-oriented policing (Goldstein, 1990), intelligence-led policing (Ratcliffe, 2002; 2003), or reassurance policing (Innes, 2006). Such innovative policing paradigms have come at a time when individual officers and policing organisations are required to engage with issues of crime and disorder in more and more complex ways. While a professional "response-driven" mode of policing (Putt, 2010) was initially thought to remedy some of the new problems encountered by police, these had little effect on some communities' experiences of crime and fear of crime. In tandem with these more structured policing innovations, policing has been required to adapt to communities' needs, and to rapidly changing legislation and policy.

At a time when vulnerable people have become key policy priorities at all levels of government, we need to take stock of police practices and operational procedures in relation to these disadvantaged groups. Our collection is therefore timely, and helps provide a rather comprehensive (albeit, worrying) picture of police roles, powers and duties towards vulnerable populations, at each step of the policing process. The various chapters in this collection have illustrated and contextualised how police "do business" in their interaction with vulnerable people, and meticulously explained the rationale of police protocols at the various points of the police process, from non-criminal interactions, to arrest/caution through to chain of custody and release into the court process.

From the various points of view of the authors, we are all agreed that procedural considerations within the policing process are labyrinthine, and that these are compounded by issues of vulnerability. Police officers, either in frontline, custody or management positions have to be versed in a number of possible complex vulnerability scenarios in order to properly cater for the needs of vulnerable individuals who come to police attention, and to ground their operations in good evidence-based practice. These types of vulnerabilities include social, cultural, intellectual, physiological, clinical, racial, sexual and gender identity, and economic disadvantage, and can present individually or in combination with one another. And yet, while it is important for police to be aware of specific vulnerabilities and be knowledgeable in aspects of policing these vulnerabilities, all authors in this collection insist that police should not and cannot be specialists in all aspects of all vulnerabilities. It is not fair to expect that police take on the roles of multiple, specialised agencies. Nor is it fair to think that the vulnerable public would receive appropriate service if the police were to do so. Clearly, a different approach is needed here.

This conclusion contributes a first time, modest attempt at a step-by-step approach that police organisations and partner agencies can use to address vulnerability-related incidents and vulnerable people in the criminal justice system and beyond. These steps concern the various dimensions of police work, from daily frontline operations to strategic and policy-driven considerations.

Vulnerable People Policing: Problem-Oriented Policing with a "Nodal" Twist?

Using the framework developed by Cope and Kalantzis (1997) and operationalised in policing by practitioners such as Maria Dimopoulos (MyriaD Consultants) and Chitrita Mukerjee (NSW Police), we conclude this collection by applying the cultural competency and productive diversity models to vulnerable people policing. Highlighting best practice and case studies introduced in earlier chapters, we provide a grounded approach for executives, managers and frontline police officers in their work with vulnerable people. If siloed approaches to vulnerabilities are ill-advised or do not cater for the most extreme cases or cross-sectional vulnerabilities, how should police approach vulnerability-related anti-social behaviour and crime? Our collection highlights some essential tools and perspectives for police, as well as warns police organisations against potential dangers.

Step One: Acquiring Good Contextualising Knowledge and Analytical Skills

While police cannot know everything about everything, it is essential, though, that they familiarise themselves with the principles of good governance of criminal issues, anti-social behaviour and, overall, what might trigger complaints from the general public. They should have in mind the various possible causes and effects of their behaviour, and be proficient in the ways to interact with vulnerable groups, investigate problem behaviour, and to ascertain and address root causes of local problems. As put by Bartkowiak-Théron and Layton, the experiences of vulnerable populations need to be recognised comprehensively, and taught in their complexity, without fragmenting them into "rote knowledge quick-fixes". These "quick-fixes" illustrate the limitations of a siloed approach to categorisation (including, redundant teaching of similar processes, warning signs, etc).

As such, responding police officers should, by way of critical analysis and due investigation processes, reach out to those individuals or agencies that are best placed to provide timely, appropriate and tailored intervention to vulnerable people. In a way, the broader framework of cultural competence that we suggest here is similar to a socially derived form of problem-oriented policing (Goldstein, 1990), with "a nodal twist" (Burris, Drahos and Shearing, 2005). Police officers observe problems, analyse their components to unveil problem "triggers", and adapt their responses to the complex facets they have uncovered. They then involve specialised stakeholders (in real time, to the extent that this is feasible), as well as target groups themselves (or carers, if need be) to facilitate quality assurance and engaged consultative mechanisms. In time, they return to the analysis stage if an assessment reveals that something is amiss. This is consistent with a SARA process (Goldstein, 1990). For frontline officers who are in contact with vulnerable people on a daily basis, the implications are considerable, in terms of their education, familiarity with vulnerable people, awareness of resources in local communities and nationally, confidence to reach out to relevant partnering agencies or contact persons, and sufficient assertiveness to change responses and opt for better solutions.

Step Two: Securing the Input of the Right Actors with the Right Model of Governance

From broader policing and policy perspectives, a more pronounced attention to the needs of vulnerable populations should allow for an expansion of the operationalisation of police protocols. By this, we mean that crime management should allow for governance from the bottom-up, involving vulnerable people early in the policing process: from the design to the delivery of initiatives that target their groups (or, as put by Wood and Marks (2008: 273), "situating knowledge from below"). This moves away from a static understanding of "police operations" as police-only derived actions and reshapes operations from within the larger community itself (that is, individuals, community groups and agencies). Good practices in such areas will undeniably impact on police performance measurement and in meeting organisational benchmarks (including, investigations, case and closure rates) through:

1. Better identification of risks, vulnerabilities and mitigation strategies
2. Better synchronisation with community expectations through consultation and participation
3. Better alignment with community-oriented principles of governance
4. Improved two-way form of community engagement
5. Increased public confidence in the police
6. Better accountability for practices
7. Improved public participation in police activities,

According to Bartkowiak-Théron (in this collection, Ch 6), the ongoing study of wicked issues (Fleming and Wood, 2006) is already contributing to a further sophistication of police roles and operational protocols, and to a more comprehensive understanding of how police should be doing business according to good governance logic. However, more is needed to ensure that police practices avoid the trap of falling into a particularisation of scarcely used services. Rather, services need to remain simple and generic, but sufficiently sophisticated to address the most composite of cases, however rare they may be (Bartkowiak-Théron and Fleming, 2012). Rather than operational quick fixes, this translates vulnerable people policing in terms of thoughtful, analytical governance mechanisms, which, according to Herrington and Clifford (in this collection, Ch 8), allow for meaningful partnerships which transcends individual organisational myopia and allows police to move beyond competing structural demands from individual organisations.

Vulnerable People Policing: Early Lessons from the Field

If we are to understand vulnerable people policing as a paradigmatic backdrop to police practice, we need to consider how it has been shaped through time, by policy and implementation. In doing so, we must admit that the practice of vulnerable people policing, however strongly embedded in policy documentation and operational manuals, looks more like a colourful patchwork than an integrated process.

Step Three: Stabilising Terminology and Consolidating Legislation

Vulnerable people policing, according to Herrington and Clifford (in this collection, Ch 8), is composed of a mismatch of resources, skills, culture, processes and expectations. With few exceptions, it has developed according to a linear, morally conservative, organisationally-focused "risk" rhetoric (Stanford, in this collection, Ch 2). Policy and practice that has developed out of this approach fails to provide clarification as to who is to be considered vulnerable, according to what criteria and at which point in time. This lack of a working definition (and its – possibly unintended – consequence on police operational protocols) was documented almost twenty years ago (Pearse, 1995), and it is high time it is approached comprehensively. The fluctuation of terminology ("vulnerable people", "vulnerable adults", "vulnerable young people", "vulnerable children", "risky people", "at risk people", the "most vulnerable people in society", etc) is an illustration of this and of the indecisive stance of policy makers about who and what constitutes vulnerability.

The use of terminology that intends, and yet fails, to be ubiquitous does not convey the sense that such legal classification of vulnerable individuals is advisable either, until we have better working definitions of vulnerability and vulnerable people, especially if they are to provide further directionality and rationale to police operational procedures (Bartkowiak-Théron and Corbo Crehan, in this collection, Ch 3). By this, we mean that legislation cannot afford to only provide a list of vulnerable groups, stopping short of providing actual definitions of disadvantage. Sections of legislation need to make meanings salient, instead of labels prominent.

Step Four: Moving Away from a Risk-Focused Deficit Model and Streamlining Protocols

This leads to an examination of whether vulnerable people policing can contribute to an improvement of the generic backdrop of police work. Until now, vulnerable people policing has operated under a deficit model. It views vulnerability as a problem, rather than as an inherent trait of social life. It has developed according to a trichotomy between the due support to capable agents (Bartkowiak-Théron and Corbo Crehan, in this collection, Ch 3) versus an over-protectiveness of defenceless individuals (with paternalistic tendencies) and against a well-documented police aversion to risk. This is detrimental to the quality of police work. To use a relatively simplistic image of the process that unfolds, initial contacts between police and vulnerable people trigger a frenetic protocol mess or a protocol panic within which police are negatively assessing the number of obstacles or risks they can encounter when they deal with a vulnerable person. This frenzy and unproductive focus on various operational traps needs to stop. We suggest that police organisations find a new, more positive (and calmer) form of assertiveness, and assume a *universal precaution strategy*, very similar to that used in the health sector. In the area of health, instead of identifying those people with HIV, Hepatitis C or any kind of vitamin or mineral deficiency (let's say, when people volunteer blood donations to support care and/or research), everyone entering the health system are treated as if they *could* be HIV positive or iron deficient, until proven otherwise. Using universal precautions protects everyone and stigmatises none, and stems from the positive perspective that care is due to all members of the public, whether they are donors, carers or *in* care (Hoy and Richmond, 2008: 146). To transfer this example to policing, it is rather unlikely that a person will come in contact with the police (either as a victim, witness or offender) without having been under duress in the lead-up to contact with the police. They could have been under the influence of drugs or alcohol, suffering a mental health breakdown, or have been the focus of an attack of any form, or in shock of having observed an accident or a crime (the list is long here). Assuming vulnerability should therefore be the norm, rather than the exception. Evidence presented throughout this collection has clearly shown that police interactions are more likely to be shaped by vulnerability than invulnerability.

According to Asquith (in this collection, Ch 10), the deficit model can also be counter-productive, and new arrangements need to be found to ensure that vulnerable people have the confidence to express their concerns to police (and report crime, if needed), that investigation techniques are culturally appropriate, and that evidence-based responses contribute to a better understanding of crime and victimisation trends. Bartels highlighted that in the past, similar risk-focused policing practices contributed to over-policing, and thus the over-representation of some communities in the criminal justice system. While this was denounced by the Royal Commission into Aboriginal Deaths in Custody (1991) more than twenty years ago, it is clear that stronger evaluations of policing practices are still needed.

Step Five: Consolidating Police Duty of Care for Vulnerable People

Importantly for vulnerable people policing officers carefully balance their duty of care with their responsibility of controlling crises and reducing risks to themselves, persons of interest and the broader community. Both care and control come hand in hand; often, though, police believe that care cannot be secured if the incident is not controlled in the first place (Hills, 1997). A police "duty of care", while foundational to police oaths worldwide, is not universally accepted in practice (see Yule, 2008 for a discussion of the judicial debate in the United Kingdom, Australia and Canada). It is not the purpose of this collection to discuss the duty of care invested in police officers in its entirety. However, it is important to consider their responsibilities in light of the legal specification of a police duty of care *in cases of vulnerability*, and its specific mention in protocols relating to individuals in custody. The courts appear to be unprepared to find a duty of care owed in all police encounters (as it may conflict with other police duties) however, duty of care is paramount in the specific cases of extreme vulnerability (such as cross-sectional vulnerability, comorbidity or high intellectual or physical impediment). Yules argues that:

> [a] duty of care would only be found if all the relevant factors were present. If there was a case where there was a sufficient relationship between the parties, *vulnerability of the plaintiff was high*, control of the defendant was high, there was coherence in the law and no interference with existing laws, and there were guidelines in place that had not been

complied with, then a duty of care could be found to exist (2008: 387, emphasis added).

As highlighted by Bartels, some police organisations, in response to the Royal Commission into Aboriginal Deaths in Custody (1991), have highlighted in their corporate documentation that there is a need for duty of care, specifically in relation to Indigenous Australians in custody (see, for example, Tasmania Police, 2008). Further, Henning (in this collection: 217, emphasis added) highlights that "[p]olice owe a *higher duty of care* to vulnerable people because their particular characteristics place them at greater risk than other people during the arrest process and in custodial situations". So in light of judicial disagreement about duty of care in general, versus an overall consensus that police duty of care is due in cases of vulnerability, then what should police *care for*, exactly?

Duty of care, according to government guidelines, usually revolves around how police communicate, listen, interact and follow up on an investigation with persons of interest. The Government of Western Australia, for example, specifically indicates that Police Duty of Care is about the respect and sensitivity due to victims, and their discretion and tact during investigations. It also involves being in regular contact with victims, supporting their needs by way of referrals and reporting, prevention and safety concerns, and information about the case (during the investigation and at court; Western Australia Government, 2012). In addition to expanding this duty of care to offenders, to accommodate the vulnerability discussed in this collection, we argue that it should also include the following:

1. Police should care about the wellbeing of victims and offenders to avoid aggravating the circumstances in which they have come to their attention (principles of de-escalation, rather than inflammation of conflict). To do this, they need to be well-informed about the diversity of their communities, and engage actively with these communities to develop good relationships with them, in order to tailor policies and practices.

2. Police need to actively audit and assess for vulnerability within a practice system of universal precaution. This would comply with both anti-discrimination practices and rule of law principles, as well as protect their own investigation and the collection of evidence (avoiding, therefore, cases being dismissed on the grounds of evidence collected while an individual was under duress). At the same time, it avoids the trap of negatively labelling a vulnerable person according to an expressed (or otherwise) disadvantage. To achieve this rather utilitarian goal, police need to be aware of broader national and international human rights legislation. As noted by both Graham and Henning (in this collection, Chs 17 and 14), they should also be aware of "the ways these ethical stances and legal structures can lead to better practice outcomes for vulnerable people and populations" (Asquith and Bartkowiak-Théron, in this collection: 14).

3. Police, whenever they interact with a member of the public, vulnerable or not, in crisis or not, need to have in mind that their actions will impact on public opinions of and satisfaction with the police as a whole.

Adopting a duty of care approach is consistent with procedural and distributive models of justice. Procedural justice refers to "people's perception of the treatment they receive during the processes involved in decision making" (Hinds and Murphy, 2007: 28). This is important for police, as it was established almost fifty years ago that "authority's legitimacy is linked to people's satisfaction with the procedural justice aspects of their encounter with that authority" (Hinds and Murphy, 2007: 28). Procedural concern with justice is paramount, for without it distributive justice is impossible. Distributive justice relates to the fair distribution of resources (including, police services, support, and by extension, operational attention) amongst customers or consumers according to principles of fairness and equity (Vermunt and Törnblom, 2007). Framed through the lenses of vulnerability, this provides us with a more sophisticated point of view on the burdens and responsibilities of police when they interact with vulnerable groups. These are exacerbated by virtue of the complexity of social disadvantage in such cases, but also, as demonstrated by Sunshine and Tyler (2003), judgment and perceptions of legitimacy of the police vary with vulnerable groups. As a normative social concept, legitimacy is heavily influenced by the moral values held by social groups. In the case of ethnic groups who have historically tense relationships with police, then it is likely that an ill-thought allocation of police services to these groups could negatively impact on perceptions of legitimacy and efficiency. This will likely have cascading consequences on issues such as compliance, reporting, intelligence gathering and investigative process. Therefore, if fairness and attention to procedures contribute to higher levels of public satisfaction with the police, and, in turn to police being more confident in the excellence of the services they provide to disadvantaged groups, then abiding by the informal and formal rules and regulations attached to duty of care will help stabilise what is currently a kaleidoscopic way of doing police business.

Current Limitations to Cultural Competency in Policing

A better and holistic approach to vulnerability needs to be the central goal for vulnerable people policing. However, many obstacles hinder the development of a cultural competency framework for operational policing. First of all, contrary to other agencies that have responsibilities in dealing with vulnerable people, police are first responders, available seven days a week, twenty-four hours a day. Their responsibility in dealing with the crises that emerge out of this function hinders their availability for ground work, and for visible forms of community reassurance, knowledge gathering and networking activities. Neoliberal pressures and economic limitations also play their part in police *proving their worth and numerically assessing their own work* on an everyday basis. Police officers often recognise the need to do better but political currents pull them in the other direction. The "hard" law and order activities (such as random breath tests, speed checks) dictated by political expediency, are prioritised over "soft" tasks of building the co-production of law and order.

Importantly, policies and practices to develop out of vulnerable people policing need to account for individual or community resilience, adaptability and agency. So far, this has been the patent flaw or rather "gap" in policy debates. Often, vulnerability is assigned to an individual, and once labelled as such, the individual is subject to a range of paternalistic practices based on the belief that they are unable to relate "adequately" to what are considered normal social conventions. Disadvantage is the focus of this discourse, not the resilience or coping mechanisms people have developed to overcome, fully or partly, their vulnerability. As argued by Bartkowiak-Théron and Corbo Crehan, the blanket labelling of generic groups as vulnerable, blatantly ignores individuals' capacities to survive and address hardships, as demonstrated by Egan-Vine and Fraser.

Performance management and benchmarking are major issues to consider when looking at the implementation limits for vulnerable people policing. If we look at this model as a framework for operational protocols, the skills required of frontline officers are expanded to include competencies (and measurable competencies, at that) in facilitating community and broader governance responses to crime and disorder. In turn, policing organisations have begun to integrate these skills and competencies into officers' professionalisation and performance development (Fielding and Innes, 2006). However, as Roberts and Herrington rightly point out, further efforts are required to move from theory to practice, including the provision of practical advice to police in relation to the identification of complex vulnerability issues. Similarly, Huntley, highlights the gap in evaluation tools for frontline officers, even for the most explicit of vulnerabilities, let alone those with vulnerabilities that render assessment difficult, such as Acquired Brain Injury.

Some authors have argued (Bartkowiak-Théron and Corbo Crehan, 2010) that vulnerable people policing can be seen as an innovation on community policing. Whether we regard it as such, or as a new utilitarian paradigm intended to assist in complex police operations, the question of its measurement needs to be considered. Like many other activities in policing, such as networking or relationship building or prevention, community policing is not easily quantifiable, especially not within monthly, quarterly and annually audits required by a results-driven organisation.

Police practitioners and academic researchers continue to disagree on how to evaluate community policing,[1] and what and who is to be assessed to account for the success or failure of the overall approach, or even individual programs (Ellison, 2006). What is becoming clearer, though, is that successful community policing requires communities with high social capital; that is, transferable networks and skills that convert to an economic benefit (Duffee, Fluellen and Renauer, 1999). Too often, it is those communities with the lowest reserves of social capital (and in some cases, an excess of bad social capital; see Winter and Asquith, this collection, Ch 5) that have become subjects of community policing approaches. This is not to argue that community policing is a waste of police time and resources; on the contrary, in a time of shrinking budgets, policing organisations need communities to become true co-producers of law and order (Webb and Katz, 1997). The strategies adopted by police to date have been largely *ad hoc*, silo responses to specific communities' demands for justice. The contributors in this collection question whether the experiences of crime, and of the criminal justice system, common to vulnerable communities can provide an integrated framework for understanding vulnerable people policing as a whole.

Solutions to these problems are provided fully or in parts by authors throughout this collection. Bartels and Richards note that practices need to be more inclusive, dialogic and participatory, in order to avoid further language, communication and by extension, operational dysfunction at all levels of the criminal justice system. According to Bartkowiak-Théron and Layton, though, this can partly be achieved if police training becomes more scrupulous in addressing vulnerability as part of a broader competency curriculum at recruit, and then corporate levels. Robinson points out that police practices, if not inclusive of these concepts of care, support, rehabilitation and reform, are likely to remain grounded in backward-looking custodial practices, and in operational automatisms that are neither likely to contribute to long-term crime reduction, nor likely to be conducive of therapeutic, rehabilitative principles, especially in the case of young offenders. Graham, though, reminds us that police are not alone in this, and that health and welfare providers need to contribute to these efforts. While such an articulation of policing governance is not new, she notes that complex, and especially cross-sectional vulnerabilities, need addressing in a coordinated manner, so as to support individual and community welfare, as well as, more importantly, desistance. Further, increasing levels of oversight have led to growing documentation of police practices, and, increasing accountability. In time, these transformations to reporting, documenting and rewarding police practices will make an imprint on the role of policing, (especially, community policing) in modern policing organisations. Mainstreaming community policing competency, in the long term, will go a long way to holistically consider vulnerability and risk in policing practices.

The Contemporary Landscape of Vulnerable People Policing

Within the criminal justice system, it is recognised that individuals from certain social groups are more susceptible to arrest, need particular attention when in police custody, and require special consideration and treatment at each point of the criminal justice process (TLRI, 2006). In the past, such groups were determined to include children and young people, indigenous peoples, mentally-disordered persons, people living with a mental illness, people living with an intellectual or physical disability and people with languages other than the official language of the country where they reside. This categorisation exercise now tends to be more comprehensive. Gender and sexually diverse communities are now commonly recognised within the framework of vulnerability. Further, Law Reform Commissions throughout the world also now recognise that forms of vulnerability should be expanded to "other persons, who, by reason of some disability, are unable to communicate properly with the police (such as the seriously visually or aurally impaired, persons who cannot speak, and so on)" (NSW Law Reform Commission, 1990, Recommendation 6). This same Commission, in 2012, also dedicated a special section of its report on bail to 'other special needs and vulnerability' (NSWLRC, 2012: 186), although the discussion, progressive in nature, remains limited and normatively restrictive. Some countries such as Ireland or some states and territories in Australia have even gone beyond this caution by enlarging vulnerable categories of adults to the elderly, and, having regard to national and international standards of care (Ireland Law Reform Commission, 2006; ACT Department of Health, 2005), to the notion of "capacity" and "guardianship".

This indicates that the problems of vulnerability and susceptibility (for both offenders and victims, and for the police) are currently paving the way for the introduction of more pragmatic, consolidated solutions or rules related to vulnerable groups in a code of arrest (TLRI, 2006: 33) or guidelines in police organisational policy. As stated by Bartkowiak-Théron (in this collection, Ch 6), Queensland Police started consolidating such practices by clearly outlining their policy in relation to vulnerable people (Qld Police, 2012), with the Queensland Department of Justice also deciding on a policy directed at the improvement of services for vulnerable people throughout the criminal justice system with:

> the development of a set of principles to guide the way the department interacts with and serves those people who may be particularly vulnerable when they come into contact with the justice system (2008: 6).

Such consolidated documents are urgently needed to clarify police operational protocols, and the documentation of police practices in regards to the most disadvantaged groups of society. Such documents are starting to proliferate in the policy and legislation landscape of Australia, either at local or state levels (see, for example, Campbelltown City Council's *Children and Vulnerable Persons' Safety Policy*). Such documents, when examined, can be fairly generic though, and are content with a juxtaposition of broad guidelines and legislation reminders about referral protocols and training. For example, the Scottish Government simply indicates in its publicly available documentation that:

> [it] works very closely with those who are responsible for shifting the balance of care so that more people are able to continue to live in their communities. Legislation, such as the Adult Support and Protection (Scotland) Act 2007, is implemented to help identify "adults at risk", to provide support to them when they need it, and to provide the means to protect them from harm (2009).

Other government organisations briefly mention their attention to the problem of vulnerability by way of similar statements, highlighting their concern to work in a concerted manner with related agencies, and reminding readers of legislation and policy in such matters. Some of these statements may or (more often) may not be accompanied by key definitions (what is a vulnerable person, who can be vulnerable, etcetera). Other organisations, though, like Surrey Police, provide the public with detailed policies and procedures, such as force policy, rationale, and police responsibilities (Surrey Police, 2011). The Northern Highland Council (UK) also provides a good example of protocol regulation and policy precision in the protection of vulnerable adults, by way of its comprehensive, multi-agency approach to abuse and discrimination. In 2005, it released a multi-agency, mandatory protocol for all statutory and non-statutory agencies working in the Highlands to follow when dealing with vulnerable adults (NHS, 2005). The document includes assessment protocols, visible signs (on the part of a victim or on the part of an offender) that may trigger a vulnerability assessment, and a list (albeit, non-exhaustive) of compounding factors (from family problems to abuse in the workplace). It provides a description of the protective mechanisms that need to unfold to ensure that police or partner agencies protect the rights and care for the health and well-being of offenders and victims, as well as a list of possible additional partnering specialist agencies[2]. This indicates two things. First, that government policy worldwide intends to place stronger foci on vulnerable people. It therefore appears that vulnerable people policing is both timely and consistent with international best practice. Secondly, this trend appears to show that while police organisations will embark on policy implementation in a fairly straightforward manner, the visibility with which they will do so varies considerably. The above examples show that some police organisations will facilitate transparent public scrutiny of their policies, while others, perhaps due to resource limitations, will provide brief statements on the subject.

The Future of Vulnerable People Policing

This collection highlights a bright future for vulnerable people policing. Recent progress indicates that police organisations and partner agencies are becoming more aware of the complexities of interacting with vulnerable people. All agree that there is a better way to address protocol mishaps than the old-fashioned, reactive and hiccuppy model of doing something differently each time a problem arises. Many police organisations have shown their proactivity in developing new structures to address vulnerability. A better awareness of diversity and new concerns about the legitimacy of policing are the main drivers of this new attention to good, evidence-based and knowledge-driven practice. As indicated by Clifford, a climate of intense scrutiny brought by the media and new communications technologies has also contributed to police organisations adopting better practices in dealing with vulnerable people. The time is now right to make sure this progress continues.

Such progress necessitates careful thought to police training and governance mechanisms, but it also asks for a shift towards universal precautions, as opposed to risk-driven procedures. If the majority of people to come in contact with the police experience some form of vulnerability, it makes sense to integrate that vulnerability into the whole policing process. Such changes will not be possible without consistency in terminology and legislation, nor without a consolidation of duty of care for practitioners dealing with vulnerable people. We hope this collection provides all with the tools to do so.

Endnotes

1 Importantly, Bartkowiak-Théron made a point recently about a necessary progressive shift from "community policing" evaluation to "police-community engagement" evaluation (Bartkowiak-Théron, 2012).

2 Please note that the Australian Capital Territory also triggered, in 2011, a state-wide consultation on guardianship and workplace risk assessment in relation to vulnerable people. The *Working with Vulnerable People (Background Checking) Bill 2010* establishes guidelines as to how to run risk assessments on people who wish or are likely to engage professionally with vulnerable groups. A "Guide to Working with Vulnerable People in the ACT" was subsequently released in February 2012. In 2006, the United Kingdom had gone in a similar direction, with the enactment of the *Safeguarding Vulnerable Groups Act 2006*.

References

Safeguarding Vulnerable Groups Act 2006 (UK).
Working with Vulnerable People (Background Checking) Bill 2010 (ACT).

Australian Capital Territory Department of Health, 2005, *Mental Capacity Act and Safeguarding Vulnerable Adults: Training Manual*, Social Care Institute for Excellence, Canberra.

Bartkowiak-Théron, I, 2012, "Universities, Policing, Law Enforcement and Community Engagement", *Australian University Community Engagement Alliance Conference: Next Steps*, Brisbane, July 2012.

Bartkowiak-Théron, I, and Fleming, J, 2012, "La catégorisation politico-sociale de la population australienne: l'exemple des politiques sanitaires et pénales (The social and political categorisation of the Australian population: The example of health and law enforcement public policy)" 117 *Information Sociales* 20.

Burris, S, Drahos, P and Shearing, C, 2005, "Nodal Governance" 30 *Australian Journal of Legal Philosophy* 30.

Campbelltown City, 2012, *Council Children and Vulnerable Persons' Safety Policy*, 37CP.

Cope, B and Kalantzis, M, 1997, *Productive Diversity – A New, Australian Approach to Work and Management*, Pluto Press, Sydney.

Duffee, DE, Fluellen, R and Renauer, BC, 1999, "Community Variables in Community Policing" 2 *Police Quarterly* 5.

Ellison, J, 2006, "Community Policing – Implementation Issues" 75 *Law Enforcement Bulletin* 12.

Fielding, N and Innes, M, 2006, "Reassurance Policing, Community Policing and Measuring Police Performance" 16 *Policing and Society* 127.

Goldstein, H, 1990, *Problem-Oriented Policing*, McGraw-Hill, New York.

Hills, A, 1997, "Care and Control: The Role of the UK Police in Extreme Circumstances" 7 *Policing and Society* 177.

Hinds, L, and Murphy, K, 2007, "Public Satisfaction with Police: Using Procedural Justice to Improve Police Legitimacy" 40 *Australian and New Zealand Journal of Criminology* 27.

Howard, M, and O'Brien, J, 2009, "Criminal Justice for Vulnerable People", *Australian Guardianship and Administration Council Conference on Social Inclusion: The Future of Ageing, Disability and Substituted Decision-Making*, Brisbane, March 2009.

Hoy, J and Richmond, J, 2008, "Standard precautions and infection control", *HIV, Viral Hepatitis and STIs: A Guide for Primary Care* (Eds Bradford, D, Dore, G, Grulich, A, Hoy, J, Kidd, M, McCoy, R, Matthew, G, Mijch, A and Strasser, S), Australasian Society for HIV Medicine, Darlinghurst, NSW, 146.

Innes, M, 2006, "Introduction: Reassurance and the 'New' Community Policing" 16 *Policing and Society* 95.

Ireland Law Reform Commission, 2006, *Vulnerable Adults and the Law*, Law Reform Commission, Dublin.

Marks, M, and Wood, J, 2008, "Generating Youth safety from below: Situating Young People at the Centre of Knowledge-Based Policing", *Handbook of Knowledge-Based Policing: Current Conceptions and Future Directions* (Ed T Williamson), John Wiley & Sons, Chichester, UK.

New South Wales Law Reform Commission, 1990, *Criminal Procedure, Police Powers of Arrest and Detention*. Viewed on 5 May 2012, <www.lawlink.nsw. gov.au/lrc.nsf/pages/R66CHP5>.

New South Wales Law Reform Commission, 2012, *Bail*, no133. Viewed on August 22nd 2012, <www.lawlink.nsw.gov.au/lawlink/lrc/ll_lrc.nsf/pages/ LRC_r133toc>.

North Highland Council, 2005, *Protecting Vulnerable Adults: Good Practice Guidance and Procedures*.

Pearse, J, 1995, "Police Interviewing: the Identification of Vulnerabilities" 5 *Journal of Community and Applied Social Psychology* 147.

Putt, J, Ed, 2010, *Community Policing: Current and Future Directions for Australia – Research and Public Policy*, Australian Institute of Criminology, Canberra.

Queensland Department of Justice and Attorney-General, 2008, *Annual Report 2006-2007*.

Queensland Police Service, 2012, *Queensland Police Service Vulnerable Persons Policy*. Viewed on 24 April 2012, <www.police.qld.gov.au/Resources/Internet/ rti/policies/documents/QPSVulnerablePersonsPolicy.pdf>.

Ratcliffe, J, 2002, "Intelligence-led Policing and the Problems of Turning Rhetoric into Practice" 12 *Policing and Society* 53.

Ratcliffe, J, 2003, "Intelligence-Led Policing", *Trends and Issues in Crime and Criminal Justice*, 248, Australian Institute of Criminology, Canberra.

Royal Commission into Aboriginal Deaths in Custody (RCIADIC), 1991, *National Report*, Adelaide.

Scottish Government, 2009, *Adult Care and Support*. Viewed on 5 May 2012, <www.scotland.gov.uk/Topics/Health/care/adult-care-and-support>.

Sunshine, J, and Tyler, TR, 2003, "The Role of Procedural Justice and Legitimacy in Shaping Public Support for Policing" 37 *Law and Society Review* 513.

Surrey Police, 2011, *Crime Prevention and Safety: Vulnerable Adults*. Viewed on 5 May 2012, <www.surrey.police.uk/safety/vulnerable_adults.asp>.

Tasmania Law Reform Institute, 2006, "Consolidation of Arrest Laws in Tasmania", *TLRI Issues Paper*, 10, University of Tasmania, Hobart.

Tasmania Police, 2012, *Aboriginal Strategic Plan*, DPEM, Hobart.

Vermunt, R, and Törnblom, KY, 2007, *Distributive and Procedural Justice*, Ashgate, Surrey.

Webb, V and Katz, CM, 1997, "Citizen Ratings of the Importance of Community Policing Activities" 20 *Policing: An International Journal of Police Strategies and Management* 7.

Western Australia Government, 2012, *Victims of Crime: Police Duty of Care*. Viewed ON 5 May 2012, <www.victimsofcrime.wa.gov.au/P/police_duty_of_ care.aspx?uid=1573-1209-0829-4281>.

Yule, J, 2008, "Negligent investigation by Police: Can a Duty of Care be Found Using the Existing Negligence Principles in Australia?" 1 *Journal of Australasian Law Teachers Association* 379.

Index